Romanian Literature and Thought in Translation Series
Matei Calinescu, General Editor

The Romanians
A History

Vlad Georgescu

Edited by Matei Calinescu
Translated by Alexandra Bley-Vroman

Ohio State University Press
Columbus

Originally published as *Istoria românilor: De la origini pînă în zilele noastre.* © 1984 by American Romanian Academy of Arts and Sciences.

Library of Congress Cataloging-in-Publication Data
Georgescu, Vlad.
[Istoria românilor de la origini pînă în zilele noastre. English]
The Romanians: a history / Vlad Georgescu; edited by Matei Călinescu ; translated by Alexandra Bley-Vroman.
p.   cm. — (Romanian literature and thought in translation series)
Translation of: Istoria românilor de la origini pînă în zilele noastre.
Includes bibliographical references (p.   ) and index.
ISBN 0–8142–0511–9
1. Romania—History.   I. Călinescu, Matei.   II. Title.
III. Series.
DR217.G4613   1990
949.8—dc20   90–7720
CIP

Printed in the U.S.A.

9 8 7 6 5 4 3 2 1

CONTENTS

ILLUSTRATIONS

PREFACE

Vlad Georgescu was working on a revised, updated edition of his book *Istoria românilor* (Los Angeles: Academia Româno-Americană, 1984) for publication in English by the Ohio State University Press at the time of his unexpected and untimely death on 13 November 1988, at the age of 52. Before his sudden fatal illness, he had all but completed the work and had read and corrected most of the English translation. Unfortunately he did not live to rewrite chapter 6, "Communism in Romania." The version that appears here, without notes, largely reproduces the text of the 1984 Romanian edition. Georgescu made a few minor changes, mostly cuts, during the last months of his life.

To update the final section devoted to the recent history of Romania, Georgescu thought of adding a new subchapter. That subchapter was going to be based, he told me, on an essay, "Romania in the Mid-1980s," conceived and written independently. In order to represent Georgescu's views about events that occurred in Romania and eastern Europe between 1984 and 1988, the year of his death, "Romania in the Mid-1980s" has been included as chapter 7 of the present volume. This essay, whose final editing was done by his friend and collaborator Vladimir Socor, differs from the rest of the book in its more journalistic perspective and tone. Its views are also now dated in light of the 1989 anti-Communist revolutions in eastern Europe, the collapse of the Ceaușescu regime in Romania, and the disintegration of the Romanian Communist Party as a political organization on 22 December 1989.

The December 1989 anti-Ceaușescu and, more profoundly, anti-Communist popular uprising, the drama of the Romanian revolution, and its aftermath constitute a major turning point in the life of that country. A book on the history of the Romanians published in the 1990s but making no mention of these events would certainly disappoint the interested general reader, to whom Georgescu's volume is in large part addressed. To give this reader a sense of the crucial importance of these recent events—the sense of the ending of a dark period in the history of the Romanian nation and of a particularly difficult but hopeful new beginning—I have decided to add to the volume an epilogue, which I wrote in collaboration with Vladimir Tismăneanu, of the University of Maryland: "The 1989 Revolution and the Collapse of Communism in Romania."

As editor I also had to resolve some special translation problems that could not be attended to by the author. One example is the Romanian term *cărturar,* used with some frequency in the original, and meaning "bookman, studious and learned man, man of learning, scholar." The translator proposed rendering *cărturari* as "scholars" throughout the book; I rejected such a mechanical translation in favor of terms and phrases better suited to the context: "intellectuals," "the learned class," "the intellectual class," "the intelligentsia," "the literati," and so on. Alexandra Bley-Vroman's translation has generally followed the original closely, but when it seemed to me to help the exposition or to clarify a certain idea for an English-speaking reader, I have recast a sentence here and there or changed a word. The reader should note that dates are given in new style, with the exception of important dates and national holidays, such as 24 January 1859 (the unification of the principalities), 10 May 1866 (the arrival of Prince Carol), and 10 May 1881 (the coronation of Carol I as king of Romania). I have also rechecked the notes and the bibliographic references. And naturally, I have corrected anything that seemed to be a mere slip, in the original or in the translation. But I have refrained from interfering with any substantive matters.

The volume testifies to the qualities of depth, lucidity, and originality of Vlad Georgescu's historical insight. Written tightly and in a sustained reflexive mode, *The Romanians: A History* is the first overall history of the Romanian people by a single author to be published in English since the masterly synthesis of R. W. Seton-Watson (1934; reprinted 1963). A couple of multiauthor official histories of Romania, sponsored by the former Communist government of Nicolae Ceaușescu, have been translated into English over the last decades and can be found in the larger research libraries in the United States, the United Kingdom, and other English-speaking countries. But the official stamp of approval, the *nihil obstat* of the ideological censor, renders them suspect, particularly in their treatment of the modern period (they invariably end with sycophantic tributes to the "greatness" of Nicolae Ceaușescu's rule). Vlad Georgescu's *The Romanians: A History,* written without fear of censorship, immediately wins the reader's trust by its remarkably straightforward tone, by its calm, balanced, and thoughtful views, by its admirable evenhandedness, and perhaps by the greatest quality that emerges from its pages—its noble serenity.

The reader of the volume will notice a change, if not in the general approach, in the focus on certain details, and more specifically on the personal characteristics of individual political leaders, as Georgescu's history gets closer to the present. For the more distant past, the author uses skillfully the various methodologies associated with the "new history," including what has been called "cliometrics," or quantitative history. In such a broad view of history (including the study of longer-term trends in the demography and the economic, institutional, and cultural life of an area or people), there is little place for the traditional "narrative history" of political events, reigns, spectacular battles, and so on. Typically, Georgescu uses the available statistical data to describe social structures, institutions, trades and crafts, and the lifestyles of the various classes and professions at length, but is very concise when writing about such traditional heroes of Romanian historiography as Mircea the Old, Stephen the Great, or Michael the Brave (the combined direct references to their biographies as major historical characters do not exceed, I would say, a couple of pages).

The author's notion of the role of personality in history—his methodology remaining basically the same—becomes more comprehensive, however, when he starts to deal with contemporary matters. More and more narrative details (political, not personal, it is true) are brought into the focus of historical attention in the chapters devoted to the two Stalinist leaders of Romania since 1945, Gheorghe Gheorghiu-Dej and Nicolae Ceauşescu. I am afraid that this trend toward a more narrative mode of presentation (and narratives imply events and characters) may have been exaggerated in the epilogue, which is unabashedly narrative as it looks from close range and in some detail at what happened in a very short period of time, the tumultuous Romanian revolution (16–25 December 1989) and its immediate aftermath up to 15 May 1990. I wonder how Georgescu would have written about the Romanian revolution and how he would have dealt with the problem of a suddenly and tremendously accelerated historical time after the eerily empty, almost "posthistorical" last two decades of the Ceauşescu period. But I am persuaded that he would have approved of the general orientation of the epilogue as Vladimir Tismăneanu and I wrote it.

I should like to point out to the reader that both "Romania in the Mid-1980s," written by Vlad Georgescu during the last year of his life for publication in a different context, and the epilogue conceived by its authors as a self-contained account of the Romanian revolution (and *not* as a continuation of the Georgescu history), refer occasionally to material already covered in chapter 6 of the book, "Communism in Romania (1948–83)." Such background information was needed to illuminate the more recent developments discussed in these two additions to the book.

Many people have generously contributed their time and competence in helping complete the manuscript for publication. Dr. Andrei Brezianu, Dr. Victor Askenasy, Ms. Danielle Gosselin, Mr. Dan Ionescu, Professor Virgil Nemoianu, Mr. Vladimir Socor, Mr. Mihai Sturdza, Mrs. Alice Zwoelfer, and in particular Mrs. Mary Georgescu, deserve the gratitude of the publisher and the editor.

Matei Calinescu
15 May 1990

CHAPTER ONE

Early Times

Origins

Thracians, Dacians, and Romans. Traces of human life appeared with the dawn of history in the territory that is now Romania: primitive flint tools discovered in the Olt River Valley and in western Muntenia, an area favorable to hunting and gathering, were possibly produced by nomadic groups of *Pithecanthropus erectus*. Neanderthals appeared around 100,000 B.C. in northern Moldavia, Dobrudja, southern Transylvania, and Oltenia. They used caves and kindled their own fires as well as taking advantage of naturally occurring ones. Objects found in caves show that the Neanderthals were rather gatherers than hunters and had tools and weapons more advanced than their predecessors'. Around 40,000 B.C. the Neanderthal gave way to *Homo sapiens fossilis*. This is the moment when races began to form, the inhabitants of what is now Romania belonging to the Cro-Magnon branch.

The Cro-Magnons, whose tools and weapons are distributed throughout Moldavia, Wallachia, and Transylvania, used tools to produce tools. They modified the old stonecutting technology, introducing pressure-flaking; they developed the spearhead, different varieties of scraper, and the flake tool. Cro-Magnon culture was undoubtedly very much affected when, toward the end of the Upper Paleolithic, climatic change led to the disappearance or migration to the north of certain animals, including the mammoth, the cave lion, the Siberian rhinoceros, and the reindeer. The remaining game was eventually reduced to most of the species found in Romania today: rabbits, boar, bear, and deer. Around 8000 B.C. the climate grew warmer and *Homo sapiens recens* developed the use of the bow and the hafted ax, invented the dugout canoe, and domesticated the dog. After 5000 B.C. the Neolithic period began.

Neolithic civilization, of which there is considerable archaeological evidence throughout Romania, came with the influx from the south of a new, heterogeneous people of preponderantly Mediterranean type, mixing proto-European, Cro-Magnon components with brachycephalic aspects similar to the Anatolian type. As in the rest of Europe, this people introduced polishing, a new way of working stone, bone, and horn, which made it possible to use other stones besides flint. This sedentary people, whose members lived in fortified settlements of stick or mud huts, had discovered the advantages of cultivating plants (the earliest archaeological evidence of agriculture in Romania dates from the sixth millennium B.C.). They domesticated animals (cattle, sheep, goats, and pigs, but not horses) and invented spinning, weaving, and pottery, developments that radically altered human life. Of the Neolithic cultures in Romania, the best known is certainly the Cucuteni, which spread through southeastern Transylvania and northeastern Moldavia and Muntenia and flourished from the end of the fourth millennium until around 2000 B.C. Cucuteni culture produced mediocre tools, but is notable for its polychrome painted pottery and for the anthropomorphic figurines, perhaps dedicated to a fertility cult, discovered at many sites. Settlements could be as large as six hectares.

At the beginning of the second millennium B.C., the region between the Carpathians and the Danube moved into the Bronze Age. As the old Neolithic tribes intermixed with nomadic Indo-European peoples who came from the steppe north of the Black Sea a new people arose, and most scholars agree that the ethnic and linguistic restructuring brought about by the arrival of the Indo-Europeans finally led to the formation of the Thracian tribes.

Although native copper had been known and used as early as the Neolithic period, the introduction of bronze metallurgy, a technology that probably came from the Mesopotamian region by way of Aegean civilization, allowed the Bronze Age inhabitants of Romania to exploit the ore from Transylvania, Oltenia, and Dobrudja fully. Bronze Age people generally preferred animal husbandry to agriculture, and they created a largely pastoral civilization very different from that of the Romanian Neolithic. Their large and fortified settlements have yielded a rich store of axes—both tools and weapons—as well as daggers and swords, suggesting that the civilization had a pronounced warlike character, which probably intensified as the first tribes appeared.

The Bronze Age, the millennium extending from about 1800 to 800 B.C., is probably the period in which the Thracians living in the region between the Carpathians and the Danube separated from the Illyrians, with whom they shared Indo-European roots. This process continued into the Early Iron Age with the Hallstatt culture until, in the sixth century B.C., we can speak of the definitive formation, recognized in Greek sources, of the Thracian tribes.[1]

Archaeological data so far put the beginning of the Iron Age in Romania in the tenth century B.C.; the technology for working the ore was probably brought from Anatolia and the Near East. In the seventh century B.C. Greek settlers appeared on the coast of Dobrudja, founding Histria (657 B.C.), Tomis (seventh century), and Calatis (sixth century), powerful economic centers that exploited the resources of territories on both sides of the Danube. In these towns the natives came in contact with the more highly developed Greek world. In the sixth century B.C. the indigenous population also faced Scythian expansion from the east and pressures from the less numerous Illyrians in the west. The Scythians' raids led to the partial establishment of their power over some of the northern Thracians. Historians still do not agree whether the people in central Transylvania called Agathyrs were Scythian or Thracian, but they do agree that Scythians were present in Dobrudja, the future Scythia Minor, and were driven out by the Macedonians only in the third century B.C.; isolated pockets of Scythians probably remained until the first century B.C.

The first result of the Scythian invasions was to drive part of the native population from the plains, push them back into the foothills of the Carpathians, and concentrate them around a few earth and stone strongholds. In Moldavia alone more than twenty of their fortresses, ranging in size from nine to forty-five hectares, have been found. Fortresses of such dimensions could serve both as aristocratic residences and as places of refuge for the local populace.

From the end of the sixth century B.C. the native "barbarians" of Thracian origin are called *Getae* in Greek sources—the Romans later called them *Dacii* (Dacians). In writing of the expedition of the Persian king Darius I to Dobrudja in 514 B.C., Herodotus, who discusses their customs at length, says that the Getae are "the most courageous and most just of the Thracians."[2] Records show that in 335 B.C. Alexander the Great undertook an expedition against the Getic chieftains from the Danube plain, destroying fields of grain and a Getic citadel. His successor on the Macedonian throne, King Lysimachus, crossed the Danube in 291 B.C. in pursuit of the same Getae, who were now under the leadership of a King Dromichaites. The Macedonians were defeated, their king captured and later freed.

Dromichaites' tribal alliance seems to have maintained strong economic ties to the Hellenic world, but his successors could not maintain the alliance, which splintered into small kingdoms until around 80 B.C.

At that time Burebista established a powerful Geto-Dacian state, extending his authority over a large area, as far as Pannonia in the west and the Greek cities on Pontus Euxinus to the south and the east. During the first part of his long rule, Burebista had his center of power on the Plain of Wallachia; the ruins of his presumed capital, Argedava, can be seen today on the Argeş River, some twenty kilometers south of Bucharest. During the latter part of his rule the king moved his residence to southern Transylvania, erecting in the Orăştie Mountains a powerful system of fortifications which his successors further developed and completed. From here he established contact with Pompey in 48 B.C., seeking to join his coalition against Caesar, whose legions were threatening Dobrudja and the whole Danube line. After the death of Pompey, the concentration of Roman troops showed Caesar's intention to attack Dacia, but his assassination in 44 B.C. put an end to the plan. Burebista died the same year, himself assassinated by an aristocracy probably dissatisfied with his centralist policies.

Burebista's extensive kingdom did not survive him. Instead Cotys, Coson, Dicomes, Rholes, Daphyx, and Zyraxes ruled over small kingdoms that, Strabo says, could not raise more than 40,000 soldiers. The political center of Geto-Dacian society now moved permanently to southern Transylvania, where the kings Decenius, Comosicus, Scorilo, and Duras continued Burebista's policies, opening the way for a great, final flowering under Decebalus (A.D. 86–106).

Dacia had long been in Rome's political and cultural sphere of influence. By 74 B.C., during Burebista's rule, the Republic reached the Danube at the Iron Gate gorge, and it extended its dominion over Dobrudja, temporarily from 72 to 61 B.C., then permanently in A.D. 46, when the whole of Dobrudja was annexed to Moesia. Conflicts between the Geto-Dacians and their new neighbors continued throughout the first century A.D. as Dacian raids south of the Danube alternated with Roman punitive expeditions north of it. Finally, under Emperor Domitian, the Romans decided to annihilate the political entity in the Orăştie Mountains as they had the Dacian kingdoms in Dobrudja and on the plain of Wallachia.

The Dacians were now led by Decebalus, to whom Duras, seeing the need for a young king as adept in diplomacy as in war, had transferred power in A.D. 86. The new sovereign found himself ruler of a vigorous and rising people. The many *davae* (the equivalent in the Dacian language of the Latin oppidum or "town") attest to a large and active population gathered around urban settlements, occupied in manufacturing and commerce, and having economic ties to the Greek and Roman worlds. Greek and Roman articles, found in abundance in Dacian archaeological sites, were bought with coins, which the Dacians had begun minting in the third century B.C. on Macedonian, Thasian, or Roman models. At Sarmizegethusa Regia the Dacians built a large fortress for the king and nobility (*tarabostes*), with sanctuaries dedicated to the gods Zamolxis, Gebeleizis, and Bendis.

Initially the conflict with the Romans went in the Dacians' favor; they sacked Moesia in A.D. 86 and in the following year defeated General Cornelius Fuscus, who had imprudently ventured into Dacia. Two years later, however, Tettius Julianus defeated Decebalus. Domitian granted the Dacians very favorable conditions for peace: in exchange for submitting to the Romans, Decebalus received a yearly stipend, artisans to strengthen his defenses, and military materiel. (The Romans often set up a client relationship when direct occupation of a territory was difficult or inopportune.) Decebalus honored his promise not to attack the Roman provinces and kept an eye on the neighboring "barbarians," preventing them from taking hostile action against Rome.

Protected by this advantageous peace, the kingdom continued to develop economically and culturally—until it became a clear threat to the empire. This explains why the Senate complained repeatedly to the emperor and why Trajan decided to settle the Dacian problem once and for all. In the summer of A.D. 101, Roman legions crossed the Danube. By winter, after a hard fight, they reached Sarmizegethusa. The Dacian-Sarmatian counterattack in Dobrudja briefly tipped the balance, but Trajan's victory at Tropaeum Traiani (now Adamclissi), later commemorated by the huge triumphal monument still to be seen at the place of the battle, removed all doubt of the outcome. The defeated Dacians accepted a cruel peace, surrendering military materiel and any deserters among the Roman artisans, dismantling their fortresses, and agreeing to Roman political control and to the presence of Roman garrisons. In A.D. 105, however, the Dacians rebelled. The Romans again crossed the Danube, this time by the stone bridge constructed by Apollodorus of Damascus at Drobeta (modern Turnu Severin), and attacked Transylvania from three directions: from the Banat, through the Olt River valley, and from Moldavia through the Oituz River valley. Abandoned by all his "barbarian" allies, Decebalus put up a brave resistance, delaying the fall of his capital until the summer of A.D. 106. He was closely pursued as he tried to flee into the mountains and chose suicide over capture. The royal residence at Sarmizegethusa Regia was destroyed, and on 11 August 106 Roman sources first include Dacia among the imperial provinces.

"The Seal of Rome." With this suggestive formulation the historian Nicolae Iorga expresses the relationship between conqueror and conquered, the Romans' rule as matrix—their capacity to impress upon the new provinces the form of their own civilization and to create structures that, though greatly modified later, persist to the present day.

Trajan included Oltenia, the Banat, and Transylvania in the new province of Dacia, and he annexed Muntenia and southern Moldavia to Moesia. The greater part of Moldavia, together with Maramureş and Crişana, was not occupied but was ruled by free Dacians, who also returned to the plain of Wallachia when Hadrian withdrew from it in 119. During the rule of Septimius Severus the Dacian border was moved back to the middle of Muntenia, and a fortified line—an earthen wall and some military camps—was constructed from modern Turnu-Măgurele to Rucăr. (The frontier remained fixed until in 245 it shifted still farther back to the Olt River.) Within these borders the Romans organized a single province in 106, then two provinces in 119, and in 158 three. Their attention to the area shows the Romans' desire to make this new conquest a strong bastion of the empire in the face of the barbarians now threatening it from the north and east.

Historians' estimates of the population of Roman Dacia range from 650,000 to 1,200,000. V. Pârvan's count of about one million seems plausible. According to his calculations 10 percent of these were soldiers—up to three legions, with additional auxiliary troops.[3] The remainder consisted of colonists from all over the empire and of course Dacians, whether native to the conquered area or free Dacians brought in later, as for instance in the time of Emperor Commodus.

The empire followed an organized, official colonization policy, granting land even to those who were not Roman citizens, founding cities, and importing whole groups of gold-mining specialists. Of the names preserved in inscriptions found to date, 74 percent are Latin. Of the divinities worshiped, 43.5 percent have Latin names, 21.3 percent are Near Eastern borrowings, and the remainder are of Dacian or Thracian origin.[4] Nevertheless it is likely that Romans formed the minority among the settlers and that most newcomers hailed from Moesia, Thracia, Dalmatia, Pannonia, and other neighboring regions. Many probably came from the Near East, from Anatolia, Syria, and Egypt. The colonizing population was clearly heterogeneous, but whatever their origins, the colonists represented imperial culture and civilization and brought with them that most powerful Romanizing instrument, the Latin language.

The theory that the Dacians were completely exterminated by the Romans was first put forward by seventeenth-century Moldavian historians and has been supported by many scholars since then, including the scholar-prince Dimitrie Cantemir and members of the Latinist Transylvanian School of the late eighteenth and early nineteenth centuries. The theory is based on Eutropius' fourth-century claim that Dacia was depopulated (*exhausta*). The passage in which he states this is not conclusive, however, for he refers only to men, leaving aside women and children. Some of the questions that arise are of what use would a vacant, uninhabited country have been in a slaveholding world? Why would the Romans have destroyed such an important source of their own wealth? A country this large could not have been fully exploited by imported labor, no matter on how grand a scale, nor could Dacia have become such a populous province in so short a time by such means alone. That the conquered territory flourished culturally and economically can be explained only by the adherence of the Dacian population to its new ruler and its assimilation of the conquerors' superior civilization. Trajan's Column, which the emperor raised in Rome in 113 in honor of his victory, shows Dacians returning to their settlements and submitting to the new authorities.

Archaeology too shows a continuing Dacian presence, with the process of Romanization clearly in evidence. The traditional Dacian style of pottery is found in the settlements alongside vessels of Roman manufacture but with local decorative elements. Dwellings were constructed largely by old Dacian methods, and the types of tools and ornaments used before the Roman conquest persisted. Research on cemeteries clearly shows that the continuing population was far too great to have been wiped out or driven away.[5] The conquered Dacians supplied the empire with many auxiliary troops, some of which actually defended Dacia's eastern border in the third century.

The official protective policy, the massive infusion of Roman settlers, and the integration of the Dacians into a higher civilization through Romanization transformed the new province from the very first into a thriving economic region. The country's resources, skillfully exploited, brought Rome considerable wealth. Dacia became one of the principal producers of grain, especially wheat, in the empire. The gold mines of the Bihor Mountains, operated by Illyrians brought in from Dalmatia, were an important resource for the empire's treasure chests. The lead, copper, silver, iron, and salt mines, which, like the gold mines, had existed in the time of the Dacian kings, were systematically worked as

well. To facilitate commerce Roman bronze coins were minted in Sarmizegethusa. The extensive network of Roman roads contributed to the
growth of the economy.

Dacia was a highly urban province. No fewer than twelve cities are
known, eight of them of the highest rank (*colonia*). Almost all were built
on the sites of the old Dacian davae and preserved their names. The
most important city in Dacia was certainly Ulpia Traiana Sarmizegethusa, the colonia founded by Trajan about forty kilometers from Decebalus' old capital and now the political and cultural capital of the
province. It boasted an imposing amphitheater and a wealth of palaces
and temples, and was surrounded by strong walls. The population of
the city was probably about 20,000. Besides Sarmizegethusa, archaeological research and other sources reveal the flourishing urban life of
Napoca (Cluj); Drobeta (Turnu Severin); Potaissa (Turda), post of the
fifth Macedonian legion; and Apulum (Alba Iulia), post of the thirteenth Gemina legion and seat of the governor of Dacia.

From the start the province's political life was not without perils.
First came the free Dacians to the north and east who, allied with their
old friends the Sarmatians, frequently attacked the province. Hadrian
had trouble in 117 dealing with such attacks, which were aggravated
by an uprising of the Dacians in the subject province, and fighting
continued both under Antoninus Pius in 143 and 157–58 and under
Marcus Aurelius. After the quieter rules of Commodus, Septimius Severus, and Caracalla, the invasions of Dacia, in particular the invasion
by the Carps (a Dacian tribe) in alliance with the Visigoths, were a
serious problem for the emperors. Some of these commemorated their
victories in Dacia by assuming the title of *Dacicus,* which the Senate also
granted to Aurelian (r. 270–75) along with that of *restitutor patriae.* But
in the years 271–75 the Roman army and administration gradually
withdrew from the province, which still bore the name (seen on coins
minted at Apulum in 250) Dacia Felix. It was hoped that moving the
border back to the Danube would make it easier to defend. With the
army went the wealthy, the city dwellers, and the merchants. The peasants, the great majority of the Daco-Roman population, stayed behind,
having no reason to leave and no place else to go.

The Dark Ages: Rise of a People. The process by which the Romanian
people was formed is not easy to follow in the written sources. Until
the ninth or tenth centuries any mention of the territory that had been
Dacia refers only to the "barbarians" dominating the area. Archaeology
probably remains the best source of information about the ethnic con-

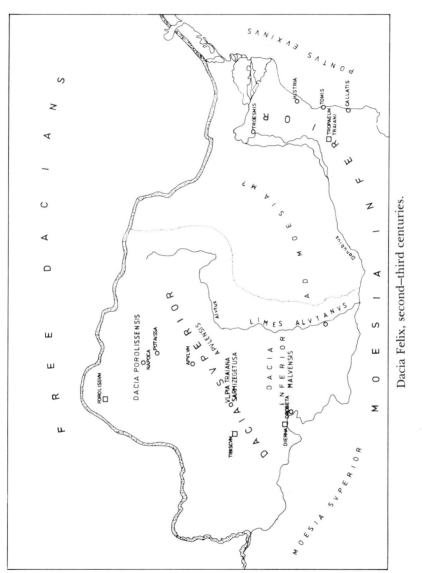

Dacia Felix, second–third centuries.

stitution of the largest population in southeast Europe. The Romanization of Dacia and the birth of a Daco-Roman people can, I think, be
considered the first stage in the long process of the formation of the
Romanian people, but this stage did not end in 275. It continued until
the early sixth century, as long as the empire, still in power along the
Danube and in Dobrudja, continued to influence the territory north of
the river. The continual circulation of people and goods across the river
and back certainly facilitated this. The Romans maintained bridgeheads
on Dacian territory all the way from Dierna (now Orşova) to present-
day Barboşi in Moldavia, even building a new stone bridge across the
Danube at Sucidava (today Celei) in 328. Their bridgeheads on the
north shore of the Danube were not abandoned until after the rule of
Justinian. Many coins issued by Aurelian's successors have been found
on Dacian territory, and they are evidence of the empire's economic
presence. Constantine the Great seems even to have restored direct
Roman control of the southern half of Oltenia and Muntenia, constructing an immense defensive earthwork more than seven hundred
kilometers long, from Drobeta to Brăila; the wall is still two meters high
in places and thirty meters wide.

Archaeological research confirms as well the presence of the Daco-
Roman population on the old provincial territory. At least a century
after the Romans' departure, the amphitheater and other public buildings at Sarmizegethusa were being used as dwellings by the poor. Evidence of similar occupation has been found at Napoca, Porolissum
(near modern Gherla), and Apulum. The cemeteries of many rural
settlements give witness to the development of a new people, Latinic,
but with customs and traditions inherited in equal measure from the
Dacians and the Romans. One such find was at Bratei (near modern
Mediaş), where the largest known Dacian cemetery has been excavated.
Its five hundred fourth- and fifth-century graves and a wealth of glass
and metal objects, coins, pottery, and fragments of weapons show a
mixture of elements: tools and pottery are Dacian or provincial Roman
in character, the contents of the graves predominantly Dacian, and the
burial ritual Roman. Comparable discoveries have been made elsewhere
in Dacia as well.[6]

After 313, the year in which Christianity was officially adopted
throughout the empire, Dacia too was largely Christianized, but not by
official act, missionary pressure, or mass baptisms. Rather, it was a
popular movement that spread spontaneously from the many Christian
communities along the Danube. Christian artifacts, for example, gems
and lamps bearing the sign of the cross, Roman altars recarved with

Christian symbols, and the fragment of candelabrum with the Latin inscription *Ego Zenovius votum posui,** have been found in many ancient Roman centers. That Rome was the source of Romanian Christianity is further attested by the Latin origin of the basic terminology: *dumnezeu* (God) from *dominus deus, biserica* (church) from *basilica, cruce* (cross) from *crux, creştin* (Christian) from *christianus, sân* or *sânt* (saint) from *sanctus, lege* (law) from *lex, înger* (angel) from *angelus, a boteza* (to baptize) from *baptizare.*

After the Romans withdrew from their territory, the Daco-Romans were subjected to constant invasions by the migratory tribes that swept across central and southeast Europe in uninterrupted succession for about a thousand years. The Visigoths ruled Dacia from 275 to 376, establishing themselves in Moldavia and on the plain of Wallachia and extending into Transylvania, too, after the year 300. With the coming of the Huns the Visigoths crossed the Danube into Byzantium; all trace of them disappeared. The Huns established their political center in Pannonia but held Dacia from there. This first Asiatic people destroyed what urban life may have remained, driving the town dwellers into remote, less accessible areas. The scarcity of the archaeological evidence for the Huns probably reflects the fact that even at their height under Attila, they preferred extorting tribute from the people (now significantly called Carpo-Dacians in documents) to establishing themselves in the former Roman province. After the Hun empire disintegrated in 454 Dacia was taken over by the Gepids, a Germanic people that had played a key role in defeating Attila's sons. Like the Huns, the Gepids had their center of power in Pannonia, and like them they left little trace. In 567 the Gepids were defeated and replaced by the Avars, who dominated central and eastern Europe for more than two centuries. They dealt a powerful blow to the Byzantine empire, breaching its northern border more than once, most seriously in 602, when their attack opened the way for the Slavs to reach the heart of the Balkans.

Archaeological evidence indicates that the Slavs had come to Moldavia and Muntenia by the beginning of the sixth century and to Transylvania by the middle of the seventh. Migrating from their homeland between the Vistula and Dniester Rivers, they had allied themselves with the Avars and established themselves in present-day Romania under Avar authority, bringing with them, to judge by the archaeological finds, a less highly developed civilization than that of the natives. Their crafts were executed with less skill; their pottery was more primitive.

---

*Translation: "I, Zenovius, made a votive offering."—ED.

Commercial ties with the lands south of the Danube were broken, and life throughout the region became more heavily agrarian and rural. When in 602 the Avars penetrated Byzantium's border at the Danube, and Emperor Maurice was assassinated, the Slavs poured into the empire, permanently establishing themselves in the Balkans. They took over the whole region as far as southern Greece, rupturing all contact between the empire and the peoples north of the Danube for the first time since the Roman conquest of Dacia. At the same time, the migration of many Slavs from north to south changed the ethnic balance, reducing the Romanic element in the Balkans but increasing its significance in Dacia. In the north, the remaining Slavic population was in the end assimilated by the Romanic. In the south the Slavs assimilated the native population, completely altering the ethnic character of one of the most Romanized provinces in the empire.

Beginning with the sixth century, then, we reach the second stage in the formation of the Romanian people. The direct impact of the eastern Roman empire is lessened, both because of the presence of the Slavs between the empire and the Proto-Romanians and because of internal changes that eventually transformed the Roman empire into the Byzantine. The Romanizing process was now over, but its effects were not lost even as the Proto-Romanians assimilated the Slavic population. Although the assimilation of the Slavs went on into the twelfth century, we may consider the constitution of a Romanian people complete by the ninth or tenth.

The formation of the Romanian people became the subject of heated controversy, primarily for political reasons, as early as the eighteenth century. Saxon and Hungarian scholars flatly rejected the persistence of Dacians in Roman Dacia and of Daco-Romans after the Roman withdrawal, and placed their source south of the Danube.[7] Bulgarian historians, unwilling to admit that the Romanians had originated in their own territory, moved them north of the Danube, denying their presence on the Balkan peninsula altogether. Russian historians also entered the controversy. They accepted the Romanians' Roman background and continuity, but only in Transylvania and the Banat, denying any Latin element in the population of Moldavia, a province upon which the Russians had designs, and which in the nineteenth century they managed to annex in part.[8]

The archaeological research of recent decades[9] has shown that the people who dominated southeast Europe numerically had no single place of origin, either north or south of the Danube. Instead, the Romanian people is the product of a long process beginning with the

Romanization of the Dacians, ending with the Romanianization of the Slavs, and taking place over an area extending both north and south of the Danube. This area was a single region until the Roman border fell in 602. After that event two branches developed. The northern one evolved into what today is the Romanian people, while the southern branch, driven west on the Balkan peninsula by the Slavs, eventually became Macedo-Romanians, the Balkan Vlachs.

Like the new people, the Romanian language developed slowly. Genealogically, Romanian is what remains of the vulgar Latin spoken in the province of Dacia, in the Balkan mountains, and along the Black Sea coast. In its earliest stage it included elements of the Thracian idiom spoken by the local population (a language of which linguists believe they can identify between 80 and 110 words), and later it was subjected to a heavy Slavic influence. But the Latin grammatical structure has remained virtually unchanged. The Slavic impact was primarily lexical: recent research has calculated that from 16 to 20 percent of the words in the basic vocabulary are of Slavic origin. The expression *torna, torna frater** used by a native soldier in the Byzantine army (A.D. 587) probably shows the evolution of vulgar Latin into Proto-Romanian. The language continued to evolve until, at the Slavic invasion, the Daco-Roman dialect began to separate from the three dialects spoken south of the Danube, Macedo-Romanian, Istro-Romanian, and Megleno-Romanian. It is likely that the four dialects became fully distinct during the ninth and tenth centuries, when the Romanians emerged as a people and began to appear in the sources.[10]

Complete formation of both people and language took place under extremely complicated international circumstances, of which the most notable is the constant flow of tribes across central and southeast Europe. Although the first Bulgarian czardom, founded in 681 and abolished by the Byzantines in 1018, had little impact, the appearance of the Magyars in the late ninth century and of the Cumans in the twelfth brought basic changes to the ethnic and political balance of the region. The return of the Byzantine empire to the Danube and its partial reconstruction of the border lost in 602 was also an important event.

The Byzantines were the first to refer to the Romanians, specifically to the Balkan Vlachs. In the late tenth century Kedrenos mentions that they were present in 976 in Greater Vlachia. Byzantine sources also mention the existence of a first autonomous political entity in 980. In

---

*Translation: "Turn around, turn around, brother." In classical Latin one would use "revertere" to convey the same message.—ED.

the second half of the eleventh century the chronicler Kekaumenos mentions Trajan's battles against Decebalus and makes it clear that the Vlachs were the descendants of the ancient settlers. Referring to the events of 1167, Kynnamos writes unequivocally that the Vlachs (in this case, those living north of the Danube) "are settlers who came from Italy long ago."[11] Nicetas Honiates too mentioned the Vlachs from north of the Danube in connection with the events of 1164. The use by Byzantine authors of *Vlach* indicates that these people were perceived as speakers of a Latin language, for this term, initially used by ancient Germans to refer to the Roman and Romanized population of Gaul, was later extended to the population of the Italic peninsula. It passed from the Germans to the Slavs and Byzantines, who applied it to the Romanic, Proto-Romanian populations on both sides of the Danube.

Byzantine sources are not the only ones to mention Romanians during this period. A ninth-century Armenian geography mentions the country "Balak"; eleventh-century texts of the Normans, who played an important role in the politics of eastern Europe, contain many references to "Blakumen" and "Blokumannland" (Vlachs and the land of the Vlachs), clearly referring to the Moldavian Romanians, with whom they came in contact. The anonymous Notary of the Hungarian king Béla III (1173–96) wrote in the *Gesta Hungarorum* (Exploits of the Hungarians),[12] based on ancient chronicles and oral tradition, that the Magyars, when they settled on the plains of the Tisza and Danube rivers, found there "Slavi, Bulgarii, et Blachi ac pastores Romanorum."* This testimony is found in other Hungarian sources as well, while the Russian chronicle attributed to Nestor says that the newcomers "began to fight with the Valachs and the Slavs who lived in those countries." *Das Nibelungenlied* mentions a "Herzog Râmunc uzer Vlachen lant" (Duke Râmunc from the land of the Vlachs).[13]

The Magyars established themselves in Pannonia toward the end of the ninth century, driven from the steppes on the Dnieper River by the Petchenegs. Their route to the plain of the Tisza River appears to have circled to the north of Transylvania and reapproached it from the west. This largely explains the name given to the province—the land beyond the forest (*trans silvas*). On reaching the Carpathian Mountains, they gave Wallachia the name "the land beyond the mountains" (Terra transalpina). According to the *Gesta Hungarorum,* the Magyars found there three voivodates: that of Menumorut in Crişana, of Glad in the Banat,

*Translation: "Slavs, Bulgarians, Blachs, and Roman shepherds."—Ed.

and of Gelu in central Transylvania, with capitals at Biharea (near present-day Oradea), Morisena (now Cenad), and Dăbîca (near modern Cluj), respectively. Archaeological research has located these voivodates, unearthing numerous settlements—twenty in Menumorut's, sixty in Glad's, and more than forty in Gelu's. Some settlements are well fortified and give evidence of a large population that engaged in agriculture and animal husbandry and traded extensively with the Bulgarians. The first two were probably politically dependent on the Bulgarian czar as well, and some historians even believe that, although Bulgaria extended to the Tisza River, Menumorut was a vassal not of the czar at Plisca but of the emperor at Constantinople.

The first Magyar attacks, led by Árpád himself, the founder of the dynasty bearing his name, were directed against the voivodates in Crişana and the Banat; the fortress at Satu Mare was taken after three days' fighting, and Menumorut's capital fell in thirteen. There the defeated natives accepted an accord in which the voivode's daughter was given in marriage to Árpád's son, so that the voivodate would revert to the Magyars on Menumorut's death. From Crişana the Magyars mounted an attack on the Banat, defeating an army of Glad's "Cumani, Bulgari atque Blachi" (Cumans [actually Petchenegs], Bulgarians, and Vlachs) and seizing the fortresses at Cuvin (Keve) and Orşova. Then one of the Magyar tribes, led by Tuhutum, made its way into Transylvania by the Gates of Mezeş, defeating Gelu, "dux Blacorum" (leader of the Vlachs) and killing him in another battle as he tried to retreat to Dăbîca, "ad castrum suum" (to his camp).[14]

With the exception of Menumorut's voivodate, which was immediately annexed, the gains from these incursions into the Banat and Transylvania were apparently soon lost. The Magyars had neither the organizational capacity nor the human resources necessary to maintain such a great conquest, whose territory ranged from Moravia and Croatia to Transylvania. Magyar archaeological remains from the tenth century are rare here. The Vlachs, as the Romanians were called in the Latin and Greek texts, Slavs, and some Magyars remaining from this first wave continued to live, together with the Petchenegs, under the framework of the old voivodates. These Petchenegs had migrated from the steppes north of the Black Sea late in the tenth century, settling mostly in Moldavia, Muntenia, and southern Transylvania. A "Romanian and Petcheneg Forest" (*silva Blachorum et Bissenorum*) is mentioned in the sources.

The next Magyar offensive took place only after Christianization, when Stephen I took the Transylvanian voivode Gyla's refusal to be christened as an excuse to occupy the region and replace him with Magyar officials (1003–04). Gyla seems to have been of Petcheneg origin, since Byzantine sources speak of the existence of a Petcheneg tribe called Gylas. A life of the monarch-saint Stephen I mentions battles with Petchenegs in the heart of Transylvania. But in spite of Stephen's victories, the voivodate did not become fully a part of the Hungarian kingdom until after the Petchenegs had been driven from Transylvania into Dobrudja in 1085. The Banat was integrated more rapidly, as Voivode Ahtum, Glad's successor (and an Orthodox Christian who had founded a monastery for Byzantine monks in his capital at Cenad), was quickly defeated and removed. In the twelfth century, to strengthen his position there, the Hungarian king settled Szeklers and Saxons along the southern and eastern borders of Transylvania and established the Teutonic Knights in the Braşov region and the Knights Hospitalers in the Banat.

During all this time the regions that became Moldavia and Wallachia underwent great economic and social changes. Archaeological digs show a dramatic increase in the number of settlements during the twelfth and thirteenth centuries. In Moldavia, the plains region east of the Siret River was inhabited by Bârladniks, who were powerful enough to support Galich against Kiev in 1159, while the south belonged to the Brodniks and Bolokhovenians; most of the Muntenian settlements are found on the lower reaches of the Buzău and Argeş rivers and along the Danube, while those in Oltenia are grouped predominantly in the valley of the River Jiu. These finds refute an old and frequently cited theory that the populace withdrew to the mountains, abandoning the plains. Until the Tatar invasion of 1241 the most heavily populated regions were the plains along the rivers, where dense forest offered good protection.[15]

Toward the middle of the thirteenth century voivodates dependent on Hungary began to form, but evidence shows that they soon sought independence from the Hungarian crown. Three voivodates were established in the future Wallachia in 1247, in accordance with the Diploma granted the Knights Hospitalers by Béla IV. Litovoi's voivodate comprised northern Oltenia, with its center of power in the vicinity of modern Tîrgu Jiu; Farcaş ruled western Muntenia; and Seneslau, called in the Diploma "voivode of the Romanians," held central and southern Muntenia.

The unification of these realms was probably hastened by the arrival of Romanians from beyond the mountains who had fled the imposition of Catholicism (undertaken by the Hungarian king at the pope's urging). The trend toward unification seems to have begun with Litovoi, who in 1277 was at war with the Magyars over lands the king claimed for the crown, but for which the voivode refused to pay tribute. Litovoi was killed in battle; his brother Barbat was captured and forced not only to pay ransom but also to recognize Hungarian rule. Barbat was probably followed by Tihomir, who was succeeded in turn by his son Basarab. This ruler systematically expanded his territory until it extended south to the Danube and east into Moldavia to the Danube delta. In 1323 Basarab's armies joined in the fighting between Bulgaria and Byzantium. In the following years they fought with the Tatars, gradually driving them out of the country. Pope John XXII sought Basarab's support for a Dominican mission in 1327, and three years later the sources show that he was again involved in the conflicts among the Balkan states, again on the side of the Bulgarians.

Basarab was a vassal of King Charles I of Hungary, who called him "our voivode," but neither his growing power nor the active foreign policy he conducted on his own account to the south and east could be acceptable to Hungary. Immediately following the Serbian defeat of the Bulgarians and Romanians at Velbujd in 1330, Charles made an expedition against the voivode, whom he called "rebellious," "unsubmissive," and "faithless," on the pretext that Basarab had occupied crown territories. When the disputed land (the Severin Banat) had been retaken, the voivode offered to pay yearly tribute and 7,000 silver marks in compensation, and to recognize the king's sovereignty; but his offers were rejected, and Charles advanced into Wallachia as far as Curtea de Argeş (Basarab's capital). But he was eventually forced to withdraw toward Transylvania without having engaged the Romanian army in any conclusive battle. Retreating through the mountains, the Hungarians were ambushed by Basarab's forces at Posada and soundly defeated, the king managing with difficulty to escape with his life. The battle of Posada marked the end of Hungarian rule and the appearance of a first independent Romanian principality.

A second Romanian principality was not far behind. After 1241 the future Moldavia was under the control of the Golden Horde, but the power shift followed the same course as in Wallachia. Although there is less documentation for the earliest Moldavian voivodates, a Romanian voivode Olaha is mentioned in 1247. In 1277 a warrior people, the Blaci, were in conflict with the Ruthenians in southern Poland. The Blaci formed a political entity somewhere in northern Moldavia, perhaps the precursor of "the land of the Vlachs" (*Walahen Land*) mentioned by Ottokar of Styria in 1307–08. To the south, where in 1297

Pope Nicholas III decided to reorganize the Catholic bishopric of Mil-
covia, it was recorded in 1281 and 1297 that another "land of the
Vlachs" was rapidly becoming a feudal state: the "maiores terrae" (as
they are called in a 1332 papal chancellery document) seized the bishopric's goods and holdings. Throughout this period rather frequent
conflicts took place between the natives and the Catholic church supported by the Magyars. "Schismatics," or Orthodox Romanians, are
often mentioned in the correspondence between Hungarian kings and
the pope.

By the middle of the fourteenth century the Golden Horde's power
was declining, and the Polish-Hungarian offensive against it was at its
strongest. After his victorious campaigns of 1345 and 1352–53, Louis I
of Hungary, successor to Charles, organized a defensive border province in northern Moldavia to be ruled by Dragoş, a voivode from Maramureş whose army had participated in the campaigns against the
Tatars. Dragoş was succeeded by his son Sas, who was followed by his
son Balc, so that the line of Dragoş seemed to have established a dynasty. But their reigns were brief: the family remained in power only
until 1359, when the local boyars, disgruntled perhaps by the presence
of Magyars and Catholics, rose up against the Romanian voivodes appointed by the king. Another native of Maramureş, Bogdan I, who had
been voivode until he led an uprising against the Hungarians, now
seized Balc's throne and declared himself independent ruler of Moldavia. None of the military campaigns undertaken by the king—and
the Hungarian Chronicle says that he "made war . . . against the Moldavians almost every year"—could force his allegiance.[16] Like Wallachia, Moldavia had joined the rolls of independent states.

CHAPTER TWO

The Middle Ages
(c. 1300–1716)

Society

Was There a Romanian Feudalism? This question, which was not even raised in Romania before World War II, is answered in the affirmative by postwar Marxist historians. They argue that feudalism was an inevitable development of the economic and social system, so the Romanians must have passed through it just as the other peoples of eastern and southeastern Europe did. This is certainly open to dispute. Official Romanian historiography is too ready to call feudal a society that was often far from the classical model of feudalism. Western historians go to the other extreme. Even when examining the same characteristics, they find no feature of feudalism in nonwestern societies. If the defining criterion of feudalism is the French or English model, then certainly neither Byzantium nor Russia nor the Romanian principalities belonged to the feudal world. But it would be wrong to deny the existence of Romanian feudalism merely because the classical forms of Western feudalism were not present in Moldavia and Wallachia. In the mid-fourteenth century when the two principalities were newly founded, for instance, the relationship between prince (*domn*) and noble (*boyar*) resembled vassalage in some respects, and the relationship between boyar and peasant and the structure of land ownership often took feudal forms. These feudal elements appeared in the principalities long after they had disappeared in western Europe, and they coexisted with elements antithetical to feudal society. Such elements included, in the political sphere, an absolute and uncontested central power, and in the economic sphere, the lively circulation of money. Romanian feudalism was peripheral, diluted, as the Renaissance and the Enlightenment would be in their turn.[1]

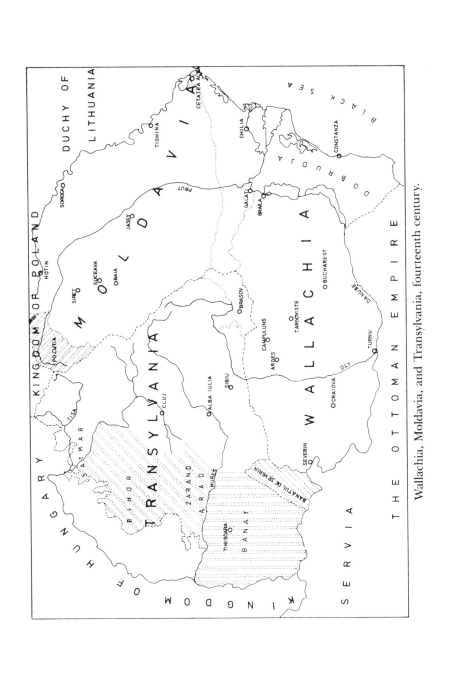

Wallachia, Moldavia, and Transylvania, fourteenth century.

The Economy. In the mid-fourteenth century Moldavia probably had a population of about 400,000, Wallachia about 500,000, and Transylvania about 900,000. The population increased gradually from the tenth century until the end of the fifteenth, when it began to fall in Moldavia and Wallachia because of the frequent wars, invasions, and internal conflicts among boyar factions or pretenders to the thrones. In the early sixteenth century Wallachia had a population of only 400,000; at the end of the century we know that there were 3,000 villages— which, estimating twenty houses per village and five inhabitants per house, suggests a population of no more than 300,000. After the reign of Stephen the Great (Ştefan cel Mare), which ended at the turn of the sixteenth century, Moldavia's population was probably smaller than when the principality was founded. It certainly had fewer people than Wallachia. In the seventeenth century periods of stagnation seem to have alternated with periods of growth, but the result was a net increase: at the turn of the eighteenth century Wallachia had 800,000 inhabitants, Moldavia 500,000, and Transylvania probably 2,000,000.[2]

The population in this period was concentrated at the foot of the Carpathians, on both sides of the range; the Danube area was also heavily populated until the coming of the Turks. The Wallachian plain and the open areas of Moldavia were rapidly depopulated as they were successively overrun by Turks, Tatars, Polish and Hungarian crusades against the Ottomans, and the campaigns of the Russo-Turkish wars.[3] Political insecurity ruined the flourishing Danube commerce and made agricultural use of the richest land in the two principalities impracticable. The plains were not farmed extensively again until after Ottoman suzerainty was limited by the Treaty of Adrianople in 1829. At that time they once more became the most densely populated parts of the country.

It is difficult to trace population migration from principality to principality in this period. There must have been constant traffic across the Milcov River, which divides Moldavia and Wallachia, although there is no record of this. Probably it was considered natural and not worthy of mention. Little is known about migrations between Transylvania and the other two principalities, either. After the waves of emigration south and east from Transylvania, which helped lead to the founding of Moldavia and Wallachia, it is likely that the percentage of Transylvanians moving to the other two principalities was variable but never significant. But this flow of people is mentioned as early as 1234, when Pope Gregory IX advised Béla, coregent of Hungary, not to permit Romanians from Transylvania to "cross the mountains," because they would become assimilated to the Wallachians. Emigration into Moldavia and Wallachia was common in the seventeenth century and is frequently noted. In 1635, for instance, the emissaries of Prince Vasile Lupu of Moldavia openly urged the peasants of the Cluj region to move to Moldavia; in 1662 Michael Apaffy, prince of Transylvania, asked the residents of Bistriţa to stop the poor from moving to Moldavia; and in 1692 the government of Transylvania notified the Habsburg emperor Leopold I that it was having difficulty limiting emigration to Moldavia and Wallachia. It became still more difficult in the eighteenth century, when the peasants learned that the regimes in Moldavia and Wallachia were less oppressive than Austrian rule in Transylvania.[4]

Throughout the fourteenth to early eighteenth centuries, Moldavia and Wallachia also received a steady flow of immigrants from other countries, mostly from the Balkans—Bulgaria, Serbia, and Greece in particular—as the Christian states south of the Danube fell to the Ottoman empire. The fact that the population grew slowly in spite of all this immigration shows the setbacks to social and economic progress caused by an unstable political zone.

Agriculture and animal raising were the principal economic activities throughout the Middle Ages. The grains raised were, in descending order, millet, wheat, and oats. Millet was the principal food of the Romanian peasant, as it was of all the people of southern Europe during the Middle Ages. Spring millet, easily cultivated, was eaten as porridge (mămăligă) even in Dacian times, and it formed the basis of the people's diet until it was replaced by North American corn in the seventeenth century. Wheat, which was used mostly by the ruling class, was imported from Transylvania but was rarely grown in Moldavia and Wallachia before the sixteenth century. This was spring wheat; winter wheat, with its higher yield and greater nutritional value, was introduced in Transylvania in the sixteenth century and in the other two principalities only in the eighteenth. After 1500 Moldavia and Wallachia too exported wheat, especially to the Ottoman empire—clear evidence that more of it was being raised, although it continued to be a luxury. Meanwhile corn was brought from Venice through Hungary and Serbia. Corn was easy to grow and, even better, did not form part of the tribute demanded by the Turks. Cultivation of corn probably began in the early seventeenth century in Transylvania and at the end of the century in Moldavia and Wallachia. From then on corn became a staple for Romanian peasants. Other grains were raised, too: oats, second only to wheat in Transylvania; barley, used in bread and beer and as fodder; and rye.

In Transylvania iron plowshares, used by the Dacians and of course the Romans, reappeared in the fourteenth century, and fertilization and triennial crop rotation somewhat later. In Moldavia and Wallachia the wooden plow was the principal agricultural tool throughout the Middle Ages. There the availability of sparsely populated uncultivated land led to the practice of using one field until it was exhausted and then moving on to another. In the sixteenth century biennial crop rotation was used, but the constant clearing of land shows that finding new land was preferred to more intensive use of the old.[5]

In addition to raising grain the Romanians had vineyards (famous even in Dacian times), orchards, gardens (in which they raised a few kinds of vegetables), and beehives to supplement the traditional diet, which was monotonous but nourishing and was generously added to by the country's considerable meat production. In the sixteenth and seventeenth centuries animal husbandry was Moldavia and Wallachia's greatest source of wealth, and it was important in Transylvania, too. People raised cattle, horses, goats, and especially sheep: the Cîmpulung region alone produced 240,000 sheep per year in the early eighteenth century. A boyar might own many flocks. For instance, in the mid-seventeenth century, the great boyar Papa Brâncoveanu had 12,000 mares, 30,000 sheep, 4,000 oxen, 1,000 water buffalo, and 4,000 pigs, and exported not only to the Balkans but to central Europe. Every year in September shepherds from Transylvania drove their flocks across Moldavia and Wallachia on their way to winter pastures on the Danube. Herding flocks from one region to another, documented as early as the rule of Mircea the Old (1386–1418) in Wallachia and involving 300,000 sheep by the beginning of the eighteenth century, was of great importance in Romanian history. Tolls levied on the animals not only brought Moldavia and Wallachia significant revenues but also served to maintain ties between the Romanians on the two sides of the Carpathians.[6]

Crafts developed rapidly in the fourteenth century in all three principalities. Cottage industries, both in boyar and in peasant households, were for a long time the only source of clothing, food, construction, and the like. Specialized production came relatively slowly—including even the distinction between artisan and farmer. By the middle of the fifteenth century, however, there was clear progress, with contemporary witnesses to metal, wood, stone, and leather working, weaving, pottery, milling, and the food industries as well-developed Romanian crafts. Some crafts, for example, clothing production, declined during the seventeenth century in Wallachia and Moldavia, but cloth manufacture continued to flourish in Transylvania. Lumbering began both for exporting logs and for making potassium carbonate for glass and soap production. The working of precious metals also became a distinct craft.

Manufacturing had a late, slow start, and was generally short-lived. Transylvania was well protected from invasion and had the benefit of technological know-how brought by Saxon immigrants, so that paper and cloth production began there in the first half of the sixteenth century, but in Moldavia and Wallachia it took another hundred years to get under way. In Wallachia Matei Basarab (r. 1632–54) built two paper mills and a glassworks that was still in use at the turn of the eighteenth century. Şerban Cantacuzino (r. 1678–88) also built a paper mill. But these efforts had only limited success, and princely manufacturing never became a real part of the country's economy. Inevitably the troubled times ahead interrupted their activity.[7]

The unstable political situation also explains why mining did not develop to its full potential. Even in the sixteenth century foreign travelers mentioned that the Romanians did not exploit their mines for fear that the Turks would take advantage of them; the Moldavian prince Dimitrie Cantemir offered this same reason again in the early eighteenth century. Only salt, abundant in all three principalities, was continuously mined, and although extraction methods were rudimentary throughout the feudal period—open pits lined with twigs—production rose steadily, for salt was much in demand in the countries south of the Danube. Other mining developed irregularly. From the time of Mircea the Old iron and copper were mined and processed at Baia de Fier and Baia de Aramă, respectively, but production fell off in the sixteenth century, and most of the Wallachian mines were abandoned for almost a hundred years. In the time of Matei Basarab, Baia de Aramă produced 700 metric tons of copper per year, but this fell to 250 metric tons by the end of the seventeenth century. In addition to salt, iron, and copper, Moldavia and Wallachia produced sulfur, amber, saltpeter, and precious metals from the fourteenth to the seventeenth centuries. Transylvania mined lead, mercury, gold, and silver. In comparison to the other two principalities, Transylvania had advanced techniques for extracting and working metals in the seventeenth century, and it was not until the end of the century that a mining crisis struck, brought about by the political upheavals that ended in the principality's annexation by the Habsburg empire.

The first evidence of drilling for oil comes from the fourteenth century, and the first wells went into production in 1440 in Moldavia and 1517 in Wallachia, but they were located only near the Carpathians and their oil was only for household use. The Romanian term *petrol,* with its Latin root, suggests but does not fully prove a continuity from ancient times to the Middle Ages.

All these products formed the basis of Romanian commerce in the medieval period. Prolonged external domination of the economy, unsafe roads, internal tariffs, and poor lines of communication worked against both domestic and international commerce, although in the Middle Ages the great trade routes that linked the Baltic with the Black Sea and central Europe with the Balkans crossed Moldavia and Wallachia even before they existed as principalities.[8] And yet, after a slow start, the domestic market developed steadily over the centuries, dealing primarily in the products of the feudal domains and the peasant farms, always at low prices. There were many fairs, markets, and bazaars (a word that entered Romanian from Turkish around 1500), and in the cities boyars, monasteries, and merchants ran shops starting in the late sixteenth century. Early in the next century *hans* appeared, massive inns within whose protective walls native and foreign merchants could break their journey and leave goods to be sold or picked up. Travelers from abroad mention no fewer than seven hans in the capital of Wallachia in 1666, including the Şerban-Vodă han, named for Prince Şerban Cantacuzino, which was still in use in the early nineteenth century.

International commerce was always lively in the principalities, as locally produced goods were exported and foreign goods transshipped through the region. In the thirteenth century, when the Black Sea trade was controlled by Genoa, the Genoese walled cities of Vicina at the mouth of the Danube and Caffa in the Crimea did a prosperous business controlling trade routes and dealing in Romanian grain and animal products.[9] At the end of the sixteenth century we find the three principalities trading mostly with central and northern Europe. The sale of cattle, hides, grain, honey, and wax to Austria, Germany, Venice, and Poland were the most profitable. In exchange the principalities bought silk and other fabrics, tools, weapons, and manufactured goods—boyar luxuries. Trade was largely in the hands of local businessmen, but merchants from Lvov, Venice, and Ragusa were also involved, while Saxons from the walled cities of southern Transylvania played an important part in shipping. The Romanian princes systematically encouraged brokers and in 1368 granted them special privileges.[10]

Romanian trade with Europe began to decrease in the sixteenth century, especially after Hungary came under Turkish domination in 1526, while trade with the Ottoman empire grew. Grain was first exported to the empire in 1502, but by the end of the century the Porte was the main market for Romanian products. This change in the direction of trade, which greatly affected the economic future of the country, did not result from natural economic causes but from political pressure. The first blow to the European trade was the fall of Genoese Caffa to the Ottomans in 1475, after which southern Bessarabia was occupied and administered directly by the Turkish empire. Trade with the West was gradually eliminated on all sides of the Black Sea, which by the close of the sixteenth century had become a "Turkish lake." Meanwhile, after the Ottoman victory over Hungary, Transylvania also came under Ottoman suzerainty, making trade relations with Europe difficult because the entire region from north of the Carpathians to south of the Danube was under direct Turkish control. The immediate result for trade was the gradual establishment, starting in 1568, of an Ottoman monopoly over foreign commerce in the principalities. By such means the Ottoman government—the Porte—was assured a constant and sufficient supply of food and other products. Until the Phanariot period the requirement to sell only on the Ottoman market was neither absolute nor entirely detrimental, for it was a profitable business. Exporting wheat and sheep—and later gunpowder and wood—to other countries was forbidden, although no limits were set on exports of the country's primary resource, cattle, or on hogs, honey, wax, and fish, among others. The restrictions had indirect effects, too. The obligatory sale of wheat to Constantinople, for example, helped to ensure the success of corn when it was introduced. More and more corn was grown for domestic consumption precisely because it was not required by the Porte.[11]

When the Ottoman empire began to dominate Moldavian and Wallachian commerce—and it retained its hold until the mid-nineteenth century—the principalities' ties with southern Transylvania and Poland, once the major trade partners, naturally became weaker. Commerce with northern and central Europe did not entirely stop, however: in the seventeenth century trade flourished anew with Poland, Venice, the German states, Russia—in 1656 Czar Alexei Mikhailovich granted Moldavia trading rights—and even with England, which by a 1588 treaty with Prince Petru the Blind had the right to buy and sell freely in Moldavia at a surtax of only 3 percent. From the mid-seventeenth century until after 1690 Scottish merchants living in the counties of Hîrlău, Cîrligătură, and Vaslui tried to develop the potassium carbonate trade, but they had to abandon the project when Moldavia and Poland, through which the trade route to England passed, became a chronic war zone.

Although we do not have complete figures, we can infer from those we have that in the early seventeenth century exports from Moldavia and Wallachia exceeded imports, and that the sale of cattle and produce brought the boyar class large incomes. As a result their lifestyle was able to combine Oriental ostentation with European refinement.

Commerce was first based on local currency, for the principalities regularly minted silver and bronze coins, first in Wallachia (1365) under Vladislav I (also known as Vlaicu-Vodă) and then under Petru Muşat in Moldavia (1377). Local currency production, which is evidence of a healthy and active economy, continued until 1477 in Wallachia and 1527 in Moldavia. After that economic and political difficulties—for example, the Porte's contesting of the princes' right to coin money— caused interruptions. Currency was issued sporadically in Moldavia (1558, 1562–64, 1573, 1595, 1597–1600, 1662–65) and rarely in Wallachia (1658 and 1713), mostly as a way for the voivode to show his sovereignty. In the end the failure of local coinage led to widespread use of Ottoman currency—along with Polish, Austrian, Venetian, and Dutch. Because of the various currencies in use, prices were linked to fluctuating foreign economies, not the principalities' internal economic conditions. Ottoman currency, for example, depreciated continuously from the sixteenth century on.

Social Classes. Evidence for social stratification has been found at archaeological sites from as early as the ninth and tenth centuries. Privileged groups apparently lived in relative wealth alongside an impoverished populace. In the ninth and tenth centuries the three voivodates mentioned in the *Gesta Hungarorum* in Transylvania and the Banat probably already had a feudal structure, although we have no evidence of a real nobility until the end of the tenth century, when the *Legenda Sancti Gerardi* mentions *nobiles*. Feudalism progressed rapidly in the eleventh and twelfth centuries, especially in Transylvania, where the Magyar kings introduced it in its Western style along with Catholicism. Sources refer to *nobiles* and *subditi* in the future Moldavia and Wallachia in 1227, and to *maiores terrae* and *rustici* in 1247, indicating that there were feudal lords and, probably, dependent peasants. Thus even before the two principalities were founded, the boyars seem to have acted as a ruling class basing itself on land ownership and having a mainly military function. Records show the class divided into at least three categories according to the size of the boyar's estate (*moşie*) and the way it had been acquired. In *Descriptio Moldaviae* (1716) Dimitrie Cantemir points out that "in ancient times" Moldavia had had 5,000 boyar courts, so that boyars made up a very large class, more than 10 percent of the population, if we go by what he says. This figure cannot be explained unless the title included officials (*dregător*) and all landowners, including free peasants (*răzeș*).

At the time the two principalities were founded the feudal lords were probably the first to become advisers and officials, for without their support no prince could rule. The earliest records do show, however, officials who were not lords and lords who were not officials. In time the two meanings of *boyar*—landowner and official—converged, as landholders began to participate in government and officials acquired land to add to their prestige. Although the government's role in creating nobles increased after the fifteenth century, the inherited estate continued to be the primary criterion for nobility until 1739, when Constantin Mavrocordat of Wallachia made rank dependent on the administrative position allotted by the prince. By then the number of boyars had decreased dramatically, first because of the bloody struggles among factions and then as economic decline caused a large number of lesser boyars to lose their titles. Boyars to whom this happened became free peasants. By the early nineteenth century boyars made up no more than one percent of Moldavia and Wallachia's population.

The boyar owed the prince "service" in Wallachia and "loyalty and service" in Moldavia, a primarily military obligation of vassalage. In exchange the boyar held land and enjoyed privileges that varied by region, sometimes including grants of immunity. Such grants transferred rights and exactions normally due the prince to the boyar. It is not entirely clear how the feudal domain came into existence, but it probably began with the seizure of village common land, both before the principalities' establishment and after. The princes also made gifts to reward extraordinary military service. They retained the right to confirm all succession, and estates reverted to the crown in the absence of male issue or in cases of treason. The principle of *dominium eminens* (the prince's legal right to all the land he ruled) was never challenged.

At first domains comprised only a small number of villages, but they grew markedly until the seventeenth century. In the fifteenth century there were domains with 50 villages in Moldavia and 100 in Wallachia. In the late sixteenth century Michael the Brave (Mihai Viteazul) received four villages as a dowry, and when he became prince of Wallachia in 1595, his domain included 44 villages. The Buzescus, a boyar family who owed fealty to Michael, began to build up their domain in 1461 and by 1656 owned 136 villages with a population of over 20,000. In Moldavia in the mid-seventeenth century, Nestor Ureche (father of the chronicler Grigore Ureche), owned 97 villages, and toward the end of the century Miron Costin had 89, and Iordache Ruset (of the boyar family later known as Rosetti) 167. These vast, rich domains yielded considerable wealth both from taxes and from the cattle trade—the great boyar Papa Brâncoveanu, who died in 1654, exported a thousand oxen annually, and the Buzescus made about 800,000 aspers per year— which explains the turbulence of boyar politics. Since the great boyars in particular were economically independent and had extensive political and military resources, they could often curb the prince's power, a setup that led to constant strife. Many domains came with immunities that permitted the boyar to take over the prince's duties in administration, law enforcement, taxation, and the courts. These accounted for 12.5 percent of recorded villages in 1500, and 20.2 percent in 1600. Administrative and judicial immunities disappeared in Wallachia in the seventeenth century, leaving only fiscal ones.[12]

During the feudal period the value of a domain was not measured by area but by number of villages, and more specifically by number of inhabitants, as the peasant was the principal resource. The peasant communes (obşte), whose origins are unknown, were the main framework of peasant life in the early Middle Ages. They were constantly undermined but never destroyed by the new institutions, from whose injustices they long succeeded in protecting much of the rural population. The communes were self-governing economic units that held land in common. They had the right to hold trials and accepted collective penal and fiscal responsibility. They disappeared gradually as their members came to own land privately. Many were infiltrated by new landowners who had acquired portions of the old common property and who brought feudal relations into the communes. As a result, many of the members lost their free status. In Transylvania the emergence of a dependent peasantry can be traced from the end of the eleventh century to the fourteenth, when the mass of peasants were bound to the land. But free communes still persisted, mostly in the predominantly Romanian regions of Făgăraş, Maramureş, and Haţeg, and in the Szekler lands of southeast Transylvania. In Moldavia and Wallachia the communes disappeared more slowly. Villages of free, land-owning peasants on the plains probably outnumbered those of serfs until the sixteenth century—even later in the mountains.

The obligations of the Romanian dependent peasants, and in Transylvania of the Hungarians, too, were those of subjugated peasants everywhere. From the lord the serfs received hereditary tenure of a plot of land, from which they could not be alienated but from which—

initially—they could move at will. In exchange for the use of the land they owed the lord a tithe—10 percent of production—and in addition a money rent and a work obligation. In Transylvania the Romanians owed another tenth of their agricultural and wine yields to the state, and Catholics paid a tithe to the church as well. The work obligation was oppressive, especially in Transylvania: one day per year until 1514, then one day per week, and in the seventeenth century three days per week. In Moldavia and Wallachia it was less, although the specific numbers of days are not known. Probably it was set to meet the needs of the boyars, who generally preferred other forms of payment (a larger tithe, for instance). As for rent, which is first mentioned in the twelfth century in Transylvania and in the fifteenth in Moldavia and Wallachia, it was never very high during the feudal period. Peasants owed more to the state than to the lord. The state also required work, as well as military service when needed.

As subjugation increased, so did exploitation. Taxes (*dar*), like the work obligation, increased steadily, tithes were eventually extended to all production, and fiscal oppression by the state grew heavier. At the same time the government continually limited the serfs' primary right, freedom of movement, until it was eliminated entirely. This happened all over eastern Europe. Peasants were bound to the land in perpetuity in 1487 in Bohemia, in 1496 in Poland, and in 1649 in Russia. In Transylvania the diet instituted "absolute and eternal servitude" in reprisal for the Dózsa uprising of 1514 in that same year. In Hungary freedom of movement was returned to the peasants in 1530, but in Transylvania hereditary serfdom continued until the end of the eighteenth century. Serfdom was the official policy of Moldavia and Wallachia, too. The depopulation of the villages caused by peasants' fleeing fiscal oppression and war with the Turks obliged Michael the Brave to bind the peasants to the land in Wallachia, probably in 1595. Similar provisions appear in the 1595 Moldavian treaty with Transylvania and in a 1628 ruling by Moldavian prince Miron Barnovski. The serfs of Moldavia and Wallachia did not officially regain their freedom of movement until 1746 and 1749, respectively.

Oppression by both the lords and the government made conditions worse for the peasants. That things were worst in Transylvania helps explain why there were two great peasant wars there in less than a hundred years. In 1437 the requirement that all outstanding taxes be paid in the newly devalued currency provoked the Bobîlna Uprising by Romanian and Hungarian peasants, who were supported by the declining lesser nobility and the urban poor. Led by Anton Nagy, "the

standard-bearer of Romanians and Hungarians," and by Mihail Ro-
mânul, the rebels overcame the boyar troops and won reduced feudal
obligations and strictly enforced freedom of movement. But after several more months of fighting the peasants were in turn defeated by a
coalition of the privileged classes—Hungarian and Saxon nobles and
the Szeklers—and lost these rights once more. Abuses by the aristocracy
sparked another peasant war in 1514, this one led by György Dózsa
(Gheorghe Doja), but this too ended in defeat and the imposition of
even harsher obligations, as the diet decreed that, to atone for the
revolt, the peasants "shall be subjected to the lords of the land in absolute and eternal servitude."[13]

In Moldavia and Wallachia conflicts between peasants and boyars
took less violent forms. Serfs ran away or joined outlaw bands; many
turned to legal means by buying the freedom either of an individual
or of a whole village, in spite of the very high prices—some villages
paid 40,000, 60,000, or even 150,000 aspers (figures from 1617). Seventy sheep were given in exchange for the freedom of one serf (1701),
and purchase of freedom was common throughout the seventeenth
century. As was true everywhere east of the Elbe River, feudal obligations did not lighten as domestic and foreign markets developed. Instead they became more burdensome, for the state and the ruling class
sought to augment their earnings not by freeing and paying their labor
force but by further subjugating it.

The urban life that had flourished in Dacia had disappeared with
the coming of the Huns, surviving only in Dobrudja and along the
Danube. Voivodal administrative centers reappeared in the ninth century, but it is impossible to determine how urbanized they were. When
walled cities were built in Transylvania by king and church (ninth century), and the Byzantine empire retook Dobrudja and the Danube line
in 976, urban life and commerce received a new stimulus, although
they declined temporarily with the Tatar invasion in the thirteenth century. But by the second half of that century the number of towns had
increased not only in protected Transylvania but also in Moldavia and
Wallachia. A list of Moldavian cities drawn up in Kiev between 1387
and 1392 mentions 14 urban centers. The number grew to 36 in the
fifteenth century and 39 in the sixteenth, falling to 37 in 1677, according to Miron Costin's complete list. The sources attest to 15 cities in
Wallachia in the fifteenth century and 29 at the end of the seventeenth.[14]

Most of these cities already existed by the mid-fourteenth century
along the active trade routes that crossed the region and promoted

urbanism. After the founding of Moldavia and Wallachia all cities, new and old, belonged to the crown, and the inhabitants' obligations were directly to the prince. The large number of cities and market towns should not lead us to overestimate their social and economic importance. Most of them had small populations, between 1,000 and 2,500, and even the large cities had no more than a few thousand. In the fifteenth century Tîrgovişte and Sibiu had about 5,000 inhabitants each, Cluj 6,000, and Braşov from 8,000 to 10,000. Only Chilia and Cetatea Albă (Akerman), the powerful trade cities of southern Moldavia, were larger—about 20,000 each in 1484 (just before they fell to the Turks). The cities grew in the seventeenth century: at mid-century Iaşi, in Moldavia, probably had about 50,000 people, and Bucharest probably had that many by the end of the century. But most towns remained small.

There was no serfdom in the cities, and their economic and administrative structure was based on privileges granted by the prince. In Transylvania cities were self-governing entities and enjoyed full rights to direct their own economic, social, and cultural development. This was especially true of the Saxon cities. In Moldavia and Wallachia, although the city councils chosen by the communes were supposed to have administrative, judicial, and fiscal powers, the prince maintained a parallel body of his own officials. These cities' autonomy was rarely honored except in trivial administrative matters, particularly after the sixteenth century, when the boyars began to build residences in the cities. The princes showed little interest in the cities, and what relations there were deteriorated until, in the eighteenth century, the Phanariot princes treated cities as personal fiefs.

Most city dwellers worked at urban occupations like the crafts and trade, but some also farmed, for agriculture continued in the cities throughout the Middle Ages, especially in Moldavia and Wallachia. The cities' semirural character was often commented on in the accounts of travelers. Differentiation among the crafts and increasing specialization led to the creation of guilds, beginning in the Saxon cities, where the first guilds were established by statute in the fourteenth century. Moldavia and Wallachia followed this lead quite a bit later: the first "brotherhood"—a professional and religious mutual assistance organization—was recorded in Suceava in 1540. The brotherhoods became real guilds only in the seventeenth century, and we first hear of a "guild" in 1641.

During the period under discussion Romanian city dwellers did not become a social and economic force capable of a significant political role; they did not form a third estate between the ruler and the nobility.

In the Transylvania of the Middle Ages cities were German and Hungarian enclaves, closed to Romanians, who generally settled on the outskirts, although a few managed to penetrate the cities late in the period. In Moldavia and Wallachia, after a promising start, cities stagnated economically or even declined. This stagnation was reflected by the urban population's lack of political influence.

Political Structures. Moldavia and Wallachia became principalities in the fourteenth century by rebelling against their suzerain, the king of Hungary. Preexisting structures provided the nascent states a solid foundation on which to build their new institutions, which was important because both principalities rejected the Hungarian model. Probably they preferred not to imitate the state whose hegemony they had just escaped.

The dispute with Hungary was both political and religious. The privileges that the king had granted the Teutonic Knights between 1211 and 1222 and the Knights Hospitalers in 1247 south of the Carpathians, to the detriment of the local aristocracy; the king's attempts to establish a Catholic episcopate in southern Moldavia in 1228, following the conversion of pagan Cumans and Orthodox Moldavians and Wallachians; and the suppression of Litovoi's uprising in 1277 all clearly show how greatly the interests of the Hungarian king and the Catholic church differed from those of the local leaders (called *maiores terrae* in a Diploma presented to the Hospitalers).[15]

It is no surprise that the Romanian rulers chose the Byzantine model. They had direct acquaintance with some of its aspects, and they knew others in their Bulgarian and Serbian forms. The Byzantine model had an imperial glitter and the additional advantage of being borrowed from a far-off land with no political presence in the region. The Romanians first copied Constantinople's religious hierarchy and structure, joining the family of Orthodox countries—with significant consequences both for politics and for culture and civilization. The metropolitanate of Wallachia was officially recognized by the ecumenical patriarchate in 1359, and that of Moldavia in 1401–02, after a long canonical debate. Besides the metropolitans, Byzantium also provided the model for certain categories of officials, and in fact for a type of civilization that lasted in Romania until the eighteenth century. It was not accidental that the first church built by a prince of the Basarab family, the Princely Church of St. Nicholas at Curtea de Argeş (c. 1352), was built in the purest Byzantine style.

In form of government, the two principalities were from the start

Princely Church of St. Nicholas (built fourteenth century). Curtea de Argeş, Wallachia.

absolute monarchies. Their absolutism was reaffirmed by all the rulers from Basarab I (prince of Wallachia, c. 1310–52) to Constantin Brân-coveanu (prince of Wallachia, 1688–1714) and Dimitrie Cantemir (prince of Moldavia, 1693, 1710–11). Although the prince lacked the advantage of investiture by Rome or Constantinople (kings of Hungary and Bulgaria possessed this privilege), his absolute power was held to be divinely ordained. From the fourteenth century the princes' correspondence and records used the expression "by the grace of God" and the pronoun Io (I), in the sense of "God's chosen one." Stephen the Great in Moldavia, Neagoe Basarab in Wallachia, and Basarab's successor Radu de la Afumaţi are a few of the princes who flatly claimed that they were God's chosen and anointed, a claim which not even the independent-minded seventeenth-century boyars questioned. Grigore Ureche said of the prince, "God has given him the right and his heavenly kingdom on earth," and the idea is repeated by many chroniclers, including Miron Costin, Dosoftei, Radu Greceanu, Antim Ivireanul, and of course Dimitrie Cantemir.

The monarchy was also dynastic. The law of the land provided throughout the Middle Ages for hereditary-elective succession, that is, for the prince to be elected by the boyars from among members of the ruling family—the Basarabs in Wallachia and the Muşatins in Moldavia. But until the seventeenth century the custom of the prince's naming his eldest son co-ruler during his own lifetime prevailed, leading in practice to dynastic succession.

Finally, the prince's absolute power proceeded from his various roles. He was the great voivode, from a Slavic term meaning leader of armies, and the *domn,* from a Latin word meaning ruler. In diplomatic correspondence and records he was also referred to by the Greek title *autocrat* or, in translation, "sovereign ruler" (*de sine stăpînitor*) or "sole ruler" (*singur stăpînitor*). He had the power of *dominium eminens* (eminent domain) so that he owned all the land in the principality, and, added to all this, legislative, administrative, judicial, and military powers as well.

Court ritual and the emblems of power further emphasized the princes' absolute power. Until the seventeenth century princes wore Western-style open crowns with three or five fleurons, worked in gold and encrusted with precious stones. Crowns were less often used after Ottoman suzerainty, but in church murals the princes were still depicted wearing them. Brâncoveanu was probably the last voivode to have a sumptuous new crown made (he did this in 1688) and who dared to wear it. Along with the crown and the mantle, the standard, the mace, and sometimes the scepter served as emblems of authority. At the height of their wealth and power the princes considered themselves successors to the Byzantine autocrats, defenders of Balkan Orthodoxy, and upholders of the Byzantine political tradition in the Balkans.

Authoritarian princely rule did not always run smoothly, and there were moments when its ability to continue was cast in doubt by the powerful class of lords. But the monarchy grew stronger as prince succeeded prince and each extended his authority and economic and military power, limiting the boyars' immunities. From the fourteenth century through the sixteenth the princes ruled absolutely, and neither

the decentralizing efforts of the boyars nor interference from neighboring powers could prevent them from consolidating power at the top.
The aristocracy manifested its opposition often and violently: there
were long civil wars like the ones fought in Wallachia from 1418 to
1456 and in Moldavia from 1432 to 1457, and the boyars plotted against
the princes, sought to replace strong authoritarian rulers with ones
more easily led, and at all times strove to weaken the prince. The boyars
occasionally succeeded in putting their candidate on the throne, but
most often paid for their thirst for power in blood.

Only after the old dynasties died out in the seventeenth century did
the aristocracy succeed in imposing what was called the "boyar state."
The boyars, like their Polish counterparts, were able to control the
central authority by electing weak princes, guiding their policies, and
preventing the formation of new dynasties. The theoretical program of
the boyars was very clearly stated in texts like the Treaty of Alba Iulia
(1595), which the Wallachian boyars made with the Transylvanian
prince against the instructions of Michael the Brave; and in *Jalba și
cererile domnilor boieri moldoveni* (Petition and appeals of the Moldavian
boyar lords [1684]), addressed to the king of Poland, in which the boyars demanded a status comparable to that of the Polish nobility. Chroniclers like the Moldavians Grigore Ureche and Miron Costin vehemently
criticized despotism and even defended regicide.

In practice, boyar rule was characterized by the installation of malle-
able princes, or direct seizure of the throne by some boyar families. For
instance, in Wallachia the Buzescus were satisfied to direct from the
wings, while the Movilăs actually wore the crown. They were the first
boyar family not of the old dynasty's bloodline to do so, and they eventually formed their own dynasty, which gave the two principalities several princes between 1595 and 1634. The Cantacuzino family too, after
a struggle with the Băleanus and a period of government through in-
termediaries (1663–78) put their Șerban on the throne. Other powerful
families who played important parts in strengthening and maintaining
the boyar regime were the Costins, the Rosettis, and the Brâncoveanus.

The power struggle between prince and boyars caused an alternation
between princely and boyar regimes. As in Poland, this struggle was
detrimental to the country, weakening it at a time of international crises.
In its weakened state it invited foreign intervention, which eventually
overthrew both prince and boyars. They were replaced by the despotism of the Phanariots.

Under the form of government and the political regimes just described, government institutions developed slowly from the time the two principalities were founded until the early fifteenth century, after which institutions stabilized, remaining basically unchanged until the 1600s. Administration was a function of the prince assisted by his council (in the late sixteenth century given the Turkish name of *divan*). Initially one aspect of the feudal obligation of *consilium*, the divan was made up of great boyars who served in the capacity of feudal lords rather than court officials. As the state grew more centralized, the divan comprised court officials exclusively. Boyars without government positions had entirely disappeared from it by the sixteenth century. When all power was concentrated in the hands of the prince, the divan had a wide range of duties, dealing with administrative, judicial, and even foreign policy problems. As a rule the princes appointed relatives and trusted advisers to the council—Michael the Brave had 36 relatives on his divans, Matei Basarab had 16, Şerban Cantacuzino 22, and Constantin Brâncoveanu 19. A position on the divan, although not paid, was a source of unquestionable power and political influence.

Throughout the feudal period, as everywhere in Europe, officials (*dregător*) served at the pleasure of the prince, not of the country, and the prince replaced them at will. Frequent changes in ruler and conflict between prince and boyars impeded administrative modernization by preventing formation of a stable civil service. Of the twenty-three officials known to have served under Prince Vlad the Impaler (Vlad Ţepeş, r. 1448, 1456–62, 1476), only three are mentioned throughout his reign, the rest having served only a year or two. Between 1501 and 1546 Moldavia had six chief secretaries (*logofăt*) and six sword-bearers (*spătar*), and from 1546 to 1600, twelve and twenty-five, respectively. Wallachia had seventeen treasurers (*vistiernic*) in the first period and forty-one in the second. Instability continued through the seventeenth century.

At the turn of the eighteenth century, according to Cantemir, there were 278 high officials in Moldavia, including eight of the first rank— a chief secretary (*logofăt*), two administrative heads (*vornic*), a military leader (*hatman*), a treasurer (*vistiernic*), a chamberlain (*postelnic*), a sword-bearer (*spătar*), and a cupbearer (*paharnic*)—forty of the second rank, and 230 lesser officials. Cantemir's figures, even if not exact, permit us to draw three important conclusions about the social and institutional history of Moldavia. First, they show that boyar rank was not yet identified with the high government position that under the Phanariots would be regarded as a boyar's natural function. Second, they reflect a tendency toward hierarchy and toward concentrating

Vlad the Impaler, prince of Wallachia (1448, 1456–62, 1476). Oil portrait, Ambras Castle, Austria.

power in a few hands, the other posts having only a secondary importance. Finally, the small number of court officials shows that the government's role was still limited.

The main work of the prince and his officials, in addition to day-to-day government, was judicial and fiscal. The administration of justice was always the absolute prerogative, unrestricted and unassailed, of the prince, in the presence of his divan. The divan was the only stable court in medieval Romanian society, but the prince could delegate judicial powers to any official, central or local, or to boyars or monasteries where their domains were concerned, or to the village communes. No distinction was made between the right to sentence and the power to punish, usually by large fines, so the administration of justice became a great source of income for all officials. Naturally it was much abused, the more so because written laws were late to appear and even then were not consistently enforced.

Common law had set standards since before the two principalities were founded, and it formed the body of jurisprudence throughout the feudal period. Roman-Byzantine law and canon law appeared (as *nomo-canons*) in the fifteenth century, when Wallachia copied the Slavic *Zakonik* (1451) and Moldavia adopted Matei Vlastares' *Syntagma,* a collection of civil and penal Byzantine laws. A great deal of church law was written either in Old Church Slavonic or in Romanian in the sixteenth and seventeenth centuries. Since the church played an important role in civil and penal matters, its law was often used. The first real civil codes date from the seventeenth century, some of them in manuscript like Eustratie's *Pravila* (Law [1632]), and others printed, like *Cartea românească de învățătură* (Romanian book of instruction [Iaşi, 1646]) or *Îndreptarea legii* (Guide to the law [Tîrgovişte, 1652]). All were based on Byzantine sources and the work of the Italian jurist Prosper Farinaccius, and the last two were still in use after 1750.

The other important domestic activity of the government, taxation, also changed considerably during the medieval period. Most of princely and state income—the state treasuries were not separated from the prince's until the sixteenth century—was supplied by revenues from the voivode's domain, from the market towns, and from the peasants. During this period tithes (*dijmă*) of grain, livestock, dairy products, wine, and the like were a great source of wealth for the government, as were labor obligations in harvesting, transport, woodcutting, and pond and mill work. Money income was provided by tariffs, salt mine leases, and fines. In the early fifteenth century the exaction of tribute (*bir*), from which boyars and clergy were exempt, augmented the monies received.

Under Ottoman suzerainty the princes' need for money grew ceaselessly—and so did the tributes. By the sixteenth century tribute had become the heaviest charge on the populace and the princes' main source of wealth. By the end of the next century the degree of fiscal oppression was severe. Besides the increased tributes, taxable goods multiplied until peasants had to make sixty different kinds of payments where there had been twenty at the turn of the century. Taxes could be collected several times a year, according to the needs of the ruler, and could also be demanded of the privileged classes when necessary. The size and number of the payments, which were collected remorselessly, the conversion to cash of many payments formerly made in kind, and the heavy fines imposed by the courts, together with salt mine leases and tariffs, brought the princes a great deal of money. The state's wealth was increasingly based on the impoverishment of its citizens, on taxation rather than economic development.

The Romanians of Transylvania. The history of the Romanians in Transylvania diverges from that of Wallachia and Moldavia. After conquering the voivodates of Menumorut, Glad, and Gelu in the ninth century the Magyars seem to have occupied only the highest levels of feudal society, replacing the old voivodes. They organized the region only in the eleventh or twelfth century, after it had been reconquered by the Hungarian king and saint, Stephen. The first mention of a "prince" (principe) of Transylvania and of the first county (comitat), Bihor, on the Hungarian border, dates from 1113. Nine more counties appeared in the twelfth century, and in 1176 a second principe is mentioned. With feudalization the nobility in Transylvania was gradually Magyarized, so that by the fifteenth century the nobles (*cneaz*) of Haţeg and voivodes of Maramureş were no longer true Romanians. Magyarized Romanians gave Hungary a king (Matthias Corvinus), a voivode of Transylvania (János Hunyadi, also known as John Hunyadi or Iancu of Hunedoara), and a Catholic primate (Nicolaus Olahus), as well as numbers of soldiers, dignitaries, and scholars.

The displacement of the Romanian aristocracy from political life really began after 1365–66. In a decree King Louis I (called the Great) required royal confirmation of noble rank, made Catholicism a qualification for holding titles and for ownership of land, and denied the rights and privileges of the clergy to members of the Orthodox church. Religion thus became a primary criterion for nobility, whereas the previous dynasty, that of Arpad, had accepted religious and linguistic pluralism in Transylvania. The establishment of an official religion was due in part to the radical religious policies of the Angevin dynasty and in part to the renewed conflict between Rome and Orthodox Byzantium and to Louis's loyalty to the papacy. No doubt the king was also motivated by Wallachia and Moldavia's having recently thrown off Hungarian rule. Magyar mistrust of the Romanian aristocracy in Transylvania was on the increase—especially since the support of the Romanian nobles in Maramureş, hostile to Hungary, had made Moldavian independence possible.

Political life in Transylvania was open only to the privileged classes, and without noble leadership the Romanians participated less and less, until they were completely excluded.[16] The leaders of the Bobîlna Uprising (1437) wanted to form a kind of peasant order or estate, and called for recognition of "the commune of Hungarians and Romanians in these parts of Transylvania" (*universitas regnicolarum Hungarorum et Valachorum in his partibus Transilvaniae*). But when the uprising was put down by the aristocracy, the opposite effect was achieved. A "brotherly union," the Unio Trium Nationum, granted the Hungarian, Saxon, and Szekler nobility a political monopoly and denied the Romanians any place in the political life of the principality. This segregation of the majority population became still stricter in the sixteenth century. First the peasants were made absolute serfs (1514, 1517), and then four privileged religions—Catholicism, Lutheranism, Calvinism, and Unitarianism—were recognized. Eastern Orthodoxy was only tolerated. When Hungary came under Ottoman domination (1526) and Buda and Transylvania became a pashalik and an autonomous tributary principality, respectively (1541), the status of the Romanians remained unchanged. Within the new state the Hungarian political leaders still would not recognize the Romanians as a "nation" equal in rights to the Hungarians, the Saxons, and the Szeklers. Like the Christian peoples of the Balkan states, the Romanians of Transylvania had no political leaders and no political standing, and the only institution that could represent their interests was the Orthodox church.

Monasteries are mentioned in Transylvania as early as the eleventh century, when Ahtum, successor of Gelu, endowed an Orthodox monastery at Cenad. We have no evidence for hierarchical organization until 1370, when a metropolitanate with jurisdiction over Oltenia, the Banat, and southern Transylvania was set up at Severin by the patriarch in Constantinople. In 1391 the patriarch established an exarchate in Transylvania headed by the abbot of the Peri monastery in Maramureş; in 1455 an Orthodox episcopate was established at Muncaci. Sometime in the sixteenth century came another episcopate at Vad, and in 1557 yet another at Geoagiu. During this time the Transylvanian Orthodox church was closely tied to those of the other two principalities. Princes of Wallachia in particular had constantly supplied money, books, religious objects, gifts, and even churches. Prince Neagoe Basarab built two, at Zărneşti and Almaşul Mare; the monk Nicodim of Tismana founded Prislop monastery in Haţeg (1398); and many princes endowed the church at Scheii Braşovului. Michael the Brave and Sigismund Báthory signed a treaty in 1595 that placed the Orthodox church of Transylvania under the canonical jurisdiction of the Wallachian metropolitan. Thereafter metropolitans of Transylvania were consecrated at Tîrgovişte in Wallachia. At Alba Iulia Michael built a new church for the metropolitan of Transylvania, and Moldavian and Wallachian princes continued to support the metropolitanate throughout the seventeenth century with annual gifts and subsidies. And they continued to build churches: Constantin Brâncoveanu built three, at Făgăraş, Sîmbăta, and Ocna-Sibiului.

But Orthodoxy, tolerated but not officially recognized, its clergy denied the rights accorded those of the "accepted" religions, could not offer Romanians the institutional framework in which to become a nation that was recognized politically. Michael the Brave did obtain some economic privileges for Orthodox clergy. But neither his brief reign over Transylvania in 1599–1601 (in 1600 he also ruled Moldavia in addition to Wallachia) nor the sympathy for Orthodoxy of the two Rákóczi princes who ruled Transylvania in the mid-seventeenth century could rescue it from inferior status. In 1691 the Habsburg empire took over Transylvania, but this too promised nothing good for the Romanians, for Leopold I undertook to respect all Transylvania's laws, including those naming the three privileged nations and four privileged religions.

The Romanians' desire to escape their unprivileged status and Austrian interest in strengthening Catholicism over Protestantism gave rise to the idea that, by joining the Catholic church, Romanians might enter a privileged category. The Habsburg court sent Jesuit envoys to propose a "church union," and the Orthodox hierarchy quickly embraced it. In 1697 a synod under Metropolitan Teofil agreed to conditions for uniting Eastern Orthodoxy with Roman Catholicism. Orthodox Christians would accept Catholic dogma while retaining Orthodox ritual and calendar; in exchange they asked that members of the new Uniate Church be granted full civil rights as loyal citizens and be admitted to Catholic schools. After a second synod, convened in 1698 by Teofil's successor Anghel Atanasie, reaffirmed the desire for union, Emperor Leopold issued a diploma (1699) extending to Uniate clergy the rights and privileges enjoyed by Catholic clergy. He freed them from serfdom, exempted them from taxes and tithes, and made them eligible for the nobility. At the insistence of Atanasie, now a Catholic bishop, Leopold in 1701 issued a second diploma extending these privileges to all Uniates regardless of social condition—even to peasants.

The "church union" was really politics under cover of religion, as Romanians sought to escape their inferior status by using the Catholic church. But the privileged nations quickly spotted the threat posed to

Michael the Brave, prince of Wallachia (1593–1601). Contemporary engraving.

the established regime, and in 1698 and 1699 they objected to the inclusion of Uniate Romanians in the ranks of privilege. As a result Leopold's second diploma never went into effect, so that the Romanians ended by gaining much less than they had asked for and much less than Leopold had promised them.

International Status and Foreign Policy

Foreign Policy Goals. Romanian foreign policy objectives naturally varied from period to period, depending on the international situation and the actions of the neighboring great powers. Like any ruling class, the Romanian boyars were constantly preoccupied with protecting the state as an entity, defending territory, and maintaining, if not independence, at least considerable autonomy.

The first princes had held themselves to be divinely ordained sole rulers and autocrats whose independence set an example to which many of their successors aspired. In 1561 the Moldavian prince Despot-Vodă declared his wish "to free this country from tyranny and to put it in good order, as it once was in the time of my illustrious predecessors." Michael the Brave of Wallachia was proud that, through him, "the principality regained its old freedom" (1595).[17] Independence was a goal throughout the seventeenth century, and princes of both Moldavia and Wallachia sought after it: Mihnea III and Constantin Şerban, Grigore I Ghica, Ştefan Petriceicu, Şerban Cantacuzino, Constantin Brâncoveanu, and Dimitrie Cantemir. Brilliant scholars like Miron Costin and High Steward (*stolnic*) Constantin Cantacuzino also held up independence as a goal. Cantacuzino was especially emphatic in his praise of the Romanians' powers of resistance, holding that they knew better than their neighbors how to maintain a separate state with its own political structures in the face of all obstacles.

Boyars and princes continually affirmed the independence of the principalities, upholding their historical boundaries and refusing to recognize annexations, invasions, or other alterations. Wallachia lost its Transylvanian possessions Amlaş and Făgăraş to Hungary in 1476, but they remained in the prince's official titles until 1688. Some voivodes, for example, Petru Aron of Moldavia, undertook "not to alienate the land or estates of Moldavia" (1456), and others promised to retake territory from the Turks, restoring the Danube boundary. Despot-Vodă openly intended to retake the Buceag; Michael the Brave spoke in 1595 of reuniting Wallachia "within its old borders and boundaries"; and Miron Costin's 1677 chronicle contains a chapter on "holdings taken by the Turks." Respect for Moldavia's territorial integrity and original borders were part of the 1711 treaty between Prince Dimitrie Cantemir and Peter the Great of Russia, and in his later writings Cantemir presented the historical arguments for this irredentism.[18]

It is difficult to discern from the documents which of the neighboring countries Romanians considered the greatest threat to their independence. Although Hungary and Poland formed an indispensable last resort in the anti-Ottoman fight, Romanians were as well aware of their Christian neighbors' designs on their territory as they were of the Ottomans'. In times of need they always turned to Buda and Krakow for help, though often fearing that their allies only wanted to take the Turks' place. Stephen the Great wrote with bitter realism, toward the end of his long (1457–1504) rule over Moldavia, "In these parts only I am left, for on two sides there is deep paganism and on the other three sides are those who call themselves Christians but who treat me worse than the pagans."[19] Fear of the neighboring Christian powers grew in the seventeenth century, when the blatant expansionism of Austria and Poland removed any illusions about their frequent promises of liberation. The Romanians were able to find no solution to the dilemma posed by their powerful neighbors during the Middle Ages.

The Ottomans' intent was at least clear from the beginning. The threat of being made into a pashalik hung over Moldavia and Wallachia for many years, and their leaders knew it, as is clear from the 1456 document in which the Moldavian boyars agreed to pay tribute to the sultan. It said that, in order "not to lose our country we must put aside need as we may and bow our heads to the pagans, and we must find a way to give them what we can to mollify them until merciful God relents and we again have God's help and find our allies as our forebears did." In 1523 Prince Ştefăniţă of Moldavia again feared that Wallachia would be made a pashalik. The documents reflect his perception of the Turks as knowing only how to despoil. "All they know and understand is the outstretched hand," wrote Neagoe Basarab, prince of Wallachia (r. 1512–21). But they were never satisfied, no matter how much was given, and their reactions were never predictable or assured.[20]

From the time that Moldavia and Wallachia were founded, the princes had adopted the attitude of crusaders defending the threatened borders of Europe. The Romanians considered themselves a bastion of Christianity, a barrier to the foe from the south who threatened to destroy Europe. The crusader spirit can be seen as early as Vladislav I of Wallachia (called Vlaicu-Vodă), the first voivode to come into direct military conflict with the Turks (1371). Later it was expressed not only by strong and actively anti-Ottoman princes like Mircea the Old, Stephen the Great, and Radu de la Afumaţi, but also in the letters of some more cautious voivodes who feared open conflict with the Turks, for example, Alexandru Aldea, Basarab the Old, Radu the Great, and Neagoe Basarab. For all of these the two principalities were the "gateway to Christianity," and if they fell, "then all Christendom would be in danger."[21] In the sixteenth century, after the fall of Hungary and the increased vassalage of the principalities to the Ottoman empire, the crusade idea lost some of its intensity and was brought up only by the princes who planned or carried out wars against the Ottomans—Despot-Vodă, Ioan the Terrible, Aron the Tyrant, and Michael the Brave. Their tone echoed that of Stephen the Great: their country was "shield to the entire Christian world," and their purpose, to unite disparate European interests against the Turkish crescent.

Michael the Brave led and lost a war of liberation (1593–1601), and after that, although references to the Ottoman empire continued to appear in the documents, they were less often openly made—and the words were less often followed by deeds. No longer did the princes state their hostility to the sultan except indirectly: they desired his defeat, they rejoiced at Christian victories, but they admitted that they could not rise against him without a decisive European victory. Nevertheless, independence remained their primary goal, and they plotted against the Turks, informed Austria and Russia of Ottoman plans, movements, and military strength, and promised the backing of their troops in case of conflict. Very few princes lacked anti-Ottoman political programs, although the international situation prevented them from carrying them out.[22]

Means and Methods. The means and methods by which the Romanians dealt with other countries also varied from one period to another. Although the use of raw military action predominated until the sixteenth century, it was supported by lively diplomacy and an efficient system of alliances. In the seventeenth century diplomacy became most important.

Moldavia and Wallachia, which had been put on the map of Europe by military victories over the kingdom of Hungary, started out with large, well organized armies intended to enforce the princes' foreign policy. The voivode would turn first to the small army (*oastea mică*), troops raised from his domain, from the cities and free villages, and from the boyars' own guards. A boyar could keep up to a hundred armed soldiers to ensure peace in his domain and court, and he lent them to the prince as part of his feudal obligation of *auxilium*. In times of extreme need the prince could also call up the great army (*oastea mare*), composed of peasants who had to serve in the prince's army on demand. Most medieval wars, especially those on foreign ground, were fought by the small army, which numbered about ten or twelve thousand soldiers in the fourteenth and fifteenth centuries, with an additional few hundred Hungarian, Polish, and German mercenaries. With the great army, first raised by Mircea the Old of Wallachia (r. 1389–1418) and last by Ioan the Terrible of Moldavia in 1574, Moldavia and Wallachia could each field 40,000 soldiers. Michael the Brave, ruling

Wallachia at the end of the sixteenth century, had the largest army, 50,000, including 10,000 mercenaries; after his reign the numbers fell steadily during the seventeenth century, when the two principalities fought few wars on their own behalf. At mid-century Vasile Lupu of Moldavia had only 35,000 soldiers and Matei Basarab of Wallachia 40,000, while in the early eighteenth century Cantemir, seeking Russian help to reorganize his army, envisioned a modest force of 17,000. He probably fought the battle of Stănileşti (1711) with even fewer.

Between the time Moldavia and Wallachia were founded and the era of the Phanariot princes the army clearly underwent a radical transformation. The great army, which alone could mobilize the whole country against a threat from without, was gradually supplanted by the small army. As government became more centralized and the boyars less a warrior class, the position of the boyars' guards was gradually taken by new troops. Such troops were recruited from among the smaller boyars and free peasants, who were eager to serve in exchange for social and economic privileges. Other social changes intervened to bring about a loss of military strength as well. As the peasants became increasingly subjugated, the pool from which the great army could be drawn grew smaller, and the prince's army, made up of professionals, gained in importance by default. The principalities found it impossible to keep up with military technology, and their armies could no longer fight wars unaided. Ottoman domination hastened the military decline, for the Turks would not permit large armies to be raised and opposed modernization lest it be used against them.

Before the eighteenth century the Romanians managed to win some decisive battles against would-be conquerors: the Hungarians, the Poles, the Tatars, and especially the Turks. As a rule the battles that stopped invasions and prevented the Ottomans from significantly altering the status of the principalities—in 1394, 1462, 1475, and 1595—were won by Romanians fighting almost alone. But even in the fourteenth century it was evident that winning a battle was not the same as winning a war. The principalities, constantly threatened from outside, clearly needed a system of alliances to stabilize their political situation and, if necessary, support prolonged resistance.

The Christian Balkan states fell to the Ottomans before the Romanians could form lasting ties with them, although the Basarab family was related to the descendants of the Serbian ruler Stephen Dushan and to the Bulgarian czars; Wallachia fought the Turks with the Serbs at Chirmen (1371) and in the Nikopol crusade (1396), but then Bulgaria became a Turkish pashalik, and the principality could do no more than offer asylum to members of the Bulgarian dynasty. Wallachia, independent of Hungary since 1330, reestablished diplomatic relations with that country in 1355, but these were often interrupted by war until Mircea the Old signed a treaty with the Hungarian king Sigismund of Luxembourg (1395). In this anti-Ottoman document each agreed to be "a friend to the friends and an enemy to the enemies" of the other, and this military and political collaboration lasted until Hungary fell under Turkish domination (1526). Almost all the Romanian princes accepted Hungarian suzerainty, and further treaties were concluded in 1426, 1455, 1507, 1511, and 1517. In 1389 Mircea the Old also formed an alliance with Poland, though with no provision for homage, as a counterbalance to Hungarian influence, and this was renewed several times before it ended in 1411. Moldavia too, independent of Hungary since 1359, concluded an alliance with that country in 1435 (renewed in 1450, 1453, and 1475). Treaties with Poland were even more numerous, the first in 1387 and the last in 1595. During this long period some Moldavian princes accepted Hungarian or Polish suzerainty.

Considering that Moldavia and Wallachia were paying tribute to the Porte at the same time, from 1456 and 1417, respectively, one should note an important aspect of medieval Romanian diplomacy: multiple vassalage. Mircea the Old accepted the suzerainty of Poland (1387), Hungary (1395), and the Ottoman empire (1417); Petru Aron knelt to the sultan and the king of Poland in the same year (1456); and while Stephen the Great paid tribute to the Ottomans, he declared himself a vassal of Poland (1459, 1462, and 1485) and of Hungary (1475), although between these acts of submission he would withhold payment of tribute (1473–87, 1500–04) or unilaterally rescind Hungarian or Polish suzerainty. Each additional vassalage effectively annulled the others, so that by playing the interests of their suzerains against each other, the Romanians in effect maintained a kind of independence.

The fall of Hungary to the Turks (1526) was a heavy blow to Moldavia and Wallachia, for it deprived them of their main ally in the struggle against the Ottoman empire; since Poland remained pro-Ottoman throughout the sixteenth century, even refusing the homage of some princes so as not to anger the Porte, the Romanians turned to the Habsburg empire. Moldavia signed alliances with the Habsburgs in 1535 and 1572, and Wallachia followed suit in 1598. This turned the principalities in a new direction, and the Habsburg alliance assumed greater significance in the seventeenth century.

Even after the failure of Michael the Brave's war of liberation (1601) the traditional course of Romanian diplomacy stayed much the same.

The international situation was less favorable. By 1672 the Ottoman empire extended into the Ukraine and southern Poland, practically encircling the principalities. Poland was in decline and unable to offer resistance or provide aid. Russia and the Habsburg empire did not take action until the close of the century. And the Cossacks, long a source of mercenaries for the Romanian princes, were more interested in sacking and looting than in fighting the Turks, and ended by accepting Ottoman suzerainty.

Lacking any real assistance from outside, the three principalities returned to their traditional policy of mutual assistance, which had worked so well from the fourteenth to the sixteenth centuries. Treaties binding the three in 1605 and 1608 did not prevent the Turks from resuming their authority over all the principalities, but in 1635–47 a new series of alliances was set up by Transylvania's György Rákóczi I, Wallachia's Matei Basarab, and Moldavia's Vasile Lupu with the help of Bulgarian leaders living in exile in Tîrgovişte. These treaties were honored by succeeding princes, and they did help stabilize the political situation, so that in 1659–61 there seemed to be a chance of throwing off Ottoman control. This of course had been the purpose of the alliance. A revolt led by Prince Mihnea III of Wallachia (1659) and the rejection of Turkish suzerainty by the diet of Transylvania (1661) were the last anti-Ottoman actions undertaken by the three principalities on their own initiative.

During the second half of the seventeenth century the Romanians were very active in diplomacy, spurred by events that later brought major political changes to Europe and put the international status of the principalities seriously in question. In an effort to keep up the old game of multiple vassalage they sought alliances with Poland, Austria, and Russia. But Poland turned them down, Austria asked for too much and offered too little, and only Russia agreed to a favorable treaty with Moldavia (1711). In the end, their shrinking diplomatic and military resources made it impossible for the Romanians to hold out against the forces redrawing the map of central and southeast Europe. Their political standing in the region diminished.

The International Status of the Principalities. The principalities' international status was a function not only of their own foreign policy goals and the means available to achieve them, but also of the relationships among the countries with whom they carried on diplomacy. Throughout the Middle Ages the situation was unstable, tilting now toward the Romanians and now toward one of the neighboring great powers. The overall picture was generally favorable to the principalities until the sixteenth century but then worsened gradually until the early eighteenth century. The international situation of that time brought them to a new low, far from their old political independence and from what their political leaders wanted and worked for.

Two factors had defined the position of Moldavia and Wallachia since the fourteenth century: the great Christian powers to the west, north, and east, and the great Islamic power to the south. The two principalities had begun by declaring their independence from the Christian powers and then accepting a vassal's obligations—but without changing their official status. Unfortunately for the Romanians, however, it was not their relations with their Christian neighbors that determined their international position during the Middle Ages, but their developing relationship with the Ottoman empire, the leading military power of the time.

Their new status, which lasted until the middle of the fifteenth century, was confirmed when Wallachia and Moldavia first paid tribute to the Porte (1417 and 1456, respectively). The Turks now considered them partially dependent territories (*dar-al-ahd*), an intermediate category between "enemy territory" (*dar-al-harb*) and Moslem territory (*dar-al-islam*). The Romanians' tribute bought peace, and except for a prohibition of actions hostile to the Turks, their political structures remained independent. This was a temporary arrangement. The Ottomans could not conquer the principalities, and the principalities could not gain complete independence, so the agreement was violated by one side and then the other as forces shifted. The Romanians, for instance, frequently withheld tribute—Wallachia did not make regular payments until 1462 and Moldavia until 1538—while the Turks repeatedly tried to make the principalities more dependent, installing pro-Ottoman princes in Wallachia from the fifteenth century. In Moldavia they first named a prince in 1538. But as long as the principalities had the support of Hungary, Ottoman domination was limited, unstable, and revocable.[23]

The battle of Mohács (1526) changed the whole political situation in central and southeastern Europe: the new king of Hungary, János Zápolyai, accepted Ottoman suzerainty in 1529 and was installed in Buda by Süleyman the Magnificent himself, and in 1541 Hungary was made a pashalik and Transylvania an autonomous tributary principality. These dramatic changes affected Moldavia and Wallachia, too. In 1538 Süleyman marched into Moldavia and replaced Prince Petru Rareş with a faithful vassal of the Porte. In Wallachia the weak rulers who succeeded Neagoe Basarab and Radu de la Afumaţi between 1529 and 1545 were instrumental in reducing their country to vassalage, and Radu Paisie (1535–45) became the first prince to be deposed and exiled at the sultan's pleasure.

Under the new regime the functions of local government were substantially reduced, some rights were usurped by the Turks, and economic exploitation was added to political domination. The two principalities retained their autonomy in domestic affairs, and the border between them and the Ottoman empire remained valid, but foreign policy was controlled by the Porte: the Romanians' right to make treaties was first restricted and then abolished, and their armies were obliged to take part in Ottoman military campaigns. Princes were still elected by the boyars for a time, but they had to be approved by Constantinople; later they were increasingly named by the sultan without consultation with the boyars. Terms of office were shortened—in Moldavia princes reigned on average seven or eight years in the period between 1359 and 1538 but only two to six years between 1538 and 1711—and the pro-Turkish princes surrounded themselves with Ottoman guards. Fortresses were demolished; the capital of Moldavia was moved from Suceava to Iaşi and that of Wallachia from Tîrgovişte to Bucharest—that is, from the mountains to the open plains and from the north to the south, nearer the imperial frontier, where they could be more easily controlled. But no matter how severe the pressure, the principalities retained their government structures, for the Turks were satisfied to enjoy the economic and political advantages of indirect rule. In this way the Ottomans avoided the risk of war and other problems that might arise from the direct administration of a Christian population with a long political tradition and a ruling class determined not to lose its political individuality.

The economic domination that accompanied political control took many forms. Tribute and additional contributions (*peşcheşurile*), payments in kind and work obligations, and a virtual monopoly over commerce were all ways for the Ottoman empire to drain the principalities' resources for its own uses. Until the mid-sixteenth century tribute was kept at a reasonable level. Some years it was lowered; some years it was not paid at all. Moldavia paid 3,000 ducats in 1456, and while the tax (*haraci*) paid irregularly by Wallachia from 1417 to 1462 is not known, we know that Prince Vlad the Impaler paid 10,000 ducats before the revolt of 1462. After 1538 political subjugation and tribute both increased. Moldavia's tribute rose to 65,000 ducats and Wallachia's to 155,000 ducats in 1593; Transylvania paid between ten and fifteen thousand ducats in the late sixteenth century.

In 1600 Michael the Brave won a brief period of independence for all three principalities, and this had an immediate effect on the tribute. It fell to 32,000 ducats under Radu Şerban in Wallachia and to 30,000 ducats under the Movilă family in Moldavia before rising again. Fifty years later under Constantin Brâncoveanu Wallachia paid 92,000 ducats, though Moldavia paid only 26,000 even in the late seventeenth century—less than Transylvania, which was paying 40,000 ducats before it passed from Ottoman to Habsburg control.

But the tribute, no matter how high, was not the worst of the principalities' obligations to the Porte. The additional contributions called *peşcheşurile* were the most onerous. These miscellaneous payments in money or in kind were at first occasional and symbolic, but later annual. By the end of the sixteenth century they cost more than the tribute, and as the number of people to be bribed increased rapidly and the expense of the *peşcheşurile* grew, the payments became hard to bear. In the Ottoman empire corruption was an instrument of power. The Romanian princes were forced to spend enormous sums for the sultan's goodwill and that of his viziers and high officials. The pashas of the Danube strongholds and practically all the dignitaries with whom the Romanians came in contact also had their price.

Huge amounts were spent to get princes appointed, too. Petru Rareş paid 100,000 ducats for the Moldavian throne in 1541, the first time we hear of this. By the end of the sixteenth century the bidding among would-be rulers sent payments skyrocketing, so that Mihnea Turcitul and Petru Cercel paid about a million ducats each to be prince of Wallachia. Later these payments fell again, although they remained high: Matei Basarab paid 400,000 ducats for the throne. Starting in the mid-seventeenth century confirmation charges were exacted from the princes as well, one to be paid yearly (the small *mucaer*) and one triennially (the great *mucaer*). The great *mucaer* was usually about equal to the amount paid to gain the throne. Charges for gaining and holding the throne were the chief means of exploiting the principalities during the sixteenth and seventeenth centuries, and they were all the more oppressive for being arbitrary.

In addition to tribute, *peşcheşurile,* and purchase and confirmation of the throne, the principalities had other obligations in cash and in kind. Money was demanded as needed for special purposes—in 1658 and

1663, for instance, Transylvania paid 300,000 ducats in military contributions. There were both fixed and occasional payments in kind, which sometimes reduced the money paid as the tribute. The first records of such payments in kind date from 1542, when the Porte demanded five hundred horses for army transport (it later increased the number). Frequent requisitions for cattle, sheep, honey, wax, lumber, wagons, and labor followed as the Ottomans fought their last offensive wars. The Ottoman monopoly over foreign commerce in the principalities, discussed early in this chapter, completes the list of forms of economic domination.

Ottoman economic pressure varied with the changing relations between Porte and principalities. It was low until the mid-sixteenth century and then increased dramatically, probably peaking in the 1580s, when Wallachia sent an average of 650,000 ducats a year to Constantinople in all. Michael the Brave's wars brought a reduction in economic pressure, so that his successor, Radu Şerban, sent about 100,000 ducats to the Porte annually. The level of exploitation rose again in the seventeenth century—Brâncoveanu paid about 200,000 ducats per year—but except during the Phanariot period it never again rose to the level of the second half of the sixteenth century.[24]

The Romanians made many attempts, sometimes violent, to reduce Ottoman domination. These succeeded in delaying outright Ottoman control of the principalities and mitigated it when it did come, at least preventing the kind of direct rule that the Turks had over the Balkan states from the fourteenth century. In the late fourteenth century Mircea the Old fought the Turks, which is undoubtedly why Wallachia survived as a political entity at a time when the Turks were liquidating the czardoms of Bulgaria and Serbia. The Ottomans invaded Wallachia in 1391 and again in 1394, when the Wallachians won a great victory in the battle of Rovine against troops led by Sultan Bayezid the Thunderbolt.

Bayezid defeated an army of crusaders joined by Wallachians in the battle of Nikopol (1396), but even the punitive expedition he made into Wallachia the next year did not bring the principality to its knees. In the years that followed Mircea took advantage of the fighting among Bayezid's descendants to consolidate his position in the Balkans and to reconquer Dobrudja. He helped Musa Chelebi become sultan (1411) and made expeditions into Ottoman territory south of the Danube. Although Musa was overthrown by Mohammed I, and a Turkish invasion in the last year of his reign obliged Mircea to buy peace once more, his long reign was decisive in the history of Ottoman-Romanian relations, for it established a political equilibrium that withstood frequent upheavals to last for many centuries.

Battles with the Turks continued throughout the fifteenth century. Sometimes the Romanians were victorious, and sometimes the Ottomans, but the Romanians still held out against Ottoman pressure. Wallachian troops joined János Hunyadi in the Crusades in the Balkans (1444 and 1445); Wallachians led by Vlad the Impaler (r. 1456–62) vanquished Sultan Mehmed II in 1462; under Stephen the Great the Moldavians won a great victory over Mehmed II at Vaslui (1475), and when the sultan launched another campaign the next year they drove him out of the principality, preventing him from reducing it to a pashalik.

Military opposition to the Turks diminished noticeably as the principalities' vassalage increased, and eventually they just could not keep up their resistance. Ioan the Terrible (r. 1572–74) did lead Moldavia against the Ottoman empire, and he won a few battles. But Ioan lost the war, demonstrating what became axiomatic: the international position of the principalities could be altered only in a favorable international situation and only with the military support of the European powers.

These conditions were met in the late sixteenth century when the Holy League (the Habsburgs, the papacy, Spain, and some German and Italian principalities) formed a new alliance whose aim was driving the Ottomans from Europe. Increased Turkish pressure, growing economic exploitation, and the fear of being made a pashalik united the various boyar factions of Wallachia. Transylvania and Moldavia joined the League in 1594. Michael the Brave, acting in alliance with Moldavia and negotiating with Transylvania, began an anti-Ottoman revolt in Wallachia in November 1594. He took the Turkish fortresses along the Danube as far as Chilia and Cetatea Albă (Akerman), leaving Giurgiu the only Ottoman bridgehead on Romanian territory. In January 1595 his troops won important victories over the Tatars (who were vassals of the Ottoman empire) at Putinei and Stănești, and over the Tatars and Turks at Ruse, Bulgaria. As fighting on the Danube line continued through the spring of 1595, the Ottomans prepared a campaign to defeat Michael decisively. For his part, he was agreeing to pay homage to Sigismund Báthory, prince of Transylvania, in exchange for military aid. In August the grand vizier Sinan Pasha succeeded in getting his forces across the Danube and headed for Bucharest. But in Călugăreni, a hilly, forested area crossed by a river and full of swamps, Michael's army won one of the greatest victories in the history of his people, stopping the Ottoman advance and forcing Sinan to retreat. The Wallachians, however, were far outnumbered and could not risk another major battle, so Michael withdrew into the mountains to await Transylvanian and Moldavian reinforcements. Meanwhile the Turks occupied Bucharest and Tîrgoviște and took steps to make Wallachia a pashalik—but not for long. Michael, with princes Sigismund Báthory of Transylvania and Ștefan Răzvan of Moldavia, drove them out, decimating them as they were retreating across the Danube.

Now that it was independent of the Ottoman empire, Wallachia's international position was considerably strengthened. Michael managed gradually to remove the disadvantageous clauses from his treaty with Sigismund, and finally rescinded the entire agreement. After fighting almost all the way to the Balkan Mountains he signed an armistice (1596) and then a peace treaty (1598) with the sultan, and another treaty with the Habsburg empire (1598), accepting Habsburg suzerainty but with no political or economic obligations. In 1598 Michael was without question the keystone of the Christian coalition in the region, and the subject peoples of the Balkans looked to him for liberation. "Perhaps you wish to make peace with the pagans: in the name of God, we beg Your Majesty not to believe anything the Turk says. . . . Here all Christians bow before Your Majesty, as they will prove at the Last Judgment," wrote Dionisie Rally, the Greek metropolitan of Tîrnovo.[25] In 1598 Michael attacked fortresses on the Turkish side of the Danube and in Dobrudja, giving encouragement and assistance to the uprising at Tîrnovo that made John Shishman III czar of Bulgaria.

After this, the fighting with the Turks having abated, Michael turned his attention to Transylvania and Moldavia, where pro-Polish and pro-Turkish princes sought to depose him and make peace with the sultan. In 1599 Cardinal Andrew Báthory succeeded his cousin Sigismund on the throne and called on Michael to abdicate and leave the country. Instead Michael invaded Transylvania with the consent of the Habsburg empire, beat Báthory's army at the battle of Șelimbăr (October 1599), and proclaimed himself prince of Transylvania. A few months later (May 1600), after negotiations with Poland ended without result, Michael invaded Moldavia, and within a month had conquered it and taken the title "prince of Wallachia, Transylvania, and Moldavia."

Thus the three principalities were united under his rule, but not for long, for Michael had made many enemies. The Habsburg empire resented his plan to keep Transylvania for himself and his descendants. The Movilă family would not give up their claim, backed by Poland, to

Moldavia. The Hungarian nobility accepted the Wallachian prince, who wanted a centralized government and who would favor the majority Romanian population as well, only under duress.

The three converging inimical interests brought about Michael's downfall. In September 1600 the nobility of Transylvania, aided by Habsburg troops under General George Basta, led an uprising against him and won a battle at Mirăslău. In the same month the Poles restored Ieremia Movilă to the Moldavian throne, and the Turks attacked Wallachia. Set upon from all sides at once, Michael fled the country, and the Poles, with Ottoman consent, put Simion Movilă on the Wallachian throne. Michael went to Prague to convince the holy Roman emperor Rudolf II of his cause and returned to Transylvania to fight the Hungarians with military support from the emperor. In Wallachia the boyars overthrew Simion Movilă. But Michael's new successes came to an abrupt end, for he was assassinated on Basta's orders immediately after the battle of Gorăslău (3 August 1601).

Michael's story could not have had a happy ending. His aims were too grand for Wallachia's military, economic, and human potential; the three principalities did not yet have common or national structures on which to base a lasting unification; and the interests of the Romanians were still in clear contradiction to those of Hungary, Poland, and the Habsburg empire. But Michael's brilliant reign had immediate and important results in mitigating Ottoman political and economic domination.

In the seventeenth century the Romanians would make only a few attempts to throw off Turkish suzerainty and reclaim their independence by force. A revolt led by Prince Gaspar Graziani of Moldavia was quickly put down (1620), but in 1658–59 a war led by Mihnea III, prince of Wallachia and an admirer of Michael the Brave, at first gave the Romanians cause for hope. Backed by the lesser boyars and allied with Transylvania, Mihnea repeated Michael's tactic of attacking the Danube line, where he took the fortresses on the Romanian side of the river and laid siege to those on the Ottoman side—Silistra, Ruse, Nikopol, and Hîrşova. But in the end he was defeated by the Tatars and forced to flee to Transylvania.

From this time until the final revolt against the Ottomans, led by Prince Dimitrie Cantemir of Moldavia in 1711, the Romanian political elite turned to diplomacy to improve their situation. Especially after the siege of Vienna (1683), the forming of a new Holy League, and the successive fall of Ottoman positions in central Europe, the Romanians played a two-edged diplomatic game. They wanted to rid themselves of

Ottoman suzerainty and yet evade whatever designs the great Christian powers of Europe might have. Princes and boyars tried to set up the system of alliances that would allow the greatest freedom of movement, preparing for military action but never stating their program openly, and never certain of the real intentions of their allies. From 1683 to 1685 Moldavia sought an alliance with King John III Sobieski of Poland, even trying to negotiate a treaty. Later the Moldavians turned to the Habsburg empire, with which Prince Constantin Cantemir concluded a treaty (1691) that was renewed by his successor Constantin Duca (1694). Two Moldavian princes, Antioh Cantemir and Mihai Racoviţă, were sent to Moscow as emissaries, and Constantin Duca proposed an alliance with Russia similar to one the two countries had formed in 1656.

Wallachian diplomacy was equally active. After years of negotiations and vacillation, Şerban Cantacuzino (r. 1678–88) offered to accept Habsburg suzerainty (1688) if his principality could remain independent with a hereditary absolute monarch, and if former possessions lost to Transylvania, including the Banat, were returned. But these conditions were not attractive to the Habsburgs, whose interests would not have been served by helping to create such a powerful Romanian state. Cantacuzino sent a deputation of two hundred, led by his brother, to negotiate in Vienna, but the talks were interrupted by the prince's sudden death (October 1688). He was succeeded by Constantin Brâncoveanu (1688–1714), who would not openly side with the Habsburgs. Instead, he turned to Russia as early as 1693. Through delegates like Gheorghe Castriotul (1698) and David Corbea (1702, 1705, 1706), he announced his intention to lead a revolt against the Ottoman empire and to ally himself with the czar, if the Russian army would provide military assistance. Like Michael the Brave, Brâncoveanu and his Cantacuzino advisers spoke for all the Christian Balkan states, demanding the liberation of all and the expulsion of the Turks from Europe. After Brâncoveanu had taken this position and conducted such negotiations, it was not surprising that Peter the Great counted on Wallachian support when he in turn led a campaign against the Ottoman empire (1711), or that he considered it treachery when Brâncoveanu chose to preserve Wallachian neutrality.

Moldavia made its last attempt to gain independence by military means during the short reign of Dimitrie Cantemir (1710–11). The sultan believed Cantemir, the son and brother of princes, to be loyal, and in giving him the throne ordered him to investigate and uncover Constantin Brâncoveanu's ties to the Christian powers. It was soon clear,

however, that Cantemir had his own ideas. He had lived in Constantinople for many years and knew the Turks well, and like many others
he was convinced that the Ottoman empire was in decline and would
lose control of Europe before long. While still in Constantinople he
promised the Russian ambassador Petr Tolstoi that as prince he would
form closer ties to Russia, and as soon as he arrived in Iaşi to take the
throne he submitted a treaty proposal that Peter the Great approved.
The treaty was signed at Lutsk in April 1711.

By the Lutsk treaty Russia, already at war with the Ottoman empire,
agreed to support Moldavia's fight for independence. Once independence was achieved Russia promised not to interfere in Moldavia's internal affairs but to permit Cantemir and his successors to rule in a
hereditary absolute monarchy. All Moldavian territory conquered by
the Ottomans was to be returned, with Russia guaranteeing Moldavia's
borders. In exchange the prince accepted the czar as suzerain and
would provide reinforcement for the Russian army as soon as it neared
Moldavia.

In May 1711, as the Russians attacked the Ottoman army, Cantemir
released a violently anti-Ottoman proclamation and gave orders for an
armed revolt. At the same time Brâncoveanu led the Wallachian army
as far as the border of Moldavia—but there he stopped, not daring to
keep his promise as Cantemir had. In July, at Stănileşti on the Prut
River, Turkish and Tatar troops surrounded the outnumbered Russians
and Moldavians and imposed a peace on them that permitted Russia
to withdraw but increased the Porte's suzerainty over Moldavia. Cantemir went into exile in Russia, followed by several thousand Moldavians.[26] Brâncoveanu lost his throne three years later when the sultan
accused him of treachery and of being a tool of the Christian powers.
He and his four sons were executed in Constantinople. Two years later
his successor, Ştefan Cantacuzino (r. 1714–16) was executed for secret
ties to the Habsburg empire.

The result of the principalities' efforts to end Ottoman domination
in the early eighteenth century was to aggravate it. The policies of
Brâncoveanu and the Cantacuzinos in Wallachia and of Cantemir in
Moldavia clearly showed the Ottomans that they could not trust Romanian princes. A more direct and efficient way of controlling the
principalities had to be found: the Phanariot regime.

Medieval Civilization: Byzantium after Byzantium

The Cultural Setting. Boyar culture dominated medieval Romanian
civilization. In contrast to the rest of southeast Europe, where peasant

culture predominated after the Ottoman conquest, cultural activities in Moldavia and Wallachia were linked to the princely and boyar courts, to the patronage and material support of the nobility, and to the upper echelons of the church hierarchy.

"Byzantium after Byzantium," the happy phrase of the great Romanian historian Nicolae Iorga,[27] sums up the paradox of Romanian cultural development. Its Byzantine aspect became prominent largely after the fall of the Byzantine empire. Archaeological digs in Curtea de Argeş, where the earliest voivodes of Wallachia lived, and in Baia and Suceava, the first capitals of Moldavia, show that Romanian boyar artifacts were originally more similar to those of Buda and Krakow than to Constantinople's. Hungary and Poland were a much more familiar world to fourteenth- and fifteenth-century Romanians than a distant Byzantium with which they had no direct tie. The princes of the Muşat and Basarab dynasties considered themselves part of the European world, defenders of a border threatened by pagans. But Byzantine influence grew gradually with Ottoman power, and markedly after the fall of Hungary and the end of Hungarian influence over the principalities. The ever-larger number of Orthodox refugees from Greece, Bulgaria, and Serbia also increased Byzantine cultural influence in Moldavia and Wallachia. As the only Christian rulers left in the Balkans, the Romanian princes saw themselves as the sole remaining representatives of an imperial tradition that no one else claimed, extending their patronage across the whole Orthodox world as the Byzantine empire once had done. Elements of protocol, costume, and some customs showed Byzantine influence, which was further encouraged by the many Greek scholars who had taken refuge in the princely courts. By the seventeenth century Byzantine forms were certainly more common than three hundred years earlier. The portraits of princes bear witness to this: Mircea the Old (r. 1386–1418) is shown dressed as a typical European knight, while Constantin Brâncoveanu (r. 1688–1714) is depicted in opulent Byzantine costume.

The contest between Eastern and Western influences hung in the balance until the early eighteenth century, and their confrontation, or, even better, their combination, gave rise to a culture that was eclectic but not without originality. Until the Phanariot regime Romanian civilization faced both east and west, both toward Europe and toward the Ottoman empire. An excellent example of this complex and highly unusual situation is found in a pair of portraits of the scholar-prince Dimitrie Cantemir (1673–1723), one in Eastern costume and the other in European. The duality created a dilemma for his generation that earlier voivodes and boyars had not faced.

Mircea the Old, prince of Wallachia (1386–1418).
Fresco, Curtea de Argeş.

Ieremia Movilă of Moldavia (r. 1595–1606) was the first prince to perceive the conflict between Eastern and European cultures in his own land and to regret the coming of the Oriental influence, which he considered foreign to the local tradition and customs.[28] But its effects were not all negative, and until the Eastern influence overwhelmed the Western in the eighteenth century, the two blended harmoniously, often resulting in interesting and original forms of expression.

Cultural Institutions. The primary institutions for the spread of cultural values were schools and books (printed and manuscript). We have no documentary evidence about schools before the fifteenth century. During the first decades after Wallachia and Moldavia were founded in the thirteenth century, instruction was probably given only by priests and monks in the monasteries, where manuscript copyists, court clerks, and the clergy would have learned to read and write Romanian and Old Church Slavonic. Monastery schools continued to be the most important and were well known in the fifteenth and sixteenth centuries— particularly those at Neamț and Putna in Moldavia and at Scheii Brașovului in Transylvania—but now princes and cities began to open their own schools. For higher studies, citizens and foreign residents of Moldavia sent their sons to Krakow and Vienna. By the time of Stephen the Great's death in 1504 eighteen Romanian students (from Baia, Bacău, Suceava, Roman, Iași, and Siret) had studied in one of those cities. Despot-Vodă, prince of Moldavia from 1561 to 1563, founded a college at Cotnari with German professors and a program of studies influenced by the Reformation. Before long the college was transformed into a Latin school with Jesuit professors; later it became an ordinary grammar school. Another Jesuit school at Iași, attended by the sons of boyars, existed from the late 1500s to the early 1700s.

Documents from this time reflect dissatisfaction with the state of education. Many called for new schools and for enlightenment through study. The metropolitan of Moldavia, Varlaam, regretted "the lack of teachers and of schooling" (1643), as did others. Visitors from abroad mention that Iași had twenty schools in the mid-seventeenth century, but the number of students attending them was no doubt small. In the villages teaching was still entirely in the hands of the priests, while the upper schools founded by the princes in the capital cities did not operate regularly.

There was no lack of attempts to create institutions of higher learning. In 1639 Prince Vasile Lupu of Moldavia opened a college in Iași. Its professors were sent by Petru Movilă, the Moldavian metropolitan

Constantin Brâncoveanu, prince of Wallachia (1688–1714).

Dimitrie Cantemir, prince of Moldavia (1710–11), in European costume.

of Kiev, and Latin was the language of instruction. In 1646 Prince Matei Basarab of Wallachia founded another college in Tîrgovişte, with teaching in Greek and Latin, but the political upheavals of the second half of the seventeenth century did not favor the development of education, and both colleges soon closed.

Elementary education made progress in Transylvania, where the Calvinists, eager to convert the Orthodox, opened schools teaching in Romanian. In 1624 Prince Gabriel Bethlen granted the sons of serfs the right to attend the schools of the principality, and in 1675 the synod ruled that every priest should run a school for the children in his village. A few village schools were even financially supported by peasants. Transylvania also produced the first pedagogical book in Romanian, an alphabet book printed in 1699.

In the late seventeenth century, higher education improved again in Moldavia and Wallachia, especially after Prince Şerban Cantacuzino of Wallachia (r. 1678–88) founded an "academy" and his successor Constantin Brâncoveanu reorganized it. The school was on the border between the European gymnasium and college levels, and renowned professors of the Christian East taught philosophy, natural sciences, classical literature, and other subjects. The Moldavian prince Antioh Cantemir founded a similar academy in Iaşi in 1707, which Prince Nicolae Mavrocordat reorganized in 1714.

From the beginning the academies were free and open to all, regardless of social position. Most students were the children of craftsmen, merchants, and poor lesser boyars. The great boyars preferred to educate their sons at home with tutors or to send them abroad, now not to Krakow and Vienna but to Padua or even to Paris—Radu Cantacuzino, probably the first Romanian student in France, studied there in 1700. The academies also had many students from the Balkan countries, and with the Great School of the Patriarchate in Constantinople they became the principal centers for education in the Orthodox southeast.[29]

Books were another important means of instilling cultural values. They were circulated largely in manuscript form throughout the medieval period, and copyists were many and well paid. Manuscript books were for the rich: in the 1500s the value of a book was about that of a medium-sized estate, and the price remained high through the next century. Manuscripts were bequeathed to heirs, they were hidden in times of danger along with other valuables, and when lost they were ransomed. Consider the history of the Humor monastery's 1473 Gospel lectionary. Sent to Transylvania in 1538 to prevent its falling into the hands of the Turks, the lectionary ended up in Constantinople, but was returned to the monastery in 1541 through the efforts of Prince Petru Rareş of Moldavia. In 1653 it was stolen by Cossacks but was ransomed by Gheorghe Ştefan (r. 1654–58) and returned to the monastery once more.

The printing press was introduced in the sixteenth century, first in Wallachia and then in Transylvania. Printing shops opened in Tîrgovişte (first book printed 1508), Sibiu (1544), Braşov (1557), Cluj (1570), Alba Iulia (1587), Sebeş (1580), and Orăştie (1582). Between 1508 and

1582 these shops published fifty-two books, fourteen in Romanian, thirty-five in Old Church Slavonic, and three in Old Church Slavonic and Romanian. Most were ordered and paid for by the princes, who repeatedly declared that they wanted to "fill the churches with books."[30] These modest shops produced only religious books with print runs of no more than five hundred. The first printers were Venice-trained Serbians, but later ones were Romanians, the best known being Coresi, a deacon, translator, and master printer who had issued no fewer than thirty-six books by 1582.

In 1582 Romanian printing ceased and did not get another start until 1635 in Wallachia, on the initiative of Matei Basarab and with the technical assistance of craftsmen sent from Kiev by the metropolitan Petru Movilă. Matei Basarab described the printing press as "a treasure more precious than all earthly treasures" and "food and shelter to the soul," sentiments echoed by Prince Vasile Lupu, who had the first press in Moldavia, set up in 1642.[31] But the successors of these two princes showed no interest in supporting printing, and it was discontinued again until 1678 in Wallachia and 1679 in Moldavia; it was also interrupted in Transylvania, where no books were published by Romanians between 1582 and 1639 and from 1656 until late in the century.

Printing flourished again only in the last decades of the seventeenth century. In Brâncoveanu's Wallachia six print shops published volumes for use by Romanians, and also for Greeks, Armenians, South Slavs, Arabs, and Turks. In all, from 1601 to 1700, 113 books were published by Romanian print shops: 61 in Romanian, 11 in Old Church Slavonic, 20 bilingual editions in Old Church Slavonic and Romanian, 17 in Greek, two in Greek and Romanian, one in Latin, and one in Armenian. A list of the books published under Brâncoveanu shows 42 books in Greek, 39 in Romanian, and 22 in Old Church Slavonic and Romanian. They were issued by Romanian presses in Snagov (established 1696), Buzău (1691), Rîmnic (1705), Tîrgoviște (1709), and Bucharest (1716), and by the Greek press in Bucharest (1690). The metropolitan of Wallachia, Antim Ivireanul, who also helped found presses in Georgia and Syria, deserves primary credit for the comparative flood of books.[32]

As for the libraries that housed these books and others bought all over Europe—the best-known were Brâncoveanu's and Constantin Cantacuzino's—their catalogs show great wealth and diversity of holdings. The institutions and instruments of culture must have made great strides during the seventeenth and early eighteenth centuries.

Literature, Ideas, and the Arts. Medieval culture, based on a mixture of local, Byzantine, and Western values and disseminated through books and schools, developed slowly, the dominant values changing from one century to the next. Romanian was not its only language, for the Romanians also used Latin. As members of the Orthodox community they cultivated the other sacred languages, Old Church Slavonic and Greek, as well. Old Church Slavonic and Greek came to be used in the churches, in the prince's correspondence and records, and in other areas.

We do not know just when the Romanians replaced the Latin liturgy with the Slavonic for reasons of religion and under the influence of the south Slavic feudal states. It was probably during the tenth century (certainly not in the fifteenth, as Dimitrie Cantemir and other eighteenth-century writers believed). The effect of the change was to integrate written Romanian culture with its Slavic neighbors' for six hundred years. During this time Latin was used rarely in domestic documents but frequently in foreign correspondence. Schools used it intermittently, but it did not come into general use as a language of culture mostly because it represented the Catholic world from which the Romanians were politically and culturally severed.

As in other countries competition between the official language and the spoken one, between the dead language and the living, began early. Translations from Old Church Slavonic into Romanian of Acts and the Epistles, the Psalms, and a psalter had already appeared in Maramureş by the end of the fifteenth century. The manuscripts were later copied in Moldavia, where direct translations of Acts and the Gospels also appeared, probably before 1532. In Wallachia, too, the Gospels were translated into the vernacular (1512–18), and Romanian came into use in private correspondence as early as 1521; by midcentury sacred books began to be printed, for as Coresi remarked in 1564, "Almost all languages have the word of God in their language, only we Romanians do not, and Christ says . . . whoso readeth, let him understand," and further, "What good does it do the Romanians if the priest speaks to them in a foreign language?"[33]

In spite of all this activity in the translation and printing of religious books in Romanian, the spoken language was adopted more slowly by the church than by the princes' clerks. Legal texts and historical chronicles began to appear in the vernacular in the sixteenth century, and the use of Old Church Slavonic in court correspondence rapidly lost favor in the seventeenth, but church services long continued in a language unknown to the faithful. Not until after a liturgy had been published in Romanian in Moldavia (1679) and a Bible in Wallachia (1688) was that shift to the vernacular made. In spite of the many claims to the contrary, the church played a conservative role in linguistic matters, and the metropolitans' presses went on printing books in Old Church Slavonic until 1731 in Moldavia and 1745 in Wallachia.

The process by which the vernacular replaced Old Church Slavonic in Wallachia and Moldavia was consciously hastened by sixteenth-century intellectuals who had rediscovered their Roman origins. They worked to prove that Romanian was a Latin language and to make it the language of culture. Coresi drew the connection between *Romanians* and *Romans,* and was the first to spell *Romanian* with an *o* instead of a *u*. In 1593 Luca Stroici, chief secretary to several princes of Moldavia, boldly affirmed the language's Latin character by transliterating the Romanian version of the Lord's Prayer from the Cyrillic into the Roman alphabet, with an accompanying explanation of the origins of the Romanian people. The chronicles of Grigore Ureche (1647) and Miron Costin (1677) include chapters on the Romanian language and its origins. And the Wallachian boyar Udriște Năsturel recorded (1647) that after discovering that "Latin is clearly related to our own language . . . there was almost no other thought in my heart and mind than to learn this language, practicing ceaselessly night and day."[34]

Dimitrie Cantemir, who published his first book in Romanian (1698) but who wrote almost exclusively in Latin thereafter, did not stop at declaring Romanian a Latin language. He believed that Old Church Slavonic had been introduced in the fifteenth century by the Moldavian metropolitan Teoctist—"the initiator of this barbarism"—through an excess of Orthodox zeal. Its continued use, added to the failure to cultivate the vernacular, had in his opinion held back the whole development of Romanian culture. He maintained that the preeminence of Old Church Slavonic had been a cause of cultural regression, while the use of Romanian in the church and in printing meant that a revival was beginning. Moldavia, he thought, was beginning "to wake up and be brought somewhat into the light from the depths of the deep darkness in which barbarism had covered it."[35]

At the beginning of the eighteenth century intellectuals viewed the Slavonic period as a time of darkness, but this is only partly true. In reality the Slavonic influence that lasted until the sixteenth century gave rise to achievements of which Romanian culture could be proud. A wealth of religious and legal literature, the first chronicles, and many translations were produced under the Slavonic cloak that covered Romanian culture for centuries.

The accomplishments of Romanian culture before the sixteenth century also included several important works of architecture built in Wallachia from as early as the fourteenth century, such as the impressive Biserica Domnească (church) at Curtea de Argeș (1352) and the monasteries at Tismana (1377) and Cozia (1387). In Moldavia civic and religious architecture flourished somewhat later, under Stephen the Great (r. 1457–1504), when the fourteenth-century fortresses and princely residences of Suceava, Cetatea Albă (Akerman), Cetatea Neamțului, Chilia, and Hotin were remodeled, reinforced, and expanded. Much of the activity took place in the short period between 1476 and 1479. The monasteries at Putna (1466) and Neamț (1487) quickly became centers of art and culture, as did many other churches and monasteries. Stephen the Great's reign also saw a flowering of the minor arts, particularly embroidery and illuminated manuscripts.

Remarkable cultural development took place during the first decades of the sixteenth century. Prince Neagoe Basarab (r. 1512–21), whose father-in-law, Prince Radu the Great, had set up the first printing press in Wallachia, wrote the first original work of Romanian literature, Învățăturile (Lessons), advice to his son Teodosie on moral, political, and military questions and matters of deportment—a type of literature that came into great favor in the seventeenth century. At Neagoe's court a monk, Gavril Protul, wrote a life of the metropolitan Nifon in Greek. And Neagoe was responsible for the remarkable episcopal church at Curtea de Argeș (1517), so striking with its Armenian and Georgian elements, so far from the Byzantine style.

Moldavia enjoyed a similar blossoming of culture. Stephen the Great's successors continued his encouragement of historiography at court, and the chronicle of Moldavia begun at his command was expanded and continued in Letopisețul anonim al Moldovei (Anonymous chronicle of Moldavia), Letopisețul de la Putna (Putna chronicle), and in what are called the Moldavian-German, Moldavian-Polish, and Moldavian-Russian chronicles. Macarie, bishop of Roman, edited a chronicle of the events of 1504–52 for Prince Petru Rareș; a Father Eftimie took up the account for the years 1541–54; and the monk Azarie brought them up to the year 1574, while in Wallachia the first "party" chronicle, glorifying the deeds of the Buzescu family, was written at the end of the century. The sixteenth century was important in the history of Moldavian art, too: the impressive painted monasteries of Bucovina are particularly noteworthy, including Voroneț (built and painted with interior murals, 1488–96; exterior murals, 1547), Moldovița (1532–37), and Sucevița (1582–96).

The achievements of the fourteenth, fifteenth, and sixteenth centuries formed the foundation for seventeenth-century culture, the high point of premodern Romanian history. Many factors worked together to permit not just the continuous development in printing and education and traditional cultural structures, but also a real outburst of creativity. First, long reigns in both principalities—Matei Basarab's (1632–54), Vasile Lupu's (1634–52), and Constantin Brâncoveanu's (1688–1714)—created stretches of domestic stability that became distinct cultural periods. Then, several rich and powerful boyar families set not only the political program but at times a cultural model as well. The constant upheavals in the international situation opened new perspectives, now raising and now dashing hopes but always inspiring the intellectuals, obliging them to think, to take positions. During the seventeenth century the principalities were in constant and close contact with Western culture. Romanians frequently traveled in Europe, and some studied there, and there were many Westerners in Moldavia and Wallachia, especially as court clerks and doctors.

A general improvement in living conditions encouraged artistic development, too. Boyars could afford to live in luxury, in spacious and comfortable mansions like those of Udriște Năsturel at Herești (built 1644) and Pîrvu Cantacuzino at Măgureni (1667), and the one built at Filipești in the mid-seventeenth century by the Cantacuzinos. The princes indulged in ostentatious display, building sumptuous palaces like those at Potlogi (1699) and Mogoșoaia (1702). They ordered extravagant crowns from Transylvania, and they combined Eastern opulence with Western refinement. On a less material plane, some large monasteries now became, with the princes' support, real cultural centers, going well beyond their ecclesiastical function. In particular, Trei Ierarhi monastery under Vasile Lupu and Hurez monastery under Brâncoveanu were devoted in equal measure to teaching, painting, and printing: each had its own recognizable style.

The most original seventeenth-century accomplishments were probably in historiography. Never before had the Romanians produced so much historical writing. *Letopisețul țării Moldovei* (Chronicle of Moldavia [1647]) written by Grigore Ureche, was still a chronicle, but historiography went clearly beyond the medieval chronicle with Miron Costin's *Letopisețul țării Moldovei* (Chronicle of Moldavia [1675]), *Cronica țărilor Moldovei și Munteniei* (Chronicle of Moldavia and Wallachia [1677]), and *De neamul moldovenilor, din ce țară au ieșit strămoșii lor* (Of the Moldavian people, and what country their ancestors came from [1675]). Constantin Cantacuzino contributed *Istoria Țării Românești* (History of Wallachia

[1716]) to the growing body of newer historiography. But the most notable efforts are Cantemir's *Historia incrementorum atque decrementorum aulae othomanicae* (1716), *Descriptio Moldaviae* (1716), and *Hronicul vechimii romano-moldo-vlahilor* (Chronicle of the antiquity of the Roman-Moldavian-Wallachians) (1723). With these the Romanians moved into solid history writing. Their facts were thoroughly documented, and most important, the new histories were full of vital ideas inspired by an emerging ethnic consciousness.

Ethnic consciousness, the Romanians' first step toward national consciousness, arose from the discovery of their origins and their unity of language and culture, and the realization that they were divided into three separate states for purely political reasons. Clearly Stephen the Great knew that the Moldavians and Wallachians were one people, since twice in a single document he used the phrase "the other Romanian country" for Wallachia (1478). There are many other such examples. Sixteenth-century chronicles commonly describe events in both principalities; Despot-Vodă summoned the Moldavian boyars to fight against the Ottomans in 1561 with the slogan, "You brave and warlike people, descendants of the brave Romans who made the world tremble"; the Wallachian printer Coresi dedicated the books he published in Transylvania (1563, 1564, 1577) to all "Romanian brothers"; a group of Wallachian boyars proposed a political collaboration with Moldavia in 1599, since "we are all of one creed and one language."[36]

The seventeenth century saw more and more expressions of pan-Romanian sentiment. They appeared in books of all kinds in all three principalities. Metropolitan Varlaam addressed himself in 1643 to "the whole Romanian people, wherever are found the faithful of this language," and Metropolitan Dosoftei of Moldavia repeated his words in 1679. Metropolitan Simion Ştefan knew in 1648 that his people lived not only in his own Transylvania but that there were "Romanians spread through other lands."[37]

But it was in historiography, from Ureche to Cantemir, that ethnic consciousness was most cohesively expressed. In his *Letopiseţ* (1647) Ureche presents many strong arguments for the claim that Wallachians, Moldavians, and Transylvanians "are all descended from Rome."[38] For Costin (see chronicles published in 1675, 1677, 1684), that "the Romanian people are descended from Italy" is a given. Costin devoted many pages to the conquest of Dacia, the Roman colonization, Aurelian's withdrawal of Roman forces, and the continuing Roman presence after the withdrawal. He believed that the Romanian people had come into being in the area bordered by the Dniester, the Black Sea, the

Danube, Pannonia, and Podolia. Costin was also the first Romanian historian to be interested in the Vlachs living in the Balkans.[39]

Cantemir summed up the whole question in the early eighteenth century. The general ideas he presented were not new, but the scholar-prince found fresh arguments in their favor. He gave the whole theory of the common origins of the Romanians and their continued presence in the territories a cohesive and unified quality that it had often lacked.[40] Because of his prestige and the wide dissemination of his writings in all three principalities, ethnic consciousness spread among political leaders and intellectuals and became the theoretical basis of the national consciousness of a few generations later.

Scholars have often asked whether the ethnic consciousness of seventeenth-century historians and political leaders was not accompanied by some degree of national awareness. Did not ethnic unity suggest political unity? Extant documents do not support such a conclusion, although some passages suggest a tendency in that direction. For example, in 1642 Vasile Lupu of Moldavia considered the conquest of Transylvania by Moldavian and Wallachian troops possible, since "in Transylvania more than a third are Romanian, and once they are freed we will incite them against the Hungarians."[41] Brâncoveanu and his high steward Cantacuzino's correspondence with the Russians also shows some political interest in Transylvania. Their letters include references to plans for pan-Balkan liberation and to "the Romanians of Transylvania."[42] But in general ethnic consciousness was not accompanied by pressure for political unification, and even as politically active a prince as Cantemir did not think of including it among his policies.

Politics and diplomacy seem to have been the principal concerns of seventeenth-century Romanian leaders. The diplomatic fervor and obsession with political problems that the documents reflect had rarely been seen before, but the rise of the Austrian and Russian empires and the gradual decline of the Turks showed the boyars that changes were coming—and spurred them to action. There were internal power struggles. Rival boyar factions formed, each ready to destroy the other to put its own candidate on the throne; plots involved now one neighboring power and now another. Previously unthinkable options now seemed possible, as political leaders seemed ready to expel the pagans and recover their independence. But often they hesitated, torn between fear of the Turks and distrust of the Christian powers. They wanted to venture but feared to risk, and they promised to revolt but stopped halfway, not trusting the assurances of Vienna or Moscow. Cantemir did lead the Moldavians in a revolt, but Brâncoveanu broke his promise to lend Wallachian support, so both attempts failed—and both princes lost their thrones in a hopeless tangle of diplomacy. The seventeenth century ended with the large-scale defeat of the Romanian ruling class, which had hoped to use the new international situation to liberate Wallachia and Moldavia from their foreign masters. Instead the Turkish grip tightened, and the Romanians lost most of their political and military power with the coming of the Phanariot princes.

The Romanians seem to have understood that they were players in a drama with far-reaching implications. They were politically active and did not mind the dangers of the game, but they were often discouraged. In their unease they were conscious of the instability of the times and eager to combat it, but they knew that they were powerless because, in Ureche's words, the country lay "in the path of evils."[43] Costin took a similarly gloomy view, because "the times are not controlled by man; rather we, poor creatures, are controlled by the times." Feeling that events were beyond his control—indeed, he was later executed by a distrustful prince—Costin took up the old theme of the Orthodox East, the precariousness of human existence, and regretted "these cruel times that overwhelm this country with dangers."[44]

Events proved the pessimists right. No century before had produced such a large concentration of wise leaders and interesting thinkers in Wallachia and Moldavia, nor had any age been as cruelly profligate of its luminaries. In only two or three decades most of those whose work had contributed to the cultural brilliance of the age were in exile (Nicolae Milescu, Dosoftei, Cantemir, Ion Neculce) or had been killed (Costin, Constantin Cantacuzino, Antim Ivireanul, Brâncoveanu). The failures of the seventeenth century opened the way to the Phanariot period.

CHAPTER THREE

Despotism and Enlightenment
(1716–1831)

Phanariots and Habsburgs

The Phanariot Period. The Phanariot period takes its name from the princes, most of whom came from the Phanar, the Greek quarter of Constantinople, appointed directly by the Porte to rule Moldavia and Wallachia during the eighteenth century. The period has been extremely controversial in both old and new Romanian historiography. Most historians have disparaged Phanariot rule, stressing its negative aspects, while others, notably the school of Nicolae Iorga, have sought to rehabilitate it to some degree. Both, however, have viewed Phanariot rule through the prism of the conflict between Romanians and Greeks, thus giving their interpretations an unwarranted nationalist twist.

While allowing that the negative elements of Phanariot rule outweighed the positive, we must try to understand that "Phanariotism" was a broader phenomenon than most historians recognize. Its roots reach back as far as the sixteenth and seventeenth centuries, and the ethnic element was not always to the fore. The Phanariots were not exclusively Greeks but Romanians, Albanians, and Bulgarians as well. Phanariot rule was a cultural, political, and social structure into which anyone could fit who wanted to accept and respect a certain value system based on conservative Orthodoxy, anti-Western traditionalism, and political allegiance to the Porte. Not all Greeks recognized these principles, and so not all Greeks were Phanariots. Some even adopted a clear anti-Phanariot position. The Phanariots formed a kind of proto-political party of mixed composition with its basis in common interests. When its ethnic diversity and interests narrowed, Phanariotism ceased to be a political and social force, and its various component groups affiliated themselves with their respective national movements, whether Greek or Romanian.

The first Phanariot *hospodars,* or princes, were more often Romanian than Greek, which clearly shows that Phanariotism could be learned or acquired, and that national origin was not decisive. The Mavrocordats had long intermarried with native families, the Racoviţăs and Callimachis (Călmaşul) were pure-blooded Moldavians, and the Ghicas, who had come from Albania, had been accepted as natives for almost a century. Until 1774 Moldavia and Wallachia were governed by Romanian Phanariots, often Hellenized but still ethnically members of the people they governed. This does not by any means imply that they were better governors than non-Romanian Phanariots. Issues of caste were more often important to the Phanariots than issues of race.

The Greeks began to predominate among Phanariots only in the second half of the century, especially after 1774, as the Romanian Phanariots gradually lost influence in Constantinople. They were first excluded from the important position of dragoman and then lost their posts as hospodars, which until 1821 were occupied exclusively by members of such Levantine families as Ypsilanti, Moruzi, Caragea, and Suţu. Some families, for example, the Racoviţăs and the Ghicas, became "de-Phanariotized," joining the Romanian nationalist movement. Others, for example, the Mavrocordats and the Ypsilantis, allied themselves to the Greek nationalist movement. Yet other families were divided: one branch of the Callimachis became re-Romanianized, but a Hellenized branch remained loyal to the Porte even after 1821.

Phanariot rule was complex, and it is impossible to accept or reject it whole. The hospodars' ethnic origin is not so important as the fact that the era was perceived, even in the eighteenth century, as a period apart from the history of the Romanians, a time when its natural course was altered and forced into decline compared to the past. In most cases the past was idealized, depicted as a Golden Age. Contemporary scholars, trained to view history as cyclic, saw their own century as a debased Iron Age.[1]

The principal feature distinguishing the Phanariot period from those that preceded it was the new character of the Ottoman regime, which had grown economically and politically far more oppressive. From 1601 on, political relations between the Romanians and the empire increasingly favored the Porte. But Moldavia and Wallachia could still for the most part maintain foreign relations and take an important role in the diplomacy of southeast Europe, until 1711 in Moldavia and 1716 in Wallachia.

With the installation of the Phanariots, the principalities were completely integrated into the Ottoman military and political systems. Their independent foreign policy and diplomacy ceased to exist. Princes became part of the imperial administration and policy, to be appointed, dismissed, reappointed at the sultan's pleasure—according to the needs not of the country but of the empire. During the whole Phanariot period the hospodars concluded only one foreign treaty, a commercial agreement with Austria (1784). Their foreign policy was limited to representing the interests of the empire, to plotting occasionally with the Russians and Austrians, and to being the Porte's informant about events in Europe.

The reduced military power of Moldavia and Wallachia (sometimes called the Danubian principalities) was a noteworthy component of their declining international role. Under Dimitrie Cantemir and Constantin Brâncoveanu the armies had still been sufficiently well organized that the Russians and Austrians wanted to collaborate with them. But after those princes' reigns no Romanian army fought under its own flag. In 1739 Constantin Mavrocordat dismantled the old military organization entirely, as it had no purpose under the new circumstances. Many contemporary sources considered that this measure was intended to weaken Moldavia and Wallachia and to leave them unprotected and at the mercy of the Porte. The native boyars repeatedly asked for the reestablishment of the army, and irregular volunteer detachments fought in all the Russo-Austrian wars against the Turks, but a regular army to defend the country did not reappear even partially until 1831.

The fact that throughout the eighteenth century the defense of the Danubian principalities was undertaken directly by the Porte was not in the Romanians' favor. After the Phanariot period began Moldavia and Wallachia became the principal battlefield for the neighboring great powers. Between the treaty of the Prut in 1711 and the treaty of Adrianople in 1829, the two principalities were occupied for twenty-five years by the armies of the warring states. Seven wars (in 1711, 1716–19, 1736–39, 1768–74, 1787–92, 1806–12, and 1828–29) were fought on their territory, bringing destruction and hindering economic development.

The principalities' diminished international status can be gauged from how often the great powers planned to divide them, and also from the losses of territory they repeatedly suffered. The first great power to annex portions of Romanian territory was Austria. In 1719 the treaty of Passarowitz ceded Oltenia to her, to the despair of the local boyars. They were terrified that once they came under the centralist, authoritarian administration of the Habsburgs, they would be "worse off than the Hungarians" (1736).[2]

Oltenia was returned to Wallachia in 1739, but Vienna annexed northern Moldavia in 1775, renaming it Bucovina. These annexations, together with repeated occupation by the Austrian military, are probably enough to account for the Habsburgs' little popularity among Romanians in the eighteenth century.

The Romanians' relations with the Russians were closer until 1792, when the border of this new great European power first reached the Dniester. From that moment Russia became just as dangerous to the interests of the Danubian principalities as Turkey and Austria. The Russian occupation of 1806–12, brought to an end by the treaty of Bucharest and the division of Moldavia, dashed any last hopes of the czar's good intentions. Time after time the boyars protested the seizure of Bessarabia; in Bucharest the people demonstrated their joy at the withdrawal of the imperial Russian armies by setting fire to Russian uniforms in the town square. Dionisie Eclesiarhul, a contemporary chronicler, best expressed the sentiments of the inhabitants for the army (which came to liberate them but stayed to treat them almost more harshly than the Ottomans): "There were not houses or places enough to hold them . . . nor food and drink enough for them, and still they stole everything they found."[3]

Conscious of the difficulty of maintaining their own political identity in a geopolitical zone so much disputed by the neighboring great powers, the boyars tried to make the problem of Moldavia and Wallachia an international one by becoming a neutral buffer state. This might have prevented conflicts arising from the divergent interests of Russia, Austria, and Turkey. The idea of a buffer state under the protection of Russia, Austria, and Prussia was first put forward by the Wallachian boyars in 1772. It was raised again and again by both Wallachia and Moldavia (in 1774, 1783, 1787, 1791, 1807, and 1829), with the acknowledged purpose of making the principalities "une barrière redoutable entre le nord et le midi" (Moldavian memorandum to Napoleon, 1807).[4]

A favorable change in relations between Romanians and the Ottoman empire and the broader international influence over the problems of the Danubian principalities that Romanians desired could be accomplished only in part during the eighteenth century. The treaty of Kutchuk Kainardji (1774) gave Russia the right to intercede with Constantinople on behalf of the principalities and permitted the establishment of consulates in Bucharest and Iaşi. Consulates soon opened, Russia's first in 1782, then Austria's (1783), Prussia's (1785), France's (1796), and England's (1801). The presence of European consuls placed some limits on the Porte's arbitrary actions. The Romanians were allowed to petition the great powers directly when Ottoman abuses became too oppressive. Thanks to consular intervention (especially Russia's), the sultan was forced to issue several edicts (1774, 1783, 1784, 1791, 1792, and 1802) placing economic relations between the Romanians and the Ottoman empire on a legal and controllable footing, at least in theory. In practice, however, the new regulations were not respected, and Turkey's economic exploitation of Moldavia and Wallachia intensified, reaching new heights by the beginning of the nineteenth century.

If the tribute exacted remained roughly constant, even being reduced after 1821 to the sixteenth-century level so that in 1831 Wallachia's annual tax (*haraci*) was only 439,500 lei, the principalities' other monetary obligations grew unceasingly, reaching astronomical sums. The endless additional contributions (*peșcheșurile*) weighed particularly heavily on the national budget, and their arbitrary and abusive nature caused considerable distress. In 1777 alone Grigore Ghica of Moldavia had to pay *peșcheșurile* of 865,888 lei; a few years earlier, in 1768, Constantin Mavrocordat had withdrawn 2,522,113 lei from the Wallachian treasury to pay the regular taxes, additional contributions, and other extraordinary demands. Payments for hospodarships, one due yearly and another larger one triennially, also rose as the custom of appointing the highest bidder became more common. The expenses connected with the purchase and, even more, the retention of the position were probably each state's greatest financial burden. More and more Romanian capital flowed into Constantinople, rising to the sum of about 120 million piasters for Wallachia alone for the period 1812–20. In 1822–23, 45 percent of all disbursements from the Moldavian treasury were to the Turks, but after the withdrawal in 1826 of the occupying armies that had put down the uprising of 1821, this figure fell to about 22 percent.[5]

The Ottoman demands for supplies, which were frequent and heavy despite the official edicts that regulated them, also had a ruinous effect on the economies of Moldavia and Wallachia. Great quantities of grain, cattle, lumber, and saltpeter made their way to Constantinople without payment, or were bought at a price well below market value. For practical purposes the Porte exercised a monopoly on Romanian foreign commerce as well. Certain products had to be sold primarily to Ottoman merchants. Exporting them to other countries was permitted only after this obligation had been fulfilled. The Ottoman right of preemption had been established in 1751, and ten years later the sultans prohibited the export of cattle and animal products except to the empire. The Romanians did not strictly adhere to all these restrictions. The amount of goods smuggled to Russia and Austria was always substantial, and the hospodar often encouraged the practice. But the empire's commercial monopoly and the Romanians' obligation to sell to the Turks at fixed prices were yet another cause of economic stagnation.

To this direct Ottoman exploitation was added Phanariot plundering at a level never before reached in the history of the Romanians, although past princes—Brâncoveanu, for instance—had not shrunk from extremely oppressive fiscal policies. The Phanariots brought with them a new political mentality. Their terms were short and they had to raise money quickly, for without gold the throne could not be bought, defended, or reclaimed. It is indicative of this new mentality that the word *chiverneo,* meaning "govern" in Greek, evolved in Romanian into *chiverniseală,* "getting rich." To the Phanariots governing meant feathering one's own nest.

The last Phanariot hospodar of Wallachia, Alexandru Suțu, is a good example. He arrived in Bucharest in 1819 with a debt of five million piasters and an entourage of 820 people, including nine children and eighty relatives, all looking for jobs. In only three years the prince had succeeded in raising, according to contemporary estimates, 28,657,000 piasters. His predecessor, Ioan Gheorghe Caragea, had accumulated only about twenty million piasters between 1812 and 1818.[6]

Increased Ottoman domination and the diminished function of the state in foreign affairs had a negative influence on the country's institutions as well, on the development of domestic affairs from the throne to the local administration. After 1716 the prince ceased to be the representative institution of the country and became just one among all the others in the Ottoman administrative system. He was a pasha of two horsetails, answerable only to the sultan for his actions. For his part, the angry sultan beheaded, with great ease and exemplary frequency, any hospodars who did not subject themselves entirely to him. Such executions, beginning with Brâncoveanu in 1714 and Constantin and Ștefan Cantacuzino in 1716, took place in 1777, 1790, 1799, and 1807 as well. Scarlat Callimachi, former prince of Moldavia, was the last Phanariot put to death on a charge of treason (1821). The hospodars' terms were considerably shortened, too. Long reigns like Brâncoveanu's twenty-six-year rule disappeared altogether. Between 1716 and 1769, for example, Wallachia had twenty hospodars in succession; in the years between the Kutchuk Kainardji treaty (1774) and the uprising of 1821 there were nineteen more. Under such unstable rule, the government of the country could not but be a hand-to-mouth affair, lacking any stability or perspective.

The decline of the prince's position is reflected by a change of title. The old independent voivodes were called *hakim* (ruler, prince) or even *tekur* (king), while the Phanariots were often called just *bey* (governor). But although their subordination to the Porte was unconditional, among their subjects the Phanariot hospodars retained most of the aristocratic attributes of the old voivodes. Traditional ceremony remained virtually unchanged. Some hospodars even used the formula "prince by the grace of God" at their coronations. To the padishah, the only real source of power during the Phanariot period, this formula had no significance; to the native people, however, it served as a reminder that the hospodar's authority was unlimited and absolute.

Hospodar despotism came into conflict first with the institution through which the boyars had in the past sought to govern the state, the Great Assembly. Its principal purpose had been to elect hospodars and to resolve certain extraordinary problems, whether domestic or foreign. Its decline, already under way in the seventeenth century, gained momentum under the Phanariots. The last election of a hospodar by the assembly took place in 1730, and its last session, held to discuss the abolition of serfdom, was in 1749. After this date, no organized institution was capable of opposing the hospodar's despotism. Boyar dissatisfaction manifested itself either in memoranda to the Porte, in plotting, or in seizing power at times of Russian and Austrian occupation, when the hospodars took refuge south of the Danube. The assembly was reborn between 1831 and 1848. Under the new name General Assembly it became, alongside the prince, the main legislative, judicial, and administrative organ of the country, the precursor of the modern parliament.

The instability and setbacks suffered by the princely institution naturally affected the whole administrative apparatus. The number of officials became excessive: within three months of his arrival in Bucharest (1752) Matei Ghica granted 120 boyar titles. The boyar's caftan was not only a social status symbol but an easy means for the prince to raise money. Just as the hospodarship was bought from the Turks, so was the boyar's title bought from the hospodar. Since the officials' income came largely from a percentage of the taxes, fines, tariffs, and various revenues, high office soon became a principal means of enrichment and a direct invitation to corruption. Under these circumstances, it is not surprising that the main function of the state during the Phanariot period was the fiscal one. The entire state apparatus, from the hospodar to the lowest civil servant, sought to wring as much money as possible from the populace. Direct tribute (*bir*), from which boyars, clergy, and some other privileged categories were exempted, was repeatedly raised. In 1819 it reached 215 talers per *liudă* (a grouping of several families for purposes of taxation), as compared to sixteen talers in 1775. In addition to direct tribute, taxpayers also paid numerous indirect property taxes (on swine and beehives, on sheep, cattle, wine, cellars, taverns, shops, and so on), as well as extraordinary levies designed to meet the hospodar's unforeseen needs. This fiscal oppression with its arbitrary and unpredictable character—due primarily to the unceasing monetary demands of the Porte—made it difficult to accumulate capital or to attempt any kind of investment.

One of the paradoxes of Phanariot rule lay in the fact that while institutional decline and economic stagnation took place, Moldavia and Wallachia enjoyed relative political autonomy from the Porte. The few Turks who had acquired property on Romanian land were withdrawn from the country for good in 1756, and after that date no Ottoman could legally acquire property north of the Danube. In 1775 the sultan formally denied Turks access to the principalities, with the exception of "numbered and regulated" merchants acting for the hospodar. In Bucharest Ottoman merchants could stay only at certain inns, while in the marketplaces the officials had "Turk-guards" to catch any who sneaked illegally into the country. Throughout this period the principalities' legislative, judicial, and administrative autonomy was never encroached upon. And yet Moldavia and Wallachia suffered a period of economic decline after 1716, while Greece, for example, enjoyed a period of prosperity under direct Ottoman administration. The case of the Danubian principalities demonstrates rather clearly that the objectives of foreign domination can easily be achieved by controlling a few key factors. Direct rule is not essential.

Economy and Social Life. Political instability, economic oppression, the frequent wars of Turkey, Russia, and Austria, and losses of territory caused Moldavia and Wallachia to suffer a period of demographic stagnation, even regression, until the mid-eighteenth century. The birthrate had slowed, and the immigration of Romanians from Transylvania, brought into Moldavia and Wallachia by the hospodar and given fiscal privileges in order to increase the labor pool, could hardly make up for the flight of villagers either to other estates or even south of the Danube. (There are no known cases of emigration to Transylvania, for the Orthodox peasants continued to find the regime in the Danubian principalities, however arbitrary and disorganized, less oppressive than the rigorous Austrian administration, which was "Papist" as well.)

It is difficult to find precise data on the fluctuation of population in the principalities. The most dependable sources seem to be Prussian, French, and Russian consular reports, which generally give similar figures. A French consular report from 1806, for instance, estimated the population of Wallachia at 1,200,000 and that of Moldavia at one million. Those numbers remained constant until 1812, when with the ceding of Bessarabia more than 200,000 Moldavians became Russian subjects. Considering the grave economic and political conditions between 1812 and 1831, it is difficult to explain why demographic indexes still show continuous growth during the two decades before the Organic Statutes.* Official Moldavian statistics in 1825 place the population of Moldavia at 1,100,490; Russian reports (1832) give the figure of 1,976,809 for Wallachia, while French sources (1831) claim a slightly greater population, 2,032,362. Allowing for the imprecise nature of these figures, it is probably safe to estimate that Moldavia and Wallachia together had, at the beginning of their modern history, something more than three million inhabitants.[7]

Agriculture and animal husbandry continued to be the principal economic activities during this period. The hospodars always held that "this is the first duty of the country, to wit, working on the land" (1802 decree), and they took many measures to ensure a sufficient supply of labor—increasingly as the eighteenth century closed. Trials involving peasants were suspended during the summer, and officials received orders to urge "all inhabitants of the estate to plow and sow as much as possible, and if any among the inhabitants does not know what is good for him . . . he should be forced against his will" (1794 decree).[8]

In spite of the hospodars' zeal, agriculture showed no visible progress during the eighteenth century in Moldavia and Wallachia, remaining very close to its pre-Phanariot productivity. The area under cultivation remained relatively limited. The fertile Danube plain could not be utilized because of frequent Turkish raids and a general state of uncertainty in that border area. Workers were few, skilled labor hard to find. Lack of capital made it difficult to introduce improved technology, and early nineteenth-century equipment differed little from that of Brân-

---

*The Organic Statutes (Regulamentul Oraganic), rendered by R. W. Seton-Watson in his *History of the Roumanians* (1934) as "Règlement Organique," were adopted in 1831 and may reasonably be described as the first constitution of the Danubian principalities.—Ed.

coveanu's time. Harvests were usually poor; good years were no more frequent than years of drought or animal epidemics. Ottoman domination and preemption of the principalities' commerce had a direct effect on the culture as corn, which was not in demand by the Turks, replaced wheat. There are no dependable figures for cereal production in the Danubian principalities before 1831. The English consul W. Wilkinson claimed that Wallachia produced ten million Constantinople *kile* (about 256,000 metric tons) per year in the period immediately preceding the uprising of 1821, but this is a very modest amount.[9] Because of the impossibility of developing efficient agriculture, cattle breeding remained the country's primary source of income until the treaty of Adrianople reopened the Danube plain to the cultivation of grain.

The Phanariot hospodars, like the Ottoman sultans, nominally encouraged the development of trades and manufacturing. In 1796 a princely decree proclaimed that "a country's primary duty is to produce more implements and handicrafts of all kinds, and other merchandise, so that not only does that country no longer need to spend so much on things that come from foreign parts, but it can even bring in money by sending things abroad. . . . And in this way both self-sufficiency and means of livelihood are increased."[10] In practice, however, this mercantilist approach to economic problems was limited by a political reality that made the development of trades and of "handicrafts" almost impossible. Foreign travelers and the consuls of the great powers remarked at the beginning of the nineteenth century, as Cantemir had a century earlier, that the Romanians consciously refrained from exploiting their rich ore deposits, so as not to enrich the hospodars and the Turks. During the Russian occupations of 1806–12 and 1828–34 the czar's officers undertook field studies. To the annoyance of the boyars and the merchants they identified several minerals, notably copper, mercury, and gold, but the Russians did not stay long enough to start exploiting them. The copper and iron mines of Oltenia had been abandoned after 1739, so that mining in Moldavia and Wallachia was limited to salt, which sold profitably in Turkey, Poland, and elsewhere, and to drilling for oil. In 1831 there were 120 petroleum workers in Wallachia; in 1834 there were 84 wells, each with an average production of 80–100 *ocas* (102–28 kg) per day. The maximum depth of the wells was no more than three hundred meters.[11]

The impossibility of setting protective tariffs, the lack of capital, and the absence of a sufficiently developed domestic market represented almost insurmountable obstacles on the road to the establishment of factories. The initiative was usually taken not by the hospodar but by the boyars and merchants. They were the only ones with the necessary money to invest. Some establishments were founded with very modest capital. The glassworks at Tîrgu Jiu, for instance, was set up at the end of the eighteenth century with only 1,004 talers; the paper mill at Ca-tichea (1793), however, started with 32,000 talers. Surrounding villages usually supplied the labor, and foreign artisans were used only where greater skill was required. The majority of manufacturers produced such consumer goods as cloth, glass, foods, clothing, paper, ceramics, tobacco products, soap, beer, and candles and supplies for oil lamps. All were intended for the domestic market. Production must have been fairly profitable, since in 1831 the Frenchman Bois le Comte counted 1,068 "factories" in Wallachia.

The difficulties encountered by the manufacturing industry are ex-emplified by the history of the weaving mill founded in Pociovalişte, Ilfov county, in 1766 by the boyar R. Slătineanu. It closed (1768), re-opened (1784), closed again, reopened once more (1794), and then moved to Bucharest (1796).[12] This kind of instability, due largely to noneconomic causes, was not conducive to prosperity in manufacturing.

Under these circumstances, the economy of Moldavia and Wallachia could offer only agricultural and animal products for foreign trade, and it had to import most other products from Europe or the Ottoman empire. The rudimentary condition of the roads—in 1796 the mail took thirty hours from Bucharest to Focşani (about 170 km) and thir-teen from Bucharest to Ploieşti (about 60 km)—made the transport of goods, particularly grain and other perishables, more difficult. So cattle remained the principal export; at the beginning of the nineteenth cen-tury Moldavia exported about 100,000 head annually, a figure that fell to 32,000 in 1822 because of the uprising of 1821. In that same year Wallachia exported 50,000 pigs to Transylvania, and at the beginning of the century Moldavia had put up about 20,000 horses for sale an-nually. Ottoman sheep buyers of the period obtained about 600,000 sheep each year from the two principalities. Other exports were skins, hides, wool, hemp, wax, fish, and, to Constantinople, wheat. Between 1812 and 1819, 57.4 percent of Romanian exports went to the Ottoman empire and 42.6 percent to Austria, Poland, and Russia. Most imports (62.1%) came from south of the Danube and the rest (37.9%) from Europe, almost all from Germany and Austria.[13]

The balance of trade showed a surplus throughout the eighteenth century, cattle export in particular bringing significant earnings, which were quickly swallowed up by Phanariot and Ottoman greed. The huge sums that went to Constantinople and to the Phanar meant that the favorable balance of trade was useless to the Romanians. It was impossible to accumulate capital under Ottoman domination. The practices of the Phanariot period considerably delayed both the birth of capitalism and the economic maturation of the middle class.

Social Classes. During the eighteenth century social structure changed little. Urbanization did continue to make progress. The number of cities and market towns in Moldavia grew from fifteen at the beginning of the eighteenth century to thirty-three in 1830. Most of these had no more than a few thousand inhabitants, but Bucharest and Iaşi grew substantially. Bucharest had a population of 50,000 at the end of the eighteenth century and 70,000 by 1832, while the population of Iaşi reached 48,148 in that year. But the urban population was never more than 10 percent of the total population, and the character of Romanian society remained overwhelmingly rural before the Organic Statutes were issued (1831 in Wallachia, 1832 in Moldavia).[14]

The boyars, despite the limitations imposed by the Phanariot regime and their own reduced political role in foreign affairs, continued to be the ruling class in the Danubian principalities. They maintained a privileged social and economic position that the Phanariots could not and probably did not wish to diminish. Immigration from Greece and other Balkan countries did little to alter the ethnic makeup of this class, for the Greek boyars most often arrived and departed with their patron hospodars. But the conflict between the native boyars and the Phanariots, which went on continuously until 1821, was not entirely without results. In 1739 Constantin Mavrocordat instituted a reform that brought significant changes to the structure of the boyar class.

Traditionally the boyars had been a warrior class. The hospodars paid for their services with estates from the throne's holdings. Later the military role became intertwined with the civil service, so that a boyar could exercise purely official functions. Nevertheless, until the beginning of the eighteenth century noble blood and possession of an estate continued to be the essential attributes of a boyar. The reform of 1739 modified the traditional character of the ruling class. The title *boyar* became simply a rank, connected neither to the ownership of estates nor to position as a high official, but merely to the goodwill of the hospodar who granted it. Anyone enjoying the hospodar's favor could be named a boyar. In this reform Mavrocordat created a very useful instrument for ensuring the proper behavior of the native nobility, who now had to stay in the hospodar's good graces to retain their social standing. The ranks were divided up into categories, from the great boyars to the country squires, each with its particular social, economic, and fiscal privileges. The most important privilege was probably exemption from taxes.

Although many hospodars sold titles as a means of self-enrichment, the number of boyars remained small. In 1832 the number of Wallachian boyar families of all categories was only 766. Even counting all their family members, the boyars of Wallachia represented less than one percent of the population of the country; in Moldavia the proportion was probably a little higher due to the greater number of lesser boyars.[15]

The eighteenth century saw continual mergers of estates and the formation of great landed properties, but the unfavorable economic situation prevented the estate from becoming a major agricultural producer. Its principal earnings came not from the sale of produce but from tavern and mill taxes, peasant taxes, and cash payments in place of the corvée or compulsory service. The few existing records show that pasture and hayfields exceeded plowlands on boyar holdings. For example, the great boyar D. Roset had only 670 hectares of his 1,741 hectare estate in use in 1825. His pastures and hayfields made up 77 percent of the land used, plowed land only 21 percent.[16] The estates did not become great grain producers until the treaty of Adrianople (1829) abolished the Turkish monopoly and opened international commerce.

As for the peasants, the process of enserfing the free peasants and binding them to the land had already begun under Michael the Brave, and it continued through the first half of the eighteenth century. Nevertheless, in Oltenia, for instance, 1722 statistics show that 48 percent of all villages were still occupied by free, land-owning peasants, a percentage that probably held for the rest of the country as well. But the continual flight of peasants from one estate to another and the frequent wars fought by Russia, Austria, and Turkey (1711, 1716–19, 1736–39) obliged the hospodars and the boyars to rethink basic agrarian relations and to propose solutions that would stabilize the country's economy and finances. As a result, in 1746 in Wallachia and 1749 in Moldavia, serfdom was abolished and the estate-bound peasants were freed. In Wallachia they were, however, obliged to pay ten talers for their freedom and to work twelve days per year for the use of a plot of the owner's land. In Moldavia there was no payment, but the corvée was twenty-four days per year, with a quota setting the amount to be accomplished in a day. The amount of land rented in this way varied from estate to estate. The former serfs thus became legally free but held no land of their own, and thus no independent means of subsistence. The official documents claimed that serfdom was being abolished because of its inhumanity. The assembly's proclamation affirmed at great length the necessity of abolishing an institution that held human beings in servitude. Serfdom was declared unnatural, to be shunned by true Christians. The real reason was entirely different: to keep the population stable and to ensure the regular collection of taxes.[17]

Liberation from serfdom in no way solved the agrarian problem, nor did it even appreciably improve the peasants' lot. At the same time, by obliging the boyar to give the landless peasants the use of plots of land, it prevented the estates from becoming freehold properties of the bourgeois type. Basically the reforms of 1746 and 1749 helped neither peasant nor boyar. They just perpetuated the old feudal style of agrarian relations, with the single difference being the new legal status of the peasant as freeman.

The relative economic backwardness of the Danubian principalities, especially the lack of stimulus that a real foreign market for agricultural produce might have supplied, kept boyar-peasant relations from reaching the explosive levels found in Transylvania. The boyars tried several times to increase the number of days of the corvée, even proposing a tithe of the days of the year, but usually not even the traditional twelve days per year could be enforced. Most often the number was left for boyar and peasant to agree upon. Until 1831 the corvée was often converted to money at a set rate. In Moldavia the price of a day's work rose from one leu at the beginning of the century to two lei toward the end; in Wallachia it went from fifteen bani (one leu is one hundred bani) at the beginning of the Phanariot period to one leu in 1818. These fees were much lower than those levied on Transylvanian, Russian, or German peasants, and even the proposed tithe of days was far less than the fifty-two-day corvée introduced by the Austrian government of Oltenia in 1722. The milder agrarian regime in Moldavia and Wallachia explains the immigration of Transylvanian and Balkan peasants. In spite of the corvée and in spite of the taxes, until 1831 the peasant's principal enemy was not the boyar but the hospodar's functionary. The state was a much more ruthless fiscal oppressor.

After the treaty of Adrianople (1829) made possible the export of agricultural produce previously subject to Turkish preemption, Moldavia and Wallachia could once again participate in international commerce. The prospect of transforming the estate into a great grain producer brought about a radical change in the nature of agrarian relations. The Organic Statutes legislated the owner's obligation to provide the peasant with land for a house, pasture, and plowland in exchange for a corvée of twelve days per year. But the work quota included in the statutes raised the corvée to fifty-six days in Wallachia and eighty-four in Moldavia. The land allotted to the peasants was insufficient for their needs. Peasants received only about 1.5 hectares of plowland in Wallachia and 2.2 hectares in Moldavia. In both principalities the allotted pasturage could accommodate only five head of cattle. Peasants were forced to contract for supplementary land on terms that amounted to slavery.[18]

The Organic Statutes were supposed to make the estate into a single property, with the peasants "placed" on the estate and paying rent in labor and taxes on the plots they had the use of. The principal oppressor of the village was no longer the state and taxation—all taxes had been combined in 1831 into a single annual poll tax (*capitație*) of thirty lei—but the landlord and the boyars. This new state of affairs explains the explosive agrarian situation after the Organic Statutes were issued.

In the eighteenth century there was no very clear concept of a middle class. Although Dimitrie Cantemir wrote in 1716, "We call people who live in cities and market towns townsmen,"[19] records from 1755 and 1762 enumerate no fewer than eight categories of city dwellers. The list begins with artisans and merchants, but goes on to include civil servants, Gypsy slaves, peasants actually farming on the outskirts of the city, and clergy and boyars. This heterogeneous character of the city and its inhabitants continued until the Organic Statutes were issued. The Phanariot hospodars repeatedly declared their interest in the growth and well-being of the middle class, but in practice they demonstrated an almost total lack of interest in the cities, simply treating them as crown estates. The eighteenth century was not a favorable time for the rise of the middle class in either a political or an economic sense. Its economic base was limited and its political influence minimal.

Until 1831 the middle class had never undertaken any political action on its own account but generally followed the boyar initiatives, especially in conflicts with the hospodar. In the West, the middle class usually allied itself with the central power against the nobility, but in Moldavia and Wallachia they allied themselves with the boyars against the hospodars. That alliance never did them much good. But the number of artisans was continually rising as guilds multiplied, first in the various branches of the garment industry and then in construction and food production. Of all the artisans, it was probably the guilds connected with construction that showed the most dynamic activity. Their members increased from 81 in 1820 to 390 in 1832 in Bucharest alone.

Judging solely by the number of stores, merchants must have been numerous even in times of economic upheaval. In 1824, for instance, there were 1,514 shops in Bucharest, most of them dealing in food and clothing.[20] The relatively large number of inns offers similar evidence of brisk commercial activity. Merchants had extensive connections with businesses in the Balkans, and the "Greek companies" based in Sibiu and Braşov did business throughout central Europe. With a few exceptions of merchants with political and financial influence, though, the middle class remained a weak economic and social force with no influence on events until the Organic Statutes. In contrast to their peers in Greece and Serbia, they played an insignificant role in the national reawakening.

The Habsburgs in Transylvania. When Transylvania came under Habsburg rule, its political status was substantially altered, its domestic autonomy limited, its foreign affairs suspended, and its Hungarian political leaders made completely subject to Vienna. The old place of the princes was taken by a governor appointed directly by the emperor without consultation with the diet. The rebellion led by Ferenc Rákóczi II, which ended with the peace of Szatmár (Satu Mare, 1711), did not succeed in changing the new regime in Transylvania at all, except to ensure that the principality was governed even more directly by the emperor. Habsburg centralism made itself felt most keenly during Joseph II's enlightened despotism, when reforms openly sought to eradicate regional differences and to create a strictly centralized state governed from Vienna. With the revocation of most of these reforms after 1790 some of the Hungarian nobility's old influence was restored, but the principality's autonomy was still very limited.

The conflict between the emperor in Vienna and the Hungarian nobility was of only modest importance to the Romanians, but they seem frequently to have nurtured the hope that the central government would help them in their conflicts with the local authorities. This was the ulterior motive for the Church Union with Rome (1697). In practice, pressure from the nobility prevented the enforcement of a second decree issued in 1701 by Emperor Leopold I granting all Uniates the rights and privileges enjoyed by the Catholics. The Romanians thus remained a tolerated "nation" with no political rights. The only immediate advantage of the Church Union was to ameliorate the economic situation of the Uniate clergy, certainly very little compared to the great hopes the union had raised.

The social structure of the population of Transylvania was not too different from that of the Danubian principalities: at the beginning of the eighteenth century peasants were 93 percent of the population, the nobility about 4 percent, and city dwellers 3 percent. Serfs accounted for 73 percent of the population, a much higher figure than in the other two principalities, where the proportion of peasants with no labor obligation remained quite large until the beginning of the nineteenth century. The predominantly Hungarian nobility was more numerous than the boyars of Moldavia and Wallachia. In 1784–87, according to Austrian statistics, Romanians made up 63.5 percent, Hungarians 24.1 percent, and Saxons and Swabians 12.4 percent of the 2,489,147 inhabitants of the principality (figures include the Banat, Crişana, and Maramureş).[21]

Religious persecution against the Orthodox, together with the more highly perfected Austro-Hungarian system of serfdom, caused many Transylvanian Romanians to flee over the mountains into Moldavia and Wallachia. There boyars in need of labor always received them well, and the hospodars accorded them special fiscal privileges. Emissaries of the boyars frequently traveled through the villages of Transylvania for this kind of recruiting, an activity the Austrian authorities tried more than once to stop. In 1746 Maria Theresa named a commission to look into the reasons for this emigration, and the border authorities were ordered to put a halt to it. The movement of people from Transylvania into the Danubian principalities had little effect on the proportions of the three nationalities in Transylvania, for the number of those who moved permanently to Moldavia and Wallachia was actually fairly low. Not more than 60,000 people fled during the period 1739–1831. In Wallachia, however, the 1832 census shows 225 villages of ethnic Romanians "from the Hungarian land."[22]

In the absence of a national aristocracy, the clergy led the battle for Romanian political rights. For about a quarter of a century this struggle was dominated by the imposing figure of Ioan Inochentie Micu-Clain, Uniate bishop (1728–51), baron of the empire, and member of the Transylvanian diet. In dozens of memoranda he demanded that Romanians be included among the "recognized nations," and he called for the abolition of their status as a "tolerated nation," to which they had been brought by the three privileged nations—the Hungarian nobility, the Szeklers, and the Saxons. Influenced by Cantemir's *Hronicul*, Micu-Clain repeatedly proclaimed the historical rights of Romanians in Transylvania, rights stemming from their Roman origins and from their continuous existence since the most ancient times on that territory. His political activism ended by displeasing Vienna, and he was forced into exile in Rome. His place was taken by clergy with less radical views, who were willing to speak, at least for the present, in the name of the Uniates and not for all Romanians.

The enlightened rule of Emperor Joseph II aroused great hopes among the Romanian peasants, who existed under ever-worsening conditions. Their corvée, set at one day per week in 1514, had risen by the middle of the eighteenth century to four days per week for serfs working as manual laborers and three for those with their own cattle. A serf's corvée could come to as much as 208 days a year, so it comes as no surprise that some peasants preferred to leave their villages and flee to the Danubian principalities, where the corvée was no more than twelve days a year.

In the context of the heavy corvée and with strong hopes for the reign of Joseph II, the peasants readily believed the rebel leader Horia's claims that the emperor had promised him aid and support in his struggle against the nobility. In October 1784 an uprising began in the Apuseni (Bihor) mountains as the peasants attempted to seize their own rights. The emperor's alleged promises soon became the program of the uprising. Horia demanded the abolition of the nobility, distribution of the estate lands, and payment of taxes by all inhabitants. In November, after negotiating with imperial emissaries, he added the abolition of serfdom and the recognition of the right of Romanians to join the border guard. Meanwhile the uprising had spread throughout Transylvania and become a bloodbath. It was brought to an end in December only with the coming of winter and the capture through treachery of Horia, together with Cloşca and Crişan, the other leaders of the uprising.

Horia and Cloşca were broken on the wheel before hundreds of peasants summoned on purpose to be intimidated and taught a lesson. But the uprising was not without less horrible results: in August 1785 serfdom was officially abolished in Transylvania by imperial decree. As in the Danubian principalities, however, this reform brought only partial improvement in the peasants' lot. The corvée of two to three days a week—that is, up to 156 days a year—and the tithe continued to oppress the peasants. Since the peasants still had no land, the personal liberty granted by the emperor was insufficient to make any radical change in their circumstances.[23]

On his deathbed in 1790, in fear of the French Revolution and under great pressure from the conservative aristocracy, the emperor revoked all his reforms, with the sole exceptions of the Edict of Toleration granting freedom of worship and the decree abolishing serfdom. Most of the rights Vienna had appropriated during the time of enlightened despotism were returned to the Transylvanian diet and the privileged nations. In the confused political atmosphere that followed the death of the emperor, the Romanians of Transylvania presented their demands and their program once again. In March 1791 they forwarded to Vienna the *Supplex Libellus Valachorum,* a long and vibrant plea for the rights of the principality's majority population.

The *Supplex* did not represent a new point of view or original claim. Almost all the ideas it contained can be found in Bishop Micu-Clain's memoranda: the affirmation of Roman origins and the theory of continuity, the demand that Romanians be included among the privileged nations and enjoy equal standing with the other three nations, and the request that their status as a tolerated people be abolished. The *Supplex* is not at first glance a very modern document, for it proposes no change in the system, only its expansion to include Romanians. In practice, however, meeting these demands would quickly have brought about a shift in the balance of power, tilting it toward the majority nationality. Vienna therefore refused to receive the petition and sent it on to the Transylvanian diet, where it was indignantly rejected.[24]

The efforts of a century, starting with the Church Union and reaching their height with the presentation of the *Supplex,* had been in vain. Economically the plight of the peasant was worse than ever; in religion Romanians were more than ever divided between Orthodoxy and the Uniate church. For the Romanians the European, Austrian regime in frock coat and periwig had proved no more favorable than the Oriental, Phanariot regime in caftan and calpac.

Reform and Revolution

Enlightened Despotism. The hard words most Romanian scholars have had for Phanariot rule need not lead us to believe that the hospodars appointed by the sultans after 1711 were merely the padishah's crude tools, lacking in culture and concerned only with rapid material gain. Some were, it is true, but alongside them we find hospodars who, without forgetting their own interests and their need for gold, still tried to rule wisely, understanding that at bottom the well-being of the country could only be to the ruler's good. Inspired by the ideas of the Age of Enlightenment and by the European models of enlightened despots,

Constantin Mavrocordat, several times prince of Wallachia and
Moldavia between 1730 and 1769.

they tried to introduce modernizing administrative and social reforms
into Moldavia and Wallachia in order to strengthen central power, put
the administration in order, and bring the rebellious boyars under the
hospodar's authority.

Constantin Mavrocordat, whose many terms—six in Wallachia and
four in Moldavia—covered the period from 1730 to 1769, was one such
enlightened despot. A man of learning, son and grandson of scholar-
princes, surrounded by Western secretaries and Jesuit advisers, influ-

enced by the books in his celebrated library (which the king of France later tried to buy), Mavrocordat introduced a series of typical enlightened reforms between 1740 and 1749. In response to the flight of peasants from the estates, which had been brought on by fiscal oppression and the numerous levies, he unified the system of taxation. He introduced a set tax to be collected four times a year and abolished many indirect taxes, for example, those on fields under cultivation and on cattle. He limited fiscal abuses, doing away with, among other things, the villages' collective responsibility before the courts. His reforms were designed to create a climate of fiscal stability and to prevent the eventual breakup of the village. This in turn implicitly meant an increase in the number of taxpayers and in the hospodar's income.

Mavrocordat also made changes in administrative and judiciary organization, bringing a sense of greater order and efficiency. For the first time, high officials were paid a salary, in place of the old system, under which they had received a percentage of the money they collected in taxes, fines, and the like. Counties were entrusted to government administrators (*ispravnici*) who were responsible directly to the hospodar. Finally Mavrocordat abolished serfdom, in 1746 in Wallachia and in 1749 in Moldavia. His explanations for this act were culled from the rhetoric of the Enlightenment, even though his real reasons were fiscal, not humanitarian.

Wanting to see his name praised in Europe, Mavrocordat issued his reforms of 1740–41 in the *Mercure de France* (1741) under the pretentious title of *Constitution*. But his reforms had no more staying power than those of the enlightened despots of Europe. They could not stand against either assaults by the boyars or financial pressures from the Porte. The need for money brought Mavrocordat to abandon the fixed tax, to increase the number of quarterly deadlines for tax payments, and to reinstitute many indirect levies. Political instability, largely caused by external factors, made the centralization of power impossible. The enhanced status of the high officials and the dissolution of the principalities' old military organization weakened the boyars, but their power was still great—and hard to control. The transfer of power from the nobility to the central government, the dream of so many enlightened despots, could be realized only partially. When Mavrocordat died in 1769, most of his improvements and reforms had already been abandoned.

No other Phanariot hospodar tried so hard to reform the social and political life of Moldavia and Wallachia. Most attempted to improve the fiscal system, but the Porte's unpredictable and ever-growing demands for money permitted scarcely a moment's respite to implement plans. Nor could the administrative apparatus be restructured, although neither ideas nor initiatives were lacking. In spite of many hospodars' hopes, the administration of Moldavia and Wallachia in 1821 was essentially unchanged from the time of Dimitrie Cantemir and Constantin Brâncoveanu.

The one area in which Phanariot enlightened despotism made some progress was the codification of laws and the drawing up of modern legal codes. The secular codes of the seventeenth century, *Pravila de la Govora* (Govora code of law [1635]), *Cartea românească de învățătură* (Romanian book of instruction [1646]), and *Îndreptarea legii* (Guide to the law [1652]), based on local custom, Roman-Byzantine sources, and the writings of the Italian Prosper Farinaccius, only incompletely reflected new social and juridical realities. In the second half of the eighteenth century the first initiatives appeared for the replacement of these codes. At the request of the hospodars Ștefan Racoviță (1764–65), Scarlat Ghica (1765–67), and Alexandru Ypsilanti (1774–82), the jurist Mihai Fotino drafted three new codes, including an agrarian one. They were not implemented, however, because they were too strongly Byzantine in character and not suited to local conditions.

The first Phanariot code, also drawn up by Fotino, was issued just a few years later in 1780 at the request of Prince Ypsilanti. This *Pravilniceasca condica* (Law register), as it was called, was in use in Wallachia until almost 1821, the year of Tudor Vladimirescu's revolution. It was replaced by *Legiuirea Caragea* (Caragea's law [1818]).

The first two decades of the nineteenth century were years of feverish legislative activity. Some initiatives, like Alexandru Moruzi's attempt to draw up a complete civil code (1804–06), never went beyond draft forms. Others, like Alexandru Donici's *Manualul de legi* (Manual of laws [1814]), were in effect for only a few years. Still others were adopted and kept in use for many years, even after the fall of the Phanariot regime. Both *Codul Calimah* (Callimachi's code [1817]) and *Caragea's Law* were drawn up for Phanariot hospodars, Scarlat Callimachi in Moldavia and Ioan Caragea in Wallachia, but by professional jurists with solid theoretical backgrounds. In Moldavia the principal author was Christian Flechtenmacher from Brașov, and in Wallachia the most influential jurist was Nestor Craiovescu. The Moldavian code was almost entirely based on the Austrian Civil Code of 1811; both are indebted to the Code Napoléon. Scarlat Callimachi was so proud of his legislative opus that he presented one of the first printed copies to the chancellor of Oxford University. The codes were useful, too. Remaining in con-

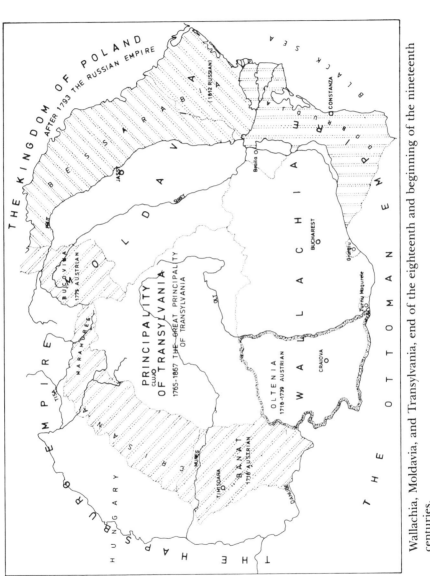

Wallachia, Moldavia, and Transylvania, end of the eighteenth and beginning of the nineteenth centuries.

tinuous use until 1865, they were probably the most enduring accomplishment of the Phanariot enlightened despots—and one of the few not eliminated by the victorious nationalist movement in 1821.

"Nothing is more just and more truly the duty of the princes to whom God has entrusted their governing, than the well-being of the people," wrote hospodar Alexandru Ypsilanti (Wallachia 1774–82, Moldavia 1787–88),[25] one of the Phanariots who wished to be not only despots but also enlightened. Unfortunately for the Phanariots and for the country, the wish usually proved illusory, as their power came not from God but from the padishah. Ypsilanti, for example, was executed in 1807 on mere suspicion of disloyalty. With such suzerains, the lights of the few enlightened Phanariot hospodars were soon extinguished. Even when their rule was indirect, Ottomans wanted no form of government but despotism.

The Boyar Reforms. The conflict between the Phanariot hospodars and the ethnic Romanian boyars dominated domestic politics in Moldavia and Wallachia from 1711 to 1821. The struggle between the "Greeks" and the "Romanians" did not divide strictly according to nationality. Sometimes Romanian boyars upheld foreign interests, or boyars of Greek origin were found in the leadership of the national parties. The conflict was political, not ethnic. It revolved around the problems of power, the status of Moldavia and Wallachia, and relations with the Turks. The Phanariots, who had their base of support in Constantinople and were appointed and kept on their thrones by the Ottomans, were naturally loyal to the sultan, bound to the Ecumenical Patriarchate of Constantinople, and hostile to any policy that might remove the principalities from the Porte's sphere of influence and civilization. The great boyars, however, kept from power, their leaders and followers alike coming in large part from the descendants of those vanquished in 1711 and 1716, naturally took a decidedly anti-Phanariot position, the only one which would permit their return to power.

The anti-Phanariot movements began as early as 1716, when the Wallachians elected as hospodar Gheorghe, son of Şerban Cantacuzino. A year later the Phanariotized Moldavian Mihai Racoviţă put down, with great difficulty, an anti-Greek uprising backed by Austria. From this time until 1739 the Moldavians intrigued almost ceaselessly, urged on by Dimitrie Cantemir's nephews and by Russia. In 1753 in Wallachia another Racoviţă, a Romanian Phanariot, was forced to send the most persistent plotters into exile in Cyprus to quell the great boyars' opposition to him. Led by Manolache Bogdan and Ioniţă Cuza, and aided by the Freemasons, who had just appeared in Iaşi, the Moldavians engaged in another conspiracy in 1778. This time the two leaders were beheaded, and other plotters were exiled to monasteries. Relations between hospodars and boyars grew steadily worse during the last two decades of the Phanariot period as plot followed plot (1813, 1816, 1818, 1820). The leaders of the nationalist movement, for example, Grigore Ghica, Constantin Bălăceanu, and Constantin Filipescu, suffered frequent arrests and banishments. The poisoning of Alexandru Suţu in January 1821 was certainly not without the involvement of the boyars. By this time the three great *bans* (boyars of the highest rank), Grigore Ghica, Grigore Brâncoveanu, and Barbu Văcărescu, had already entrusted Tudor Vladimirescu with the leadership of a national revolt, and a month later the Moldavians, led by the great treasurer Iordache Rosetti-Rosnovanu, would take advantage of the international confusion created by the beginning of the Etairia movement to force Mihail Suţu, the last Phanariot hospodar, to leave the country.

In some periods the great boyars had power. During the many wars between Ottomans and the Christian countries the hospodars generally retreated to the border fortresses, leaving the divans to govern. This happened in 1736–39, 1769–74, 1787–92, and 1806–12, and on each occasion the boyars set forth their agenda for governing in documents, significant in their political orientation and in the direction they proposed to take the country. The most important among these were the Moldavian-Russian convention of 1739, the Wallachian and Moldavian memoranda of 1769, 1772, and 1774, the Wallachian divan's program of 1791, the Moldavian reform proposals of 1802, 1807, and 1810, the Wallachian boyars' violent anti-Greek memorandum of 1811, and the Moldavian memoranda of 1817–18.

The main concern of these programs was the problem of the form of government in Moldavia and Wallachia. Between 1716 and 1821 the boyars requested forty times that the Phanariots be replaced with elected Romanian princes, the request being issued to Constantinople, St. Petersburg, Vienna, and Paris almost without change, whenever it appeared likely or possible that the foreign hospodars could be eliminated. The boyars were always hostile to any kind of Phanariot despotism, enlightened or otherwise. Regaining political power was the keystone of their political agenda until after 1821.

The boyars' plans did not all agree on the most suitable form of government for the principalities, however. In 1769, for instance, the

nationalist movement, led by the metropolitan Gavriil Callimachi of
Moldavia, wanted to establish an aristocratic republic led by twelve great
boyars vested with broad legislative and judicial powers; direct administration, that is, executive power, was to be left to the lower- and mid-
level boyars. The proposal provided for government based on a legal
code, for economic and cultural reforms, and for an administrative
reform affecting the hospodar's high officials. A similar plan was proposed by Dumitrache Sturza in his *Plan, sau formă de oblăduire republi-
ciască aristo-dimocraticească* (Plan, or aristocratic-democratic republican
form of government [1802]), but here executive power would have been
held by a divan made up of great boyars, the judicial by another divan
composed of second-level boyars, and the legislative by the two divans
together. Sturza also proposed to establish a third divan with largely
fiscal duties, to be elected from all social categories.

Other plans called for a boyar state headed by a prince with "limited"
powers. In 1782, for example, the program entitled *Unirea boierilor pă-
mînteni* (Union of native boyars) proposed to ensure that no prince,
whether Moldavian or Phanariot, would damage "the honor of the boyars and the good of the country and [that] we should all, openly and
otherwise, do our duty so that the boyar state and our homeland may
be given their due rights and privileges." In 1817–18, Iordache Rosetti-
Rosnovanu drew up no fewer than eight proposals, outlining the installation of a regime in which the throne would be just for oversight
and control, the real power passing into the hands of a general assembly
and a divan controlled by boyars.[26]

The Age of Revolutions. The long military occupations by Austria and
Russia in 1769–74 and 1787–92 helped to breach the wall the Phanariots had tried to build to keep out the influence of European ideas.
After 1774, the boyars' libraries were filled with books of the Enlightenment. The Freemasons, active in Bucharest since 1743, founded their
first Masonic lodge in Iaşi in 1772 under the guidance of Russian officers. The Ecumenical Patriarchate of Constantinople pronounced an
anathema against them; the hospodars, Nicolae Mavrogheni in particular, bitterly opposed them; but this did not prevent them from increasing in numbers and from coopting many high-level clerics, boyars,
and many leaders of the nationalist movement.[27]

Both boyars and hospodars greeted the outbreak of the French Revolution in 1789 with surprising sympathy. They did nothing to prevent
revolutionary propaganda from pouring into Bucharest and Iaşi under
the protection of the French consuls, some avowed Jacobins like Hor-

tolan, others like Fleury, who boasted that he had contributed to the fall of Louis XVI. Both of these frequently visited the salons of the great boyars.

In Iaşi, to the indignation of the Russian consulate, Ion Piuariu Molnar recited verses that were circulating in Transylvanian villages, addressed to Napoleon: "Bonaparte is not far off, please come here, give us our rights." Talleyrand himself took care to send the emperor's proclamations and official bulletins to the principalities from Paris. Except during Napoleon's Egyptian campaign, the hospodars showed great interest in establishing relations with France, maintaining an assiduous and eloquent correspondence through the embassy in Vienna.[28]

Probably neither the boyars nor the hospodars clearly distinguished between republic and empire. The Phanariots cultivated France because that country had good relations with the Porte and because they hoped to gain leverage in the complex play of influence with Constantinople. The boyars, however, moved by the ideas of national liberty propagated both by the republic and by the empire—ideas so well suited to their own political agenda—calculated that the French could help them oust the Phanariots and regain power. They had taken in only part of the revolutionary message, only the foreign policy and the revival of nationalism, completely ignoring its democratic aspect, social equality. They sent the emperor many memoranda (1802, 1807, and 1810) proposing very advanced political reforms, speaking of independence, alliances, and national progress, but leaving aside any measures for domestic reorganization that might benefit the peasantry or the middle class. The great boyars thought that they could use French influence to drive out the Phanariots so that they might replace them with their own aristocratic state.

The end of the eighteenth century witnessed the political awakening of the lesser boyars, more liberal in philosophy and anxious to play a role of their own in governing the country. Their surviving documents, for instance the manifesto addressed to the metropolitan Iacob Stamate of Moldavia (1796), stress the need for domestic reforms and threaten uprisings or, as an 1804 pamphlet puts it, "thoughts of French insubordination." Another manifesto written some years later expresses surprise that the great boyars "do not read newspapers, otherwise they would know what is happening now in Spain, in Naples, and in other countries, and that the rights of the people are increasing everywhere."[29] The conflict between the conservative great boyars and the liberal lesser boyars, held in check until 1821 by their common fear of the Phanariots, exploded when that danger was removed and became a principal element in Romanian domestic politics until the middle of the nineteenth century.

The Romanians did not need to look as far as Spain and Italy to see ideas of a political renaissance transforming the lives of the people. Closer to home, in Serbia, a bitter struggle for national independence had begun in 1804. Both princes and boyars viewed it with approval and supported it with money and materiel. The formation of the Etairia in 1814 brought the Balkan revolutionary spirit still closer to the Romanians. Many of the Greek boyars joined this organization, whose avowed purpose was liberating the Balkans from the Turks. During the last decade of Phanariot rule Christian southeast Europe was going through a continual process of political radicalization. Some change could be expected, for various reasons, at almost every social level.

It was in this context that the Wallachian *bans*, Grigore Ghica, Grigore Brâncoveanu, and Barbu Văcărescu, organized a revolt to restore the principalities' old rights, long violated by the Turks and the Phanariots. As its military leader they chose (probably in December 1820) Tudor Vladimirescu, a lesser boyar from a family of free peasants and a former commander of the pandours (a kind of soldier) during the Russo-Turkish War of 1806–12. Vladimirescu had military experience; he enjoyed the protection of Russia, having been granted honorary Russian citizenship when a lieutenant in the Russian army; he had close ties to the Etairia from the months he had spent in Vienna; and above all he was known for his anti-Phanariot and anti-Turkish outbursts and hostility. As landlord and tax collector, as a former local administrator and a one-time member of the household of the boyar family Glogoveanu, Vladimirescu had shown himself to be a typical representative of the rising new class, grown rich in the international cattle trade, often harsh in dealing with peasants, ambitious, and anxious to play a political role.

In December 1820, Vladimirescu and the head of the Etairia, Prince Alexandru Ypsilanti (grandson of the hospodar of the same name and an officer in the Russian army), agreed on a military collaboration, and on 15 January 1821 the three *bans* officially commissioned Vladimirescu in writing to lead the revolt: "We have chosen you to raise the people in arms and to proceed as directed," for "the good of Christian people and of our homeland." The next day the three boyars appointed Dimitrie Macedonski as Vladimirescu's lieutenant and made the purpose of the whole movement still more explicit: "The right time . . . has come and it is possible that with God's help we may free ourselves."[30] With a military guard provided by Grigore Brâncoveanu, Vladimirescu and

Tudor Vladimirescu, leader of the 1821 uprising in Wallachia.

Macedonski left Bucharest for Oltenia during the night of 17–18 January 1821, to incite the pandours to revolt. The death of hospodar Alexandru Suțu, probably poisoned by members of the Etairia, was announced on 18 January. The three *bans* proclaimed themselves *caimacams*—temporary replacements for the prince—and took over the government of the country. The next day the Russian consul Pini, who had been in on the plot, recognized the new government.

Although the movement's program, known by the title *Cererile norodului românesc* (Demands of the Romanian People), is dated 17 January, it was written in Bucharest in December 1820. It was very anti-Greek and appeared to be directed against the Phanariots, not the Porte. But the removal of the Greeks was just the first step on the road to independence. Vladimirescu himself told the pandours, "This undertaking was ordered by Czar Alexander I of Russia and concerns not only our own freedom but that of the whole Greek nation. . . . We will enable Prince Ypsilanti to cross the Danube to free his homeland. The Russians will help us overpower the Turkish fortresses on our side of the Danube, and then they will leave us, free and independent."[31] This speech reveals the essential elements on which the revolt was based: the alliance with the Etairia and the conviction that Russia would give the two anti-Ottoman movements unconditional assistance.

Events took an unexpected turn, however. The Greek and Romanian rebellions came just at the moment when the monarchs of the Holy Alliance were at the congress at Laibach (Ljubljana), consulting on how to stem the revolutionary tide raging in Italy and Spain. As a founder of that conservative Vienna alliance, Alexander I could not openly support an uprising against a legitimate monarch even if his personal sympathies might lie in that direction. It is unlikely that the czar ever gave the members of the Etairia anything more than assurances of sympathy, but they had taken them for promises of aid and had passed them on to the Romanians as such. The whole revolt of 1821 was based on mistaken hopes. On 18 February the Russian consul in Bucharest publicly disavowed Vladimirescu, and on 23 February Ioannis Count Capodistria himself, as foreign minister of Czar Alexander I, withdrew the decoration, citizenship, and army rank he had granted Vladimirescu during the Russo-Turkish War. A few weeks later in Ljubljana the czar condemned Ypsilanti's revolt as well, so that the Etairia, Vladimirescu, and the *bans* who had organized the revolt found themselves without the support they had counted on, support they had persuaded themselves was imminent and without which they could not emerge victorious from a military confrontation with the Ottomans.

Once abandoned, Vladimirescu and Ypsilanti soon exhausted what little trust they had in each other. The Romanians had allied themselves with the Etairia on condition that that group should proceed to Greece —a plan now rendered impossible. Ypsilanti stayed, taking control of the northeast section of Wallachia, which brought him into conflict with the local people: they did not want to have escaped from the Phanariots only to come under Etairia rule. Meanwhile Vladimirescu occupied Bucharest, sequestering some of the great boyars and running the country almost as a prince. He put a white top—the insignia of a hospodar—on his calpac and took the title "commander of the nation's armies." On 17 April he reaffirmed that his principal aim was to "free the country," and he took measures for the military defense of the capital.

The nature of the movement had also perceptibly changed in the meantime. The social element had become more important than the national. Vladimirescu did not intend to unleash a peasant rebellion. He had taken no greater step for social reform than just to ease taxes. Most often he had tried to restrain the peasants and protect the boyars, whose political support he needed. In any case the peasants had not joined him, so that the movement lacked the broad foundation that might have made it a popular rebellion. Still, social tensions certainly increased, and one landlord wrote, "I cannot give orders to the peasants or the merchants, for they have changed. . . . Now they are the masters, and I am afraid of them"; and "nobody obeys us."[32]

The czar's disavowal, the increasingly social aspects of the movement, and the imminent entry of Turkish troops into the country were enough to make most of the boyars flee to Transylvania. The three *bans*, Ghica, Văcărescu, and Brâncoveanu, were in the lead. Left alone, Vladimirescu tried to solve the crisis by approaching the Turks and presenting the movement as strictly anti-Phanariot and in no way hostile to the Porte. On 15 May he left Bucharest for northern Oltenia, where he intended to create a stronger and more stable base of resistance until he could reach an agreement with Turkey. But the Etairia guessed his plans and seized him in Goleşti. He was hastily tried as a traitor by an Etairia tribunal and executed in Tîrgovişte in June. After his death, which the rebels long refused to accept, the pandours dispersed in preference to fighting for Ypsilanti, and in August the Etairia detachments were completely routed by the Turks in the battle of Drăgăşani.

The revolt had fallen short of its aims, but through skillful diplomacy the boyars succeeded in achieving worthwhile gains for the country. In 1821 and 1822 they wrote no fewer than seventy-five memoranda and reform projects, which they forwarded to Russia, Turkey, and Austria. They were demanding international recognition of many national rights, including the most important, the right to have Romanian rulers again. In September 1822 the Porte agreed to replace the Phanariot hospodars with native princes: Grigore IV Ghica in Wallachia and Ioniță Sandu Sturdza in Moldavia.

The period between the revolt of 1821 and the issuing of the Organic Statutes is probably one of the most interesting times in the modern history of the Danubian principalities. Contemporary writers were caught up in a frenzy of hope, the hope for change, and the belief that their sufferings and those of the country were at an end: "Here is justice, here is the golden age," exclaimed the Moldavian boyar Ionică Tăutu, voicing the general confidence in the future. Between 1821 and 1830 dozens of memoranda and reform plans, appeals and proclamations, were written in Wallachia and Moldavia, discussing from all angles how to establish the era the poet Barbu Paris Mumuleanu hailed with the words, "Brothers and compatriots, a new age has dawned."[33]

The new age was not a golden one for all, especially for the peasants, whose life the replacement of Phanariots by Romanians had not changed. As for the boyars, after 1821 they were divided into two hostile camps, each striving to hold power and to govern according to its own political vision. The political and ideological conflict between great and lesser boyars now became a factor to be reckoned with in the Romanian political scene, as nineteenth-century conservatism and liberalism both had their origins in this battle of ideas.

The confrontation between the two groups was particularly serious in Moldavia, where Prince Sturdza took advantage of the flight of the great boyars to surround himself with innovative lesser boyars who wanted to reform the system according to the principles described by Tăutu in his 1822 *Constituție a celor 77 de ponturi* (The 77-point constitution; also known as *Constituția cărvunarilor* [The Carbonari constitution], from the Italian revolutionaries). They proposed setting up a constitutional regime in Moldavia, with separation of powers and an improved and modernized administration, and they included numerous measures to encourage industry, agriculture, commerce, and urban development. Tăutu's regime did not embody representation for all classes; political power was left in the hands of the boyars. But the Carbonari used the term *boyar* in a very broad sense. For them the boyars included many bourgeois and intellectuals, and they excluded the great boyars from government, so it is not surprising that these attacked Tăutu's constitution. Many documents by the great boyars accuse it of revolutionary spirit, of anarchism, and of wanting to over-turn the legitimate social order. Even Prince Grigore IV Ghica of Wallachia joined this denunciatory chorus, calling the idea of a "constitution . . . and representative form of government" unsuitable and ridiculous.[34] But in 1827 he appointed a commission to draw up a basic statute, really a constitution.

The Ottomans continued their military occupation of the Danubian principalities, and it proved difficult to reorganize the administration under these conditions. The two princes strove to exercise their autonomy—in 1824, for example, they tried to recreate the national army the Porte had abolished in 1739—but almost every initiative was opposed by Turkey. The obstructive Ottoman presence and influence persisted until the convention of Akerman (1826), which promised Moldavia and Wallachia real autonomy and allowed them to proceed with their internal reorganizing. But in less than two years they were again occupied, this time by Russia, under whose control they remained until 1834.

The Russo-Turkish War of 1828–29, which ended with the treaty of Adrianople, had important consequences for Moldavia and Wallachia. It put their relations with the Porte on an entirely new footing, increased their autonomy, abolished the Ottoman monopoly on commerce, and removed them, except for a modest tribute, from the empire's political and economic control. The treaty also provided for the prompt reorganization of their domestic administration on the basis of the Organic Statutes, which had begun to be drafted even before the war ended. One version was sent to St. Petersburg. The final version of the statutes, after being debated for a few months in the Extraordinary General Assemblies for Oversight in Bucharest and Iaşi (1831), was issued in Wallachia at the end of 1831 and in Moldavia on 1 January 1832.

The Organic Statutes were a curious and eclectic first Romanian constitution including, beside a statement of general principles for societal organization, form of government, and social structure, articles on all kinds of administrative and organizational details. The Wallachian statutes contained 371 articles and the Moldavian 425, many adopted from the more than one hundred drafts that had been written during the preceding decade. The institutional provisions were certainly new and modernizing in effect. They introduced a constitutional monarchy in which the prince's authority was counterbalanced by a general assembly with broad legislative powers and controls. There was complete separation of powers, a new concept in the political life of the principalities. The administration was modernized and streamlined. There were many measures to stimulate the economy, including free commerce on the domestic and foreign markets. And order was brought to the system of taxation, the old fiscal chaos being replaced by a single poll tax.

But many measures intended to advance modernization stopped halfway. The boyars were still exempted from taxes. The monarchy was constitutional, but the assemblies, made up almost exclusively of boyars, were not representative. And the restructuring of agrarian relations was not in the peasants' favor, in spite of the good intentions of Count Pavel Dmitrievich Kiselev, the progressive Russian administrator of both principalities from 1829 to 1834.

The main change in foreign relations introduced by the treaty of Adrianople and ratified by the statutes was Russian protection of the Danubian principalities. The sultan was still the nominal suzerain, but the czar was now the real ruler. Russian influence grew yet stronger with the appending to the statutes in 1837—over the General Assembly's objections—of the so-called Additional Article. It gave St. Petersburg the right to veto any domestic reform deemed unfavorable to Russia. As a result Romanians began to look on the statutes as an instrument of Russian interference in internal affairs. For the peasants and the middle class, they were also an instrument promoting domination by the great boyars. For that reason, as the years passed, the negative elements of this first Romanian constitution began to outweigh its positive ones. In 1848 the revolutionaries denounced it passionately as an obstacle to progress. Later they burned it in the public marketplace.

But the statutes had had their merits. Even biased as they were, they formed a basic constitutional document such as had never existed in any of the neighboring autocratic great empires. In only a few years they brought the Romanians back into the European modern world from which Phanariot rule had kept them for more than a century. By 1848 the statutes had indeed become an impediment to social and political progress, but in 1831 they were a necessary first step toward the modern age.

Enlightenment and Nationalism

Between East and West. During the eighteenth century contact between Europe and the Danubian principalities was severely limited, and the former ties that the ruling classes and scholars had had with the rest of the Continent were greatly reduced. Texts from the beginning of the century make no distinction between the principalities and Europe, which means that, despite Ottoman rule, the Balkans were not considered outside the pale of European civilization. Dimitrie Cantemir, for instance, said his country resembled in its basic features "the foremost peoples of Europe,"[35] and none of his contemporaries would have considered a trip to Poland, Hungary, or Austria a visit to another culture and civilization.

The Phanariot period changed the sense of community that the seventeenth-century Romanian scholars had with Europe. The new regime, representing a sovereign hostile to the Christian powers not only politically but also in all other areas of life, made direct contacts with the West difficult and viewed with suspicion any who maintained such contacts, unless they belonged to the small circle of dignitaries whose allegiance could be readily ascertained. The Porte viewed even contact between Phanariots and Europeans with distrust. When the hospodar Alexandru Ypsilanti's sons went to Vienna without permission in 1782, the prince immediately stepped down from his throne, knowing all too well that the sultan would no longer trust a ruler whose sons had fled to the West.

During the Phanariot period, the Romanian concept of Europe grew narrower. Europe became a separate cultural zone known only indirectly. Very few Romanians now traveled beyond their western borders until after the treaty of Kutchuk Kainardji in 1774. Europe was a far-off ideal, inspiring admiration for the light it cast and regret that it did not shine brightly enough in Moldavia and Wallachia. The archimandrite Grigore Romniceanu best summarized these sentiments in the preface to his *Triodul* (Triodion) in 1798: "The people of Europe have sharp minds, they are fine princes, orators, doctors, and lawmakers, who have domesticated, instructed, and conquered all the other peoples of the world with the power of their minds, their tongues, and their hands. . . . Science, trades, and good habits flourished and still flourish there." For all these merits, the archimandrite concluded, "It is right that this Europe should be called the jewel of the world."[36]

After 1774 Romanian contact with Europeans and with the philosophy of the Enlightenment began to increase and became harder for the government to control; there was an increase too in the number of those traveling to the West and having the opportunity to see with their own eyes what they had previously known only through books or by other indirect means. These travelers could then compare the two realities and meditate on the reasons for their differences. The admiration of many began to be colored with a feeling of inferiority, of regret that Romanian civilization was not at that level, as they felt it deserved to be. Europe, with which Cantemir and the chronicler Miron Costin had dealt on an equal footing, was now held up as an example of development that Romanians were advised to follow if they wanted to return to the cultural sphere to which they had once belonged. They even reproached the West for permitting the sultan to torture them "tyrannically in the middle of Europe." The desire to catch up with "the people of the other Europe," as the boyar Dinicu Golescu said in 1826, became obsessive. Only Europe was "enlightened," only Europe could be taken as a model. Like Eufrosin Poteca—"Couldn't we borrow something from them?"—most intellectuals were ready for a loan.[37]

That Romanian civilization in the Danubian principalities was far more Eastern in 1800 than it had been in 1700 or 1600 is not hard to prove. We need only glance at pictures of the great boyars or read the marriage contracts or wills of the period. In his sumptuous Oriental costume Dinicu Golescu looks almost like a Turkish pasha, whereas in 1574 one of his ancestors had been represented on his gravestone as a European knight. Fabric and jewelry were now imported not so often from Venice or Germany, as in the seventeenth century, but from Constantinople. Elements of Eastern costume were adopted in part for political motives, for no great boyar or Phanariot prince would dare appear before the padishah in the clothes of the infidels. For that matter the uncertainty of life, the frequent incursions of the Turks from their border fortresses, and the many wars against Christian nations all had a direct influence on the Romanian way of life. For example, the open courtyards and palaces of Constantin Brâncoveanu's time were abandoned, and the boyars now built themselves fortified residences (culă) or added defenses to their great halls. The new buildings were easy to defend but lacked the comfort of the older boyar houses at Hereşti, Mărgineni, or Filipeşti.

This did not mean, of course, that the boyars' life was without brilliance or wealth. Although fashions had certainly changed, the boyars' lifestyle under the Phanariots continued to be rich and ostentatious, and it was so described by more than one foreign traveler who passed through the principalities. At the beginning of the nineteenth century, when a large estate could be bought for about 15,000 talers, Iancu Golescu spent 20,000 talers for his wife's wedding gown. The boyars' passion for luxuries and the reckless way they went through fortunes worried both the church and the government. Sumptuary laws were often written—but almost never enforced. There were temporary im-

Fortified mansion (*culă*) (built second half of eighteenth century). Oltenia, Măldăresti.

port restrictions on silks and other fabrics from Aleppo, India, and Constantinople, and also, in 1797, on European-made carriages. This measure must have been quickly forgotten, because the great boyar Barbu Ştirbei returned from Karlsbad at the end of that same year with not one but two new carriages, both ordered in Vienna. And a few years earlier (1784) another boyar had ordered from Austria "one of those small fluffy dogs . . . it should be very small, so that there will be none other like it in all Europe."[38]

The wars between Russia, Austria, and Turkey, the presence of European officers in Bucharest and Iaşi, and after 1774 the opening toward Europe brought about, as in the example of Ştirbei's carriages, the gradual replacement of the Oriental way of life by the European. The boyar women were the first to abandon the Eastern style of dress, which they did as early as the Russo-Austrian occupation of 1787–92—a period renowned in the Moldavian capital of Iaşi for the balls Prince

Potemkin gave. The younger boyar men began to give up their exqui-
sitely embroidered caftans and to exchange their Turkish trousers and
headgear for narrow trousers and top hats after the next Russian occupation (1806–12). The great boyars and the older men kept the old
styles until around 1830, and some even after the issuing of the Organic
Statutes.

Many intellectuals called for an end to Oriental dress as a necessary
step in the process of modernization. By 1833 an advertisement for the
Bogosz Brothers' Latest Fashions Shop had almost no Oriental flavor.
The store imported European jewelry, dressmaking goods, fabrics,
porcelain, furniture, carpets, firearms, carriages, chocolate, "foreign
wines," perfumes, cologne, and Havana cigars for the citizens of Iaşi.

An examination of the documents of the period leaves the impression of a most picturesque and lively age, despite Turks, Phanariots,
wars, and military occupations. The "disease of love," so called by Eufrosin Poteca in 1829, appears to have occupied the time of most boyar
men and women. Divorces, elopements, and rapes seem to have formed
a part of day-to-day life in the city, as they are detailed and described
with seeming pleasure in the court registers. Hunting parties were organized with ostentatious display, each boyar priding himself on his
outfit, which included a variety of breeds of dogs. In 1818 the hospodar
Ioan Gheorghe Caragea astonished the capital by attending a balloon
ascension on the outskirts of Bucharest.

Conflict between these "new European customs" and "traditional values" is often mentioned during this period. I do not believe, however,
that the Oriental lifestyle of 1800 can be considered traditional. Three
or four generations earlier it had been as new as the European style
now was. Only the peasants carried on a traditional mode of life without
interruption. Its basic structure was neither Eastern nor Western. The
lifestyle of ruling class and city dwellers, however, swung like a pen-
dulum from age to age, because it was bound not so much by local
traditions as by the international situation and the cultural impact of
the dominating great power.

The Romanian Enlightenment. Was this society, set on the border between East and West, founded on the values generally held in the Age
of Enlightenment? By what route did the ideas of the Enlightenment
find their way into the principalities, and how deep did they penetrate?
Can their effects be considered a part of the European Enlightenment?

For political reasons the Phanariot period brought with it an active
Easternizing tendency. Because of the Phanariot period Cantemir, Cos-

tin, and Constantin Cantacuzino had no direct intellectual successors. There is a clear hiatus: the first half of the eighteenth century was culturally unoriginal and impoverished, and virtually all Romanian contact with Europe, except for a small privileged group on the fringes of the princely courts, was cut off.

Not until the second half of the eighteenth century were European ideas again current in Moldavia and Wallachia. Boyars began to study French, and the fashion spread of hiring family tutors from the West. After 1774 the number of private secretaries, doctors, piano teachers, gardeners, and cooks brought in from Austria, Germany, and France increased. Secretaries and tutors came primarily from France, and were paid far better than servants brought from Austria and other countries closer to home. At the beginning of the nineteenth century, for instance, the state treasurer Iordache Rosetti-Rosnovanu paid Fleury the tutor 4,570 lei a year, plus 300 for his valet; Iosif the cook meanwhile had to make do with 765 lei, while Miller the gardener received only 125.[39]

Clearly in their daily life the ruling classes were increasingly influenced by Western ways. Residences were built in the new neoclassical style, especially in Moldavia, where Polish influence was strong. Interior decoration altered, too, as Middle Eastern furnishings gradually gave way to those brought from Europe. Knowledge of French enabled the boyars to read the literature of the Enlightenment and facilitated its introduction into the principalities. Even without direct human contact, even without travel, the ruling class and the leading intellectuals inevitably became part of what was later called "L'Europe française."

The few library catalogs remaining to us reveal their owners' tastes, as do the letters hospodars and boyars wrote ordering books from Austria, Germany, and France. Most books were shipped through dealers in Braşov and Sibiu, but there were also some boyars—the Mavrocordats, the Rosettis, the Balşes—who had direct connections with the French capital, sometimes even with purveyors to the court. Thanks to these, their libraries were well stocked both with Greek and Latin classics and with the works of such seventeenth-century political thinkers as Hugo Grotius and Samuel Pufendorf. The writers of the time— Montesquieu, Voltaire, Rousseau—are also well represented in the libraries along with much historical and political literature about the French Revolution and the epic events of the Napoleonic wars. The *Encyclopédie* was available on demand at the Rîmnic episcopal office in 1778. At the beginning of the nineteenth century Western books were by far the most numerous both in private and in church libraries. For example, the Rosnovanu library at Stînca had in 1827 493 books in

French, 75 in Greek, and eight in German. The 1836 catalog of the Bucharest library of the metropolitan lists 2,275 titles in Latin, 1,497 in French, 1,278 in Italian, 300 in Greek, 49 in German, 18 in Turkish, 13 in English, and one in Russian.[40]

The fact that so many members of the intellectual elite had direct acquaintance with the literature of the Enlightenment in the original probably explains why so few attempts were made to translate it into Romanian. Translations from the literature of the Enlightenment were uncommon in Transylvania and even rarer in the Danubian principalities. Voltaire was first translated in 1772 (*Le Tocsin des rois* and *Traduction du poème de Jean Plokoff*) and in 1792 (*Histoire de Charles XII*), Rousseau and Montesquieu in 1794 (*Narcisse* and *Arsace et Ismène*, respectively). But none of their great works appeared before 1830, when Stanciu Căpățîneanu translated both *Le contrat social* and *Considérations sur les causes de la grandeur des romains et de leur décadence*. François Fénelon's *Télémaque*, however, had circulated in Romanian translation as early as 1772. Early nineteenth-century translators' literary tastes seem to have embraced both Enlightenment and pre-Romantic works. Between 1800 and 1830 works by Jean Pierre de Florian, Edward Young, Alexander Pope, Constantin François de Volney, Jacques-Henri Bernardin de Saint-Pierre, the abbé Prévost, and the earl of Chesterfield were translated.

Education contributed to the spread of the ideas of the Enlightenment, although it developed in contradictory ways and not always in the interests of the national culture. The princely academies (established between 1678 and 1688 in Wallachia and in 1707 in Moldavia) did represent oases of culture in the Orthodox East, but under the Phanariots they soon fell under the exclusive influence of Greek teachers. As a result the national schools (upper-level schools where Romanian was the language of instruction) were stifled until the beginning of the nineteenth century. In 1814 Gheorghe Asachi set up his engineering course, and Gheorghe Lazăr opened his school. Both taught in Romanian. By doing so they challenged the Hellenized princely academies. These princely academies, which were attended by Romanians, Greeks, Serbs, and Bulgarians, often brought ideas of the Enlightenment into Moldavia and Wallachia. Christian Wolff, Alexander Baumgarten, and the abbé Condillac were the philosophers with the greatest influence on the professors at the Bucharest academy, while at Lazăr's St. Sava School the philosophy courses were inspired by the works of Immanuel Kant.

It apparently fell to the church to run the schools, with the state levying a special tax on monasteries and priests to supply funding. The interest in and the preoccupation with the problem of education in the principalities demonstrate a mentality formed by the Enlightenment. Both hospodars and boyars repeatedly affirmed that only through education can people "live according to reason," "come to know works and persons," and become "well-disposed, since . . . they use only reason and have no other aim than the common good" (Alexandru Ypsilanti, *Charter* [1776]). Such arguments clearly stem from the Enlightenment, as did the effort made by the throne between 1741 and 1743 to require that all children learn to read and write. The boyars too were aware of the significance of education, proposing in 1746 that attendance at the princely academy be compulsory for their offspring "because they are worse educated than those beneath them."[41]

In spite of this Enlightenment mentality, education made slow and disjointed progress in Moldavia and Wallachia. The reforms of 1748, 1776, 1813, and 1818 really made education only slightly less restricted and old-fashioned. In 1776 the princely academy in Bucharest had only nine professors, teaching grammar, arithmetic, geometry, astronomy, history, physics, theology, Latin, French, and Italian; natural sciences were added later. The number of students was always very small, only about ten in each of the five grades throughout the eighteenth century. In 1834 only 1,129 Moldavians and 3,050 Wallachians attended public schools; a comparable number may have studied with family tutors or at private schools.[42]

The situation was not much better in Transylvania, although intellectuals there too shared the attitudes of the Enlightenment. At least the number of schools, professors, and students was much greater than in the Danubian principalities. There were three Romanian high schools, at Blaj (founded 1754), Braşov (1829), and Beiuş (1829), and three theological institutes, at Blaj (1754), Sibiu (1811), and Arad (1822). The census taken by the Austrian general Bucow in 1761 counted 2,719 Romanian teachers in the principality.[43]

Another manifestation of the spirit of the Enlightenment was the interest in publishing books. Between 1700 and 1800, 799 books were published by Romanians, 617 in Romanian and 182 in Greek, Latin, Old Church Slavonic, and other languages. The percentage of nonreligious books was much greater than that of religious ones, a good indicator of changes in attitude. Between 1717 and 1750, for instance, secular books represented only 15.6 percent of publishing in the Danubian principalities, but grew to 53.2 percent in the decade 1790–1800 and to 74.8 percent in 1820–30.[44] In the middle of the eighteenth century the lay printers, mostly merchants or printers by trade, first broke the church's monopoly on publishing. Publishing passed most rapidly into lay hands in Transylvania, where books were published in Romanian not only in Uniate Blaj but also in Vienna (from 1771) and Pest (from 1777).

In the Danubian principalities the atmosphere of the Enlightenment had a particularly strong effect on political and legal thinking. The reform movement was clearly influenced by European ideas, as was the feverish activity in creating the new legal codes issued in 1765–70, 1780, 1814, 1818, and 1820–26. The influence of Cesare Beccaria, Gaetano Filangeri, and the French and Austrian civil codes were readily noticeable. Outside law and politics, however, the culture of the Danubian principalities was less creative than it had been at the beginning of the eighteenth century. Historiography in particular lost ground. The principal works in the field, like chronicler Mihai Cantacuzino's *Istoria Ţării Româneşti* (History of Wallachia [1776]) and boyar Ienăchiţă Văcărescu's *Istoria prea puternicilor împăraţi otomani* (History of the all-powerful Ottoman emperors [1794]) were clearly inferior to the works of Costin, Cantemir, or Constantin Cantacuzino.

The decline of historiography in Moldavia and Wallachia was compensated for in some measure by its progress in Transylvania, where the level of Romanian culture was superior to that on the other side of the mountains throughout the Age of Enlightenment, in sharp contrast to its status in the seventeenth century. Now there was constant, and fertile, contact with the world of Austrian and Hungarian culture. The Romanian intellectuals in Transylvania felt they belonged to European culture. The prejudices of the Hungarian ruling class and of the court in Vienna may often have hampered their efforts—as in 1795, when the authorities banned the formation of the Great Romanian Philosophical Society of Transylvania, or when they frustrated several projects to establish Romanian journals between 1789 and 1820—but still there were many notable accomplishments, mainly in linguistics and history. Samuil Micu-Clain (nephew of the Uniate bishop Ioan Inochentie Micu-Clain) and historian Gheorghe Şincai brought out *Elementa linguae daco-romanae sive Valachicae* (Elements of the Daco-Roman or Wallachian language) in 1780. Micu-Clain also wrote *Brevis historica notitia originis et progressus nationis daco-romanae* (Short historical note on the origin and development of the Daco-Roman nation) in 1778 and developed the theme further in *Istoria, lucrurile şi întîmplările românilor* (The history, works, and fortunes of the Romanians), an extensive study published in part in 1806. In 1808 Şincai completed *Hronicul românilor și a mai multor neamuri* (Chronicle of the Romanians and of other peoples), probably the most erudite history written by a Romanian to that date. Finally, in 1812 Petru Maior wrote *Istoria pentru începuturile românilor în Dacia* (History of the beginnings of the Romanians in Dacia).

The effect of the Enlightenment on the Romanians of Transylvania was not limited to these leaders of the Transylvanian School. It could also be seen in the formation of literary societies, in the publication of school textbooks intended to bring the ideas of the Enlightenment to the general population, in the publication of popular science, and in the translation of rationalist texts aimed at the elimination of superstition and the triumph of reason. One such text was Șincai's adaptation of a work by the German physicist H. Helmuth under the title *Învățătura firească spre surparea superstiției norodului* (Elementary education designed to stamp out the people's superstition).

The Transylvanian intellectual elite without a doubt attained a higher level of culture than their counterparts in Wallachia or Moldavia, and they were more numerous as well. The newest and most radical political ideas, however—independence and unification—developed not in Transylvania but in the Danubian principalities. This seeming paradox demonstrates once again that the primary factor in the emergence of a national consciousness is less the general degree of culture in the population or the presence of Western cultural influences than the existence of strong local leaders willing and able to take independent political action.

The Rise of National Consciousness. As we have seen, seventeenth-century men of learning had defined a Romanian ethnic consciousness by asserting that all Romanians—Moldavians, Wallachians, and Transylvanians—sprang from a common origin, and that their language derived from Latin. The first half of the eighteenth century brought no visible development in this early stage of national consciousness. Most scholars, including Bishop Micu-Clain, the chronicler Ion Neculce, and bishops Clement and Inochentie of Râmnic, repeated the old claims without much change, basing their historical notes almost exclusively on the writings of Cantemir. Romanians were declared to be purely "Roman," and since none had yet contested this, it was treated as established fact, beyond dispute.

One of the first changes in this old interpretation resulted from a rise of interest in things Dacian in the second half of the eighteenth century. Writers still believed in the Roman origins of the Romanians, but now they rejected the claim of Eutropius, and later of Cantemir, that the Dacians had been wiped out after Trajan's conquest. They were as proud of their Dacian as of their Roman origins, and they took pains to trace their national roots through the Dacians back to the beginning of history.

Pro-Dacian sentiment arose almost exclusively among Moldavian and Wallachian scholars. It began with Mihai Cantacuzino's *Istoria Ţării Româneşti* (History of Wallachia), written in Romanian between 1774 and 1776 and published in Greek in Vienna in 1806. Cantacuzino's was the first book to speak of the symbiosis of the two peoples and of the amalgamating of their languages. Similar ideas were expressed by Ienăchiţă Văcărescu in his 1787 *Gramatica rumânească* (Romanian grammar), and Văcărescu was also the first author to draw a favorable portrait of Decebalus. After this the idea of the Romanization of the Dacians became a permanent feature of Romanian historiography. It was expounded in great detail in such works as Dionisie Fotino's *Istoria Daciei* (History of Dacia [1818]) and Naum Râmniceanu's *Despre origina românilor* (On the origin of the Romanians [1820]). Fotino concludes that "the Romans and Dacians, crossbreeding, created a distinct, mixed people"; Râmniceanu, that "after the Dacians learned the Roman language, not only did they get along well together, but they also intermarried, Romans marrying the Dacians' daughters and marrying their own daughters to the Dacians." The effect, Râmniceanu writes, was that "the Dacians became Romanized and the Romans Dacianized."[45]

This idea of Roman "crossbreeding" was not accepted in Transylvania except by the great scholar and poet Ioan Budai-Deleanu. All other Transylvanian men of learning held to Cantemir's line, asserting that the Romanians were of pure Roman blood. Their theory was put forward in many texts, from Micu-Clain's *Brevis Historica Notitia Originis et Progressus Nationis Daco-Romanae* (1778) to the erudite histories of Şincai and Maior mentioned above. When doubts began to be cast on this theory for political reasons, the Transylvanian scholars engaged in heated debates with the Saxons and Hungarians who contested and attacked it.[46] These arguments about history even found their way into political works like the *Supplex* of 1791, the ancient and continuing presence of the Romans in Transylvania—in other words their historical right—now becoming a useful political weapon and a principal justification for the Romanians' claims.

The idea of a single origin for all Romanians led naturally to the idea of political unity, and it is no accident that this was first expressed by the political leaders, who were historians as well. The earliest proposal for the unification of Moldavia and Wallachia came in 1772 from

Mihai Cantacuzino. His proposal was included in memoranda presented to Russia, Austria, and Prussia on the occasion of the peace negotiations at Focşani.[47] It was taken up again by Nicolae Mavrogheni (1788), Ion Cantacuzino (1790), and Ştefan Crişan-Körösi (1807). Crişan-Körösi was probably the first writer to suggest the name Dacia for the proposed new united Romanian state.[48]

By the beginning of the nineteenth century the idea of political unification had extended to include not only Moldavia and Wallachia but Transylvania as well: Râmniceanu's *Cronica Ţării Româneşti* (Chronicle of Wallachia [1802]) was probably the first to suggest the possibility of recreating "Dachia, whose borders, oh! if God would but grant us to return them to their original sovereignty, as we desire." Budai-Deleanu too flirted with the idea of the unification of the three principalities (1804), but he thought they should be united under Habsburg rule. The definition of a pan-Romanian nation, formulated by Moisie Nicoară of Banat, dates from this period as well. "The nation," he wrote in 1815, extends "from the Tisza to the Black Sea, from the Danube to the Dniester."[49]

There were no further proposals for uniting the Danubian principalities with Transylvania until 1838, when Alexandru G. Golescu reworked the theme of Greater Dacia.[50] But the unification of the Danubian principalities, or Lesser Dacia, became an oft-repeated element in Moldavian and Wallachian memoranda and reform proposals after the 1821 revolt. Unification was again officially requested in 1830, when the Organic Statutes were being drawn up, but Russia rejected the plan because it called for electing a foreign prince not from any of the neighboring (including Russian) dynasties. The statutes did recognize the need for eventual unification based on the common interests, customs, religion, language, and origins of the inhabitants of the two principalities. They also institutionalized the concept of a single, Moldavian-Wallachian citizenship, which had until then been accepted only by local custom.[51] With the explicit inclusion of the idea of unification in the first modern Romanian constitution, the national consciousness, until now expressed only by small and isolated political groups, became the official program of what was considered from then on a single modern nation.

The development of political nationalism, as seen first of all in the idea of a united Romanian state, coincided, in the second half of the eighteenth century, with the birth of patriotic feeling. Dimitrie Cantemir had spoken of "love of country" (1716), but the idea then referred only to Moldavia; the first work to write of love of the whole territory

Romanians inhabited was probably *Triodul* (Triodion [1831]) by Bishop Inochentie of Râmnic. There the regional sense is gone, and the book is addressed equally to Wallachia and to "all parts that form a Romanian homeland." The concept of homeland (*patria*) had gone beyond arbitrary political boundaries and was applied to all areas with a Romanian population.[52]

For the next generation patriotism, love of country, became a frequent concern. Ienăchiţă Văcărescu, for example, published his grammar in 1787 "for love of country." It was now a matter of pride to be Romanian, which was the sentiment that led Samuil Micu-Clain to write his histories. Scholars had the good of the people in mind and considered that they had a duty to their country. Even a legal text like Andronache Donici's *Manualul de legi* (Manual of laws) held that "to serve one's country . . . and to love one's compatriots is one of the absolute duties."[53] The anthropomorphized homeland took on the face of a mother rebuking or praising her sons, rejoicing or weeping over their conduct. Such injunctions as "Love thy country, love thy neighbors," "And who is nearer to you if you are Romanian than a Romanian?" (*Ithicon* [Manual of good manners; 1822]) appeared in many documents. Some works were actually devoted wholly to patriotism, for example, Iancu Nicola's *Manualul de patriotism* (Manual of patriotism [1829]) or the anonymous *Ispită sau cercare de patriotism* (Temptation or trial of patriotism) that circulated during the period.[54]

The Romanian intelligentsia knew that homeland and patriotism have two coordinates: the vertical—historical continuity and community, and the horizontal—the common interests of its members. The first writings to treat this subject usually conflated patriotism with boyar interests and the homeland with the boyar state. But after 1800 more authors believed, with Tudor Vladimirescu, that "the country means the people and not the robber class." Vladimirescu promised to be "the best son my country has," a "true son of my country," and to sacrifice even his life in its interest.

Patriotism implied a duty, personal sacrifice. As the boyar Ionică Tăutu wrote in 1829, "I have no other interests but those of my country, no other wish except her happiness, nor do I seek any other honor than that of the nation."[55] Just after Tudor Vladimirescu's revolt in 1821, intellectuals seem to have had a romantic faith in the possibility of establishing social harmony and equality of interests, of converting everyone into a "good patriot."

Independence and unification were primary components in the newly political national consciousness. In the eighteenth century an active cultural nationalism developed as well, no doubt under the influence of the Enlightenment and the idea, quoted from Prince Ypsilanti's 1776 *Charter,* that if they "live according to reason," people will become better citizens, will discover truth and beauty, and will grow in virtue.[56] This idea, with minor variations, took hold of most of the intellectual elite in all three principalities, although the Transylvanians perhaps showed somewhat greater concern for the concrete, practical measures for bringing the Enlightenment to everyone, commoners as well as privileged. All agreed that culture was a key factor in the rebirth of the nation, a great good that must be consciously developed in the people and distributed to them—almost injected. The authors of the programmatic *Vestiri filozoficeşti şi moraliceşti* (Moral and philosophical communications [1795]) believed this. So did Gheorghe Lazăr (writing in 1820) and Dinicu Golescu (1826). For Golescu the Enlightenment was to bring "brilliance, praise, and all kinds of improvements to a people that wants to be numbered among the great and enlightened peoples."[57] The Enlightenment was a means of emerging from the darkness and of coming to stand beside the advanced nations of Europe.

The Romanians realized that from the standpoint of culture they were behind other countries and peoples. This led them to examine their past, searching for reasons for their slow cultural development. Following Cantemir's trail to the discovery of their origins and an appreciation of Roman culture, they quickly concluded that the blame for their being left behind Europe must fall on Slavic influences.

Such an unfavorable view of Slavic culture, a culture that until the eighteenth century had been so important in the Danubian principalities, was relatively new. Udrişte Năsturel had been translating from Latin into Old Church Slavonic in 1647, and the metropolitan Antim Ivireanul had published a Slavonic grammar as late as 1697. For seventeenth-century men of learning the Slavic influence on Romanian culture had been an inseparable part of the Orthodox faith. Even though, as Ivireanul said, Slavonic was "foreign, not our own," he considered its use not reprehensible, but rather of special cultural merit.

The interest in Latin origins changed this viewpoint. As we have seen, Cantemir first put forth in *Descriptio Moldoviae* (1716) his theory that Old Church Slavonic had been a dead foreign language introduced in the fifteenth century by the metropolitan Teoctist, who was of Bulgarian origin, in order to make a break between the Romanians and the West and to keep them in the Orthodox world. The theory now spread from Cantemir to almost all Romanian scholars, who held first Slavonic and later the Cyrillic alphabet to be foreign forms and unnatural for expressing the Latin essence of Romanian culture. Similar accusations were brought against the influence of Greek culture, and even more readily, since it was generally connected to the Phanariots. Although the study of Greek language and culture flourished in the Danubian principalities during the eighteenth century and was very useful to both Romanians and Greeks, the scholars of the Romanian renaissance often condemned it in very harsh terms. For Grigore Ple-șoianu, for instance, author of *Cuvînt asupra limbii românești* (A word about the Romanian language [1821–22]), Greek professors were "adders and scorpions" trying to take everything valuable that the Romanians possessed without giving anything in return.

Among the various instruments for cultural growth, education received the most constant attention. In Transylvania there were ceaseless demands for the right to education, often repeated in Bishop Micu-Clain's memoranda and in the writings of the Transylvanian School. In the Danubian principalities writers frequently bemoaned the lack of instruction and pled for the establishment of schools. In 1756 the metropolitan Iacov I Putneanul of Moldavia made public a circular entitled *Învățătură pentru ca să-și dea fiește care om feciorii lui la carte* (Education so that all may send their children to school). In 1770, boyar memoranda proposed the founding of an "academy of sciences, arts, and languages," while around 1800 another Moldavian metropolitan, Iacob Stamate, an admirer of Montesquieu, drew up a remarkable plan for modernizing education. Many of these ideas were taken up again in the Organic Statutes, which stated explicitly the government's obligation to organize and improve public education.

Like all other national movements in eastern Europe, the Romanian one gave special attention to the problem of language: the national language was seen not only as an important tool of the cultural renaissance but also as representative of the rise of the nation. At the beginning of the eighteenth century scholars had reached three principal conclusions about the Romanian language: its Romance character, its use in all countries inhabited by Romanians, and, they insisted, the need to develop and cultivate it. Many Romanian intellectuals of the age thought that promoting the national language was a patriotic duty, a first step toward catching up with the Enlightenment. Without the national language, they believed, no other cultural instrument could successfully function. This explains the many "patriotic" grammars like Văcărescu's. The educated class in the Danubian principalities never got beyond making general statements, but in Transylvania they went further, actively undertaking to cleanse and purify the language, to

bring it closer to its presumed model and to the Latin soul of the Romanian. Ion Budai-Deleanu, in his writings between 1812 and 1820,
and Petru Maior, in the works he published between 1812 and 1819,
were probably the most enthusiastic adherents of removing foreign
words from the language, of replacing the Cyrillic alphabet with the
Roman, and of permitting lexical borrowings only from Italian or
French. After 1830 this became a Latinist exaggeration among many
Transylvanian linguists, who attempted to create a pure language artificially. As in other eastern European countries, linguistic purity was
abandoned in the end in favor of the spoken language—a position most
Wallachian and Moldavian thinkers had held all along.

The development of national, political, and cultural consciousness
led among other things to the idea of a renaissance. The theme of
awakening appears frequently in the first decades of the nineteenth century. Gheorghe Şincai romantically expressed it in the phrase "Awake
. . . my beloved people," Naum Râmniceanu in the words, "Do but come
in the name of God, let us restore our people to life and create our
country."[58]

What was new here was that this awakening was to be not only a
political but a general spiritual renaissance; the literate classes seem to
have wanted a basic transformation, the modernization of the fundamental structure of society, not just of its outer form. Only thus, warned
Grigore Pleşoianu just before the Organic Statutes were issued, could
Romanians be called "Europeans in fact, not just in name."[59]

CHAPTER FOUR

The Age of National Revival
(1831–1918)

Capitalism and Modernization

The Economy. One of the most important social phenomena of the period following the treaty of Adrianople in 1829 was the population explosion in the Danubian principalities, particularly on the Danube plain. The Turkish fortresses (called *rayas* in Romanian) at Turnu-Măgurele, Giurgiu, and Brăila had made the economic exploitation of the rich plains impossible. With their removal the southern portion of the principalities was opened to agriculture and the Danube to grain traffic. The population increased quickly.

In 1859 the two Danubian principalities elected the same prince and formed a single country, the United Principalities of Moldavia and Wallachia: a census taken shortly thereafter counted 3,864,848 inhabitants; in 1899 their number had reached 5,956,690, and by 1912 the last prewar census showed 7,234,920. Of this number 93.1 percent were Orthodox, 3 percent Jewish, 2.6 percent Catholic and Protestant, and 0.7 percent Moslem. The 1912 census also showed that 18.4 percent of the population lived in cities and 81.6 percent in country villages. According to official Hungarian figures, Transylvania had 5,548,363 inhabitants in 1910: 53.8 percent ethnic Romanian, 31.7 percent Hungarian, and 10.6 ethnic German.[1]

The economic structure of the Danubian principalities was not too different in 1831 from what it had been a century earlier, for the eighteenth century had been a time of economic stagnation. Until the 1840s livestock was still the main source of income and the primary export. Most of the country had long been in pasturage, hayfields, and forest, but the percentage of cultivated land now grew steadily, from 370,000 hectares in 1831 to 1,415,000 hectares in 1865 and 5,180,000 in 1912.

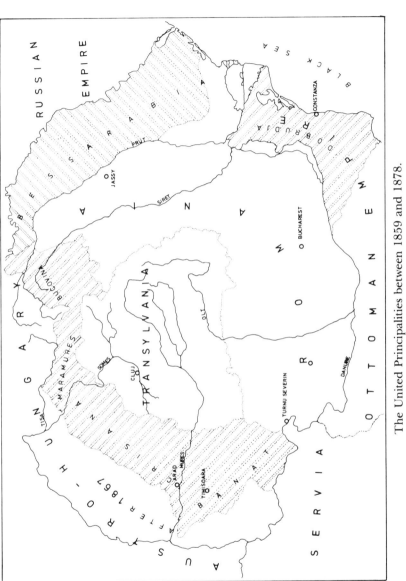

The United Principalities between 1859 and 1878.

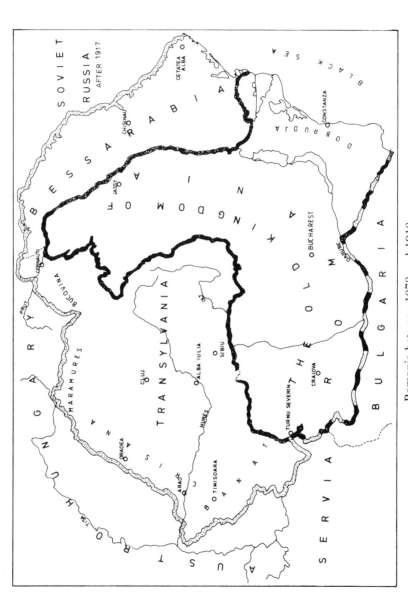

Romania between 1878 and 1918.

In 1860 19.9 percent of all land was under cultivation; this increased to 41.6 percent in 1905 and 46 percent in 1915.[2] By the middle of the nineteenth century agriculture had clearly become the mainstay of the Romanian economy.

As to what Romanians raised, an ever-increasing area, by 1915 84.2 percent of all cultivated land, was in grain production, with the remainder in textile- and oil-producing plants (1.6%), vegetables (1.6%), plants used in industry (0.5%), and other crops (12.1%). Agriculture was obviously not diversified but one-sidedly favored grain production. The value of agricultural produce in 1914 broke down this way: grain 79 percent, vegetables 7.4 percent, fodder 7.2 percent, plants for industrial use 2.2 percent, vineyards and orchards 4 percent.[3]

In the mid-nineteenth century wheat replaced corn as the primary grain under cultivation, and grain production rose sharply. By 1913 Romania was the fourth largest wheat exporter in the world, after Russia, Canada, and the United States. But Romanian agriculture was still rather primitive. Lacking both technical equipment and skilled workers, the great landowners—the principal grain producers—concentrated on extensive rather than intensive agriculture, possibly also because so much land was still uncultivated and the soil was so fertile.

As early as 1834 a group of landowners formed an agricultural society with the purpose of introducing Western methods and of importing farm machinery. The first machinery was imported in 1835, but the estates and especially the peasant farms were always short of equipment. In 1860 Moldavia had only ninety-eight steam-powered threshing machines in use, and at the beginning of the twentieth century only 40 percent of the great estates, which held half the cultivated land, were mechanized. Peasant plots were farmed entirely by human and animal power. From 1903 to 1916 agricultural mechanization progressed markedly. The number of steam-driven threshing machines rose from 4,585 to 20,000, and tractor-drawn plows increased from 55 to 300.

Lack of technical equipment and backward farming techniques—insufficient use of fertilizer, lack of selected seed, and a preference for spring over fall planting (along with the use of the old single-crop system on the peasant plots)—were all hindrances to the development of intensive agriculture. The fertile land, however, permitted fairly good yields of up to 1,818 kilograms of wheat and 1,104 kilograms of corn per hectare (1905). In 1913 the kingdom produced 2.7 million metric tons of wheat, and just before World War I Romania was exporting an average of one million metric tons of wheat annually.[4]

From Crafts to Large Industry. As we have seen, the Phanariot period saw very little industrial development. Time after time efforts to establish manufacturing failed, mostly for extra-economic reasons, while mining fell below even the levels reached in the seventeenth century. This was not for lack of raw materials. A report on the principalities' mineral wealth that the administration of the Russian occupation completed in 1833 and its accompanying map (1834) show silver, lead, and copper deposits, as well as salt and oil. A Russian traveler, A. Demidov, added gold, coal, lignite, and mercury to this list a few years later.

Real industrial production, however, did not exist at this stage. Steam power was first introduced in a Wallachian mill only in 1845, more than a century after the invention of the steam engine (1725). Austrian Transylvania was slightly more advanced. There the first steam engine was put to use in 1838 in the mining industry at Zlatna. Until the mid-nineteenth century the word *industry* in the Danubian principalities generally referred to the processing of agricultural and food products. The few "factories" were actually small shops producing paper, glassware, wool fabric, rugs, tobacco products, soap, macaroni, and supplies for oil lamps. Mills and the alcoholic beverage industry—largely made up of raki stills but also including some breweries—were important parts of this fledgling industry, too. To these can be added the production of saltpeter and gunpowder, of wooden paving blocks, and the construction industry. Until the mid-nineteenth century the only mining worthy of mention was still that of salt. Two-thirds of the product was exported.

Just before the two principalities united in 1859 the petroleum industry, until then rudimentary, began to develop. In 1857 it produced only 275 metric tons, but a year later Marin Mehedințeanu established the first Romanian refinery, at Ploiești in Wallachia. A second was built in Moldavia the same year. The oil they produced was used chiefly for lighting in their respective capital cities. Oil production increased steadily after unification to 12,000 metric tons in 1870, 16,000 in 1880, 53,000 in 1890, and 250,000 in 1900. The prewar record of 1,847,875 metric tons was set in 1913. At that time 57.2 percent of the Romanian oil yield was exported.

In 1894 eighty-four of the eighty-seven refineries ran on local capital and only three on foreign capital, but the Mines Law of 1895 opened the way to foreign capital, and by 1900 most of the refineries were controlled by German, Dutch, English, and American companies. The Steaua României refinery was established in 1896 by English, American, and German capital; American capital backed the Româno-Americana plant (1904); and the English and Dutch invested their money in the Astra plant (1908). By 1914 German capital controlled 30 percent of production and 8 percent of processing capacity. The Astra controlled 25 percent of production and 40 percent of processing.[5]

The pace at which new companies were founded picked up after Romania became independent of the Ottoman empire in 1877. In 1902 there were 625 enterprises under the heading "large industry" (at least twenty-five employees or a capital of 50,000 lei); in 1915 there were 1,851. In the grain processing and distilling industries companies began to merge and form corporations in the last decade of the nineteenth century. In the first years of the twentieth the paper, glass, and sugar industries followed suit (first merger in 1902), as did oil and lumber (1903 and 1910, respectively). The oil companies were most liable to merge, followed by mining and lumber. In 1914 there were 182 corporations registered in the kingdom of Romania, compared to only four in 1890.

The rapid development of "large industry" in the late nineteenth and early twentieth centuries was largely the effect of two laws (1887 and 1912) designed to encourage local industry. These provided for the loan of funds on favorable conditions to anyone opening a factory. Companies could get both tax exemptions and exemptions of duties on imported equipment and raw materials, as well as free rail transport for the finished product. Factories could be established with foreign labor so long as the work force was two-thirds Romanian within five years. Romanian industrialization, based on local raw materials, made steady if slow progress. In 1914 the value of production ranked as follows: food production, 49 percent; oil and petroleum-products, 29 percent; lumber and construction materials, 14 percent; and metallurgy and energy production, 8 percent.[6]

Commerce. The treaty of Adrianople had finally done away with the Ottoman monopoly on trade, making it possible for the Danubian principalities to trade freely with Europe, so that by midcentury the direction of Romanian commerce had substantially changed. Imports from south of the Danube fell steadily: in 1857, for example, only 13 percent of Moldavian imports came from the Ottoman empire, the rest from Austria and Germany (32%), England (29%), France (19%), and Russia (7%). Exports to various Ottoman provinces remained significant until after unification. In 1857 73 percent (by value) of Moldavian exports went to the south, and only 24 percent to central Europe (the remainder went to western Europe).

Until the middle of the nineteenth century animals and animal products were the two principalities' main export. In 1833 they represented half the value of all exports, while grain exports were only one-sixth. But as agriculture developed grain exports increased continually, so that between 1871 and 1875 cattle represented only 11 percent of the value of all exports, while wheat accounted for 36 percent, corn 28 percent, oats and barley 10 percent, and other exports for 15 percent. On the eve of independence the greater part of Romanian exports was going to Austria-Hungary, which remained Romania's principal trading partner until the First World War, when that role was taken over by Germany. In 1913 Romanian foreign commerce (imports and exports) ranked as follows by value: Germany, 23 percent; Austria-Hungary, 19 percent; Belgium, 16 percent; England, 8 percent; France, 8 percent; Russia, one percent; other, 25 percent. In the year that war broke out grain exports represented 68.6 percent of the Romanian total, followed by petroleum products (10.3% in 1912) and lumber (3.8% in 1912). In spite of the incomplete statistics we can draw two basic conclusions, first, that Romania had become a great grain exporter, and second, that Romanian foreign trade, whether measured by value or volume, was now predominantly with the Central Powers.[7]

This orientation was not always in the interests of local industry. On the one hand, the various governments encouraged private enterprise in the opening of factories, but on the other, they favored free trade and opposed protective duties. Very few products were protected by tariffs of even 20 percent of their value. In number such products even fell from 209 in 1886 to 81 in 1891. Duties were lowered again in 1893, and the trade conventions signed with Germany and Austria-Hungary in 1893 were not such as to protect the nascent local industry.[8] Until World War I trade policy favored the grain-exporting landowners more than the industrial middle class.

For a long time another obstacle to commerce, foreign commerce in particular, was the lack of a modern transportation system. The principalities' rivers were not navigable, so trade routes were almost exclusively on land, and the modernization of roads was not begun until 1840. As a result the cost of transporting grain the three hundred kilometers from northern Moldavia to Galați was greater in those years than that of transport from Galați to England.[9] Improvements were made very slowly. In 1864 only 970 kilometers of highway were paved with cobblestones, increasing to 1,910 kilometers (of a total of 5,420 km of public roads) in 1876, and 26,992 kilometers (of about 45,000 km) in 1910. Plans for the construction of a railroad were issued in

1842, but the first line, from Bucharest to Giurgiu, was not completed until 1869. There were trains in the Banat from 1856, and in Turkish Dobrudja the Constanța–Cernavoda line was opened in 1860. Once begun the railroad system grew quickly. There were 938 kilometers of railroads in 1873, 2,424 in 1890, and 3,600 in 1914.[10]

The lack of a national currency and banking institutions also slowed economic development. In 1831 the leu was just a coin used for purposes of calculation, and actual transactions were carried out in piasters, ducats, or rubles—currencies with fluctuating values that the principalities, with their limited autonomy, could not control. For this reason one of the first concerns of the nationalists was to issue a national currency. (It had diplomatic significance too, since issuing currency was considered a mark of sovereignty.) But the efforts of Princes Mihai Sturdza (r. 1834–49) and Barbu Știrbei (r. 1849–56) in this direction were blocked by the Ottoman suzerain.

Under Alexandru Ioan Cuza, the first prince of the United Principalities, and into the beginning of the reign of Carol I, who succeeded him in 1866, Vienna objected that the legend "Prince of the Romanians," which Bucharest proposed for the new currency, was irredentist. Constantinople was ready to permit the circulation of small Romanian coins if they bore a seal reflecting the country's dependence on the Turks. Finally in 1867 the government minted a bronze coin with no seal and no legend but with the national coat of arms. A few years later (1870), over Ottoman objections, a silver and a gold coin bearing a portrait of Carol and the restrained legend "Prince of Romania" were struck. A national currency had been created in spite of Austrian and Turkish opposition.

Romania met difficulties too in establishing banks and the credit system that would be the principal instrument of investment in agriculture and industry. The founding of a national bank was first proposed in the Organic Statutes, but it was not until 1856 that the National Bank of Moldavia opened. It stayed in business, in various forms, until 1877. After unification the number of banking institutions began to grow, starting with the Savings and Loan Bank (1864), the Rural Landowners Credit Union (1873), and the Urban Landowners Credit Union (1874), and culminating with the National Bank of Romania in 1880. This bank, modeled on the national bank of Belgium, was at once a circulation, discount, and note issuing institution. It also functioned as a limited company in which the state held one-third and the stockholders two-thirds of the shares. In 1901 the state withdrew from this partnership and the National Bank became a private institution. Under Liberal Party control it played a key role in national industrialization and in the economic consolidation of the middle class.

In Transylvania the first Romanian bank, the Albina of Sibiu, opened in 1872, followed by the Aurora of Năsăud in 1873; the number of Romanian banks in Transylvania grew from 41 in 1892 to 150 in 1905, when they totaled 4 percent of all banking institutions in the kingdom of Hungary.[11] Meanwhile in Romania credit institutions continued to grow in number and importance, from only five in the 1880s to 197 in 1913, by which time 40 percent of their capital was held by foreign banks—German, Austrian, French, Belgian, and English. Nine banks (four Romanian and five foreign) held 824.5 million lei of a total banking capital of 1,176 billion lei. Like industry, finance was becoming highly concentrated.

As in any underdeveloped country, industrialization depended largely on foreign capital. In 1914 the top branches of industry were dominated by foreign interests, which controlled 94 percent of the oil and sugar industries, 74 percent of metallurgy, and 69 percent of the lumber industry; local capital predominated in the cellulose and paper industry (54%), in food production (69%), transport (73%), and textiles (78%). After World War I an active protectionist policy was introduced, and foreign capital lost the importance it had had in the prewar economy.

Social Structure. Because of slow economic development and late and incomplete modernization, no real change took place in the social structure of the Danubian principalities until after unification—which is also the period for which we have the first fairly detailed statistics. In 1860, for instance, the official census of Wallachia registered 2,218,636 farmers (this included both peasants and boyars), and in the "free professions" 91,826 artisans, journeymen, and servants, of which 85,378 were in commerce and 5,081 in manufacturing. The Moldavian census used different categories, unfortunately just as imprecise: 1,076,951 farmers (again including boyars), 107,713 artisans, 21,954 people in commerce, and 46,088 clergy. This social structure did not alter significantly until the end of the century, when the statistics show some growth in the number of laborers and a regular expansion in the number of civil servants. In 1859 Moldavia had only 2,188 public servants, but by 1903 the two principalities together had 102,560. By contrast, industry employed only 169,198 people, and of these only 39,746 worked in "large industries." Transylvania, which was more developed, had 222,300 laborers in 1910.[12]

Nineteenth-century Romanian society was dominated politically by the aristocracy. Through the Organic Statutes, the boyars had in 1831 asserted even more power than before, at the expense of all other social classes and at the cost of seriously weakening the central power. In restructuring the boyar class the statutes followed the Russian model, but also discouraged hereditary rank, as the old Phanariot reforms had. Prince Constantin Mavrocordat had made the boyar title, until then inherited, a reward for service: this was a Phanariot blow against the seditious boyars, making them dependent on the prince, who alone could confer position. At the same time it gave access to boyar rank to those who lacked noble blood but found favor with the court. The Organic Statutes went further toward eliminating hereditary rank. Now the title of boyar was not tied to performance but was simply granted by princely decree. The great boyars still retained the highest titles, but the lower ones were freely distributed both as rewards for special merit and for money. This explains the increase in the number of boyars in Wallachia, for instance, from 766 in 1832 to 3,013 in 1858. And in 1851 the nineteen ranks of Moldavian boyars (in Wallachia there were only nine) included 2,375 individuals.

Except for first-rank boyars, the majority of whom came in fact from the old bloodlines, the new boyars did not enjoy any special privileges, and in time the title ceased to have any special meaning, inspiring more irony than respect. "Esquires are asses," said one "forty-eighter" (as the leaders of the 1848 revolution were called). Boyar titles were so devalued that their elimination in 1858 aroused almost no opposition. In practical terms, however, the hereditary boyars still had great influence, now arising not from rank but from the economic power they wielded as estate owners. The great boyars had become great landowners. To the peasants, the difference in terminology meant very little.

The changing status of the boyar class can be explained largely through their changing economic function. Under the Phanariots, the boyars' principal income derived not from their estates, which could not be made profitable under the Ottoman commercial monopoly, but from their positions as state officials, so they sought government positions and neglected farming. But when the treaty of Adrianople brought free trade, the cities and the domestic market expanded. General progress was stimulated by the Organic Statutes and by the gradual reintegration of the Danubian principalities into the European cultural and economic systems. The monetary value of the official post shrank, and that of the estate grew. Now the old system of dividing up the estate into plots given to the peasants for their use and a small reserve for the boyar no longer served the interests of the owners. They wanted to increase the reserve and turn their estates to large-scale production of marketable grain.

Property laws did not encourage the boyars to modernize the countryside. The boyars owned the land, but they were required by law to divide it, except for the reserve, among the peasants who had lived in the estate villages for generations, since the time of serfdom. The boyars' ownership was conditional, while the peasants were legally free but landless except for what they received by agreement from the boyar.

As long as the land had no economic value this system worked smoothly, and relations between boyars and peasants were relatively calm. The real oppressor of the villagers was not the owner but the tax collector. But this began to change as soon as the estate became a potential producer of large profits. The boyars demanded that the estates be converted to completely independent freehold ownership, while the peasants demanded the appropriation of the plots they were using. The Organic Statutes kept the old ownership system but made things even worse for the peasants. They still had the use of the land, but the plots were now too small, and the best land was kept in the boyars' reserve. In exchange for this land they had to supply an increased corvée, with a work quota. Without this labor the boyars could not have made their reserves profitable. This hybrid system, which worsened with every succeeding modification, was regarded with hostility by the peasants from the start. Whole villages emigrated across the Danube and the Prut in 1833–34.

The oppression of the peasants under the Organic Statutes and the increasingly severe corvée can be explained in purely economic terms. Owners increased the corvée both in number of days and in amount of labor to be provided, because they had no other way to make their estates profitable quickly. Lacking capital, equipment, and knowledge of economics, this was the only solution. In the short run the method did bring in the anticipated income, but in the long run it became a serious obstacle to the free development of agriculture. It also meant mortgaging social relations to an outdated feudal institution.

For more than three decades, until 1864, the corvée was the most pressing social problem in the Danubian principalities. The peasants asked that it be ended and demanded that they be given their plots outright; the owners considered it a rent paid by the peasants for the use of land not legally theirs. The owners even called repeatedly for an end to their obligation to distribute land to the peasants and for a new, capitalist-style relationship between peasant and owner, which they called "freedom of work, freedom of ownership." The peasants would sell their labor and the owners would buy it for a salary in order to make their estates productive. This would have been equivalent to dispossessing the peasants and transforming them into a farming proletariat.[13] But the great majority of the ruling class, and indeed of the intellectuals, rejected this radical change in owner-peasant relations, preferring a type of agrarian reform that would transfer a portion of the property to the peasants.

During the revolution of 1848 in Wallachia there were heated discussions on how to achieve such a reform. Owners and peasants met face to face in the property committee convened by the provisional government, but no decision was reached. In 1851 new agrarian legislation brought some relief to the peasants, increasing the size of the plots the estate owner had to allot, reducing some of the labor obligations, and simplifying the requirements for moving from one estate to another. But the basic system remained unchanged. The peasants were still tenants on the estate who had to pay in labor for the land they used. Heated discussion of agrarian reform continued in the years preceding unification and throughout Cuza's reign.

No consensus had been reached by May 1864, and on Prime Minister Mihai Kogălniceanu's advice the prince dissolved parliament and promulgated a relatively radical agrarian reform by decree. The peasants were granted outright ownership of the land they had been using, although the total to be distributed might not exceed two-thirds of the boyar's estate, excluding forests. Ownership could not be transferred for thirty years. And the corvée and all other forms of feudal servitude were discontinued, with the payment of compensation to the owner. By this reform 2,038,640 hectares were distributed to 511,896 peasants, so that peasants eventually owned 30 percent of the cultivated land. The other 70 percent remained in the hands of the great landowners.[14]

The principal defect of the Agrarian Law of 1864 was that the peasants were given too little land. In order to supply their needs they were obliged to contract with the landowners for supplementary land, and these were crushing contracts, enforced by the army with an iron hand until 1882. The peasant uprisings of 1888 brought a degree of relief in the agricultural system, but the distribution of property continued to be in the peasants' disfavor. In 1907, which would see an even bigger peasant uprising, the distribution of land was as follows: 40 percent of all cultivated land was in units of 10 hectares or less; 9 percent in units of 10–50 hectares; 2 percent in 50–100 hectare units; 10 percent in 100–500 hectare units; and 38 percent in units of more than 500 hectares. But 24 percent of the peasants had no land at all, and 34 percent of them owned between one-half and three hectares.[15]

The peasants' situation was made still worse by the leasehold (*arendășie*) system, under which the landowner received a fixed income with no effort. On the eve of the great peasant uprising of 1907, 62 percent of the great properties in Moldavia were leased out, 44 percent of them to ethnic Romanian tenant managers (*arendaș*), 43 percent to Jews, and 13 percent to foreign Christians. In Wallachia only forty of the 180 great landowners ran their own estates; the rest preferred to lease theirs out. In Moldavia especially there were actual consortia of tenant managers, the best-known being the Fischer Trust, which in 1905 held leases on no fewer than 159,399 hectares.[16]

Then came the 1907 uprising, which began in Moldavia but soon engulfed the whole country and went on for more than a month before being put down. Countless people died, and dozens of villages were destroyed. The revolt made clear just how fragile the social equilibrium was and how pressing the restructuring of agrarian relations had become. At the urging of the Liberal Party's left wing and with the king's assent, the liberal platform of 1913 included the distribution of the great landed estates to the peasants. Ferdinand, who succeeded Carol I as king of Romania, signed the reform bill in 1917. Because World War I was then being fought, the bill did not go into effect until 1921.

Property ownership in Transylvania did not differ substantially from that in the kingdom of Romania. Serfdom proper had been abolished by the Hungarian revolution of 1848, but here too the measure was not followed by land reform, and the peasants' land rights were recognized only in small steps from 1853 to 1896. As in Romania, the land allotted each peasant family was utterly insufficient to support it. In 1902, 6,963 great landowners (about one percent of all landowners in Transylvania) held 39 percent of the cultivated land, while 884,638 peasants (99 percent of the landowners) farmed 60 percent of it. When one breaks it down by nationality, it becomes apparent that the situation was least favorable to the Romanian peasants, 80 percent of whom owned on average only about a quarter of a hectare; the remainder held 36.8 percent of the 25–50 hectare farms, 20.3 percent of those with 50–500 hectares, and 5.7 percent of the great units with over 500 hectares; the rest belonged to ethnic Germans and Hungarians.[17] As in Romania, radical reforms—the Agrarian Laws of 1921—virtually eliminated the latifundiary estates.

Politics, Institutions, and the Power Structure. The Organic Statutes only partially resolved the question of who was to wield power in Romania. Certainly the statutes modernized the administration, but only to the extent of replacing the old princely despotism with an oligarchy that concentrated all power in the hands of a few great boyar families who had overthrown the Phanariots—and whose representatives had written the statutes. Although the statutes had the blessing of Russia and Turkey, the political system they mandated in no way resembled the despotism practiced in St. Petersburg and Constantinople. The national assemblies' legislative and financial powers were so constructed that the prince, whose power was theoretically sovereign, could not govern without the consent of the great boyars who controlled the assemblies. This gave rise to continual conflict between the central government and the boyars, conflict that dominated the whole period of the Organic Statutes in both Moldavia and Wallachia.

The structure of the extraordinary national assemblies convened to elect the princes is significant for demonstrating the assemblies' elitist nature. The Wallachian assembly of 1834, for example, was made up of 190 deputies, including four prelates, 50 first-rank boyars, 73 second-rank, 34 district deputies (also boyars), and 27 deputies of urban corporations, with not a single peasant delegate. It was actually less representative than the old medieval assemblies, which at least included the freeholders. The ordinary national assemblies that met annually for about two months were even more socially restricted. In Wallachia the assembly consisted of a metropolitan, three bishops, 20 great boyars, and 19 lesser boyars, and in Moldavia there were, besides metropolitan and bishops, 16 great and 16 lesser boyars. These deputies were "elected" by the boyars every five years, as provided by the statutes.

While recognizing that the Organic Statutes established an oligarchic political system, one should not lose sight of the real modernizing elements they introduced, such as the prince's oath to uphold the statutes and the law of the land, the creation of a civil list to distinguish the prince's assets from the national treasury, the central authority's partial responsibility to the assembly, and above all a separation of powers such as had never before existed. The document also brought some order to the administration by creating a "council of ministers," with six to eight members named by the prince and answerable to him. The names of the departments and their small number will give an idea of the relatively limited functions considered suitable for the state at this stage: the department of state (for general matters and foreign relations), finances, domestic affairs, the army, faith (later called religions), and justice. Later two new departments were added, public works and financial control. The state apparatus remained small in the number of ministries and of civil servants in general throughout the period of the Organic Statutes. In 1833 the Department of Finance had only 37 employees, the Department of Domestic Affairs 38, and the Department of Justice 25.

The oligarchy established by the statutes remained unchanged until 1848, when for four months (June through September) the victorious revolutionaries dismantled it in a frenzy. They burned both the statutes and the *Book of the Nobility* (*Arhondologie*) in the public square and adopted a constitution based on the most liberal principles possible. The combined Russian and Turkish invasion of the Danubian principalities in September 1848 swiftly ended the experiment in liberalization and brought back the discredited statutes and the boyar oligarchy. But this too would soon cease, for external events—the end of Russian influence as the Crimean War began in 1853, the intensified struggle for unification, and the growing strength of its supporters, many of them forty-eighters—led to the gradual disintegration of the system. The old administrative provisions remained, but the political structure was continually modified in favor of the liberals, most of whom were lesser boyars.

The treaty of Paris (1856) provided for the convocation of ad hoc assemblies, in which Romanians could express their wishes for the future organization of the country. Electoral legislation enfranchised 10,141 voters in Wallachia (810 great boyars, 6,308 small landowners—largely boyars, too—1,257 urban landlords, 116 free professionals, 1,498 merchants, and 152 artisans), and 2,954 voters in Moldavia (507 great and 261 small landowners, 1,153 urban landowners and free professionals, 896 merchants and artisans, and 137 peasant delegates). On the basis of this legislation, voters for the Wallachian assembly in Bucharest elected 34 great and 17 small landowners, 31 urban and 17 peasant deputies. The Moldavian assembly in Iaşi elected 28 deputies to represent the great landowners and 14 for the small, 20 for the cities and 15 for the peasants; selected clergymen were added in both principalities.[18] These figures demonstrate why for the first time in the history of the Romanian assemblies politics was not controlled by the great boyars. They had been defeated by the liberal boyars and the middle class with the help of the peasants. It explains as well why there was such broad-based discussion, not so much about unification and the international position of the principalities—on these subjects there was almost total consensus—but about domestic reform.

The Paris convention of 1858 replaced representation by class with a minimum income qualification for voters, which divided them into first two categories (1858), then four (1866), then three (1884), called "colleges." Although the minimum income had gradually been lowered, in 1913 no more than 1.9 percent of the population had a direct vote: 0.4 percent for the Senate, and 1.5 percent for the Chamber of Deputies. Add to this the 15.7 percent of the population with an indirect vote (just 1,139,301), and one sees that on the eve of World War I only 17.6 percent of the kingdom's population could vote in one way or another. Romanian parliamentary democracy clearly had its limitations. But it had unquestionably made progress since 1831, when only about eight hundred boyars had the franchise.

The minimum income requirement remained relatively high, the primary reason for the small electorate: for the First College the qualification was 1200 lei per year in 1911–15. All city residents who paid at least twenty lei a year in direct taxes voted in the Second College, as well as reserve officers and members of the free professions, and anyone who had completed four years of school voted in this college regardless of income. All who paid taxes, no matter how little, could vote in the Third College. Those who paid over three hundred lei per year in taxes voted directly if they could read and write, as did priests, teachers, and tenant managers who paid rents of more than a thousand lei; the remaining electors voted indirectly. Although the great majority of the electorate voted in the Third College, they sent only thirty-eight deputies to parliament. The First College elected forty deputies.[19]

Romanian parliamentary democracy was clearly imperfect, but it functioned surprisingly well, without violent swings or upheavals. The principle of constitutional monarchy, which Cuza generally upheld, was adopted in 1866 as part of a new constitution that remained in effect (with minor alterations) until 1923. The personality of Carol I and his long reign (prince 1866–81, then king until his death in 1914) also helped to stabilize the institutions and to ensure a continuity that could not have existed formerly, with the frequent turnover of rulers. But even so it was some time before the parliamentary system was fully in effect, and for a while after unification the new civil service was as undisciplined and unprofessional as the boyar class had been in its reign. A modern administration could not be installed overnight. Cuza appointed twenty different governments in the two principalities during the first three years of his reign in an attempt to modernize the administration. But after 1866 no more changes of government were made without consulting the electors. The prince appointed the government. The government held parliamentary elections and ran the country with the help of parliament until the appointment of a new government and the setting of new elections. A great many elections took place: between 1866 and 1871 they were held annually. By the 1870s the political parties had crystallized better, and the frequency of elections began to diminish. Liberals and conservatives regularly alternated in office. Parliamentary elections and their concomitant changes of government occurred in 1871, 1876, 1879, 1883, 1884, 1888, 1891, 1892, 1895, 1899, 1905, 1907, 1911, 1912, or roughly every three or four years. This rotation created a remarkably stable political situation with none of the violence and instability experienced by other Balkan nations during the nineteenth century.

The deputies took their work very seriously: parliament opened each year in November and usually remained in session until March, but would often go on well into the summer to allow further discussion and legislation. Judging by the debates published in *Monitorul Oficial* (Official monitor), there was much activity in parliament, and the lawmakers displayed a passion for legislation. In 1879, for instance, they voted on seventy-two bills in just a few months. Many new laws were needed, for many new situations arose in these years as a modern Romanian society was being built—although there was an undeniable tendency to excessive legislation and to the repeated amendment of laws already adopted. The Civil Code, introduced in 1865, was amended in 1900 and again in 1904, 1905, 1907, and 1909. The Trade Code passed in 1840 was modified in 1864 and then replaced in 1887 with a new code, which was modified in 1895, 1900, 1902, and 1906. Articles in the Penal Code adopted in 1865 were changed in 1874, 1882, 1893, 1895, 1900, 1910, and 1912.

The state's domestic functions remained rather limited throughout the nineteenth century. In 1862 Romania's government had only eight ministries: domestic affairs, foreign affairs, finance, public works, justice, religions and public education, war, and financial control (the future court of accounts). There was no economic post until 1864, when Cuza created the Department of Domestic Affairs, Agriculture, and Public Works. In 1869 domestic affairs was split off, followed by public works in 1893, and the name became Department of Agriculture, Industry, and Commerce. The changes clearly reflect the government's growing concern for economic problems.

Little weight was given to the post of minister of domestic affairs (the minister was in charge of the police force), and it was often combined with that of public works or of the economy. Romanian society was relatively open in the nineteenth century, so that the department had no great repressive function. The rural gendarmerie was not organized until the end of the century, while the Department of General Security did not appear until 1908, following an attempt on the life of the liberal leader Ion I. C. Brătianu.

The main defect of the regime set up in 1866 was probably that it was not very representative. The constitution, the laws, and the form of government were all modern, and liberal for their time, but in practice they served much too small a percentage of the population. Perhaps this reflected the generally backward social condition of the country. The real obstacle to participation in politics, to the right to vote, was not the income qualification, which was quite low for the Third College, but the literacy requirement. The conservatives—and other political leaders, too—believed that to enfranchise citizens who could not read or write would create a voting majority that might be easily swayed by any demagogue. Despite this not unreasonable objection, the Liberal Party included a demand for universal suffrage in its 1892 platform, and a year later the Social Democratic Party did the same.

The limitations of the system and the fact that democratization was proceeding far too slowly were brought into violent relief by peasant uprisings. On paper, in the constitution, in parliament, things were going well, but by 1877 the agrarian reform of 1864 still had not been completed. The uprisings in 1888 hastened the pace of agrarian reform somewhat, but at the turn of the twentieth century the greater part of the peasantry still lived in abject poverty. Their response to the promises of chronically delayed reforms was the great peasant uprising of 1907. According to official statistics more than a thousand peasants lost their lives when the revolt was put down with unnecessary force by the Liberal government (under Ion I. C. Brătianu in the Department of Domestic Affairs and General (later Marshal) Alexandru Averescu in the Department of War).

The amount of bloodshed in that uprising made it clear that some basic reforms were necessary. The conservatives, whose leaders were old and slow to change, upheld the old order and would accept only a few superficial improvements. But the Liberal Party followed the lead of its left wing, in particular that of Constantin Stere, down the road to institutional and political reform. In September 1913 Brătianu, who had headed the party since 1909, issued a program of reforms with the king's consent, including among other things universal suffrage and appropriation of land to the peasants. A month later this program became the official party platform. In February 1914 a liberal-controlled parliament began to discuss the reforms, and the conservatives, divided but resigned and feeling pressure from the palace, raised only pro forma objections and only at the beginning of the discussions. They were not fully aware that they were signing their own political death warrant. The chamber of deputies adopted the bill embodying the program of reforms on the third reading, with 143 votes in favor and one opposed. On 5 June, a few months before the start of World War I, parliament declared itself a constituent assembly and began to discuss constitutional reform along the lines of the newly passed bill. Work continued in spite of the war until December 1914, when it became clear that in view of international circumstances foreign affairs must take precedence over domestic ones. On Brătianu's suggestion parliament's work was suspended, to be resumed after the war.

Political Life

Domestic Policy. The era of the Organic Statutes in the Danubian principalities began with their violation. The czar and the sultan, not trusting the boyars to be faithful to them, insisted on appointing the first princes themselves instead of allowing the general assemblies to elect them. They placed Mihai Sturdza on the Moldavian throne and Alexandru Ghica on that of Wallachia. Sturdza ruled until 1849 and Ghica until 1842. Both princes came from old and influential boyar families that had produced other princes, and both were men of European culture, determined to modernize society in their principalities. Sturdza was in addition one of the authors of the Organic Statutes.

Throughout his reign Sturdza had the support of Czar Nicholas I and the Russian consulate in Iaşi, Moldavia's capital. This made it easy for him to control the plotting of the great boyars, whose hostility toward him was intense throughout his reign; the dissatisfaction of the lesser boyars, who, led by Leonte Radu, conspired against him in 1839; and even the increasingly dangerous unrest among the young intellectuals, who brought revolutionary ideas from the West, where the prince himself had sent them to study. Authoritarian and acquisitive yet subservient to the Russians, Sturdza was not highly esteemed by his contemporaries, but he was well educated and familiar with the ideas of the Enlightenment. He modernized the administration, built roads, and encouraged culture. Some of his measures were radical for his time, for example, partially nationalizing church lands (1844) and emancipating the Gypsy slaves of the state and monasteries.

There was more political turmoil in Wallachia. In 1834 Russia insisted that an "Additional Article" be appended to the newly adopted statutes stipulating that no change could be made in the constitution without the consent of the suzerain and of the protectorate governments. Sturdza easily obtained the Moldavian assembly's consent (1835), but the Wallachian assembly, already hostile to Ghica because of his fiscal policies, bitterly opposed this reduction in their autonomy. The debate raged until 1838, when the Russian consul broke the deputies' opposition by delivering a firman from the Porte in which Turkey ordered the assembly to accept the "Additional Article." In that same year Ghica had to deal with a revolt planned by Ion Câmpineanu, the representative of the liberal boyars. Câmpineanu held that the statutes and the appointment of princes by czar and sultan were illegal. He demanded a constitution and unification of the Danubian principalities as an independent state. His very liberal, virulently anti-Russian platform, especially what was called the "Constitution of the Romanians," called for a representative, constitutional government, equality for all before the law, and very broad civil liberties, to be achieved by a "war of independence." But the planned revolt, to be coordinated with the uprising in Poland, was discovered just as its organizer returned from a trip to England and France.[20]

Liberal boyars plotted rebellion again in 1840, led this time by Mitiţă Filipescu, with the very young Nicolae Bălcescu among his supporters. In contrast to Câmpineanu, who had wanted to change everything and settle every problem at once, Filipescu wanted gradual improvement by peaceful means. His program was less concerned with such foreign policy matters as independence but was more radical on social issues, proposing to end the corvée and to solve the agrarian problem by distributing land to the peasants. This movement too was discovered, and its participants given long prison sentences.[21]

All these upheavals—together with two uprisings by ethnic Bulgarians in Brăila (1841–42), who wanted to go to Bulgaria to start a rebellion against the Porte—gradually undermined Russia's and Turkey's faith in Ghica. Violating the Organic Statutes once more, they dismissed him in October 1842. The general assembly elected Gheorghe Bibescu to the throne by 131 votes to 49. He was a lesser boyar of large property and one of the few Romanians of the time to have studied law in Paris.

Bibescu proved a good ruler but indecisive, and he was by no means prepared for the revolutionary storm that swept him from his throne in June 1848.

The Revolution of 1848 fits naturally into the framework of revival and modernization that began after 1821. The forty-eighters even considered their movement a direct continuation of Tudor Vladimirescu and the Cărvunari (the Romanian Carbonari), whose writings they rescued from obscurity and whose ideas they adopted. The way was prepared for a revolution by the earlier rebellions, and it was organized and led by political and intellectual figures whose beliefs were already well known. After 1840 the need for a change was expressed in almost all political circles, but most strongly among the young intellectuals, mostly boyars, who had studied in France. In 1843 the Wallachian liberals Nicolae Bălcescu, Ion Ghica, and C. A. Rosetti organized a secret society called Frăţia (Brotherhood), with aims not very different from Câmpineanu's or Filipescu's. Social thought of the decade before the revolution took a decided turn toward democratization—the abolition of class privilege and the resolution of the peasant question. Nationalist ideas followed Câmpineanu's proposals for union and independence. In the 1840s there was also a passion for history, which was used in political arguments as a justification for nationalism. Intellectuals and scholars were obsessed with ancient Dacia and with the union of the three principalities Michael the Brave had formed in 1600. The sixteenth-century treaties between the Christian powers and the Ottoman empire (called by the Romanians *capitulaţiile,* "capitulations") were again brought up and used to justify the demand for an altered relationship with the Porte.

But before they could explode, the revolutionary movements of the 1840s needed the right international setting. The fall of Louis-Philippe and the proclaiming of the French Republic provided such a setting and were greeted with much enthusiasm by Romanians then in Paris (Vasile Alecsandri sent home a scrap of cloth from the throne). On 20 March 1848 Moldavian and Wallachian leaders agreed that the revolution should start in both principalities simultaneously. It turned out to be difficult to coordinate the two actions, however, as events in the two capitals followed different courses.

The Moldavian revolutionaries believed a peaceful victory would be possible, and over a thousand people gathered at the Hotel St. Petersburg in Iaşi on 8 April to adopt a petition to the prince. Most of the petition's thirty-five articles concerned civil liberties, improving the lot of peasants, an end to qualifications for voters, economic and administrative reform, and support for cultural development.[22] These were not extremely radical, and Prince Sturdza seemed ready to accept them. But he did reject two key demands, the dissolution of the general assembly and election of a new one "truly representative of the nation," and the establishment of a "citizen guard." Upon being urged to accept the petition with no changes, the prince took refuge in the militia barracks and ordered the revolt put down. Three hundred revolutionaries were arrested. Many others fled to Austrian Bucovina and from there to the West. The Iaşi revolution, launched too early and with too little preparation, lasted only a few days.

In Wallachia the revolutionaries were better organized, and they managed to seize power in June and hold it until Russia and Turkey invaded the principality in September. In May a broad-based revolutionary committee with representatives of the intellectuals and of all the liberal boyar factions, set 21 June as the date for launching the revolution, sending deputies to the various counties to put the plan in motion. On the chosen day revolution was proclaimed in the town of Islaz in Oltenia, where the revolutionaries had the support of the military units commanded by Gheorghe Magheru and Nicolae Pleşoianu; two days later, on 23 June, another uprising began in Bucharest. The Islaz proclamation, which the revolutionaries called "the constitution," was presented to Prince Bibescu, who unlike Sturdza accepted it and agreed to the formation of a provisional government. Two days later, however, he fled secretly to Braşov, leaving the country in the hands of the revolutionaries but depriving them of the legitimacy that his presence had lent the new regime. On 27 June 30,000 people, gathered in Filaret Field in Bucharest, swore to uphold the constitution and acclaimed a new government dominated by radicals, most notably the Brătianu and Golescu families.

The proposed constitution had a literary introduction, probably written by Ion Heliade Rădulescu, beginning "The Romanian people awake . . . and recognize their sovereign right," and twenty-two articles, most of which had been on political agendas for some time. Legislative and administrative independence from the Porte, political equality, a representative general assembly, responsible ministries and princes, freedom of the press, a national guard, an end to the peasants' corvée, an end to Gypsy slavery, dissolution of boyar ranks, and civil rights for the Jews were all included. The constitution further provided for the immediate convening of an extraordinary general assembly to draw up a final constitution based on these twenty-two points.[23]

Most of these principles—abolition of rank and of the income qualification for voters, emancipation of Gypsy slaves and rights for the Jews, and establishing a national guard—went into effect at once. The representative assembly (called the Constituent Assembly) and the solution to the peasant problem proved more difficult. In the debate over the Constituent Assembly, supporters of universal suffrage (led by Bălcescu) argued with supporters of selective franchise. At last, on 31 July, the provisional government issued instructions for the elections. The franchise was extended to all Romanians "of free condition," good behavior, twenty-one years of age, and permanently residing in the town in which the election was held. These would vote on a number of delegates in primary elections; the delegates in turn would meet at the county seats to elect the assembly deputies. There was no income qualification for voters, but since the voting took place at two levels, the great majority of the population had only an indirect voice. It was still a great step forward from the Organic Statutes, but unfortunately the invasion put an end to the revolution before the first elections for the Constituent Assembly could be held.

The franchise was extended without much opposition from the "reactionaries," but discussion of agrarian reform was prolonged, heated, and in the end fruitless. On 21 July the provisional government set up a property committee with equal numbers of landowners and peasants, and this committee finally voted to end the corvée and to appropriate land to the peasants in exchange for compensation payments. But the two groups could not agree on how much land should be given, and at this point the government, worried by the situation abroad and fearing the accusations of "communism" being leveled against it, suspended the committee's deliberations until a later date.

The danger of foreign intervention was certainly growing. By the end of July Ottoman troops under the command of Suleiman Pasha had crossed the Danube and were quartered in Giurgiu, while Czar Nicholas I had informed the governments of Europe that he was not pleased with the liberalizing course of events in Wallachia. The revolutionaries had with considerable diplomacy induced Suleiman to recognize their regime (now a regency instead of a provisional government), and they were to send their constitution to Constantinople for approval. But at the czar's insistence the sultan refused to receive the delegation that brought it (which included Bălcescu, Ştefan Golescu, and Dumitru Brătianu, among others). Then the two great powers resolved to reinstate the old order by force of arms: on 25 September Turkish troops marched into Bucharest under Fuad Pasha, quickly putting down the resistance of the Dealul Spirii fire brigade, and two days later Russia's

Cossacks entered the capital under General Aleksandr Nikolaevich Lü-ders. The neighboring empires ended Wallachia's experiment in liberalization forcibly and against the most basic laws of the land; it had sinned in being too close to their borders.

The union of Moldavia and Wallachia was unquestionably the paramount ideal of the postrevolutionary period both politically and intellectually. At first glance it appears that neither domestic nor international conditions favored this dream, which leaders in both countries had mentioned so often since 1772. The occupying armies reinstated the Organic Statutes, and in May 1849 the two great powers signed the convention of Balta Liman, which further limited the autonomy of Moldavia and Wallachia. According to the convention, Russia and Turkey would appoint princes, depriving the general assemblies of an old right actually granted by the Organic Statutes. The term of rule, which under the statutes had originally been life, was reduced to seven years. The general assemblies, which had proved so recalcitrant, were dissolved and replaced with new assemblies made up exclusively of boyars. Even under these conditions the two emperors were not sure the revolutionary spirit had been suppressed, and they continued to occupy Moldavia and Wallachia until 1851.

At Balta Liman Barbu Ştirbei was named prince of Wallachia and Grigore V Ghica prince of Moldavia. Ştirbei was a convinced anti-revolutionary and conservative, while Ghica, a unionist, favored the forty-eighters (as the leaders of the revolution continued to be called in later years). The forty-eighters, unlike their Wallachian counterparts, had been permitted to return immediately and even to occupy important administrative positions. In June 1853, with the outbreak of the Crimean War, the Danubian principalities were again occupied by Russia, and then by Austria in August 1854. The Austrian occupation continued throughout the war, ending only in January 1857.

The unionist movement and the struggle for a more liberal society had to be carried on at a time of international upheaval and under foreign occupation hostile both to political liberalization within the two principalities (Russia's position) and to pan-Romanian nationalist aspirations (Austria's and Turkey's). Nonetheless the National Party (Partida Naţională), as the revolutionaries and the unionists had begun to call themselves, gained strength steadily both in ideology and in organization.

The idea of unifying Moldavia and Wallachia had been current for many generations. It had been included in reform bills and boyar political agendas ever since 1772, and even the Organic Statutes, which also included a modern definition of *nation*, said it was necessary. After 1831, most organizations, no matter what their political orientation, supported unification. It was called for alike in 1838 by the followers of Ion Câmpineanu, the liberal great boyar, and in 1839 by the adherents of Leonte Radu, the conservative lesser boyar; by Mihai Sturdza, the conservative Russophile (1838); by the intellectuals who later led the revolution of 1848, for example, Ion Ghica (1838), as well as by writers and intellectuals who refused to participate in it, like Costache Negruzzi (1839). During the revolution both Moldavians and Wallachians avoided calling for unification in their official agendas so as not to increase Russia's and Turkey's fears, but allusions to unification were far too frequent and transparent for the great powers to ignore, particularly after Wallachia sent a memorandum to the Porte in June 1848 saying that it would be natural for Romanians "to be reunited in a single state." Exiled Moldavians too, in a pamphlet entitled *Principiile noastre pentru reformarea patriei* (Our principles for the reformation of our homeland [May 1848]), made unification the stated aim of the nationalist movement. And from 1848 until 1859, the issue was discussed in hundreds of books, memoranda, and reform bills, in petitions to the great powers, and in newspaper articles. The question of unification dominated the politics of the Danubian principalities.[24]

During the decade before unification, Romanian propaganda in other countries was intensive and successful. At first the Wallachians who were in exile until 1857 made their appeals mostly to European revolutionaries like Giuseppe Mazzini and Alexandre Auguste Ledru-Rollin, with whom they shared a belief in a general European revolution and membership in their revolutionary Central Committee in London. But after 1852, with Napoleon III in power and the revolutionary movement waning, the forty-eighters directed their propaganda to the European courts that seemed most sympathetic to the Romanian cause, sending countless memoranda to Paris and London and publishing numerous articles in the French, English, and Italian press. In this way the unionists managed to arouse a good deal of sympathy in most of the capitals of Europe.

Back at home, the unexpected outcome of the Crimean War had immediate repercussions in the Danubian principalities. The end of the Russian presence, which had dominated Romanian politics for almost twenty-five years, strengthened the position of the nationalist movement and enabled it to organize openly. The Treaty of Paris (March 1856) placed Moldavia and Wallachia under the protection of the seven great European powers. Ad hoc assemblies would be created to express the wishes of the people, and a European commission sent to Moldavia and Wallachia would act upon those wishes. The great powers would establish the principalities' new status, basing their actions on the Romanian proposals.

When their seven-year terms ended in July 1856, Barbu Ştirbei and Grigore V Ghica were replaced by regents (*caimacam*): Alexandru Ghica, a unionist who had been prince under the Organic Statutes, was again appointed in Wallachia, and in Moldavia the regent was Theodor Balş, a conservative who supported Turkish rule and whose designs on the Moldavian throne made him a separatist. In Wallachia the unionist Central Committee, formed in the summer of 1856, was free to carry on its activities, but in Moldavia Balş, aided by Austria and Turkey, reinstated the qualification for voters that his predecessor had abolished just months earlier, stifled the unionist press, and systematically persecuted members of the nationalist movement. Balş's death in March 1857 brought no relief, since his successor, Niculae Vogoride, was controlled by Turkey and continued Balş's antiunionist policies, hoping for the crown for himself. The manipulated and falsified elections for the ad hoc assemblies in Moldavia yielded a clear majority of separatists; Wallachia elected almost exclusively unionists. A compromise on what to do about the principalities was reached by England, which favored the Porte, and France, which supported the union. England agreed to persuade Turkey to invalidate the fraudulent election results, while France consented to only partial unification. The two principalities would be declared a single state, but most of their institutions would be kept separate.

New ad hoc assemblies with an overwhelming majority of unionist deputies met in October 1857 to make known the wishes of the Romanian people as agreed at the Paris convention. Both assemblies passed a four-point program demanding a guarantee of national autonomy, unification, a foreign prince from one of the ruling dynasties of Europe, and a representative and constitutional form of government. The Wallachians postponed discussion of domestic reforms so as not to endanger the nationalist and unionist agendas, but the Moldavian assembly, which included a group of very active peasant deputies, extended its session until January 1858 for prolonged discussions of all the social, institutional, and political changes that should be made in the newly united country.

The European commission presented its report in April 1858, and in May the representatives of the great powers met in Paris to make a final decision on the domestic and international status of Moldavia and

Wallachia. France, Russia, Prussia, and Sardinia were in favor of unification; Austria and Turkey were firmly opposed; and England's position was not clear-cut. Discussion at the European conference, dominated by Count Alexandre Walewski, the French foreign minister and a great supporter of the Romanians, went on until August and ended with the adoption of the Paris convention to serve as a constitution in place of the Organic Statutes.

Because of the stubborn opposition of Austria and Turkey, not one of the Romanian proposals was accepted in its entirety. The new state's autonomy and neutrality were recognized, and it was placed under the collective protection of the great powers, but the Porte's suzerainty was sustained. The two principalities were permitted to unite, but each would have its own prince—a Romanian, not a foreigner as requested— and its own government. And the new country was called not "Romania" but "the United Principalities of Moldavia and Wallachia." The armies shared a single chief of staff, and a commission was set up in the border city of Focşani to unify the laws of the two principalities. The boyar ranks were abolished in favor of equality before the law, but the electoral regulations were much more restrictive than those under which the ad hoc assemblies had been elected in 1857. The constitution the great powers agreed to was far less liberal and modern than the nationalist movement had wanted, and it left unresolved most Romanian problems, both domestic and international.

Preparations began at once to choose the electoral colleges that would select the princes. The situation was promising in Moldavia, where the provisional government was dominated by liberals, but more uncertain in Wallachia, where the Conservative Party now had greater influence. Fortunately for the nationalist movement, conservatives in both principalities were divided: in Moldavia there was a split between the followers of former prince Mihai Sturdza and those of his son Grigore, and in Wallachia between former princes Gheorghe Bibescu and Barbu Ştirbei. This made it easy for the Moldavian unionists to push through the candidacy of Colonel Alexandru Ioan Cuza, commander of the army and descendant of a family that had been active in the nationalist movement for many decades. He was unanimously elected prince on 17 January 1859.

Only a day later the foreign minister of Austria was predicting that the Wallachians too would elect Cuza prince, flouting the intent of the Paris convention. The idea of electing the Moldavian prince in Wallachia, too, had actually been under consideration in unionist circles for some months, and in mid-January 1859 it was officially proposed to

Alexandru Ioan Cuza, elected prince of the United Principalities
(1859–66).

Wallachia by a delegation taking the Moldavian election results to Constantinople. Ties between Freemasons in the two principalities fur-
thered the double-election solution, and the Wallachian conservatives,
unable to agree on a candidate of their own, finally agreed to support
the nationalist one. On 24 January, o.s., Cuza was elected prince of
Wallachia, again unanimously. The restrictive terms of the Paris convention had skillfully been evaded. Presented with a fait accompli, the
Porte gave in and recognized the union, but only for Cuza's reign. For
the Romanians, however, the double election was just the first step on

the road to a complete and permanent union. The two administrations were gradually consolidated, and in January 1862 the separate governments resigned so that the first single government of Romania could be formed in Bucharest.

Cuza's reign (1859–1866) was unquestionably a period of great social and political change. The prince ruled prudently until 1863, bringing the major political orientations to power in turn, both conservative and liberal (the first government of the United Principalities was conservative; Barbu Catargiu was prime minister). Until 1863 Cuza concerned himself largely with consolidating and centralizing the administration, finances, army, and justice system. He was able to ignore the coming explosion of social problems, among which the peasant question ranked foremost.

From October 1863 until January 1865 Mihai Kogălniceanu presided over a new, liberal administration. Kogălniceanu favored some radical domestic reforms. In 1863 the estates of the monasteries were nationalized, a measure that had been on political agendas since the 1820s. In spring 1864 the government opened discussion on agrarian law, proposing to allocate to the peasants, upon payment of compensation, the land they were using. When parliament opposed this measure, Cuza suspended the legislative session (May 1864) and assumed all power, governing the country by decree. He first issued the Agrarian Law, then followed it with a new constitution entitled "Additional Document of the Convention of 19 August 1858."

This authoritarian government was not without advantages. The prince introduced a large number of laws and reforms in a short time, including legislation on public education and a reorganization of the judicial system. In 1865 new penal and civil codes were adopted, as well as a code of criminal procedure. But the prince had lost the support of both the conservatives and the liberals by his coup d'état. Conservatives resented his agrarian reforms and liberals his dictatorial style. As a result he faced a united opposition determined to remove him from office. Isolated, and lacking both the old friends and advisers his actions had alienated and any real will to stay on, the prince often said he would step down at the end of his seven-year term. He did nothing to prevent his coming ouster, not even offering any resistance when a group of conspirators entered the palace during the night of 23 February 1866 to compel him to abdicate and leave the country. He died in Heidelberg in 1873.

As early as 1802 the nationalist movement had wanted to bring in a foreign prince. By choosing a foreign prince the Romanians hoped to put an end to internal power struggles and at the same time ensure more

Carol I von Hohenzollern, prince (1866–81) and king (1881–1914) of Romania.

dependable diplomatic support from abroad. After Cuza abdicated, the crown was offered first to Philip of Flanders, who refused it, and then, with the support of Napoleon III and Bismarck, to the young Carol (Charles) von Hohenzollern. After a long, adventure-filled journey in the company of Ion C. Brătianu, traveling in disguise so as not to be recognized on Austrian territory, Carol arrived in Romania on 10 May 1866, o.s., to begin his productive reign, which lasted almost half a century.

The first event in the reign of Carol I (1866–1914) was parliament's unanimous adoption of a new constitution in June 1866. The constitution remained in effect until 1923. Carol handled the various factions and parties with modesty and moderation, and as a result this was a period of remarkable political stability. The political elite, still small and dominated by a few leaders, adapted without apparent difficulty to the new rules of the game, giving up the old anarchic struggle for power. The influence of a foreign prince had brought about the stability the nationalist movement had wanted since 1802.

Another stabilizing factor was that the ruling class organized itself into two parties that alternated regularly in office. The division between liberals and conservatives had been discernible from the very beginning of the century and had become clearer still after 1821 when, for about a decade, the Carbonari-style reform bills proposed by the liberals clashed with those of the conservative great boyars. The forty-eighters had their origins in that period too, reviving the memory and writings of Ionică Tăutu, while their adversaries identified with the more traditionalist spirit of the Organic Statutes. In 1848 the liberal camp, itself made up largely of boyars, was accused of being communist, and its members were known as "the Reds" for many years. The distinction between conservative and liberal views further increased after 1848, especially over domestic reforms and the agrarian question. But there were not yet any clearly delimited organizations, although the word *party* was used after 1859 to refer to the two camps. These parties of the time were more like loose associations centered around certain dominant personalities, such as Ion C. Brătianu for the liberals, and Barbu Catargiu and later Lascăr Catargiu for the conservatives.

When a modern parliamentary system with periodic elections was instituted (1866), real parties quickly began to organize, although factions and dissidents long continued to exist. The first years of Carol's rule saw a tremendous turnover in governments. Between 1866 and 1871 the prince formed no fewer than thirteen administrations, some moderately liberal (like those of Ion Ghica or Mihai Kogălniceanu) and some moderately conservative (like that of Dimitrie Ghica). The radical liberals led by Ion C. Brătianu and C. A. Rosetti, who had contributed so much to the effort to secure a foreign prince, were left out, for Carol was afraid of their revolutionary reputation. The conservatives—who had their unofficial headquarters at an Iaşi club from 1871 (the Liberal Party was formally constituted in 1875)—had less trouble winning the prince's trust. With Lascăr Catargiu as prime minister they stayed in office from 1871 to 1876, the longest any Romanian parliamentary government had yet held power.

In 1876, when the international situation was in chaos and the Russo-Turkish War appeared unavoidable, the prince appointed Ion C. Brătianu prime minister, with Nicolae Ionescu and later Mihai Kogălniceanu as foreign minister. This administration lasted until 1888. During these twelve years independence was declared (1877) and granted (1878), the kingdom was proclaimed (1881), and a quantity of modernizing legislation was passed covering such subjects as ministerial responsibilities (1878), village structure (1878, 1882), the organization of education (1879, 1883) and of the army (1878, 1883), and the founding of a national bank (1880). In 1884 the liberal chamber of deputies passed a new electoral law that reduced the number of electoral colleges from four to three, considerably increasing the number of voters in each. During the second half of its long term, this Liberal government obtained parliament's approval for a large number of economic measures designed to develop industry and increase the country's economic independence, among them a new protective tariff and a bill to encourage local industry (both 1887).

Opposition was slow to organize. In 1880 the Conservative Party was formally constituted with party rules, county-level offices, and a newspaper, *Timpul* (Time), edited principally by Mihai Eminescu. The conservatives' road to power was smoothed by conflicts within the Liberal Party, a break between Ion C. Brătianu and his brother Dumitru giving them their greatest opportunity. This split allowed a united opposition to form in 1888, bringing down the Liberal government. After a series of short-term transitional Conservative governments (led by Theodor Rosetti, Lascăr Catargiu, and Ioan Emanoil Florescu), the king asked Catargiu to form a new government, which remained in office until 1895. It was an enlightened administration, and parliament, swayed by Petre P. Carp in particular, passed a number of laws governing agriculture, mines, and the organization of the clergy.

The two parties now rotated almost automatically, the liberals in office 1895–99 (Dimitrie A. Sturdza, prime minister), 1901–05 (again under Sturdza), and 1907–10 (under Sturdza and Ion I. C. Brătianu, son of Ion C. Brătianu); the conservatives were in power 1899–1901 (led by Gheorghe Grigore Cantacuzino), 1905–07 (Cantacuzino again), and 1910–14 (Carp and Titu Maiorescu). In January 1914 parliamentary elections brought back the liberals—Ion I. C. Brătianu had replaced Sturdza as party leader in 1909—and that government lasted until the end of World War I in 1918.

With the conservatives and liberals monopolizing politics (conservatives generally represented the interests of big landowners and liberals those of small property holders and the middle class) there was not much room for other political forces. The Conservative-Democratic Party, dissident conservatives led by Take Ionescu (formed in 1907), and the Nationalist-Democratic Party organized by Nicolae Iorga in

1910 had a negligible role in politics. There were various attempts to found a nationwide peasant party—by Constantin Dobrescu-Argeş (in 1882 and again in 1885), or by Vasile Kogălniceanu and Ion Mihalache 1906)—but all failed for lack of popular support. The socialists achieved a degree of organization but did not manage to have any real influence on the country's politics. The first two socialist deputies were elected to parliament as independents in 1888; a few years later, in 1893, sixty-two delegates from all over the country met in Bucharest to form the Social Democratic Party of the Workers of Romania, which was only partially a workers' party, and which collapsed in 1899 when its leaders went over to the liberals. Although they regularly nominated a slate of candidates, the social democrats never had more than a single deputy in parliament; the party was set up again in 1910 under the name Social-Democratic Party, but gained importance only after the end of the First World War.

Romanian nationalism in Transylvania in the nineteenth century achieved nothing like the political successes of Moldavia and Wallachia. It was caught between Magyar nationalist sentiment and the changeable but generally anti-Romanian policies of the court in Vienna. Until almost 1848 its program was limited to repeating demands from the *Supplex*, which Austria and Hungary had been rejecting since 1791: recognition of the Romanians as an equal nation and of the Orthodox faith as an official religion. Except for minor details, and some social and cultural issues, these two points had for a century made up the basic but unfulfilled Transylvanian Romanian program.

In contrast with Moldavia and Wallachia, where church and clergy played only a marginal role in politics, the nationalist movement in Transylvania was long led by the church. The division between Uniates and Orthodox and the rivalry between leaders as well as between flocks did not help the political struggle. The Uniate bishop Ioan Lemeni and the Orthodox bishop Andrei Şaguna generally adopted a prudent attitude of waiting. In 1842, however, the Uniate church did issue a violent protest against a decree that made Hungarian the official language of the principality, calling it dangerous to "our nationality."[25] After 1840 the initiative passed gradually from the clergy to the intellectual class, among whom the most important were probably Gheorghe Bariţiu, editor of the Braşov *Gazeta de Transilvania* (Transylvania gazette) and its literary supplement, *Foaie pentru minte, inimă şi literatură* (Paper for the mind, the heart, and literature), and Simion Bărnuţiu, professor at the Uniate lyceum in Blaj. Bariţiu was the author of several articles that aroused a great response, including "Românii şi panslavismul" (Ro-

manians and Pan-Slavism [1841]), "O tocmeală de rușine și o lege ned-
reaptă" (A shameful agreement and an unjust law [1842]), "Ce să fie
românii?" (What is to become of the Romanians? [1842]), and "Națio-
nalitate" (Nationality [1844]), Bărnuțiu was a philosopher and juridical
thinker whose ideas directly inspired the revolutionary activities of
1848.

In the Danubian principalities the 1848 revolution was, as we saw,
carefully planned; in Transylvania it was more spontaneous, although
the approaching storm had long been sensed in the villages. The revolution at Pest was sympathetically regarded at first, as its liberal program raised hopes for similar reforms in Transylvania. But on 21
September the ethnic Hungarians called for unification of the principality with Hungary. Three days later Bărnuțiu urged ethnic Romanians to defend their rights as a nation, and a few days after that a
deputation led by Alexandru Papiu-Ilarian petitioned the government
of Transylvania for, among other things, recognition of ethnic Romanians as an equal nation and the abolition of serfdom. By April the
mood of insubordination had reached such a level that the authorities
began to arrest the "demagogues" on charges of rebellion and of disturbing the public order.

The March Laws enacted by the diet of Hungary at Pozsony (Bra-
tislava today) proclaimed social equality and the abolition of serfdom,
but only if Transylvania united with Hungary, which recognized only
one nation and one language: Hungarian. The Romanian response was
a two-day meeting at Blaj (15–17 May) at which a sixteen-point "National Petition" to Vienna and to the Transylvanian diet at Cluj was
adopted before an impressive crowd: it called for equality of the Romanian nation with the others, recognition of the Orthodox church,
use of the Romanian language in administration and legislation, abolition of serfdom without compensation payments, and a Romanian
national guard. There were also demands for the economic, social, and
cultural rights that the Romanians, being a second-class nation, had
never had. As for union with Hungary, the meeting asked that the
decision be delayed until a new diet could be formed with Romanian
representation—an assembly that would reject the plan out of hand.
The meeting also resolved to create a national guard and a Romanian
national committee to be headquartered at Sibiu.[26]

But on 29 May the union of Transylvania and Hungary was proclaimed by the diet of Transylvania, in which the majority population
of ethnic Romanians had only two deputies, not elected but appointed
by the king. The positions of the two ethnic revolutionary movements

were now irreconcilable, and a conflict began that would hurt both equally and would last until the Hungarian revolution was put down by the Russian and Austrian armies.

In August the Hungarian government accused the whole Romanian National Committee of being rebels and traitors, but before they could be arrested the Austro-Hungarian conflict broke out. The Romanians took advantage of that by collaborating with the imperial authorities in Transylvania against the Hungarian revolutionaries. Supplied with Austrian advisers and arms, the National Committee set up twelve Romanian "legions," which disarmed the Magyar revolutionary guards and established a Romanian administration in the southern counties. This was the situation in December, when General József Bem marched into Transylvania with the Hungarian revolutionary army; by March his army had driven the Austrians out and occupied Sibiu. Most of the members of the Romanian National Committee went into exile in Wallachia. The first stage of the Romanian revolution had ended in absolute defeat.

After the fall of Sibiu and the dispersal of the National Committee, the center of revolutionary activity moved west to the Apuseni (Bihor) Mountains, where Romanians led by Avram Iancu defeated Magyar efforts to put down the rebellion or to persuade them to join the Hungarian revolution. They held out until July, Iancu sometimes immobilizing as many as 20,000 Hungarian soldiers, troops that Buda could have put to better use elsewhere (particularly against the Russians). To the joy of the Romanians, the Russians marched into the principality in June. Nicolae Bălcescu and other Wallachians now living in exile wanted the Romanians and the Hungarians to join forces against General I. F. Paskevich's troops: Bălcescu's plan included some limited rights for ethnic Romanians, but the Hungarian leader, Lajos Kossuth, did not agree to it until July. At the insistence of the Wallachian activists, meanwhile, Iancu agreed to remain neutral. His neutrality could be of no use now to the Hungarian army, which in August was forced to surrender at Șiria, near Arad.

Habsburg rule was restored, but the Romanians were not granted the rights they had expected. Not one of the demands made in dozens of memoranda to Vienna was met. Reforms were repealed, serfdom reinstated, and Avram Iancu, whose men had fought the Hungarian revolutionists for the emperor, was actually arrested, although he was then freed for fear of popular reaction. Transylvania suffered under Baron Alexander von Bach's centralized despotism and his active policy of cultural Germanization, which stifled any expression of nationalism for several years. The imperial government's only concession was to create a Uniate metropolitanate at Blaj in 1854, and the former bishop was consecrated as metropolitan; ten years later the Orthodox bishop Şaguna also became a metropolitan.

In October 1860 Vienna made Transylvania autonomous again, and a period of liberalization that lasted until 1867 began. The Romanian nationalist movement began to organize again, and a national congress held at Sibiu in January 1861 brought the program of the Blaj meeting up to date and submitted it once more to the emperor. A month later the government of Transylvania held a conference on minority nationalities (called "the nationalities") at Alba Iulia, with twenty-four Hungarian delegates and eight each for the Saxons and Romanians. The Hungarians opposed autonomy and demanded unification with Hungary, while the Saxons and Romanians opposed annexation and voted for greater autonomy.

For reasons not easy to understand, probably a combination of circumstances, Austria took a liberal position and convened a new provincial diet also at Sibiu, the delegates to be chosen under new and very liberal electoral laws. This election yielded forty-eight Romanian deputies, forty-four Hungarians, and thirty-two Saxons, with an additional eleven Romanians, twelve Hungarians, and ten Saxons appointed by the emperor. For the first time in the history of Transylvania ethnic Romanians would have direct influence over legislation and could change the country's institutions by legal means. And change them they did. On 26 October they passed a law granting equal rights to the Romanian nation, placing the Romanian population and their two churches, Uniate and Orthodox, on an equal footing with the original three privileged nations and the four accepted faiths.[27] Bishop Ioan Inochentie Micu-Clain's program was finally carried out—more than a century after it was formulated.

Meanwhile government policy in Vienna had changed direction once more, and fearful of minorities—Slavs and Romanians—Austria had already decided on a compromise with Hungary that led in 1867 to the creation of the Austro-Hungarian Dual Monarchy. In 1865 the emperor repealed the legislation of the Sibiu diet and convened another diet at Cluj to present views on the union of Transylvania with Hungary. To forestall unpleasant surprises, the crown appointed 191 of the deputies (137 Hungarians, 34 Romanians, and 20 Saxons). An additional 103 were elected by a small number of voters, whose very high income allowed them the franchise. Most of the Romanian deputies, calling themselves passivists, refused to participate in this assembly, and the

Hungarians voted that the Transylvanian diet be integrated into a new national parliament at Pest. The national parliament quickly voted to reinstate the 1848 constitution, repealed the principality's autonomy, and united it with Hungary in February 1867. The Romanian nationalist movement that had briefly thought itself victorious was back to Micu-Clain's starting point, the *Supplex,* and the meeting at Blaj.

After annexing Transylvania, Hungary instituted an active "Magyarization" policy, which was carried out with singularly poor judgment until the breakup of the dual monarchy in 1918. The Nationalities Act (1868) recognized a single nation, the Hungarians. The Electoral Act (1874) instituted qualifications for voters that were low in the mostly Magyar cities but high in the countryside, where the population was largely non-Magyar. Voting rights were increasingly restricted, to the point that a bill proposed in 1917 would have given the franchise only to speakers of Hungarian and graduates of state schools. An 1878 law against antigovernment agitation allowed the repression of all nationalist opposition. A series of laws on education, starting with the 1868 Nationalities Act and ending with the Apponyi Laws (1907), gradually replaced the minority languages with Hungarian in institutions of learning. And in 1896 the Banffy Law legislated the Magyarization of a number of towns and villages.

The Romanians had outspokenly opposed proclamation of the dual monarchy from the first. On 15 May 1868, on the twentieth anniversary of the revolution, in the very city where the 1848 meeting had been held, the leaders of Romanian Transylvania issued the *Blaj Pronouncement,* a detailed statement of the nationalist agenda. This was actually a repetition of the 1848 statement. Their primary demand was the repeal of the union with Hungary and a return to the principality's old autonomous status, with all minorities recognized. The authors were immediately arrested, but were pardoned by the emperor. In March 1869 they held a conference at Miercurea and founded the Romanian National Party under Ilie Măcelariu. A similar party had been set up a month earlier in the Banat, headed by Alexandru Mocioni, and in 1881 the two joined forces to form a single Romanian National Party.

At the Miercurea conference the party adopted "passivity" as a political tactic. They refused, for example, to participate in the parliamentary elections on the grounds that they did not recognize the 1867 union. They continued this tactic until 1905. The nationalist struggle continued outside parliament, and the great hope was that the Austrian government would support it.

The most significant event of this period was certainly the *Memoran-*

dum of 1892. As early as 1870 Ioan Rațiu had conceived the idea of a memorandum that would explain the Romanian viewpoint to the Habsburg court and the outside world. A first draft had come out in 1882, and the party had discussed different variants from 1887 to 1892, finally settling on one written by Iuliu Coroianu. Before issuing it they sent the text to Bucharest, where Carol I approved it and promised his support. No new demands or issues were presented in the *Memorandum*. It expressed opposition to the 1867 union of Transylvania with Hungary, criticized the restrictive electoral legislation and the anti-"nationality" education laws, and demanded rights for the "nationalities." These demands came at a time when Budapest was escalating its Magyarization program, and the authorities' response was harsh. Those who had collaborated in writing the *Memorandum* were condemned to prison terms varying from two months to five years. In 1895, at the request of King Carol and others, the emperor pardoned those who were still behind bars.[28]

Relations between the Budapest government and the Romanian National Party continued to deteriorate, as did those with the Serbian and Slovak communities with whom the Romanians had founded the Congress of Nationalities in 1895. Finally the party conference was banned in 1896, and the party newspaper, *Tribuna* (Tribune), suppressed in 1903. At the multiparty national conference of 1905, party leaders resolved to change their tactics, giving up passivity in favor of participation in parliament and politics. That year eight Romanian deputies were elected to the parliament in Budapest, along with one Serb and one Slovak (who together immediately founded a minority coalition); the number of Romanian deputies rose to ten in 1906 but fell to five in 1910. There were 393 Hungarian deputies. Clearly not even political activism would yield the results that the Romanians had waited for and laid claim to for so many generations.

By the last years of the dual monarchy, the leaders of the party had split into several factions, some openly favoring union with the kingdom of Romania (like Octavian Goga and Vasile Lucaciu), some preferring to wait and see what would happen (like Iuliu Maniu), and some (like Aurel Popovici) seeing a federalized Austria as the solution to the Romanian problem. Whatever the means, all agreed on the need for a complete change in the present state of affairs, and none wanted to accept the dual monarchy as it stood. The possibility of any understanding between people with an agenda like this and the Budapest government was nil.

In October 1913, in the tense atmosphere preceding the world war,

the new prime minister, Count István Tisza, proposed opening negotiations to improve Romanian-Hungarian relations, but it was too little
and too late. The Romanian National Party considered the government's concessions unacceptable and broke off talks in the summer of
1914.

Foreign Policy. The Danubian principalities emerged from the Russo-
Turkish War of 1828–29 with a dramatically altered international status. Under the Treaty of Adrianople and the Organic Statutes, they
were now subject to both the Ottoman suzerain and the Russian pro-
tector (this had been tried in the Balkans before, for the Republic of
the Ionian Islands, at the beginning of the century). In practice Ottoman suzerainty was nominal. The Russian consul in Bucharest and his
adjunct in Iaşi were the real imperial governors of the two principalities.
The "Additional Article" further extended the influence of St. Petersburg, granting it the right to approve any changes in the constitutions
and in domestic institutions. This hybrid regime persisted until the
Congress of Paris (1856) replaced the oppressive Russian protectorate
with the collective protection of the seven great powers. The Romanians
then finally achieved the international status they had been demanding
since 1772, and they kept it until independence in 1877.

The interference of Russia and Turkey as well made it difficult for
the princes to undertake any independent foreign policy, but the
various plans and projects drawn up by the revolutionaries in both
principalities, largely demands for independence, are of considerable
interest. Many of their activities were tied to the Polish revolutionary
movement led by Adam Czartoryski, whose representatives were on
good terms first with Ion Câmpineanu and later with the forty-eighters.
The arrogance of the Russian protectorate had driven both Poles and
Romanians to consider Russia, not Turkey, their primary foreign enemy, and a great deal of anti-Russian literature sprang up during this
period. Most of it was written in French to attract a European reader-
ship.[29] The Romanians appear to have believed it would be possible to
come to a peaceful understanding with the sultan, and to have considered Czar Nicholas I the main obstacle to domestic reform. Nor was
any love lost on Austria in Bucharest and Iaşi, as many forty-eighters
prematurely anticipated a swift collapse for the Habsburg Empire.[30]

The suppression of the revolution of 1848, followed by the Austrian
occupation of the Danubian principalities from 1853 to 1857, further
intensified anti-Russian and anti-Austrian feelings among the Roma-

nians and drove them to closer ties with the Hungarians, another victim of the two autocracies. Negotiations between the Hungarian exiles and Prince Cuza at this time reached a fairly high level when they formed an alliance against Vienna (1859). Although both parties wanted closer ties, attempts at cooperation came to an end in 1863 over the issue of Transylvania, with the prince telling the Hungarian general István Türr that he could not support the Magyar rebellion unless Hungary agreed to grant Transylvania's ethnic Romanians their rights.[31]

The Polish and Hungarian movements had adopted federalism as a platform, just as the Romanian nationalists had done at the time of the 1848 revolution. In July of that year, for instance, A. G. Golescu-Arapilă proposed a confederation of Slavs, Hungarians, Romanians, and Austrians, with its capital at Vienna but under German protection. In November, after the revolution had been put down, he extended his proposed federation to include "all the nations of the East." Other forty-eighters envisioned more limited federations. Ion Ghica wanted a loose Serbo-Croatian-Hungarian-Romanian federation (1850), with each national state retaining its own identity but sharing foreign policy, defense, and public works at the federal level. Bălcescu too proposed several confederations (1850), including a United States of the Danube comprising Romanians, Magyars, and Serbs. Other forty-eighters like Ion Heliade Rădulescu had ambitious dreams of a "Universal Republic of Europe," or at least of a framework that would reunite the Latin peoples, as in Vasile Maniu's 1869 plan.[32]

The only results of any of these projects were agreements made with Balkan states. Cuza maintained close ties with Serbia, and the two states even established diplomatic relations in 1863, before Romanian independence and over the head of the Porte, which was by then impotent as a suzerain. This connection continued under Carol, in 1868 becoming an alliance. During this period there were also discussions with Greece (1866, 1869) about joint actions against Turkey. These steps, and the active Romanian support of the Bulgarian revolutionaries, show how important both Cuza and Carol considered the Balkans for Romanian diplomacy.

From the very beginning of his reign, Carol made it clear that he wanted a change in relations with the Ottoman empire, in fact that he wanted to regain complete sovereignty. In announcing to the czar his accession to the throne he wrote that "the hour marked by providence for the emancipation of the Orient and of the Christian world" had come. A few years later, in June 1876, he again wrote that the only solution to the Eastern question would be the destruction of the Otto-man empire. In the cabinet he raised the issue of independence as early as 1873.[33]

In this the new ruler agreed with the political leaders, who had never given up the hope of renewed independence. But after Carol's accession in 1866 the members of this group had different ideas on the way to achieve their end. Most of the liberals, including Ion C. Brătianu, Mihai Kogălniceanu, and Vasile Boerescu, favored closer ties to Russia and open anti-Ottoman action. The idea of approaching St. Petersburg may seem odd at first glance, especially coming from forty-eighters who had been thrown out of office by the czar's Cossacks. But after Russia's defeat in the Crimean War, most forty-eighters ceased to regard it as the main threat to the nationalist cause, their hostility and fear turning instead toward Austria and even more toward Austria-Hungary. At the same time Russia seemed to be the only great power with any interest in the Balkan nationalist struggle and in the destruction of the Ottoman empire. For these reasons Carol and the liberals gradually established closer ties, and eventually an alliance, with Czar Alexander II.

The conservatives were long opposed to this foreign policy; for some time they even feared independence, holding that the regime of joint European protection established by the Treaty of Paris in 1856 was the best defense against Russian expansionism. The conservatives were largely Moldavians who had studied in German-speaking countries and retained connections there, and for them danger came from the east, not from Austria-Hungary. They were more interested in Bessarabia, whose southern portion had been returned to Moldavia in 1856, than in Transylvania.

In 1876, as the crisis in the east grew worse (with Serbia and Mon-tenegro at war with Turkey), and as it became clearer that Russia wanted to emerge from isolation and regain its own pre-1856 status, Carol dismissed the conservative administration that had governed since 1871 and brought in Ion C. Brătianu as prime minister, with Nicolae Ionescu and later Mihai Kogălniceanu as foreign ministers. At first the new government hoped to gain independence by diplomacy. Dumitru Brătianu was sent to the Constantinople Conference (Novem-ber 1876) to obtain "la consécration de l'état politique de la Roumaine, par une garantie spéciale de la neutralité perpétuelle du territoire rou-main" (The consecration of the political status of Romania, with a spe-cial guarantee of the neutrality of Romanian territory in perpetuity).[34] But Turkey responded by issuing a new constitution claiming that Ro-mania was an integral part of the Ottoman empire, although recognized as a special province. The government protested, saying Midhat Pasha's constitution was illegal under Romanian-Ottoman treaties—and then turned resolutely to military means of gaining independence. Prime Minister Ion C. Brătianu met with Czar Alexander II and his chancellor, Prince Aleksandr Mikhailovich Gorchakov, in Livadia in the Crimea as early as October 1876 to negotiate a Russian-Romanian military convention. The convention, signed in Bucharest on 16 April 1877, permitted Russian troops to cross Romanian territory en route to the Balkans. Among other things, St. Petersburg agreed to respect "the political rights of the Romanian state . . . and to maintain and defend Romania's territorial integrity."[35]

Russian troops began to cross the border on 24 April, heading quickly for the Danube, but did not reach the mouth of the Olt River until mid-May. Meanwhile Turkey began to bombard and attack the Romanian side of the Danube. The Romanian government declared war on the Ottoman empire, and on 21 May 1877 Mihai Kogălniceanu proclaimed in parliament, "We have severed our bonds to the High Porte. . . . We are independent, we are an independent nation." After his speech the chamber of deputies passed a motion, with seventy-nine in favor and two abstentions, declaring "the absolute independence of Romania."[36]

A general mobilization order had been issued in early April, and the army soon numbered about 100,000: 60,000 were active troops and the remainder militia, border guards, and other auxiliary units. Since the Russian command had rejected Carol's offer of military assistance made just after war broke out, the role of the Romanian divisions was limited to holding the Danube line until the arrival of the Russian forces: in April and May the country's small flotilla of four ships was in the lower Danube region helping to immobilize and sink Turkish monitors that could have obstructed access to Bulgaria, and in June the Russians crossed the river with almost no resistance from the Turks. But the Russian operation was soon brought up short at the heavily defended fortress at Plevna (Pleven), and after two unsuccessful assaults Grand Duke Nicholas applied in some alarm for Carol's support. The Russians also agreed that Carol should be supreme commander of the combined Russian and Romanian troops there, and by the end of August 40,000 Romanian soldiers had reached Plevna, where they played a decisive role in the battle. Even before Osman Pasha, the Turkish military commander, surrendered (10 December) Carol's troops were fighting in the battle of Rahova, and in January they fought at Smîrdan and Vidin.

For all that, the Romanian representative was not received at the Russian-Turkish armistice negotiations that produced the treaty of San Stefano (3 March 1878), and although Ion C. Brătianu and Mihai Kogălniceanu were allowed to present the Romanian view at the Congress of Berlin, they had no voice on the treaty, which had already been drawn up and was signed on 13 July. This accord made official the independence that Romania had proclaimed more than a year earlier. But although the Russo-Romanian convention of 16 April 1877 expressly guaranteed the kingdom's territorial integrity, Romania lost southern Bessarabia, while gaining northern Dobrudja.

Romanian reaction to the treaty of Berlin was bitter and resentful, and the loss of Bessarabia was seen as a violation of the nation's sovereignty. As a result Russia again became, both to the government and in public opinion, public enemy number one, who would use and then betray a wartime ally. With France in a weakened condition after 1871 and with the lack of interest in Balkan matters shown in Paris and London, the only countries that could balance Russian influence and stop Russian expansion were Germany and Austria-Hungary. Although relations with Vienna were strained, not only over Transylvania but over navigation rights on the Danube and various commercial interests as well, Ion C. Brătianu's Liberal government gradually improved them. In 1883 Romania formed an alliance with Austria-Hungary, which Germany and Italy joined later. The treaty was renewed in 1902 and 1913, but its terms were kept secret, known only to the king and the prime minister. The terms were never revealed to parliament for fear that that body would reject them.

Given Romania's position under the treaty of Berlin, joining with the Triple Alliance had the favorable effect of getting the kingdom out of diplomatic isolation and consolidating its position in southeast Europe, while the opening of the central European market to Romanian products brought some economic advantages. But it stifled the struggle for national unification and made it harder for the country to support the Romanians in Transylvania. In the long run the alliance with the Central Powers was perceived as going against the national interests as well as against the sentiments of most Romanians. It was not honored when war broke out in 1914, or in 1916 when Romania joined in the hostilities.

In the decades following independence Romania showed little interest in Balkan diplomacy. Relations with Greece were generally poor, particularly in regard to the Aromanian population of Greece. Bucharest was trying to develop this group's awareness of their Romanian heritage, while Athens sought to Hellenize them. Relations with the Porte were almost nonexistent, and those with Bulgaria, whose designs over northern Dobrudja were viewed with suspicion, were cold. Only with Belgrade did Romania have friendly relations, based on Bucharest's general attitude of open opposition to the anti-Serbian policies of Austria-Hungary.

The political and military rebirth of France toward the end of the nineteenth century coincided with a real explosion of pro-French sentiment among Romanian intellectuals comparable to that of the unionist period. This made it possible to begin a gradual diplomatic reorientation that ended with Romania's switching allegiance from the Triple Alliance (Germany, Austria-Hungary and Italy) to the Triple Entente (France, England, and Russia). The press and parliamentary debates showed more anti-Austro-Hungarian sentiment every year, particularly after Italy began to show signs of wanting to leave the Alliance.

In 1908–09 parliament discussed ending the alliance with the Central Powers and returning to the traditional policy of closer ties with France. During the crisis caused by Austria-Hungary's annexation of Bosnia, Ion I. C. Brătianu spoke emphatically on Romanian opposition to Austria-Hungary's anti-Serbian Balkan policy. After a brief visit to Bucharest, Crown Prince Wilhelm reported in Berlin (1909) that "in case of war, Romania will at best refuse to carry out her obligations as an ally, if she does not actually decide to join the other side." In December 1913 old King Carol himself told the German ambassador in Bucharest that because of the Austro-Hungarian policy on nationalities "the Romanian people will not side with Austria in war. . . . It is not enough for us to have treaties, they must have popular backing."[37]

The Balkan wars briefly turned public attention from the deepening conflict between Romanians and Hungarians in Transylvania. Titu Maiorescu's Conservative government brought Romania into the second Balkan War and then mediated the peace at Bucharest (1913) by which Romania annexed southern Dobrudja (which had been given to Bulgaria by the Congress of Berlin in 1878). This unwise step poisoned relations with Bulgaria for years to come and created a fatal weakness in the southern front when Romania entered the war in 1916.

World War I and the Formation of Greater Romania. The idea of Transylvania's union with the other two principalities came into vogue at the beginning of the nineteenth century with the rise of national consciousness. It was first expressed by Naum Rămniceanu (1802), a Wallachian of Transylvanian origin, and Ioan Budai-Deleanu (1804), a Transylvanian. Rămniceanu proposed that the Danubian principalities annex Transylvania, and Budai-Deleanu that Transylvania annex the principalities.[38] Both proposals were clearly premature, and they were not repeated until in 1838 Alexandru C. Golescu-Albu and Ion Câmpineanu made the union of the three principalities the cornerstone of their agenda.[39] In 1848 the Wallachian revolutionaries Golescu-Albu, Ion Ghica, Bălcescu, and Ioan Maiorescu, reflecting ideas current among European revolutionaries, claimed that the Habsburg monarchy was on the point of collapse and that this would enable the union of Transylvania with the Danubian principalities. This kind of idea, unrealistic for the time, circulated among the Transylvanian revolutionaries too, who proclaimed at the Blaj meeting in May 1848, "We want to be united with our country."[40]

The failure of the revolution in all three principalities did not end the unionist projects. In 1852 Dumitru Brătianu was already coining the term "Greater Romania."[41] And although Ion Ghica, Dimitrie Bolintineanu, and Gheorghe Barițiu feared that the triumph of reaction and despotism had reduced the prospects for unification, other political and intellectual figures—Ion C. Brătianu, Mihai Eminescu, Vasile Maniu, Alexandru D. Xenopol—continued for a while to believe, in B. P. Hașdeu's words (1870), in the "possible division of Austria."[42] In 1871 the young Xenopol, the future great historian, gave an impassioned irredentist speech at the grave of Stephen the Great—then in Austrian Bucovina—in which he called union inevitable.[43]

With Transylvania part of an allied empire it was difficult to support irredentism openly there, but the Transylvanian nationalist movement secretly received support and encouragement from Bucharest, especially from the Liberal governments. The focus of the struggle shifted from the political to the cultural field, directed largely by the Cultural League established in Bucharest in 1891, to which many Transylvanian intellectuals belonged. The league's political character became clear in 1914 when it changed its name to League for the Political Unity of All Romanians.

Nationalist ideas thus received loud and public expression, increasingly so after 1900, but at the outbreak of World War I in 1914, Romanian political leaders were far from agreeing on the direction the country should take. The liberals, with the exception of the pro-German Constantin Stere, believed that Romania's place was with the Entente, a view shared by Take Ionescu's Conservative Democratic Party and by most intellectuals. But the conservatives were divided into three factions: Petre P. Carp wanted the 1883 alliance with Austria-

Hungary honored, Titu Maiorescu and Alexandru Marghiloman urged friendly neutrality toward the Central Powers, and the pro-Entente group led by Nicolae Filipescu advocated immediate entry into the war against the Central Powers. As for the socialists, they pronounced themselves true to the international socialist position, and opposed Romanian participation in a war that they held to be imperialist. Following antiwar demonstrations in the streets, the Social Democratic Party Congress of August 1914, showing little sensitivity to the question of national unification, declared that it was firmly against participation in the war and in favor of permanent neutrality. It remained opposed even in 1916 when Romania entered the war.

The king appealed to the government's leaders to honor the 1883 treaty, but a crown council meeting in Sinaia (3 August 1914) decided on neutrality: one by one the participants explained their reasoning and voted that the treaty with the Central Powers did not apply, since it bound the signatories to go to war only if one of them were under attack. Only Carp, with his historical view of the war as yet another confrontation between Germanism and pan-Slavism, favored joining at once with the Central Powers. He claimed that they represented a far lesser danger to the Romanian nation than did Slavic expansion.

Romanian neutrality (1914–16) was actually no neutrality at all, for as early as autumn 1914 Ion I. C. Brătianu's government began to negotiate terms for entering the war with the Entente. King Carol died in October 1914, and the pro-Entente position of the new king, Ferdinand, gave a further impetus to the talks. Meanwhile, Russia recognized Romania's right to Transylvania as of 1 October 1914, in exchange for Brătianu's promise that the kingdom would remain neutral and enter the war only at the right moment. In February 1915 Romania and Italy signed a mutual defense accord, and in May Romania and Russia began talks in St. Petersburg about Brătianu's conditions for entering the war. The prime minister claimed Transylvania, the Banat, and Bucovina, according to its 1775 borders. Russia's foreign minister, S. D. Sazonov, made no objection about Transylvania but offered only part of the Banat, excluding Timişoara, and only southern Bucovina. A series of defeats forced the imperial government to moderate its position somewhat, and in July Sazonov accepted the Romanian demands on condition that the kingdom enter the war by 5 September, but Brătianu considered that date too early, particularly in view of recent German victories along the eastern front. Negotiations were broken off, reopening only in January 1916 under strong pressure from England and France.

Ferdinand I, king of Romania (1914–27).

After much discussion, two conventions were concluded, one political and the other military. Both were signed at Bucharest on 17 August 1916 by Ion I. C. Brătianu and representatives of the English, French, Italian, and Russian governments. According to the political treaty, Romania would acquire Transylvania, the Banat, and Bucovina. The military agreement stated that Romania should immediately declare war on Austria-Hungary with the support of the Triple Entente, including a general Russian offensive onto the Hungarian plain, an offensive against Bulgaria by the allied troops of the Salonika front, defense of Dobrudja by Russian troops, and the regular provision of arms and munitions to Romania.

These two treaties were brought before the crown council at Cotroceni on 27 August, where King Ferdinand informed the ministers, party chiefs, former prime ministers, and other assembled dignitaries that the decision to enter the war had already been made and that military operations were already underway. The army crossed the Carpathians that night; it easily took Braşov and part of the Szekler region, then dug in outside Sibiu. The northern offensive, however, was brought to a halt by the unexpected fall of the southern front. Bulgarian troops attacked in force beginning on 1 September. General Alexandru Averescu attempted a counteroffensive at Flămînda, but after some initial success he was beaten back. By the end of October German and Bulgarian troops had taken Turtucaia, Silistra, Constanţa, and Cernavodă. These defeats resulted largely from the failure of Romania's allies to honor the terms of the military convention, which specified that General Maurice Sarrail's offensive from Salonika should coincide with the Romanian attack on Transylvania, immobilizing Bulgaria and protecting Romania's back. Not even the promised Russian defense of Dobrudja was carried out, and Romania was put in quite a different position from the one foreseen when the conventions were signed and war declared.

The disaster on the Danube changed Romania's military situation fundamentally. The offensive in Transylvania had to be halted and forces concentrated on the southern front. The Romanians held their own against the Bulgarian and Austro-Hungarian troops, but when German reinforcements arrived (commanded in the north by General Erich von Falkenhayn and in the south by Marshal August von Mackensen) the tide soon turned. General Eremia Grigorescu managed to defend the Moldavian passes, but Averescu could not hold the Wallachian border, and Bran and Predeal fell before the end of October. But the German armies failed to break through the Carpathians, and by the end of November the northern front was relatively stable.

Ion I. C. Brătianu's fears had proven sadly justified, and all the caution with which he had negotiated Romania's entrance into the war had been useless. Not one of the terms of the military convention had been respected by his allies. Sarrail's failure to mobilize had permitted the opening of a new southern front, forcing the very small Romanian army to fight on two fronts instead of concentrating on its Transylvanian offensive; with no general Russian offensive against Hungary, the Central Powers had had all their forces free for use against Romania; Russian military assistance in Dobrudja had been nonexistent; and the promised arms and ammunition never reached their destination. Romania's fate in the war was sealed.

In November the Romanian military suffered one defeat after another. Falkenhayn penetrated the line of defense on the River Jiu in the middle of the month and went on to take Craiova. At the same time combined German and Bulgarian forces crossed the Danube at Zimnicea, directly threatening the nation's capital. The indecisive battle on the rivers Neajlov and Argeş (1–3 December) could not save the city, and on 6 December Mackensen marched into Bucharest not long after king, government, and officials had been evacuated to Iaşi. By the end of January 1917 the front was in southern Moldavia, leaving three-quarters of the country in enemy hands.

Although Moldavia was surrounded by the Central Powers on three sides, the Romanians were able to defend themselves as long as Russian troops protected their northern flank and as long as they had their direct lifeline to the west through Russian territory. In summer 1917, for example, Romanian troops won victories at Mărăşti and Mărăşeşti, putting an end to Mackensen's hopes of conquering Moldavia. But with the fall of the Kerensky government and the founding of the Bolshevik regime, continued resistance became impossible. The imperial Russian army collapsed so quickly that on 3 December 1917 General D. G. Shcherbachev, commander of Russian troops in Moldavia, began to negotiate an armistice with Germany. Romania elected to be a party, and the treaty was concluded on 9 December. The principal danger was not now from the Germans but from Communist Russians. Cristian Rakovski, a Bulgarian-Romanian Bolshevik, led a campaign that threatened the existence of the Romanian state. Russian troops in Iaşi broke down into anarchy and had to be disarmed, while in Galaţi, Paşcani, and other towns, fighting between Romanians and Bolsheviks went on until January 1918, when the last of these allies-turned-enemies were expelled from Moldavia. At the end of January, claiming that Romanian troops were invading Bessarabia, the Soviet government officially broke off diplomatic relations with Romania.

The Romanian government now had very little choice: with the consent of their allies they began new talks at Focşani in early February, determined to negotiate a real peace this time. At the same time Ion I. C. Brătianu was replaced as prime minister by General Averescu, who still hesitated to accept the harsh conditions imposed by the Central Powers in their ultimatum of 1 March. But with the 3 March signing of the Treaty of Brest-Litovsk, which permitted Germany to occupy the Ukraine so that Moldavia was completely surrounded, the government was finally forced to accept the terms. On 7 May 1918 the Treaty of Bucharest was signed. Romania lost Dobrudja and a strip of mountains including the peaks of the Carpathians and 170 villages. Economically the country became a fiefdom of Germany, which assumed control of its industry, commerce, and finances. Romania's participation in World War I had turned into a major disaster. The only good that came of it, one which no one had foreseen in 1914 or 1916, was the return of Bessarabia.

In spite of the Russification it had undergone since its annexation to Russia in 1812, Bessarabia had retained its largely Romanian character. In 1817 86.7 percent of the population had been Moldavian, and the Russian census of 1897 counted a mixed population—47.6 percent of the people were still Romanian, 19.6 percent were Ukrainian and Ruthenian, 8.2 percent Russian, 11.8 percent Jewish, and 13.8 percent other.[44] As in all the non-Russian provinces of the former empire, during the revolution there had been calls in Bessarabia first for autonomy and later for independence. The Romanians of the province had formed a National Moldavian Party (April 1917), proclaimed Bessarabia autonomous, and elected a national council as the highest governing body (October 1917). At the beginning of December the council had declared that the Moldavian Democratic Republic was within the Russian federation for the time being; in January 1918 the republic declared its independence; and in March the council voted to unite Bessarabia with Romania.

The harsh treaty of Bucharest had not yet gone into effect—nor even been ratified by parliament—when, in August 1918, Marshal Ferdinand Foch's counteroffensive broke through on the Somme. In September Sarrail finally began the offensive from Salonika that was to have covered the Romanian army in 1916. He succeeded in breaking through the Bulgarian lines. This change in the military situation brought down Alexandru Marghiloman's pro-German government, and a new "government of generals" led by Constantin Coandă immediately mobilized all forces and sent troops into Transylvania (16 November), where Romanians and Hungarians had been vying for control ever since the collapse of the dual monarchy in October.

On 18 October Alexandru Vaida-Voievod had read a declaration of Transylvania's independence from Hungary in the name of the Romanian National Council before parliament at Budapest. Iuliu Maniu, who was in charge of foreign and military affairs for the council, assembled 70,000 Transylvanian troops in Vienna under General A. Boieriu and Colonel Alexandru Vlad. It was not difficult to seize control of Transylvania, for the Hungarian administration fell apart unexpectedly quickly. Its role and functions were taken over by local branches of the Romanian National Council and the Romanian national guard. When the last attempts at negotiations between Romania and Hungary fell through (13–15 November), the council, with Ştefan Cicio-Pop as president, called an assembly at Alba Iulia, and on 1 December 1918, with a crowd of more than 100,000 present, the 1,228 deputies voted to unite Transylvania with Romania. They also elected a directing council under Iuliu Maniu to govern the province until it could be integrated into the kingdom of Romania. The Romanian National Council in Bucovina had voted for union with Romania a few days earlier (28 November). The new borders were eventually recognized in the treaties of Saint-Germain (September 1919), Neuilly (November 1919), and Trianon (June 1920), signed with Austria, Bulgaria, and Hungary, respectively.

National Culture

We have seen that during the eighteenth century, as Ottoman political, economic, and value systems were forced upon it, Romanian society had difficulty keeping open its channels of communication with Europe. Although the adoption of Turkish ways was incomplete and temporary, it still meant a distinct break with the ideas and tastes favored during the reigns of Constantin Brâncoveanu and Dimitrie Cantemir a century and more earlier. The nineteenth century, in contrast, was seen as a time of regeneration, of a return to origins, to the "true" values.

Civilization. "This is the age of machines," proclaimed the anonymous Wallachian author of *Haracterul epohi noastre* (The character of our era [1830]). "The strength of humankind is certainly increased by these means to astonishing proportions, and we gratefully note that today, with a modest amount of work, we have better housing, better clothing, and better food."[45] The documents of this period, including advertisements, are eloquent of the changing habits and tastes under the Organic Statutes. In less than a generation, Turkish pants were replaced by "German clothes," the Turkish divan by the French couch, and the hookah by cigars.

The architecture of boyar and middle-class houses was immediately affected by the new styles and the new taste for comfort. The boyars no longer built fortified houses (*culă*) as in the eighteenth century, preferring sumptuous open palaces reminiscent of the time of Brâncoveanu—but now with a neo-classical flavor. The new style, brought to Moldavia through Polish and Russian channels, quickly spread not only in the cities but also among the boyar estates. Early examples were

Ghica-Tei Palace, Bucharest (built 1822).

Prince Grigore IV Ghica's 1822 palace at Tei on the outskirts of Bucharest and the 1835 palace built in Bucharest for Barbu Ştirbei, the future prince. Architecture flourished throughout the century, evolving from neo-classicism through romantic or classical eclecticism (Bucharest National Theater, 1852; University of Bucharest, 1869). Later the Paris of the Second Empire inspired imposing structures (Bucharest National Bank, 1885; Romanian Atheneum, 1888; the Central Library of the University, 1893; Central Post Office, 1900; Central Savings Bank, 1900; and the Cantacuzino Palace, 1900; and in Craiova and Constanţa the Palace of Justice, 1890, and the casino, 1910, respectively). Romanian architects were unusually active in the nineteenth century not only because of the country's improved economy and rel-

The Atheneum, Bucharest (built 1888).

ative wealth but also because the country had produced several important ones, including Alexandru Orăscu and Ion Mincu, who were
trained as much in the West as at the Bucharest School of Architecture.
At the turn of the century Romanian architecture was trying to define
a traditional style based on the Brâncoveanu model and on peasant
buildings. The Buffet (1892) and the Minovici villa (1905), both in
Bucharest, were among the first examples of this tentative indigenous
style.

Only a small proportion of the population benefited from the new
trends in housing. Statistics from 1859–60, 1906, and 1913 show that
most people lived in dwellings that were far from modern. In the Wallachian province of Oltenia, for instance, in 1859 only 3.5 percent of
the houses were of brick or stone, and almost all of these were in cities.
Eighty-three percent of all houses in the province were built of wood,
but in the capital city of Craiova 90 percent were of stone. The same
census shows a density of three persons per room. The 1860 census
for all Wallachia counted 1,213,950 houses: 55,320 of brick, 830,219
of wood, and 328,411 of adobe. Only 76 houses had three stories and
5,444 two stories; the remaining 1,208,430 had only one.[46]

Cantacuzino Palace, Bucharest (built 1900).

Analysis of these figures over time shows that living conditions gradually improved, most significantly at the beginning of the twentieth century. Between 1906 and 1913, for example, the number of *bordeie* (primitive mud houses) fell from 3.8 percent to 2 percent of the total, and the number of rooms per house increased. In 1906 only 14.6 percent of houses had three rooms and 4.5 percent more than three, in 1913 42.3 percent had three rooms and 19.1 percent had more. In Bucharest one in ten houses had more than six rooms. In 1913 16.6 percent of all houses in the kingdom were built of brick, 32.8 percent of wood, and 48 percent of wattle and daub, or adobe. Only 19.6 percent had running water; 97.7 percent were privately owned. The 1913 census takers concluded that 39 percent of the urban population and 25 percent of those in the country lived in "unsatisfactory" conditions.[47]

Although in general urban modernization was slow, the principal cities changed quickly between 1831 and 1918. The size of houses is reflected in the water rates initiated by the city of Bucharest in 1857: from two "gold pieces" a year for one- to five-room houses up to thirty "gold pieces" for thirty- to forty-room dwellings. (There were only a few dozen of these, boyar houses with outbuildings.) Electric lighting came to Bucharest in 1882 and to Brăila and Galați in 1892. By 1913 the number of power stations had risen from six to thirty-four. During the same period the number of generators in Transylvania grew from fourteen to sixty. Bucharest built a trolley system in 1893 and began city bus service in 1904; telephone service began in 1884 with three hundred subscribers. In 1896 the first moving picture was shown in the city, and in 1912 the first Romanian film, *Independenţa României* (Romania's independence), was issued. In 1889 Barbu Bellu brought the first automobile into the country (a four-horsepower Peugeot), and by 1904 there were sixty-four cars in Bucharest. The city felt obliged to draw up "regulations for the policing of traffic" and set a speed limit of fifteen kilometers per hour.

The first auto races in Romania were also held in 1904. The winner, Prince Valentin Bibescu, drove his forty-horsepower Mercedes from Bucharest to Giurgiu and back in 109 minutes and 30 seconds. The upper classes began to take up sports. Public fencing matches and target shooting began in 1864, and gymnastics competitions in 1872. The Jockey Club, which combined interests in horseracing, politics, and society gatherings, was established in 1862. After 1880, when the journal *Sportul* (Sports) first came out, there began to be interest in more democratic, less "boyarish" sports like track and field and even soccer. In track and field the first championship competition took place in 1882. Soccer did not hold such a competition until 1909, which was also the year the Romanian team made its international debut, losing ingloriously to Turkey, 10–0. Tennis, ice skating, bowling, *oina* (a Romanian game played with bat and ball), and cycling became passions with the urban elite.

As for nutrition, early nineteenth-century records (for example, official price lists) show an abundance of foods in the public markets, and at least for the boyars and the middle class food was plentiful and varied throughout the century. Buying power in the cities was fairly high, even for workers. In the early 1900s a lathe operator made up to 0.75 lei per hour and a coppersmith up to 0.90 lei; sample food prices include, in 1906, 0.25 lei per kilogram for bread, 1.11 lei per kilogram for sugar, and 1.04 lei per kilogram for pork. On the eve of World War I city people at all social levels were living better than they had for a century.[48]

The same cannot be said of the rural population. The peasants had a monotonous corn-based diet, largely without meat or wheat and far below minimum dietary requirements. As the number of cattle fell— and it fell constantly during the nineteenth century—so did milk and meat consumption, leading directly to the appearance of pellagra. The medical control of diseases that had previously caused great destruction, such as cholera and the plague, improved the peasants' lot somewhat. But their place was taken by others unknown or at least unattested in the eighteenth century, like malaria, tuberculosis, and pellagra, which village medical facilities could not combat. Under the Organic Statutes Moldavia and Wallachia were ill equipped to meet their medical needs. The Wallachian statutes allowed only 150,000 lei for health costs and the Moldavian 120,000 lei. Vaccination for smallpox began in 1832, but in 1833 there were only forty-two physicians in Wallachia—many of them with degrees from Paris—and the number of practitioners stayed low for many years, rising only with the creation of the Board of Health (Direcţia Sanitară) in 1862, the founding of the Bucharest School of Medicine (1867), and the passing of the first health legislation (1874). Although the position of County Doctor was created in 1862 and the Health Law of 1881 provided for rural hospitals, in 1906 there were only 215 doctors practicing in the villages.[49] The school of medicine did make remarkable progress, however, even receiving European notice in some fields. Victor Babeş wrote the first treatise in the world on bacteriology (Paris, 1886), and Gheorghe Marinescu, founder of the Romanian School of Neurology, was internationally known for his work on the nerve cell (Paris, 1909).

Cultural Modernization. In form and in content the educational system in the newly united principalities was far from modern or from meeting the country's cultural needs. Boyars' children could be educated by foreign tutors or in private schools, but in 1834 public school enrollment in the two principalities together was only 725. By 1850 this number had grown to about 10,000, rising sharply to 117,575 in 1875–76 and to 535,470 in 1913–14. In 1864 Prince Alexandru Ioan Cuza's first education legislation made four years of elementary school free and compulsory. Cuza was responsible for establishing Romanian higher education, too. During his reign, both the University of Iaşi (1860) and the University of Bucharest (1864) opened. The University of Iaşi grew steadily from its modest beginning with only three departments (law, philosophy, and theology), eleven professors, and eighty students until 1900–01 it had 5,130 students. Official records mention 2,924 in law, 841 in medicine, 784 in letters and philosophy, 69 in the school of civil engineering, and 512 in other technical departments.[50]

Transylvania showed no such progress, at least for ethnic Romanians. Although in 1851 there were 44,000 students, the percentage of Romanians was small, and of the 2,164 elementary schools only 742 were for Romanians. In 1872 there were 24,590 students enrolled in Hungarian public high schools, 3,948 in German ones, and only 2,270 in

Romanian ones. After the union of Transylvania and Hungary in 1867, the government's Magyarization policy was carried out even more forcefully than before. Although the Eötvös Law of 1869 provided for some schools to teach in languages other than Hungarian, first the laws passed in 1904 and 1905 and then the Apponyi Laws of 1907 led to the closing of many Romanian language schools. By 1912 only 964 Romanian public elementary schools were left in Transylvania, while higher education was not available in Romanian, the majority language, until after unification with Romania.[51] In 1914 illiteracy was widespread: 40 percent of the population in Transylvania, 60 percent in the Old Kingdom (Wallachia and Moldavia), 60 percent in Bucovina, and 94 percent in Bessarabia could not read or write. Although progress had been made in education, much more was needed.[52]

The circulation of books increased considerably at this time. In the eighteenth century books were virtually unknown outside boyar and church libraries, but in the early nineteenth century lists of borrowers show a distinct rise in the number of middle-class readers. Reading room catalogs published between 1838 and 1850 allow us to observe the tastes of the times. Middle-class readers borrowed primarily novels, then memoirs and letters, short stories and tales. The most widely read authors were Balzac, Dumas, Hugo, and Chateaubriand, with Byron trailing faintly. The general public almost entirely stopped reading works of the Enlightenment. Most books borrowed from reading rooms between 1838 and 1850 were in French (4,048), followed by English (481), German (88), Italian (23), and Russian (13).[53] Since no duties were levied on foreign books, importing them was easy throughout the history of the two principalities.

After many unsuccessful attempts from 1789 on, Romanians at last established newspapers in both Moldavia and Wallachia in 1829. Within five years there were three papers with 650 subscribers, and the press began to take an active part in intellectual debate. The number of newspapers—of all orientations and for all tastes—grew exponentially in the second half of the century, while the number of literary journals was 106 by 1900.

Publishing was fairly restricted between 1831 and 1862. The Russian military administration instituted strict censorship in 1831, and publication of texts that might lead to "disturbance of the peace" was prohibited. This decree remained in effect for the duration of the Russian protectorate, and nothing could be published without the approval of the authorities. Censorship was abolished for a few months during the 1848 revolution, but was reinstated immediately thereafter. It was again abolished by the Press Law of 1862 and outlawed by the 1866 constitution, remaining illegal until 1934, so that during a long period of nearly seventy years the Romanian press enjoyed a remarkable degree of free expression.

Literary societies played a significant role in the political and cultural revival in all three principalities. In the years preceding the revolution of 1848, literary societies (founded in 1821, 1827, 1833, and 1845) usually harbored revolutionary and nationalist activity. This changed in Moldavia and Wallachia after unification, but continued in Transylvania throughout the rule of Austria-Hungary. The most notable of the societies was ASTRA (Asociaţia Transilvană pentru Literatura Română şi Cultura Poporului Român [Transylvanian Association for Romanian Literature and the Culture of the Romanian People]), founded in 1861. This society, whose leaders included almost all the foremost nationalists of Transylvania (Andrei Şaguna, Gheorghe Bariţiu, Vasile Ladislau Popp, Timotei Cipariu, Iosif Şuluţiu-Sterca, Vasile Goldiş) promoted nationalist values just when they were most in danger of disappearing under Magyarization.

In the United Principalities the societies were not very concerned with politics, concentrating instead on culture and offering important guidance in a period of rapid social and political change. The Junimea (Youth) society, established in Iaşi in 1864 by Titu Maiorescu, Petre P. Carp, Theodor Rosetti, Vasile Pogor, and Iacob Negruzzi, presented the ideas of the conservative left. Meanwhile in Bucharest, C. A. Rosetti prevailed upon the government to approve the founding in 1866 of the Literary Society (Societatea Literară), modeled on the Académie Française. Within the year it became the Romanian Academic Society (Societatea Academică Română) with sections for literature and lexicography, history and archaeology, and the natural sciences.

Intellectual Climate. The intelligentsia did not emerge as a distinct social category in the Danubian principalities until after 1830. For centuries professional scholarship had existed only on the technical level—manuscript copyists, tutors, printers, painters, miniaturists. Until the early nineteenth century the boyars, the clergy, or the middle class might engage in creative intellectual activity, but they did not form a cohesive social unit.

This situation began to change under the Organic Statutes, and a fairly large group began to take form—professors, writers, and others who shared certain intellectual characteristics, interests, and social status. Such people came to play a very influential role in national culture through their various professional organizations (the Iaşi Society of Doctors and Naturalists [founded 1834]; the Philharmonic Society of Bucharest [1833]; the Society of Romanian Students at Paris [1845]; the Medical and Scientific Society of Bucharest [1857]) and the literary societies and reading groups that were springing up in Romania and Transylvania alike. Later these groups coalesced into associations of great political and cultural influence (for example, ASTRA, the Cernăuţi Cultural Society [founded 1862]; Junimea, the Romanian Academic Society [1866], the Cultural League [1891], and the Association of Romanian Writers [1912]).

The new intelligentsia was active in politics, too. Many participated directly, and throughout the century a large number of political leaders were university graduates. Most of these degrees came from foreign universities, which was another difference between them and the scholars and leaders of the eighteenth century, who rarely went abroad. Starting in the 1830s Moldavians and Wallachians studied abroad, mainly in France but later at German university centers as well. Transylvanians usually gravitated toward Vienna and Budapest. The influx of European ideas and the emergence of an intelligentsia favored modern ideas over traditional values, and Romanian society now turned to a new value system.

First, religion's diminished importance is striking. In Transylvania the clergy continued to play a significant part in Romanian leadership throughout the nineteenth century, but in the United Principalities they were gradually pushed out of politics. As early as 1854 princes, boyars, and scholars proposed curtailing the rights of the metropolitans and bishops in the general assemblies and administering church properties through the Ministry of Religions. Two years later they recommended making priests salaried state employees and limiting the number of monks. In 1857 the Moldavian ad hoc assembly passed a resolution to make the church subordinate to the state, with the members of the hierarchy chosen by the assembly, a salaried clergy, and control of monastery lands in government hands. Cuza's church laws of 1863, 1864, and 1865 succeeded in subjecting the church to the state, over the opposition of some church leaders who demanded autonomy for the church as a national institution and part of the nationalist revival. Under pressure from the ruling class, the Orthodox church yielded its considerable economic and political power unresistingly to lay authority in Romania, much as it had in Greece after 1821 and in Serbia after 1830.[54]

The dominant idea in nineteenth-century Romania, nationalism, had appeared before 1800 with the desire for political and cultural regeneration and was consummated early in the twentieth century when the three principalities united as Greater Romania. In the "age of nationalities" much more was accomplished than in the previous period, but the lack of new concepts was striking. Most of what was won politically— unification, independence—had been discussed since before 1830, and even the idea of cultural support for nationalism was not particularly new, while Romanian origin and language issues had been examined since the Enlightenment.

What nineteenth-century thinkers did achieve was not innovation but dissemination among a larger public of ideas that until then had circulated only among the ruling class. The ad hoc assembly of Moldavia described the "Romanian nation" this way in 1857: "We have the same origins, the same language, the same religion, the same history, the same institutions, the same laws and customs, the same hopes and fears, the same needs to be met . . . , the same borders to defend, the same past sufferings, the same future to ensure, and finally the same mission to fulfill."[55] Because it reflects the "mission" of uniting all Romanians in a national state, this is more aggressive and forward-looking than the formulation in the Moldavian Organic Statutes. The historical argument for Romanian unity was now somewhat in decline, although for many intellectuals and political leaders it remained a motivating principle.

The Romanians of Transylvania (like August Treboniu Laurian and Alexandru Papiu-Ilarian), for example, were still basing their political claims on the theory of Roman origins and a continuous Romanian presence. Educated Transylvanians still held to the belief that the Dacians had been exterminated and that the Romanians were of purely Roman origins, but in the kingdom of Romania most intellectuals, like Bogdan Petriceu Haşdeu (in a major work published in 1860), Ion Ghica (1864), and V. A. Urechia (1868), disagreed with that theory. They valued the Dacian element in the Romanian makeup at least as highly as the Roman, if not more. The historical argument was also brought into the debates with ethnic German, Austrian, and Hungarian scholars that had begun in the eighteenth century and continued throughout the nineteenth. Until the mid-nineteenth century the Romanian view was presented mostly by Transylvanians, but after Robert Rössler's *Rumänische Studien* came out in 1871, scholars from the kingdom took the lead. The most important reply to Rössler came from A. D. Xenopol, first in his book *Teoria lui Rössler* (Rössler's theory [1884]) and then in his six-volume *Istoria Românilor din Dacia Traiană*

Alexandru D. Xenopol, Romanian scholar.

(History of the Romanians of Trajan's Dacia [1888–93]). Xenopol, a historian and philosopher of history, recognized that both Romanians and Hungarians were wrong to base present claims on the past. He was perhaps the first Romanian scholar to say that territorial rights should be granted not on the basis of origin or continuous presence but on the right to self-determination.

Even before 1848 Romanian intellectuals largely opposed mixing historical values with political ones and the historical demagoguery so common in developing countries. In 1843, for instance, Mihai Kogăl-niceanu harshly attacked "Romanomania"—the obsession with Roman origins—as well as the use of history for the political needs of the moment. The Junimea group followed, speaking out against historical "megalography" (Titu Maiorescu) and the creation of a "nationalist

Bible" (Gheorghe Panu).[56] This gave such Moldavian and Wallachian historians as A. D. Xenopol, Alexandru Philippide, Dimitrie Onciul, and Constantin Giurescu a much firmer scientific footing than the Transylvanian School of history, which still suffered from Latinist excesses and a romantic historicism much influenced by politics.

The debate over how to modernize, and how quickly, is a characteristic example of changing ideas in the nineteenth century. Unlike their Russian or Serbian counterparts, Romanian intellectuals were not divided between supporters and opponents of Westernization. The problem of Western versus Eastern forms of civilization had been resolved before the Organic Statutes. But there were differences of opinion on how quickly new forms should replace the old, and fears that innovation might somehow alter the basic national spirit. The idea that development and modernization need not imply a break with the past, without which there can be no future, was first expressed by the Moldavian Alecu Russo (works published in 1840, 1851, 1855) and later by Alexandru Moruzzi (1861), Prince Barbu Ştirbei (1855), and of course in the writings of Junimea members, who created what Maiorescu called a theory of "forms without content" (1868). By this he meant that simply to adopt Western forms would be to modernize so quickly and superficially that their content could not keep pace. It would lead to a society based on false—because imitated—values. Maiorescu considered that a people could endure the lack of culture, but not false culture. In works like Theodor Rosetti's study *Despre direcţia progresului nostru* (On the direction of our progress [1873]), Junimea members called for a rediscovery of the "vital kernel," the recovery of original values, and the rejection of imitation.[57]

But no one, neither the Junimea writers nor the traditionalist literary trend represented by the journal *Sămănătorul* (The sower [founded in 1901]), knew what that vital kernel was or how modernization might jeopardize it. Almost all the members of Junimea had studied in Germany, and most of them were in politics (Maiorescu, Carp, and Theodor Rosetti became ministers and prime ministers) and responsible for setting up new cultural and other institutions. Their fear of political change had much to do with their class and party, for the conservative boyars were afraid of the effect that the modernization of institutions might have on politics and on their own social status.

Liberals, on the other hand, without denying the need to respect tradition—in fact Ion C. Brătianu, C. A. Rosetti, and Mihai Kogălniceanu, the "reddest" liberals, kept reaffirming it—held that tradition must not be an obstacle to progress. Xenopol, a former member of

Junimea, best summarized the arguments of those who wanted swift, far-reaching progress. In a reply to Maiorescu in 1869 he argued that the present problems were inevitable in a country undergoing the kind of profound changes Romania had experienced in less than half a century, and they in no way showed that Romanian society was unprepared for progress. Rather, he concluded, progress must be made even faster, since there was no choice but to adopt unhesitatingly the model of Western development.[58]

To the former forty-eighters that meant first of all adapting to Romanian needs the most liberal western European constitution of the time, the Belgian one, and encouraging rapid industrialization. The conservatives, starting with Nicolae Suțu in his *Aperçu sur l'état industriel de la Moldavie* (1838), would accept at most such industries as would complement agriculture, and in general wanted to remain what Suțu called "an eminently agrarian country." But the liberal economists Petre S. Aurelian (writing in 1860) and Ion Ghica (1865, 1870) argued that industrialization was a guarantee of independence. As Ghica said, "A nation without industry cannot be considered civilized." Ion C. Brătianu expressed the nationalist view of the best way to reform the economy most concisely: "by ourselves" (*prin noi înșine*). His idea gained great influence just after World War I.[59]

The tremendous social changes in Romania in the nineteenth century, and the generations-long pursuit of the nationalist ideal, led to a mixing and interdependence of political and cultural values to the detriment of aesthetic ones. The forty-eighters and their followers believed in using culture for social purposes. Ion Heliade Rădulescu considered literature political manifestation, and Hașdeu thought that politics enriched literature. But the members of Junimea vehemently denied that politics and aesthetics were even compatible. Maiorescu held that political poetry, even patriotic poetry, had no artistic value, was not even an art form. The dispute went on for years, becoming even more contentious when it was joined by Constantin Dobrogeanu-Gherea and the Socialist journal *Contemporanul* (The contemporary [1881–91]). In theory the problem remained unresolved, but in practice the Junimea line emerged the clear winner. Almost every great writer of the time was either a member of the group or a follower of its mentor, Maiorescu.

There were some who went beyond the Junimea position to say that introducing too much politics into cultural areas could be harmful not only to literature but to society at large. Intellectuals, starting with Teodor Diamant in 1834, wondered why Romanians preferred positions as officials and functionaries to direct involvement in economic activity.

Constantin A. Crețulescu (Kretzulescu) wrote in 1860 that a political career brought with it too many social and economic benefits, which, as Ghica said (1861), made officials into parasites. Dimitrie Drăghicescu, in *Psihologia poporului român* (Psychology of the Romanian people [1907]), and Constantin Rădulescu-Motru, in *Cultura românească și politicianismul* (Romanian culture and politicism [1910]), *Psihologia ciocoiului* (Psychology of the upstart [1911]), and *Psihologia industriașului* (Psychology of the industrialist [1911]) went further, declaring that Romania could not be considered truly modern as long as its citizens preferred political and administrative work to direct economic activity.

Junimea brought literature out of the stagnation it had fallen into after decades of sociopolitical manipulation and opened the way for the poetic genius of Mihai Eminescu. Among the outstanding writers who emerged during this time were the dramatist Ion Luca Caragiale, the novelist Mihail Sadoveanu, the literary critic Garabet Ibrăileanu and the philosopher Vasile Conta. Modern historiography emerged in the middle of the century with Nicolae Bălcescu and Mihai Kogălniceanu, was dominated toward its end by A. D. Xenopol, then later by Nicolae Iorga. Hașdeu's writings formed the basis of modern Romanian linguistics. Toward the end of the century a number of Romanian scholars gained respectable reputations in Europe, for example, Matei Drăghiceanu and Grigore Cobălcescu in geology, Emil Racoviță in biospeleology (he was the first Romanian to go to the Antarctic, in 1898), and David Emmanuel, Traian Lalescu, and Spiru Haret in mathematics. Aeronautics made advances between Traian Vuia's self-propelled airplane (1906) and Henri Coandă's experiments with jet-propelled aircraft (1910), while George "Gogu" Constantinescu laid the foundation for the science of sonics (1916).

But the most interesting phenomenon in this period was the emergence of avant-garde art and literature. The painters Ioan Andreescu and Ștefan Luchian, for instance, both influenced by Impressionism, brought painting far beyond the academicism of Theodor Aman and Nicolae Grigorescu, while Constantin Brâncuși revolutionized modern sculpture. Similar innovations took place in literature, where Eminescu imitators and *Sămănătorul*-style idealizations of village life were energetically denounced by the Symbolists.

Symbolism, an urban movement that concentrated on protest and the search for a new value system, anti-Junimea, anti-Eminescu, anti-*Sămănătorul*, antipopulist, antisocialist, and negativist, was founded by Alexandru Macedonski in the journal *Literatorul* (The littérateur [1880]). Symbolist poet Ilarie Voronca would later observe, "Of all nations I choose the imagination," a key phrase in the understanding of this group, which after 1900 included Tristan Tzara, the founder of Dada, as well as Ion Minulescu and Ion Vinea. It was also at this time (1907) that a precursor of absurdist literature began to write under the name of Urmuz [Demetru Dem. Demetrescu].[60] All these avant-garde movements came out of a society in transition and continued to be important elements in Romanian culture between the two world wars.

Achievements at Home and Abroad. The Romanians made gradual progress in nationalist foreign policy throughout the nineteenth century and on to the end of 1918, although it came fairly slowly. Long intervals elapsed between such major events as the fall of the Phanariots (1821), unification (1859), independence (1877), and the creation of Greater Romania (1918). There was always a delay between the formulation of a political idea or objective and its accomplishment. The union of the Danubian principalities, for instance, was first requested by the Wallachian boyars in 1772 but carried out only in 1859. The leaders set independence as a political objective many generations before it was regained in 1877. And union with Transylvania, first proposed in the early nineteenth century, had to wait more than a century. Many domestic policy aims, too—a national bank and currency, free foreign commerce, an independent customs department, and numerous cultural programs—were long on the nationalist agenda but were held back by external factors.

The process of state building and modernization was slow in part because of unfavorable international circumstances. For many years the country lacked not a goal, not direction or a plan, but the opportunity to achieve them because of the great powers' meddling in local politics. Many long-hoped-for programs were realized only by seizing moments of international change. Tudor Vladimirescu's revolt in 1821 was made possible by the outbreak of the Greek war of independence. The Russo-Turkish War of 1828–29 led to the treaty of Adrianople and the adoption of the Organic Statutes. Without the defeat of Russia in the Crimean War in 1856 Moldavia and Wallachia probably could not have united in 1859, nor could independence have been gained in 1877 if a new Russo-Turkish war had not begun. And it is hard to imagine that Transylvania could have joined the kingdom in 1918 but for the simultaneous collapse of the two neighboring empires that for centuries had dominated eastern European policy.

But the international situation, although it facilitated them, did not create Tudor Vladimirescu's revolt, the unifications of 1859 and 1918, or independence. Events abroad, however, might make or break a plan—as the history of other peoples shows—if political leaders failed to exploit promising situations. Romania seems always to have had political leaders with a talent for foreign relations, quick to make use of conflicts among the great powers and to push their programs through at the moment when those powers were not in a position to refuse. Almost every nationalist victory overturned some earlier decision of the great powers, as the Romanians played them against each other. This was true both of Vladimirescu's revolt and of unification, rejected by the Paris congress in 1858 but achieved in 1859. No great power supported Romanian independence in 1877, and Russia opposed the kingdom's entry into the Russo-Turkish War until the last moment, but Romania won independence on the battlefield and then at the Congress of Berlin. Few expected a military revival in 1918, but as soon as the war was over Romanian troops invaded Hungary, marching all the way to Budapest. The ruling elite succeeded in fulfilling the national program by holding to it tenaciously and making the most of circumstances.

The same kind of success in domestic matters, however, eluded them. Conservative boyars and liberal middle class agreed on basic objectives in foreign affairs, but their views on domestic questions were diametrically opposed. Because of the opposition of the great boyars and great landowners who made up the Conservative Party and the weakness of the middle class, the revolutionary program of 1848 was only gradually executed, and the most radical provisions—universal suffrage and agrarian reform—did not pass parliament until 1914, going into effect only in 1917 and 1921, respectively.

Although progress was slow, nineteenth-century domestic politics had many positive aspects. The kingdom of Romania was far from democratic, but it was certainly liberal, and while participation in the political process was limited, freedom of speech and movement were not. The principal institutions may not always have functioned efficiently, but they were at least not repressive, as they had been before Prince Cuza and as they would be again after 1938.

An indication of the relatively open character of nineteenth-century Romanian society is the way first Moldavia and Wallachia and later the kingdom of Romania drew immigrants. They had begun coming in the Middle Ages, but their number increased dramatically at the time the modern national state was being formed. Balkan peoples from south of the Danube had always come to the principalities seeking a richer and more peaceful life, and they continued to do so until 1877. Tens of thousands of Bulgarian, Greek, and Albanian subjects of the Ottoman empire became citizens of Romania. A great wave of Jewish immigration into Moldavia began in 1834 and was strongly encouraged by the authorities between 1834 and 1849. By 1899 there were 269,015 Jews in the kingdom, 4.5 percent of the total population. (The proportion shrank to 3.3 percent [239,967] within thirteen years because of emigration.)[61] Most Jews who came to Romania were Galicians from the Austrian empire and Poles and Ukrainians from the Russian empire, but after 1859, and even more after the accession in 1866 of the Hohenzollern prince, Carol I, many "technocrats" came from Austria, Germany, Transylvania, and France, to Romania's considerable benefit. And there was none of the peasant emigration to America so widespread among ethnic Romanians and Hungarians in Transylvania and Hungary at the end of the century.

The initiative to modernize generally came from above in nineteenth-century Romanian society, from the ruling class and in particular from its radical core of liberal boyars, who considered that they were upholding the ideas of the revolutions of 1821 and 1848. But even this "red" party implemented its reforms slowly and carefully. It was not until the early twentieth century that it became truly radicalized, partly because of a new generation of leaders centered around Ion I. C. Brătianu and partly in response to popular pressure, especially after the peasant uprising of 1907. Nineteenth-century reforms were always incomplete, postponed, or only half enforced. At the outbreak of World War I, which would bring about the formation of Greater Romania, the kingdom still lacked many of the structures that define a modern society.

CHAPTER FIVE

From Greater Romania to Popular Democracy

(1918–47)

Greater Romania

The Political Regime. By the time World War I was over, Romania had changed fundamentally. In the first place it had expanded with the addition of Transylvania, the Banat, Bessarabia, and northern Bucovina from 137,000 to 295,049 square kilometers. There was a great demographic difference, too. Whereas the population of the Old Kingdom had been overwhelmingly Romanian, greater Romania had a significant number of inhabitants of other nationalities. According to the 1930 census the total population was 18,057,028, of whom 71.9 percent were Romanian, 7.9 percent Hungarian, 4.4 percent German, 3.2 percent Ruthenian and Ukrainian, 2.3 percent Russian, 4 percent Jewish, 2 percent Bulgarian, 1.5 percent Gypsy, one percent Turkish and Tatar, 0.8 percent Gagauz,* 0.3 percent Czech and Slovak, 0.3 percent Polish, 0.1 percent Greek, and less than 0.1 percent Albanian, Armenian, and other. In Transylvania, where the potential for ethnic conflict was greatest, the census showed three principal groups: 57.8 percent were Romanian, 24.4 percent Hungarian, and 9.8 percent German.

The 1940 statistics indicate that by 1939 the population had risen by almost two million to 19,933,802, an increase that is the more surprising since it was due almost entirely to an increase in the birthrate.[1] (After 1918, in contrast to the previous century, the number of emigrants from Romania outstripped that of immigrants.) The 1925 migration law established the right to freedom of movement, and by the

*The name given to Christianized Turks in Dobrudja and southern Bessarabia.

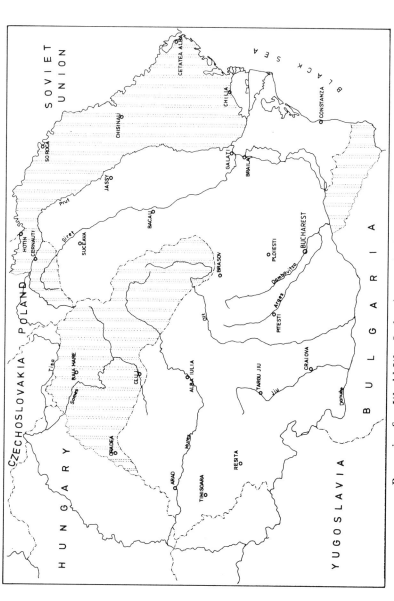

Romania after World War I, showing territorial losses from 1940.

end of 1938, 79,806 Romanian citizens, largely Hungarians, Germans, Jews, and Russians, had emigrated from Romania. Emigration dipped after 1930: 1,372 in 1932, 1,179 in 1933, 1,371 in 1934, 2,423 in 1935, 1,534 in 1936, 1,337 in 1937, 1,642 in 1938. The ethnic groups emigrating in 1936, for example, were Jews (1,251), Germans (138), Hungarians (93), and Romanians (52). In 1938, a year before World War II began, the official emigration figures were 907 Jews, 303 Germans, 229 Russians and Ukrainians, 126 Hungarians, and 77 Romanians.[2]

Socially, greater Romania resembled the Old Kingdom. In 1930 the population was about 79 percent rural and 21 percent urban; there was one city of over half a million (Bucharest, at 631,288), four of more than 100,000 (Chişinău, Cernăuţi, Iaşi, and Galaţi), and nine of more than 50,000 inhabitants. In 1930 a partial accounting showed that 72.3 percent of the population worked in agriculture, 9.4 percent in industry, 4.8 percent in public service, 4.2 percent in commerce and banking, and 2.8 percent in transportation and communication.[3]

A series of reforms in 1917–23 brought radical changes to the country's social and political structure and gave rise to a new and different set of institutions. The 1913 liberal program, which parliament had been discussing before World War I, went into effect gradually from 1917, when King Ferdinand promised agrarian reform and an electoral system based on universal male suffrage. Provisions for land reform were enacted in 1918 and 1920, and then in 1921 the Agrarian Law was passed, for practical purposes putting an end to the great estates and making Romania a nation of small landowners. The first elections under the new electoral system were held in 1919. By 1937, 4,651,959 people had registered to vote in the election for the chamber of deputies.[4]

The passage of agrarian and electoral reform laws, both planks in the liberal platform, brought about an immediate change in the internal balance of power. The first casualty was the Conservative Party, which fell apart after the new reforms were introduced. Alexandru Marghiloman's government (March–November 1918) fell when Romania reentered World War I. The party returned to power just once, for only thirty days, under Prime Minister Take Ionescu (1922) before disappearing for good. In the 1919 elections it won less than 4 percent of the vote (sixteen seats in parliament), in 1920 less than 3 percent (four seats), and in 1922 not a single seat.

The liberals became the strongest party of the interwar period. With only the brief interruption of Marghiloman's government, they held office from 1914 to 1919. But then, like other liberal parties of Europe, the party lost the elections as a result of the universal suffrage for which it had worked so long. After retrenching and reorienting themselves, the liberals were returned to office and governed with undeniable authority from 1922 to 1928 (except for March 1926–June 1927) and from 1933 to 1937. The period of greatest liberal achievement was probably 1922–26, when Ion I. C. Brătianu's government dealt perceptively with the difficult problems of organizing the new state. These years also saw both economic reconstruction and the adoption of the liberal and democratic constitution of 1923, which remained in effect until 1938. In 1926 the Liberal Party was at the height of its powers, at last carrying out the mission it had undertaken in 1848. After 1930, although still in office, it grew weaker, losing one leader after another as Ion I. C. Brătianu (1927), Vintilă Brătianu (1930), and Ion Gheorghe Duca (1933) died, then splitting into two main factions. As a result the party lost its influence and the December 1937 elections, although the two liberal factions together won nearly 40 percent of the vote.

The political scene that had been so stable before 1914, with two major parties alternating in power, now became fragmented. The main opposition party during the period between the wars was the National Peasant Party, created in 1926 by the union of Iuliu Maniu's National Party of Transylvania with the Peasant Party Ion Mihalache had founded in 1918 in the Old Kingdom. Although they had a much broader base of support than the liberals, the National Peasant Party had difficulty becoming an efficient governing party, and held power only briefly (1928–31 and 1932–33). Their leaders were well intentioned and morally sound, but not politically able and flexible like the liberals. They made tactical errors, like permitting Prince Carol II to reclaim the throne in 1930 and forming an "alliance" with the Iron Guard for the 1937 elections, by which they hastened the collapse of the budding Romanian democracy and its replacement with a dictatorship. Not until 1944 did the National Peasant Party take the lead in both numbers and popularity, and by then neither numbers nor popularity could bring it to power.

Various other parties took turns in governing Romania. The People's Party, led by Marshal Alexandru Averescu (1920–21, 1926–27), the National Democrat Party, led by Professor Nicolae Iorga (1931–32), and the National Christian Party, led by the poet Octavian Goga and by Alexandru C. Cuza (1937–38), all had their day in power. As early as 1921 the political spectrum was further broadened as new parties formed on the extreme left and right. These never controlled the government but did play an active role in politics, especially after 1930. In contrast to other eastern European countries like Czechoslovakia, Bulgaria, and Yugoslavia, where both socialists and Communists had some influence, left-wing parties had little voice in Romania. In 1921 a rupture in the Social Democratic Party between partisans of Leninism, adherents of the Third International (Comintern) in Moscow, and loyal social democrats led to the creation of the Romanian Communist Party.

Communist Party membership was always small, and it dropped from about 2,000 at the time of the Second Congress (1922) to 1,500 in 1931 and less than 1,000 during World War II. In 1923, after a period of political vacillation, the party fell into line with Soviet views and followed a strident anti-Romanian policy, so that it found favor mostly among the minority nationalities—Hungarians, Jews, Bulgarians—who all opposed greater Romania for different reasons but with the same determination. With the single exception of Gheorghe Cristescu (1922–24), all the general secretaries (after 1924 called first secretaries) were non-Romanians, chosen in Comintern-sponsored congresses held abroad or else appointed directly by Moscow without regard for party regulations and bylaws. Elek Koblos, alias Bădulescu (1924–28), a Hungarian, was chosen at the Third Congress at Vienna; Vitali Holostenko, alias Barbu (1928–31), a Ukrainian, was chosen at the Fourth Congress at Kharkov and was succeeded at the Fifth Congress at Moscow by another Ukrainian, Alexandru Danieluk, alias Gorn (1931–35); Boris Stefanov (1935–40), a Bulgarian, was then appointed by a central committee that met in Moscow, and his successor, the Hungarian István Fóris (1940–44), was also named directly by Moscow. With this kind of leadership (and the central committees, politburos, and secretariats were also dominated by minorities) and the dismemberment of greater Romania as its principal objective, it is small wonder that the Communists remained a marginal party.

In 1923 the Communist Party under Cristescu adopted the Cominform's position on nationalism and self-determination and passed a resolution suggested by Nikolai I. Bukharin, which they held to until World War II. The resolution declared Romania a multinational state artificially created by Western imperialism. A series of party resolutions affirmed the minority nationalities' right to self-determination "to the point of the complete disbanding of the presently existing state." The party never recognized Bessarabia's union with Romania, and it approved the Ukraine's demand for the annexation of Bucovina (at the Fourth Congress in 1928). In 1933, after years of supporting the Comintern's call for an independent Dobrudja, they threw their weight behind Bulgarian annexation of that province.[5]

Ion I. C. Brătianu's Liberal government used the Communists' anti-nationalist line and their involvement in a secessionist uprising in Tatar-Bunar, Bessarabia as excuses to outlaw the party (1924). In spite of its loyalty to Moscow, the Romanian Communist Party was not spared by Stalin's purges, and many of its leading members—Cristian Rakovski, Alexandru Dobrogeanu-Gherea, Marcel Pauker, and Gheorghe Crosneff, the Bulgarian editor-in-chief of the newspaper Scînteia (The spark)—disappeared without a trace into the Soviet gulag. Paralyzed by factional fighting between 1928 and 1931 and then decimated by Stalinist repression, led until the eve of World War II by a politburo headquartered abroad, the Communist Party could play only a minor role between the wars.

In 1930 Béla Kun, speaking for the Comintern, accused the Romanian Communist Party of lack of influence over the working class, claiming that the Lupeni strikes (1929), for example, had had no Communist participation.[6] The Comintern representative was right; the union and workers' movements were more socialist than Communist. Although the former Social Democratic Party had no more than a thousand members at the time of the 1921 split, through the unions it indirectly controlled about 200,000 people. These formed the base of support for the federation formed in 1922 by socialist parties from Transylvania, the Banat, and Bucovina, together with the old Social Democratic Party. All four joined in 1927 to form a single Social Democratic Party led by Titel Petrescu. The new party won nine seats in parliament in 1928 and seven in 1931. After that it gradually declined, in part because of the emerging dissident left wing, including the Unitary Socialist Party (founded 1928) and the Romanian Socialist Party (1933). In 1937, in the last elections held in greater Romania, the social democrats won just under one percent of the vote, not enough to elect a single candidate.

The legionary movement had its beginnings in 1922–23, when Corneliu Zelea Codreanu formed first the Association of Christian Students and then, with Alexandru C. Cuza, the National Christian Defense League. But it was not officially established until the Legion of the Archangel Michael was founded in 1927. After 1930 it was also called the Iron Guard. Nationalist, anti-Semitic, anti-Western, messianic, and with a cult of the leader such as had never before existed in Romanian politics, this organization had all the characteristics of the other right-wing extremist movements of the period. The legion owed its existence to the domestic situation in Romania. Initially it had no ties to the Nazis or the Italian Fascists, nor did it borrow from their ideologies. But it

Carol II, king of Romania (1930–40).

was clearly aided by other countries' rightward shift and by direct or indirect support from such countries.

Under the guidance of Ion I. C. Brătianu and the other strong personalities that had created greater Romania, and with the prudent King Ferdinand on the throne, political stability continued until the end of the 1920s. But the king's unexpected death (1927), the loss of the three main liberal leaders (Ion I. C. Brătianu, Vintilă Brătianu, and Ion G. Duca) over the next six years, and vacillation and dissension within the National Peasant Party leadership left the way open for Carol II and the Iron Guard. Carol had been forced to renounce his right to the throne in 1926 because of controversy over his mistress Elena Lupescu (born Magda Wolff), and his six-year-old son Mihai had been crowned in his place. Carol had promised to stay abroad for ten years, but in 1930 he took advantage of Iuliu Maniu's weak government to return to the country, get the 1926 law repealed and remount the throne. The Iron Guard was outlawed first in 1931 and again in 1933, but reappeared in 1935 under the name All for the Country. The movement grew steadily in popularity, aided by the economic crisis, the rise of anti-Semitism, the corruption of the ruling classes, and the incapacity of the old parties to solve the country's problems.

A long period of classic liberalism and civility in Romanian politics ended with the assassination of Prime Minister Ion G. Duca by members of the Iron Guard (Sinaia, December 1933). Censorship was reintroduced in 1934 for the first time since 1862, and the administration began to govern by decree. The liberals were divided, some supporting Constantin "Dinu" I. C. Brătianu, another son of Ion C. Brătianu and a political leader of the old Brătianu tradition, others favoring Gheorghe Brătianu, son of Ion I. C. Brătianu, a great historian but a mediocre politician, and still others preferring the palace's man, Gheorghe Tătărăscu. This last faction was in office from 1933 until December 1937 with Tătărăscu as prime minister. It grew increasingly conservative and dependent on the king, and with the exception of some older leaders, increasingly corrupt and unpopular, so that it lost the December 1937 election.

That thirteen major parties and fifty-three secondary organizations ran in the 1937 election shows how splintered politics was. The incumbent liberals got about 36 percent of the vote, falling short of the 40 percent which, by the 1926 electoral law, would have allowed it an absolute majority in parliament. Gheorghe Brătianu's dissident liberals won about 4 percent, Maniu's National Peasant Party about 20 percent, the All for the Country Party (Iron Guard) about 16 percent, the National Christian Party 9 percent. The remainder of the vote went to two dissident Peasant Party factions (4%), the People's Party (1%), the Labor Front (1%), the Hungarian Party (4%), the Jewish Party (1%), and the Social Democratic Party (1%).[7] Three percent of the vote went to various other minor parties and groups. The king chose the National Christian Party, ranking fourth in the voting, to form a government! The distinct movement to the political right both in Romania and elsewhere in Europe posed a serious threat to the traditional parliamentary system.

At this point the two liberal factions reunited, and in January 1938 they began negotiating with Maniu to form a "constitutional block" that might be able to save something of the democratic institutions. The right wing too was trying to consolidate its forces. It had obtained one-quarter of the popular vote in the elections, and prime minister-designate Octavian Goga entered into talks with the legion. Fearing a right-wing consolidation, Carol dissolved parties and parliament and established a royal dictatorship (10 February 1938). Greater Romania, or at least the political structure created by its founders, ceased to exist. The democracy, imperfect as it had been, was replaced with an authoritarian regime for the first time in the country's modern history.

Greater Romania's foreign policy did not undergo the kind of changes and contradictions seen in its internal affairs. Except for the Germanophile Iron Guard, all other political forces from the parties to the palace worked to create a general security policy that would guarantee, under the League of Nations, the international status granted by the treaties of 1918–20. To this end Romania, Czechoslovakia, and Yugoslavia formed the Little Entente in 1921, a defensive and anti-revisionist alliance to uphold the Treaty of Trianon. Shortly thereafter Romania formed a series of other alliances. With Poland it joined in a "convention of defensive alliance" in 1921, replaced in 1926 by a mutual defense treaty. It sealed an "amity treaty" with France in 1926. In the same year it signed a "pact of amity and cordial collaboration" with Italy, which at the time still supported Romania's current boundaries. Bucharest was a party to the Kellogg-Briand Pact of Paris, condemning war as a means of resolving disagreements, in 1928, and in 1929 it approved the Moscow Protocol, in which the countries of eastern Europe and the Soviet Union echoed that pact. In 1933 it signed both the convention defining an aggressor in London and the Saavedra Lamas nonaggression and conciliation pact in Rio de Janeiro.

Romania was always eager to strike up regional pacts guaranteeing the country's new boundaries, of which the Little Entente was one of the first. Another important one was the Balkan Entente, worked out in four annual Balkan conferences (1930–33) and signed in Athens, by which Romania, Greece, Yugoslavia, and Turkey respected the integrity of one another's frontiers. Foreign Minister Nicolae Titulescu and other Romanian diplomats played an active role in the League of Nations, too, opposing the invasions of China (1931) and Ethiopia (1935), and the occupation of the Saar (1935). In 1934 Romania followed France's example and reestablished diplomatic relations with the Soviet Union, and in 1935–36 was even preparing to sign a mutual assistance pact with that country, guaranteeing Romania's 1918 borders.

But after 1936 Carol II was driven by international developments—

notably the growing importance of Germany and inactivity and lack of firmness on the part of the Western democracies—to reorient his foreign policy in order to prevent the country's political isolation. As a first step, Titulescu, closely identified with the pro-French policy and the League of Nations, was removed from office (1936), and the planned Soviet alliance was abandoned. When the royal dictatorship was established in 1938 the political leadership clearly lost what unity they might once have had, and there were now deep divisions between those who wanted to continue the old foreign policy and those who supported a rapprochement with the totalitarian regimes. Where Maniu and the older political generation considered that "any Romanian who wants to bring Romania's foreign policy directly or indirectly into the German orbit is an outright criminal" (January 1938), Codreanu declared, "I am against the great democracies of the West. I am against the Little Entente and the Balkan Entente. I have no use for the League of Nations. Within forty-eight hours of the triumph of the Legionary movement, Romania will have a close alliance with Rome and with Berlin" (1937).[8] It is hardly surprising that the king thought dictatorship might be a means to solve the crises in his domestic and foreign policies in the late 1930s.

The Economy. Records show that between 1920 and 1940 Romania was fourth in Europe in area under cultivation, and was the fifth largest agricultural producer in the world. More than 60 percent of Romanian land was in agricultural use in 1930, and five-sixths of that land was used for raising grain. Toward the end of the thirties grain production fell as cultivation of vegetables and plants for industrial use increased, but throughout the period Romania continued to be a great grain producer and exporter, as it had been before World War I. Nonintensive agriculture was still used, however, and modernization was extremely slow.[9]

The founders of greater Romania considered agricultural modernization and updated agrarian relations key factors in the new society. In 1913 60 percent of all agricultural and forest land had been in the hands of the great landowners, while the peasants owned only 40 percent of it. In 1918 44 percent of peasant families owned less than three hectares and 15 percent less than one. About 300,000 peasants had no land at all. Land reform was finally legislated but proceeded very gradually. In 1917, in its temporary headquarters in Iaşi, parliament wrote into the constitution the government's right to expropriate land. The law went into effect region by region, first in the Old Kingdom in

December 1918, then in Transylvania, Bucovina, and Bessarabia. In 1921 parliament passed the Agrarian Law distributing 5,811,827 hectares to 1,393,353 heads of family, who received six hectares apiece in Bessarabia, five in the Old Kingdom, four in Transylvania, and two and a half in Bucovina. This reform changed the entire structure of agrarian property, and Romania went overnight from being a country of large estates to one of small landowners. Parcels of less than ten hectares accounted for 95 percent of all property. Most holdings (83%) were smaller than five hectares. Once huge estates were reduced to 100–500 hectares. To envision how the changes affected the great landowners, consider that 46,422 hectares were appropriated from the crown, 38,669 from the St. Spiridon Trust (in Iaşi), 31,866 from the Hungarian countess Christina Wenkheim (in Arad), and 3,668 from the conservative former prime minister Alexandru Marghiloman.[10]

Things looked very good on paper: most of the inequities of the past century had been righted, and most of the wishes of the progressives fulfilled; the peasants at last owned land and the tenant managers (arendaş) were gone, along with the absentee landlords. But the reformers soon found that socioeconomic theory does not always work in practice. The peasants lacked the capital and the equipment they needed, knew little of modern farming techniques, had inadequate financial assistance from the government, and were saddled with an inheritance law that continually divided their newly acquired land. Under these circumstances they soon proved worse farmers than the great landowners, especially when they were hit by the world economic crisis of 1929–33. National grain production did not reach prewar figures again until 1929. During the years 1923–27, wheat production was only 850 kg per hectare and corn only 1,100 kg per hectare (less than half the average for normal years in the prewar period), although cheap labor kept profit indexes at world levels.

Although the land reform was the work of their party, the Liberal governments of 1922–28 took few practical steps to support agriculture. Credit extended by the National Bank doubled to reach 4,024,991 lei in 1927, but since the peasant farmers could not get the long-term loans necessary for the practice of modern agriculture, the increased credit by no means met their real needs. The government also set very high export duties on grain until 1929, and then the collapse of farm prices (48% of 1929 prices in 1932 and 45% in 1933) put an end to the hopes of the small landowners—and of the politicians and economists—that breaking up the great properties and appropriating land to the peasants would solve all the problems of Romanian agriculture.[11]

The thirties brought a welcome change in agrarian policy. Export duties were abolished (1931), and the government actively encouraged grain exports to reduce the backlog. In 1931–32 export premiums reached 10,000 lei per railroad car of wheat and 13,000 lei per carload of flour, an outlay that was recovered through taxes on bread. In 1933–34 the government tried to stabilize prices by making large-scale grain purchases, and in 1935 it set minimum prices for agricultural products to guarantee the producers' income. Then in 1937, when three-quarters of all peasant landowners had less than five hectares, a new law was passed organizing and encouraging agriculture in an attempt to prevent the further subdivision of these small holdings.

Because of these measures and because Germany suddenly began to buy and stockpile Romanian agricultural products in preparation for war, the last years before World War II were years of progress for agriculture. The number of tractors rose from 3,257 (1927) to 5,732 (1939) and that of threshing machines from 12,779 (1927) to 18,828 (1939). In 1938 there were 1,500 agricultural engineers, 500 subengineers, and 25,000 graduates of lower-level schools of agriculture. Rates of production had risen so that in the same year wheat, for instance, was up to 1,450 kg per hectare in Bessarabia, 1,600–2,542 in Wallachia, 1,600–2,000 in Transylvania, and 2,000–2,750 in Moldavia. Although the hopes placed on restructured agrarian relations in 1921 had not all been fulfilled, Romanian agriculture still made a remarkable contribution for a developing nation. Agriculture accounted for 55 percent of the net national product (1937) and produced enough both to feed the population and to export significant quantities of grain.[12]

Although agriculture was slow to develop, industry made continuous and fairly rapid progress throughout the interwar period, reaching its height in 1938. In the twenties there were heated debates about industrialization. The liberals, taking up Ion C. Brătianu's watchword "by ourselves," preferred domestic means of industrialization, without outside help or foreign capital. This was not an entirely disinterested position, for the Liberal Party controlled the National Bank and most of the credit system. The National Peasant Party, on the other hand, favored an open-door policy and wanted to bring foreign capital into the Romanian economy. In practice, since the liberals were in power for longer periods of time and not during the worst of the Depression years "by ourselves" won out over open-door. Only 36 percent of all capital in the Romanian economy was foreign in 1929, shrinking to 21 percent in 1938. Most of it was in heavy industry (70% in 1929, 41% in 1938).

In 1938 England was the biggest foreign investor, followed by France, the United States, Italy, and Germany, in that order.[13]

The liberals were responsible for an active protectionist policy. Protectionist laws were passed in 1924, 1927, and 1929 and extended in 1931, 1935, and 1936. As a result the import of manufactured goods fell steadily between 1920 and 1938, and industrialization increased at one of the highest rates in Europe, more than 5 percent for the years 1920–29 and more than 3 percent for 1929–38. (The lower figure is due primarily to the world economic crisis: for 1933–38 the growth rate was better than 6 percent.) Although only 10 percent of the population worked in that sector, industry accounted for 35 percent of the gross value of output in 1929 or 23 percent of the net national product. The value of industrial production in 1926 was 20,331 million lei in the Old Kingdom, 19,133 million in the Banat and Transylvania, 3,246 million in Bucovina, and 896 million in Bessarabia. The highest degree of mechanization was in glass manufacturing (69%), followed by construction (66%), metallurgy (54%), electrotechnology (46%), and the chemical industry (45%). The chemical industry had the highest productivity (wood products had the lowest) and also the greatest level of capital investment and production values. The petroleum and methane industries were particularly well developed.

The Great Depression interrupted this rapid development, and by 1932 industrial production had fallen to 57 percent of its 1929 level. After 1933 the growth rate returned to its former levels, stimulated by measures taken to encourage industry (such as a 1936 law favoring new entrepreneurs), by its concentration in fewer hands (in 1936 thirteen billionaire stock companies held 48% of all industrial capital and 90% of the metallurgical industry), and by the accelerating preparations for war across the Continent. If production of consumer goods grew at only a modest rate because of the limited domestic market, in a country with a relatively low standard of living, other branches, metallurgy in particular, showed a remarkable growth rate. In the decade 1930–39 production of housewares and home furnishings increased only 39 percent, but production of sheet metal rose 82 percent, machinery 112 percent, and cast iron and steel parts 258 percent.[14] Oil production increased too, to a high of 8.7 million metric tons in 1936, after which production fell to stabilize at 6.2 million metric tons in 1939.[15]

This relatively rapid industrialization was achieved even though factories did not work to capacity, particularly in food and consumer goods. In 1938, for example, breweries were working at 40 percent of capacity, producers of cooking oil at 60 percent, and cement works at 56 percent. The limits of economic progress had clearly been reached, and could not be extended further until Romanian society had been restructured and the people's buying power increased.

Between the wars commerce was directly affected by changes in the economy as well as by the international situation. Where France and England had been Romania's principal trading partners from 1918 to 1929, Germany gradually took over this role and after 1933 showed increasing interest in buying raw materials and grain and in selling industrial goods and arms. In 1938 29 percent of imports (by value) were from Germany, 9 percent from England, and 6 percent from France. Of Romanian exports 37 percent went to the Reich, 8 percent to England, and just under 8 percent to France. Trade with Germany further increased after it annexed Austria, and went still higher once it took over Czechoslovakia, formerly another of Romania's major trade partners.

The character of imports changed as industry developed, the proportion of manufactured goods falling as raw materials rose. Raw materials went from about 10 percent of imports in 1930 to 34 percent in 1939, while finished products fell from 65 percent of imports to 33 percent. Semimanufactured goods rose from 25 percent to 33 percent. The most significant change was in grain exports, which fell from half the value of Romania's total exports in 1927 to just under one-quarter in 1938.[16]

Society. Like any other developing society, Romania was a land of contrasts. Teams of sociologists studying village life in the thirties reached fairly gloomy conclusions. The peasant diet was poor. They ate too much starch, too little protein and fat, too little meat, and too much vegetable matter. Statistics for 1923–27 show fairly high per capita grain consumption, 436 kg yearly.

Income naturally varied by occupation, with the average middle-class Romanian earning about 40,000 lei per year, enough to live reasonably well on. The prime minister's salary was almost a million lei per year, a sum that would have been exorbitant before World War I, when ministers depended more on private income than on state salaries. The 1938 census, taken at the peak of the country's development, shows that 716 Romanians made at least a million lei (seven made more than ten million a year), 70,529 made over 100,000 lei per year, and 304,400 earned between 20,000 and 40,000 lei.[17] Industrial workers were relatively well off, which may explain the weakness of the union movements.

Significant strikes and street demonstrations occurred only in 1920, 1929, and 1933, and after the economic recovery of the thirties began, social unrest was minimal.

In the cities, however, economic development brought great changes. Prewar Bucharest, with its boyar houses surrounded by greenery, changed greatly after 1918. The city center was systematically redesigned, the main avenues were widened, and many imposing buildings were erected, including a new royal palace, banks, ministries, colleges, and apartment buildings. Still, although the population tripled and industrial areas sprang up, the city retained the pleasant, open aspect that had given it the name "Little Paris."

Prices, especially food prices, rose sharply after 1913 (incomes went up appreciably, too) to a 1929 high and then fell by about one-third. By 1938 average prices were 22.50 lei per kg for beef, 29.90 lei per kg for pork, 39.50 lei per kg for feta cheese (a staple among the poor), 8.70 lei per kg for white bread and 7.20 for black, 1.73 lei apiece for eggs, and 3.25 lei per kg for potatoes. Urban dwellers' per capita consumption rates in 1938 were 123 kg of wheat, 5.8 kg of sugar, and 42 liters of wine annually. The 1935 records show 19 kg of meat, 34 kg of fruit, and 165 liters of milk as well. Rents were high—2,916 lei per month for three rooms in 1929 and 1,595 in 1938—while clothing was cheaper on the eve of World War II than it had been ten years earlier. The cost of cloth for a man's suit had fallen from 806 to 534 lei per meter, and a pair of shoes from 766 to 605 lei.[18]

Public education also made progress after 1918, although illiteracy went down more slowly between 1920 and 1938 than between 1899 and 1914. By 1930 three-quarters of the urban population and half the rural population could read (57% of all Romanians). Literacy varied by region. In first place stood the Banat, with 72 percent literacy, then Transylvania with 67 percent, the Old Kingdom with 56 percent, and last Bessarabia, with 38 percent. Of those who could read, only 3 percent had studied at the university level; 83 percent had completed only primary school, while the remainder had attended trade or secondary schools.[19]

The Liberal governments of 1922–28 made great efforts to improve education. They almost tripled the budget, from 954 million lei in 1922 to 2.6 billion in 1926. The Education Law of 1924 increased required schooling from four to seven years, established stiff penalties for parents who did not send their children to school, set up adult literacy classes—enrolling 730,000 in 1925—and restructured teacher training institutes. The number of graduates from these institutes increased from 25,000 in 1922 to 37,000 in 1926, while primary schools increased in number from 12,000 to 23,000, secondary schools from 297 to 370, and trade schools from 174 to 344.

Higher education experienced the greatest change. In 1922 Romania had four universities (Bucharest, Iași, Cluj, Cernăuți), a business school at Cluj, a law school at Oradea, and a theological institute at Chișinău. Enrollment at these institutions grew throughout the twenties to 27,903 in the 1926–27 academic year (4,390 Jews, 509 Hungarians, 465 Germans, and the rest Romanians) and 38,869 in 1933–34. The government also allocated large sums each year for study abroad.

In this period law drew the most students (39% in 1928–29), followed by letters and philosophy (27%). The hard sciences stood in third place (17%), and smaller numbers studied medicine and pharmacology (12%), theology (6%), and veterinary medicine (1%; all percentages are rounded).[20] These figures cannot be followed in other years for want of complete statistics, but enrollment in general went down in the late thirties. The order of preference remained the same, however. Most Romanian students apparently wanted to become lawyers and magistrates, no doubt with an eye to a career in public life.

Cultural activity in the years between the wars was very different from that of the preceding period, lacking that generation's overriding concern with political nationalism. During most of the nineteenth century aesthetic values had been consciously sacrificed to the cause of nationalism, but with the advent of greater Romania intellectuals could at last turn from narrow regional concerns to universal questions. Doubts were now cast on the old values, and names once venerated no longer inspired unanimous admiration. The work of Nicolae Iorga, for example, was now contested (unjustly) by a whole new school of historians led by Constantin C. Giurescu, Gheorghe Brătianu, and Petre P. Panaitescu, which put facts and documentation before what they considered romantic interpretation. Many of the old writers, like Octavian Goga, who had been so active in the nationalist struggle before 1918 did not fit in the new world. In their place a new generation had burst forth, young, iconoclastic, unconcerned with the old ideals. Some of these, like Constantin Brâncuși in sculpture, and Ion Barbu, Ion Vinea, Ilarie Voronca, Benjamin Fundoianu (Fondane), Tudor Arghezi, and George Bacovia in poetry, engaged in innovative and aggressive Modernism. Liviu Rebreanu and Mihail Sadoveanu wrote brilliant novels. Urmuz, who died young in 1923, gave impetus to the literature of the absurd, which was later so brilliantly developed by Eugène Ionesco. The literary and artistic avant-garde, close to leftist circles in many cases, was very active.

Passionate confrontations between ideas characterized this period. Heated debates among intellectuals centered around several widely read journals—*Gândirea* (Thought), *Viața românească* (Romanian life), *Sburătorul* (The genie), *Revista fundațiilor regale* (Journal of the royal foundations)—and included themes like the relationship between traditionalism and Modernism, the problem of the national character, and the role of the Orthodox religion in Romanian society. Some declared themselves traditionalist and anti-Western. Nae Ionescu and Nichifor Crainic are probably the most notable examples of this widespread trend. Both rejected Western Modernism, trying to define a specifically Romanian mentality and to return national culture to its traditional Christian origins, which they felt had been perverted by Western materialism. Ionescu, a philosophy professor who was close to the legion, considered Orthodoxy the essence of Romanian-ness. Crainic, a journalist and poet who became minister of culture under Ion Antonescu, preached militant Orthodox mysticism, authoritarian and anti-Western, and called for a corporatist system based on "native values."

Other intellectuals avoided the anti-Western excesses of the extreme right as they sought a traditional national character. Among these was Lucian Blaga, a solid philosopher and fine poet who was also a diplomat in Warsaw, Prague, Vienna, Berne, and Lisbon. Blaga is best known for his theory of the "Mioritic space" (which he named after a folk ballad, *Miorița*), a philosophical attempt to explain the Romanian spirit through the Romanian landscape, which he saw as the stylistic matrix of Romanian culture. Several young intellectuals who gained international renown after the war also began their literary and philosophical work at this time—Eugène Ionesco, Emil Cioran, Mircea Eliade, and Constantin Noica among them. With the exception of Ionesco, who was in the 1930s an antitotalitarian literary anarchist, all of these took the anti-Western, traditionalist position of the right. The rightist intellectuals showed an overriding interest in their Dacian heritage, which many considered more significant to the development of Romanian spiritual values than the Roman—that is, Western—influence.

The thinkers on the political right certainly played an important role in Romanian culture of the period, but they accomplished less or at least less of lasting value than the adherents of Western values whom they attacked. The new school of history, for example, was less influential than Iorga, and although philosophers like Constantin Rădulescu-Motru and Ion Petrovici were probably less brilliant than Nae Ionescu, like Titu Maiorescu they shaped the thinking of a whole generation of students. Similarly Tudor Vianu, George Călinescu, and the important literary critic Eugen Lovinescu, with his Western spirit, brought back the moderation and common sense often lacking in the cultural extremism of the thirties.

Cultural development was much influenced by the appearance of intellectuals in such social sciences as political economy and sociology. Dimitrie Gusti created an original school of sociology, while Virgil Madgearu, Victor Slăvescu, Mihail Manoilescu, and Gheorghe Zane laid the foundations of modern Romanian economic thought. After 1920 a large number of research institutes were quickly established: the central institute of statistics, several institutes of Romanian and world history, an institute of chemistry, and institutes for research in economics, forestry, energy, animal husbandry, immunology, and sociology.

Greater Romania was the creation of the leaders of old Romania, who found a way to make use of international circumstances to reunite the country. Without these able politicians of the Old Kingdom, the new one could never have come into being. But greater Romania did not mean only wider boundaries and reunited provinces: it also meant a new social and political system, the passage from undemocratic liberalism to liberal democracy. The political leaders who created greater Romania were the products of nineteenth-century liberalism. In Wallachia and Moldavia there were the Brătianus and their supporters, and in Transylvania the Memorandists and Iuliu Maniu. All adhered to democracy and Western values and introduced radical reforms intended to modernize the economic, social, and political structures of the new state from the ground up.

These reforms naturally upset the social equilibrium before they could reestablish it. Agrarian reform only partially solved the problems of the peasants. Universal male suffrage, while positive in itself, brought new extremist political forces to political activism and ultimately to power. The radical reforms of 1917–23, imposed from above on a society with only limited democratic traditions and without a really modern social structure, simply did not have enough time to settle in and alleviate the complications of the postwar situation. It was also the country's misfortune that the founding generation was so soon gone. The few who remained were quickly swept away by the wave of newcomers and by international events, especially the rise of fascism. The new political generation that came after 1930 in the wake of the reforms did not at all resemble the old generation. Corruption, violence, and opportunism replaced the civility of the old political elite in Romania as elsewhere in Europe. The new people, who could not have seized power without the political liberalizations of the early twenties, and who ought to have consolidated greater Romania, actually destroyed it long before it was dismembered by the totalitarian powers. By 1938 the old dreams of Ferdinand and the Brătianus, and Maniu's fundamental democracy, were dead.

The Authoritarian Regimes

The Royal Dictatorship. With the establishment in 1938 of the first dictatorship in its history, greater Romania, or at least its basic institutions, ceased to exist. In the past legislation had often been poorly implemented, and institutions had not always functioned adequately, but their general direction had been progressive and benevolent. But now the very spirit of the law was so perverted as to impede progress and healthy development. The royal coup reversed the course of Romanian history since Tudor Vladimirescu's 1821 uprising.

Instead of elections there was now a referendum, which in the new climate required that the populace not only give its approval but do so with enthusiasm. There were 4,297,581 votes in favor of the constitution of 1938 and only 5,483 against. Formerly elections had usually been won with majorities of under 60 percent. The results of the referendum reflect how fully authoritarianism had suppressed the parliamentary spirit.

Carol II's constitution retained almost none of the democratic institutions introduced by the constitutions of Carol I (1866) and Ferdinand (1923). There was no mention of civil rights and obligations; it was forbidden, among other things, "to promote in speech or writing a change in the form of government," so that the idea of political offense was reinstated somewhat as it had appeared in Callimachi's code (1817).[21] Death was the penalty for disrupting the public order, something no previous constitution had permitted in peacetime. Carol II abolished the separation of powers, assuming both executive and legislative roles himself. The autonomy of parliament, which had often sat from early autumn until early summer, was virtually abolished. Parliament was to meet only at the king's command, "at least once a year." The 1938 constitution resembled the Organic Statutes more closely than it did the constitutions of 1848, 1866, and 1923.

The "historical" political parties were dissolved, although they retained much of their organizational structure. At first Carol had hoped to draw them into the new regime, but neither the National Liberal nor the National Peasant Party wanted to cooperate. They repeatedly protested the dictatorship and demanded a return to the parliamentary system. In the end Carol decided to form a single new party, the National Renascence Front, which public servants and all other citizens were invited to join. In January 1939, within a few weeks of its foundation, the front had 3.5 million members. It was the first party with mass membership in the history of the country, and membership in it soon became a prerequisite for social advancement.

The royal dictatorship was not, however, a fascist or Nazi regime. It was only moderately nationalistic and anti-Semitic, and citizens retained some civil rights. Rather, it was marked by a kind of monarchic missionary zeal for domestic peace and social harmony. No written program defined its principles and structure; it was cumbersome and gave an impression of improvisation and superficiality. For instance, the National Renascence Front was formed on 16 December 1938, ten months after the dictatorship was established. Its regulations were published on 5 January 1939. Regulations for the front uniform came out on 20 February and were modified on 24 November. The administration had a similarly ad hoc character. The Legislative Council was restructured eight times in 1938 and 1939, the Foreign Ministry six times, the Ministry of the National Economy five times, and the Ministry of Agriculture four. In 1939 the palace published a 278-page volume of essays for the use of the public entitled *Royal Sayings*. In it Carol offered advice to everyone from farmers to intellectuals. This "manual" can be seen as the first expression of the cult of personality in Romania.

In spite of its efforts the new regime was not supported by the other political forces. Carol called for a nationwide reconciliation to protect the country from danger from abroad, but this was never achieved, and from February 1938 to September 1940 the king and the Iron Guard were locked in a bitter power struggle that led to the deaths of hundreds of Guardists, including the entire leadership of the movement. The Guard's founder, Corneliu Zelea Codreanu, was assassinated in prison in November 1938, and Guardists responded by murdering Prime Minister Armand Călinescu, the king's strongman, in September 1939.

Pressured by Nazi Germany, the royal dictatorship tilted ever farther to the right. By spring 1939 the old system of alliances, set up with such care after 1918, had been destroyed by growing German influence and the appeasement policy of the great Western democracies. During the crisis over Czechoslovakia that dominated the first year of the new regime Carol II stood by the old alliances with remarkable tenacity. Romania upheld the Little Entente, granted Soviet aircraft permission to use Romanian air space, and refused to join in the partition of the sub-Carpathian Ukraine, just as the dictator Ion Antonescu would later refuse a share of the Yugoslav Banat (1941).

In November 1938 Carol went to London and Paris in search of more substantial support but received only empty assurances: the spirit of Munich was still strong in the West. On his way back he stopped at Berghof in Bavaria for a brief interview with Hitler, which did nothing to allay their mutual distrust. Immediately after this meeting, while he was still on the train, Carol ordered the execution of thirteen Guardists including Codreanu, further straining relations between Bucharest and Berlin. At the same time he was trying desperately to strengthen economic ties to Britain and France in order to avoid becoming an economic satellite of Germany. During fall 1938 Romanian diplomats warned London and Paris repeatedly of the danger caused by the increased German economic presence in the Balkans, but to no avail. Neville Chamberlain even told Carol that although Great Britain did not favor the idea of dividing southeast Europe into spheres of influence, it was inevitable that Germany should dominate the area economically.

After much pressure, followed by an ultimatum, Romania was forced to conclude a trade agreement with Germany in March 1939, putting the petroleum industry and the country's entire economy at the disposal of the Reich. Now Britain and France became alarmed and hastily signed trade accords with Romania, although they were too limited to be of any use. In April 1939 they also offered to guarantee Romania's independence, though not its territorial integrity. Carol accepted anyway.

When World War II broke out Romania declared itself neutral and delayed shipments of raw materials to Germany as much as possible in hopes of a quick Anglo-French victory. On the day before the war began a restricted crown council predicted the Allies would win, and just a few months earlier Prime Minister Călinescu had said, "If there should be a general war we will go with England, for that is where victory will be, and that is where public sentiment lies."[22]

The swift German offensive of May 1940 and the fall of France in June caught Bucharest by surprise, leaving the country without allies and at the mercy of Hitler and Stalin, who had agreed as early as August 1939 to divide eastern Europe into spheres of influence. On 26 June 1940 Stalin, with the Reich's agreement, took advantage of

Romanian confusion to demand that Romania immediately give up Bessarabia and northern Bucovina, to which Carol agreed on German advice. In August Romania and Bulgaria began to renegotiate the Dobrudja border, again with German approval. The Treaty of Craiova returned southern Dobrudja, annexed in 1913, to Bulgaria. Only one political party in Romania, the Communists, approved of the transfers of territory and the dismemberment of greater Romania. They had greeted the Soviet ultimatum with enthusiasm and had sent "the warm greetings of the people of Bessarabia and northern Bucovina, who have been freed from the yoke of Romanian imperialism."[23]

After the fall of France Carol hoped to save his throne, his regime, and the country's territorial integrity by quickly forming closer ties to Germany and adopting domestic measures that he thought Hitler would favor. On 1 June Romania abrogated the ineffective British and French guarantees, and on 10 July it withdrew from the League of Nations. The National Renascence Front was renamed the Nation's Party, the pro-Western prime minister Gheorghe Tătărăscu was replaced with the pro-German Ion Gigîrtu; and the Iron Guard, which had been banned and its leadership decimated, was invited to join the government. The Guard's surviving leader, Horia Sima, was made undersecretary of state in the Ministry of Public Education, and later minister of arts and religions. Anti-Semitism, moderate until now, became official policy. On 9 August a decree prohibited "marriages between those of Romanian blood and Jews," and three weeks later another decree severely limited Jews' access to all public education.[24]

But these last-minute measures could not save the royal dictatorship. Unpopular at home and viewed with suspicion in Berlin, the dictatorship broke down after Hitler's ultimate test, the Vienna Diktat (30 August 1940). Under threat of German military intervention, Romania was forced to cede northern Transylvania to Hungary, an arrangement that would allow German troops to reach the Ploieşti oilfields quickly. Faced with general hostility and the beginning of an uprising led by the Iron Guard, Carol granted General Ion Antonescu dictatorial powers and allowed him to form a new government. Within twenty-four hours Antonescu had demanded that Carol abdicate and leave the country. Mihai I, now nineteen years old, became king again, as in 1927–30, while Antonescu took the titles chief of state and president of the council of ministers.

The National Legionary State. With the Soviet ultimatum, the Vienna Diktat, and the Treaty of Craiova, greater Romania had lost 92,743

Mihai I, king of Romania (1927–30, 1940–47).

square kilometers and over six million inhabitants. Thanks to Hitler and Stalin, about three million Romanians lived outside of this lesser Romania. Immediately after the Vienna Diktat Italy and Germany guaranteed the new borders, to the annoyance of the Kremlin and the relief of Romanians, who feared the threat from the east far more than the one from central Europe.

Antonescu ruled for four years; a general, and later, after the battle of Odessa, a marshal, he preferred the title *conducător* (leader). From the first he wanted to work with the traditional parties, but both the

National Liberal and the National Peasant parties, true to their democratic principles and to their conviction that Britain would win the war, refused to be associated with the dictatorship. So Antonescu brought the Iron Guard, or legion, into the government and on 13 September 1940, declared Romania "a national legionary state." Sima was named vice prime minister, and other Guardists became foreign minister and ministers of public works, public education, labor, and religions. Other government posts went to members of the military and a few technocrats.

Inevitably misunderstandings soon arose between Antonescu and the Iron Guard. Both considered the alliance temporary and went on trying to broaden their base of support and their influence in the country. An exchange of letters between the *conducător* and his vice prime minister only a month after the establishment of the national legionary state clearly shows the conflict between the two different policies and ideologies. Antonescu, a law-and-order man whose roots were really in the old world, pro-British by conviction and pro-German only from necessity (as he had left his post as military attaché in London he had remarked that "Great Britain must always be victorious, because civilization must always be victorious over barbarism"),[25] was distressed by the radical and unprofessional Iron Guard leadership, which was ill prepared to govern. Sima reproached him for not doing away with the old world, pointing out that even in economic matters "the emphasis must be on the political element," that the society of the future could not be built by technocrats but only by "new men." The legion found Antonescu too tolerant of the old structures. He would not install a real totalitarian regime but only a political dictatorship. Sima complained that the parties were allowed to work behind the scenes, that there was no absolute monopoly on power, that the press was only partially controlled, and that the economy was still based on liberal principles. "The old world puts up formidable resistance," his accusation concluded, adding that the Guard, "the new world" that "would like to work, to establish the new order, . . . is prevented from doing so."

It is easy to understand why Antonescu viewed with mistrust the Iron Guard's experiments in governing. They were inept in economic and administrative matters. To politics they brought anarchy and total disregard for the law. And they set up a parallel government that made it almost impossible for the official administration to function. Antonescu wrote to Sima, "It is not by destroying, not by striking a new blow every day, not by blocking economic activity with foolish measures . . . not by these means that economic order can be restored." Getting rid of the non-legion technocrats and public servants would only weaken business, he continued; a government cannot run with two policies, two systems of justice, two philosophies of government, and two sets of economic and political leaders; "two heads of state cannot rule at the same time; the government must first of all be separated from the party."[26]

Antonescu himself put country before party. In separating the two he revealed a nontotalitarian outlook unacceptable to the Iron Guard, which identified nation with party. Relations between them deteriorated steadily, especially after November, when sixty-four former dignitaries and officers imprisoned at Jilava for their involvement in the assassination of Corneliu Zelea Codreanu were themselves murdered. In separate incidents Nicolae Iorga and Virgil Madgearu were also assassinated. These killings helped discredit the Iron Guard. As further offenses became daily occurrences and people were beaten, humiliated, and abused, the National Peasant Party's Iuliu Maniu wrote to Antonescu demanding that "the authority of the constituent powers be re-established in the State" and that measures be taken so that "citizens of all social categories may again be secure in their lives and property."[27]

The legionary movement emphasized the cult of personality and brought a death cult to Romanian politics. Horia Sima was presented as "chosen by God . . . the man chosen in our age to take our destiny in his hands and restore it to its place in history." Mythic qualities were attributed to him: "He arose in the very midst of the storm. His beliefs were unshaken. He never wavered for a moment . . . as resolute as a rock at the head of his forces"; "Our Horia, slight though his earthly form may be, is bigger than the mountains. He has the form of an angel and the sword of an archangel. . . . Horia is thought, Horia is feeling, Horia is our light, our will, and our strong arm."[28] This cult of personality went far beyond Carol's timid attempts and even those of the *conducător,* who though he spoke of himself only in the third person always considered himself just a soldier brought in to aid his country in its moment of need.

On 10 October 1940 Antonescu admitted German troops to Romania, and on 23 November, after brief visits with Mussolini and Hitler, he signed the Tripartite Pact. Hitler preferred the sharp, aggressive Antonescu to the undependable Sima, and after its recent excesses he did not want the Iron Guard in control in a country whose stability was important to Germany for strategic and economic reasons. The Nazis sacrificed their ideological comrades to support the Romanian military.

On 14 January 1941 Antonescu visited Hitler at Berchtesgaden, where he learned the details of Operation Barbarossa and was also given a free hand to eliminate his rivals.

Meanwhile in Bucharest the most extreme elements of the Iron Guard were forming a death squad to assassinate him, and another faction was holding talks with the leftist leader Petru Groza about a possible collaboration. On 16 January Nicolae Pătraşcu, secretary-general of the legion, warned, "There will be shooting from every window." Rallies were held and paramilitary detachments organized on 17, 18, and 19 January. The Iron Guard was apparently not aware that Hitler had already abandoned it and that the outcome of its conflict with Antonescu had already been determined at Berchtesgaden.

Antonescu began to take action against the Iron Guard as soon as he returned to Bucharest. He immediately abolished the Commission for the Romanianization of Businesses, removed Minister for Internal Affairs Constantin Petrovicescu and Police Director Alexandru Ghica, and replaced all their prefects with military personnel. The Iron Guard recognized this as a move to eliminate it and responded with street demonstrations and calls for an all-legion government. Certain of victory, they began a rebellion in Bucharest on the morning of 21 January. Barricading themselves inside the public buildings under their control and occupying the radio station and some neighborhood town halls, they engaged in armed street fighting and devastated the Jewish quarter.

During the night of 21–22 January, a legion delegation led by P. P. Panaitescu and V. Chirnoagă presented Antonescu with two main demands: that Sima appoint a government comprising Iron Guard members exclusively, and that he be made prime minister. Antonescu agreed to discuss these demands, probably to gain a little time, for he rejected them outright. At two o'clock the next afternoon he commanded the army to restore order. Within a few hours the main centers of resistance were occupied, including the legion headquarters, and by evening the rebellion was over.

Hitler telephoned Antonescu that evening to urge him to take whatever measures he liked and to offer the support of the German troops already in the country. He explained, "I don't need fanatics. . . . I need a healthy Romanian army." Antonescu refused assistance and promised that order would be restored within twenty-four hours. That same evening Hermann Neubacher, in charge of German affairs in Bucharest, and General Erik Hansen, commander of German troops in Romania, informed Sima that Hitler was supporting Antonescu, adding, "Important events are in preparation for this part of Europe that require order and peace in Romania. The Führer appeals to the legionary movement's patriotism and asks that the disturbances cease." At five the next morning Sima ordered an end to resistance.[29]

It had taken the army only a few hours to put down the rebellion, which had not spread beyond the capital, so that it was already over when the Germans intervened. Hitler's call and Neubacher and Hansen's mediation may have been intended to salvage something of the Iron Guard rather than to help Antonescu; the German army also smuggled seven hundred legion members into Germany. About eight thousand rebels were arrested and given long prison sentences. The last of them were not released until 1964. According to government figures, 416 died in the rebellion (370 in Bucharest and 46 in the provinces); 120 of these were Jews. The same records show that the Iron Guard was responsible for 73 deaths between 6 September 1940 and 20 January 1941, including those killed at Jilava. A new government composed almost entirely of generals was formed on 27 January, and on 14 February the national legionary state was abolished.

The Military Dictatorship. Antonescu came of a middle-class Wallachian family and had played an important role in the First World War as the principal author of the defense of Moldavia during the 1917 German offensive. Strongly anti-German, he had opposed the separate peace with the Central Powers and had called for resistance to the end. He was a military attaché in Paris and London and later general chief of staff (1934). Although he was a strong critic of the king's policies, Carol asked him to be minister of defense in the government headed by Octavian Goga and Alexandru C. Cuza (1937–38). He was critical of the king's policies and was arrested briefly in July 1940, but after the loss of northern Transylvania Carol appointed him once more on the advice of Iuliu Maniu and Constantin I. C. Brătianu. But Antonescu was primarily a good soldier; his political abilities were never adequate. He was not a Nazi, a fascist, or even pro-German, but as a soldier he came to expect a German victory. To regain Bessarabia, and in the naive belief that Hitler would reward him with the return of northern Transylvania, he led Romania into a war in which it had much to lose. He never missed an opportunity to remind the Führer that the Vienna Diktat was unjust and that he was awaiting its repeal. Hitler kept him hoping that the borders would be redrawn after the final victory, just as he kept Hungary's regent Miklós Horthy, hoping that *his* country's borders would remain unchanged.

Ion Antonescu, prime minister of Romania (1940–44).

Antonescu ordered Romanian troops across the Prut River (22 June 1941) on his own initiative, without consulting any of the national leaders and without any treaty or convention with Germany to establish the conditions and limits of the collaboration. By 27 July, when Bessarabia and northern Bucovina had been liberated after heavy fighting, he had to decide whether to fight on beyond the Dniester, which Hitler had not requested, or to halt his army on the restored border. Unlike the Finnish commander Baron Carl Gustav Emil Mannerheim, who stopped after retaking Karelia, Antonescu continued his offensive into the Soviet Union along with the German army "to preserve faith, order, civilization." On 6 August Hitler gave Romania the administration of the territory between the Dniester and Dnieper Rivers ("Transnistria"), and on 15 October Romanian troops took Odessa with great losses. They continued to serve as part of the German advance, fighting beside the Wehrmacht in the battles for the Crimea (1941–42), Stalingrad, the Caucasus (1942–43), and the Kuban (1943), and then again in the defense of the Crimea (1943–44).

The retaking of Bessarabia and northern Bucovina had been popular with most Romanians, but the continued fighting beyond the Dniester was viewed with hostility. King Mihai was firmly against it, as were the chief of staff, Ion Iacobici, and other generals. Maniu protested in strong terms, "The Romanian armies should not invade territories that have never belonged to them. . . . It is inadmissible for us to present ourselves as aggressors against Russia, which is now allied with England . . . it is inadmissible for us to link our fate with the Axis in a war of aggression and conquest." Maniu's demands that the army withdraw from the Soviet Union (as in his memorandum of January 1942) so infuriated Hitler that he asked Antonescu why he tolerated a man who "consciously works to weaken resistance on the domestic front."[30]

The eastern campaign complicated Romania's relations with Britain and the United States, and although Antonescu maintained, "I am an ally of the Reich against Russia, I am neutral in the conflict between Great Britain and Germany. I am for America against the Japanese" (December 1941),[31] nonetheless, at the request of the Soviet Union, Britain sent Romania an ultimatum (1 December 1941) as it had to Finland, demanding that troops be withdrawn behind the Dniester within five days. When Antonescu did not comply, Britain declared war on Romania (7 December 1941). Romania declared war on the United States in December 1941, but there was no response until June 1942, and when it did reply the United States noted that Romanian participation in the war was not of its own free will but under German coercion and control.

National Liberal and National Peasant party opposition had been in contact with the British Middle Eastern command since summer 1941 by means of a radio transmitter the British legation had left behind when it fled Bucharest. Early in 1942 Maniu informed Britain and the United States of his wish to stage a coup d'état and have the army fight against Germany—if the Allies would recognize Romania as an independent country, guarantee its borders, and send an expeditionary force to the Balkans. In the spring Britain tried to draw the Kremlin into these discussions, but even when Maniu indicated his willingness to drop the demand for pre–World War II borders between Romania and the Soviet Union, Stalin showed no interest. The opposition parties communicated through Swiss and Turkish diplomats in Bucharest and through Eduard Beneš and his Czechoslovak government-in-exile in England.

One British plan to launch an offensive on central Europe through Yugoslavia was firmly rejected by the United States (January 1943), and Britain now insisted that Romania could not enter into any peace negotiations without Soviet participation. Anthony Eden declared in March 1943, "Our policy towards Roumania is subordinated to our relations with the Soviet Union and we are . . . unwilling to accept any commitments or to take any action except with the full cognizance and consent of the Soviet Government." As a result of change in the Soviet attitude, the British agreed to meet with Maniu. As the Soviet foreign minister said to Eden, Maniu represented "the only serious opposition in Romania." A few months later, in an apparent effort to console Romania for the Soviet reannexation of Bessarabia, Vyacheslav Molotov told Beneš that the Transylvanian problem "was not resolved in a way that is just for Romanians."

Within Romania there were growing signs of opposition to the war. On 1 January 1943 Mihai told the diplomatic corps assembled to wish him a happy new year that he hoped for a "peace based on justice, liberty, and understanding." Even Antonescu revealed uneasiness and some doubts at this time, and in October 1942, after having vainly opposed the planned attack on Stalingrad, he made the astonishing observation, "Germany has lost the war. Now we must take care . . . that we don't lose ours."[32] Antonescu's new outlook was no doubt related to the cautious inquiries into how Romania might withdraw from the war, which Foreign Minister Mihai Antonescu (no relation to the *conducător*) had been making in Italy, Spain, Portugal, and Switzerland, and by Alexandru Cretzianu, the new ambassador to Ankara. Initially Mihai Antonescu had hoped to be able to act as mediator between Britain and Germany, but this plan, which he sent to the German foreign minister, Joachim von Ribbentrop, so enraged Hitler that the idea was quickly dropped. The Romanians were left to act on their own account, behind the backs of their German allies.

The principal negotiations were conducted at Ankara (September 1943–March 1944), Stockholm (November 1943–June 1944), and Cairo (March–June 1944), in the names of both Marshal Antonescu and the opposition parties. Maniu and Brătianu repeatedly asked that Romania

be permitted to surrender to the western Allies only, while Britain insisted on an unconditional surrender, to which the Soviet Union would
also be party. Antonescu, although never seriously interested in real
negotiations on these terms, had told Maniu as early as the end of 1943
that he was willing to retire if that would ensure better armistice conditions. To secure those conditions Prince Barbu Ştirbei, a former
prime minister and a brother-in-law of Ion I. C. Brătianu, was sent to
Cairo in March 1944.

Meanwhile the military situation had changed radically. The Red
Army had retaken northern Bessarabia and had reached the Prut River
(March 1944). On 2 April the wily Molotov declared that the Soviets
had no intention of altering Romania's social or political system nor any
designs on Romanian territory, and on 12 April, in Cairo, Ambassador Nikolai V. Novikov presented Prince Ştirbei with a proposed
armistice convention. Romania would cease hostilities, change sides,
accept the June 1940 borders, pay reparations, and release and repa-
triate prisoners of war. At the same time the Soviet Union declared the
Vienna Diktat unjust and promised assistance in liberating northern
Transylvania. Antonescu rejected these conditions on 15 May, but after
some hesitation the Liberal Party and Peasant Party representatives
accepted all the Allies' terms on 10 June. The Allies were informed
that King Mihai would take the necessary steps to overthrow the government and change sides.

But the Allies never responded. The Red Army had marched into
northern Moldavia in May, occupying Suceava, Rădăuţi, and Botoşani,
and it not longer showed much interest in peace talks. Britain and the
United States, busy with their plans for the Normandy invasion, had
abandoned the idea of landing in the Balkans. Britain had proposed
to the Soviet Union that Europe be divided into spheres of influence,
with Romania under Soviet care and Greece in British hands. In June,
after some objections, the United States agreed to this arrangement on
condition that it last only three months. Under these conditions, with
no restraints and with victory in sight, it is hardly surprising that the
Soviets ignored the earlier peace talks with Romania.

On the advice of London, Maniu and Brătianu decided to include a
representative of the Communist Party in their negotiations with Moscow. In June, with Mihai's knowledge, the National Liberal and National Peasant parties joined with the Social Democratic and Communist parties to found the Democratic Parties Bloc, which immediately
accepted the Allies' conditions—switching sides, overthrowing Antonescu, and establishing a democratic government. But with no military

organization of their own they had no way to bring this about. Only the young king, in his role as supreme commander, could attempt that. Mihai had often shown himself openly hostile to the *conducător*, and with the promise of the dictator's removal the king began detailed preparations. Anxious to make peace before the Red Army marched any farther into Moldavia, Mihai had already approached the commanders of several large active units in May. These had promised him their loyalty but advised him to wait for the withdrawal of some motorized German troops that were due to be sent to Poland. Representatives of the palace, the army, and the political parties met on the night of 13–14 June 1944 to form a joint plan.

Two more months were wasted waiting for the Allies to accept the proposed armistice and deciding whether to take action. But when the Soviets launched a new offensive on 20 August only two possible solutions remained: either to withdraw from the war at once, or to be occupied by the Red Army, which by the evening of 22 August had reached the line formed by Tîrgu-Neamţ, Huşi, and Chişinău. On 5 August and again on 22 August Antonescu unconvincingly stated his agreement "in principle" to a truce (apparently to gain time, for he was putting his faith in the atomic bomb Hitler had told him of at their recent meeting in East Prussia).

But now Mihai at last took the initiative. On 22 August Antonescu returned from the front, where the German general Hans Friessner promised continued resistance on the Focşani-Galaţi line. He met that evening with Ion Mihalache of the National Peasant Party and the next morning with Gheorghe Brătianu of the National Liberal Party, and finally agreed to resign if the leaders of the two parties would state in writing that they approved the terms of the armistice. Summoned to meet with the king that afternoon, Antonescu accepted only when Brătianu had promised to bring the signed statement immediately (in fact it was never delivered). At the palace preparations were complete for a coup d'état in case Antonescu should refuse to sign the armistice. When he arrived at five o'clock, he still insisted that with the Focşani-Galaţi line holding there was hope for better terms. In the end Mihai ordered Antonescu arrested, along with his foreign minister and the other principal ministers. At ten o'clock on the evening of 23 August Mihai's proclamation of the end of the Antonescu regime was broadcast throughout the country, and Romanian troops were ordered to stop fighting and to retreat south of the Focşani-Galaţi line as quickly as possible. The Red Army seized this opportunity to take prisoner some

130,000 Romanian soldiers and officers, who were at once deported to the Soviet Union.

On the morning of 24 August, having appointed General Constantin Sănătescu to head a government composed almost exclusively of military personnel, Mihai went to northern Oltenia to avoid being taken prisoner by the Germans. He returned to the capital on 10 September. Fearing that the Germans might attack the palace to free Antonescu, Sănătescu handed over both Marshal Antonescu and Mihai Antonescu to representatives of the Communist Party as soon as the king had left. When the Russians entered Bucharest at the end of August, the former dictator was deported to the Soviet Union. He was returned in 1946 for trial and execution.

Romanian Marxist historians have never acknowledged that the Holocaust reached Romania and that the first great pogrom after the outbreak of war took place in June 1941 in Iaşi.[33] Russian and Bessarabian Jews were among the victims of summary executions when Romania seized Bessarabia and marched into Transnistria—a territory that acquired an ugly reputation for receiving, until June 1942, some 150,000 Jews deported in inhuman conditions.[34] Much of the Jewish population of Bessarabia and Bucovina was affected, though in the Old Kingdom almost all Jews survived. At first Antonescu ordered the synagogues closed, but he soon rescinded his decision. In September 1940, pressed by Gustav Richter, Adolf Eichmann's representative in Romania, he ordered the wearing of yellow stars, but a few months later withdrew that decree at the urging of Patriarch Nicodim and others. In summer 1942 Antonescu promised the Germans that all Romanian Jews would be deported to the extermination camps in Poland, but he annulled the deportation order at the insistence of Mihai, Maniu, and the Orthodox hierarchy. Jewish high schools remained open throughout the war in the major cities, and in Bucharest a Jewish theater (the Baraşeum) and an orchestra continued to function.

At the end of 1942, the government acceded to the request of Zionist organizations and the Jewish Agency for Palestine in Bucharest to facilitate Jewish emigration to Palestine. Bucharest became a kind of conduit for Jewish emigration to Palestine from Slovakia, Hungary, northern Transylvania, and Poland.[35] At the war's end the official records showed 355,972 Jews living in Romania.[36]

Hacha or Mannerheim? Aware of his tenuous position, the *conducător* himself had asked this question in January 1941—would his role be to give up, like the president of Czechoslovakia, Hacha, or to walk a fine line between Germany and the Soviet Union, as the Finnish marshal did? Neither Hacha nor Mannerheim, he concluded, but Antonescu. At the end of his nearly four years in power he would probably have reconsidered that confident answer.

From Authoritarianism to Totalitarianism

The International Context. King Mihai had asked that the German army withdraw peaceably from Romania, and General Alfred Gerstenberg, commander of the German aviation mission in Romania, had agreed, but Hitler ordered the "traitors" liquidated. On 24 August 1944 German troops and aircraft stationed in the area attacked Bucharest, causing great damage. The new government responded from its temporary headquarters in the basement of the National Bank by declaring war on Germany and calling on the Allies to bomb the German troops concentrated at Băneasa on the outskirts of the capital. The Allies complied on 26 August, and this, together with the resistance of Romanian troops, put an end to the attack. Several thousand Germans surrendered in the capital that day, and when the Red Army marched into Bucharest on 31 August there were no German soldiers left in the city.

As soon as Romania changed sides, Nikolai V. Novikov, Soviet ambassador to Cairo, communicated with the government confirming the armistice conditions that had been proposed in April, with the additions agreed upon in Stockholm, including a free zone where the Romanian government could operate—a necessary condition for a truly independent state. But the provisions of the April draft soon fell victim to the rapidly changing international situation.

At the Kremlin's request the western Allies agreed that the armistice should be signed in Moscow rather than Cairo, and that the signatories should be Romania and, in the name of all the Allied powers, the Soviet Union alone. The Romanian delegation (Barbu Ştirbei, Constantin Vişoianu, Lucreţiu Pătrăşcanu, Gheorghe Pop, and Dumitru Dămăceanu) arrived in Moscow on 4 September, but Soviet Foreign Minister Vyacheslav Molotov did not receive them until 10 September, by which time the Red Army was in complete control of Romania, and the new convention for the armistice had already been drawn up. Not one of the Romanian requests appeared in this final form, which was very different from the Cairo draft formulated just a few months earlier. While the United States and Britain stood aside, the Soviets withdrew their promise of an unoccupied zone. Romania was required to support the army of occupation and pay war reparations worth 300 million dollars within six years. The Romanians asked that provision be made for the evacuation of troops after the end of the war, but Molotov refused, and Averell Harriman, United States ambassador to the Soviet Union, advised the delegation not to insist, saying there could be no doubt that the Soviet troops would then withdraw from Romania. Romania was also refused cobelligerent status, although the armistice allowed twelve Romanian divisions to take part in the fighting. These twelve became twenty in fact, and between August 1944 and May 1945 there were nearly 170,000 Romanian casualties in Transylvania, Hungary, and Czechoslovakia. (Altogether about half a million Romanian troops were killed, wounded, or missing in the war.)

The Allied Control Commission formed to oversee the armistice was entirely Soviet-dominated. Its American and British members did not even have the right to travel freely in Romania without the permission of the Soviet authorities. Harriman said immediately after the signing that he would give the Russians "unlimited control of Romania's economic life" and "police power for the period of the armistice."[37]

Was Romania deliberately abandoned to the Soviets? From the time it became clear that the United States would not agree to an invasion through the Balkans for military considerations, Britain had pragmatically granted Moscow a dominant role in Romania. In October 1944, when the Red Army had occupied Bulgaria and reached the Greek border so that the whole peninsula was in danger of falling to the Russians, Winston Churchill made his famous percentages proposal to Joseph Stalin, dividing the Balkans into spheres of influence. Ninety percent of Romania was to go to the Soviet Union, 50 percent of Yugoslavia, and 10 percent of Greece. The remainder would be for Britain and "the others." Britain intended this agreement to be temporary. The fate of all southeastern Europe would be decided at a peace conference.[38]

The percentages agreement was not known or even guessed at in Bucharest, nor was any Romanian privy to the 1944 discussions between Stalin and Tito, in which Stalin said, "This war is not like those in the past: whoever occupies a territory imposes his own social system on it."[39] Romania had great hopes for American and British mediation at Yalta (February 1945), but the vague "Declaration on liberated Europe" issued by the conference proved to be no obstacle to Soviet expansion. Only a month later, when Molotov's deputy Andrei I. Vyshinsky visited Bucharest to oversee the appointment of Petru Groza, the prime minister chosen by Moscow, he answered the king's objections with, "Yalta— I am Yalta." Together with the occupation of Poland, the brutal trampling of constitutional rights in Romania finally opened the eyes of leaders in the West, especially Franklin Roosevelt's, to Soviet policy. On 9 August 1945 his successor, Harry Truman, said of Romania, Hungary, and Bulgaria, "These nations are not to be spheres of influence of any power."[40]

This wish did not come true. Soviet aims were clearly understood in London and Washington, but the West was anxious to avoid confrontation and had limited means to stop the continual slide of eastern Europe, including Romania, into Soviet control. After hesitating for eleven months they finally recognized the Groza government in spite of the abusive way it had been imposed. On 10 February 1947 they signed the Treaty of Paris with Romania. The treaty not only imposed even harsher conditions than those in the armistice convention, but also legalized the Soviet military presence on Romanian territory without any stated term of withdrawal.

The Communist Takeover. The same tactics were used in Romania as in other eastern European countries. The Communist Party at first supported a coalition government, then gradually increased its influence until, with direct Soviet pressure and intimidation, it drove out all others and was left in total control. Empty promises of reform bought the party some popular support among both peasants and workers, but in any case the Communists met with only limited resistance from their disoriented and divided opposition.

Among the old political parties in the Romanian coalition, the liberals and the social democrats were the first to be jettisoned, largely because of their weak leadership and the factionalism that had virtually neutralized them. The National Liberal Party had split in autumn 1944 when Gheorghe Tătărăscu, the former prime minister, was elected president of a new National Liberal Party. The old one continued under the leadership of Constantin "Dinu" I. C. Brătianu. Tătărăscu joined the Groza government in March 1945 as vice premier and foreign minister in hopes that he could temper Communist extremism and introduce some points from the liberal program. For instance, in July 1945 he stated that his party favored a parliamentary monarchy and opposed the nationalization of industry and the expropriation of agricultural land. But this attitude only contributed to the disintegration of the opposition without saving Tătărăscu or his party, and on 6 November 1947, when the Communist Party no longer had need of its fellow travelers, his party was unceremoniously dropped from the government. The old National Liberal Party voluntarily suspended activities in summer 1947, but Dinu Brătianu was nevertheless arrested, although not until 1950. He died at the age of eighty-three after months of harsh imprisonment.

Like Tătărăscu, the social democrats hoped to moderate the Communists' stance by playing along with them. When the Communist ministers brought down General Constantin Sănătescu's government by resigning in a body (16 October 1944), the social democrat Titel Petrescu followed their example. Later he agreed to even closer ties between the social democrats and the Communist Party. The Communists profited by infiltrating and finally splitting his party (March 1946). Petrescu's supporters immediately formed a new Social Democratic Party, called "Independent," but they never had any real power or influence, and Petrescu shared the fate of all the non-Communist leaders of old Romania: arrest, imprisonment (1948–55), and premature death (1957).

The only political party that was not undermined from within was the National Peasant Party, which explains the particular determination with which the Communists fought them and killed off most of their leaders. On 16 October 1944 the National Peasant Party unveiled its reform program, which followed, in broad terms, the one adopted in 1935: expropriating rural properties larger than fifty hectares—a demand first made by Ion Mihalache in 1920; nationalizing first heavy industry and then other industry to create a state-supervised economic sector; and establishing agricultural cooperatives and industrialization based on domestically produced raw materials. Because the new platform was more radical than the 1935 program, the party received greater mass support. Its real mistake, for which President Iuliu Maniu was largely responsible, was the failure to take power when King Mihai offered it in August 1944. This deprived the country of the only leadership that could have been strong and popular, the only party that could have rallied the people around a truly democratic program. In refusing to take over in 1944, Maniu showed the same indecisiveness as he had in 1930, 1937–38, and 1940. But this time it caused a power vacuum into which the Communist Party moved.

Protected by the Red Army and aided by some very effective propaganda, fed by the hopes of some and the opportunism of others, the Communist Party's ranks grew steadily. They were swelled first by the minority communities—Hungarians, Jews, and others—who had suffered real or imagined persecution and who now considered it their turn to play an important role in politics. The ethnic composition of the party leadership, and of rank and file as well, was for many years predominantly non-Romanian, in spite of the fact that former legion

Ana Pauker, Communist leader.

members were also admitted by a special arrangement made between
the Communist leader Ana Pauker and the former secretary-general
of the Iron Guard, Nicolae Pătraşcu. In absolute terms, the party grew
from less than a thousand members in 1944 to 35,800 in March 1945,
then 256,863 in October 1945, 717,490 in June 1946, and 803,831 in
December 1947. The troika (Constantin Pârvulescu, Iosif Rangheţ, and
Emil Bodnăraş) that had replaced First Secretary István Fóris in April
1944 was itself replaced in autumn 1947 by a foursome: Ana Pauker,
Vasile Luca, Teohari Georgescu, and Gheorghe Gheorghiu-Dej.

For strategic reasons Moscow pushed Gheorghiu-Dej to the fore, and
he was elected first secretary in October 1945. But the real power in
the party remained in the hands of the "Muscovites"—Pauker, Luca,
and Bodnăraş, together with Iosif Chişinevski and Leonte Răutu. All
of these had spent years in the Soviet Union. The domestic contingent

Foreground, left to right: Communist leaders Vasile Luca, Teohari Georgescu, Emil Bodnăraş.

of Gheorghiu-Dej, Lucreţiu Pătrăşcanu, Chivu Stoica, and Gheorghe Apostol found less favor in Stalin's eyes. This was no accident, for both Gheorghiu-Dej and Pătrăşcanu had made statements that aroused Moscow's suspicions. Gheorghiu-Dej had published a pamphlet, *O politică românească* (A Romanian policy [1944])—whose very title was suspect for a Communist of the time—while Pătrăşcanu had declared that he considered himself a Romanian first, and a Communist second. Gheorghiu-Dej seems to have quickly realized that he had made a tactical error. After 1945 he toed the Stalinist line, avoiding complications and gaining room to maneuver against the Moscow faction until at last he emerged victorious. Pătrăşcanu was less adaptable, and he became less and less influential until in 1948 he was dropped from the party leadership.

The Communist Party had started on its road to power when the Antonescu regime was overthrown and Maniu passed up the opportunity to form a coalition government. King Mihai had no choice but to appoint Sănătescu prime minister, and Pătrăşcanu was made minister of justice, an important position that enabled him to begin purging the army and the government of non-Communists as early as September 1944. The so-called People's Tribunals also began to function in September. Created to try war criminals, these were useful instruments for disposing of any and all opponents.

The Sănătescu administration had the task of running the country under completely unnatural conditions, and it lasted only two months. The constitution of 1923 was again in effect, though in name only. Moldavia, for example, was administered directly by the Soviet army, which had installed its own local officials. Soviet censorship was instituted in the whole country on 12 September. Nothing could be published without advance approval of the military authorities. On 12 October the Communist and Social Democratic parties withdrew from the Democratic Parties Bloc to form, together with other leftist groups, the National Democratic Front, and four days later the Communist ministers brought down the government by resigning. They had hoped to seize power immediately, and indeed, although the new government was again formed by Sănătescu, the participation of the Communists and their collaborators was broadened, and they were given key positions. Petru Groza became vice prime minister, Teohari Georgescu deputy minister of the interior, Gheorghe Gheorghiu-Dej minister of communications, and the socialist Ştefan Voitec minister of education. Pătrăşcanu remained minister of justice.

The reorganization of the government did not end public unrest, which rather increased, and the second Sănătescu regime lasted only seven weeks. King Mihai refused to appoint another prime minister from the National Democratic Front, and instead named General Nicolae Rădescu, a well-known anti-fascist who had spent two years in a concentration camp. But even he was not permitted to operate normally. On 13 November, on the pretext of maintaining order, the Soviet Union took over direct administration of northern Transylvania and increased pressure on the king. In January 1945 the Soviets began to deport Saxons and Swabians from Transylvania to the Soviet Union. And in February Communist demonstrations calling for a National Democratic Front government reached a new high. Stubbornly Rădescu dismissed Georgescu from the Ministry of the Interior and declared that he would stop at nothing, even civil war, to establish order. Certainly he could not have won such a war, with a million Soviet soldiers in the country. Then on 26 February Andrei I. Vyshinsky arrived unexpectedly in Bucharest to tell the king that Rădescu must go, and that Groza was the only replacement acceptable to Moscow.

Mihai opposed this heavy-handed Soviet interference in Romanian domestic affairs and turned to the West for diplomatic support, but Britain and the United States informed him that the Yalta Declaration would not go into effect until the war had ended. Meanwhile Vyshinsky kept up the pressure by pounding tables, slamming doors, bringing

Soviet tanks out on the streets of Bucharest, and finally threatening an end to the independent state of Romania, until on 6 March, with Maniu and Gheorghe Brătianu still advising him to resist, Mihai gave in. He thought that at least he would have some control over the Communist government, but that was an illusion.

The administration of northern Transylvania was returned to Romania, as the king wished, but the policies of the Groza government, which was made up exclusively of members of the National Democratic Front and Tătărăscu's National Liberal Party, led to the rapid implementation of Communist policies. An agrarian reform measure directed against landowners and rich peasants was adopted on 23 March, and a purge of government employees began a week later. A detention camp for political prisoners was set up at Caracal. At first it was filled with legion members, but later with anyone opposing the regime, and the activity of the People's Tribunals intensified. In summer 1945 the first joint Soviet-Romanian companies (Sovroms) appeared. Through them Romania's economic resources were siphoned off to the Soviet Union.

In view of all this Mihai called on the Groza government to resign so that he could replace it with a representative one. Britain and the United States had not yet recognized the Groza administration precisely because it represented only the Communists and their allies, not the majority of the population. In June Truman informed Stalin that the United States would not sign a peace treaty with Romania and Bulgaria, since they were ruled by governments "which do not accord to all democratic elements of the people any rights of free expression, and which in their system of administration are, in my opinion, neither representative of nor responsive to the will of the people."[41] The British government issued a similar statement.

Groza refused to resign—which was illegal, since it was the king's constitutional right to appoint and dismiss the prime minister—and in August Mihai went "on strike," refusing to sign the decrees and laws forwarded for his approval. The government continued its activities unabated, however, without regard for legal or constitutional niceties, knowing that it was protected by the occupying army and by Moscow. This situation caused widespread resentment, and on 8 November 1945, the king's birthday, clashes between some 50,000 anti-Communist demonstrators and Communists with police support left eleven dead, hundreds injured, and even more arrested.

While Mihai remained on strike and a strained atmosphere pervaded Romania, and while Britain and the United States continued to refuse to recognize or treat with the Groza government, the Allied foreign ministers met in Moscow to discuss the problem (December 1945). Their solution, delivered to Bucharest by Vyshinsky and the American and British ambassadors to Moscow, Averell Harriman and Archibald Clark Kerr, was this: two posts of minister without portfolio were created for one member of Dinu Brătianu's National Liberal Party and one member of Maniu's National Peasant Party; and the prime minister was made to promise that all the democratic rights demanded by the West would be granted and free elections held. In vain did Mihai warn the Western ambassadors, "But what is the use of pressing for elections when the county is in the hands of these people? . . . Unless you supervise the whole business with observers throughout the country, the lists and voting will be falsified and the government will get a large, faked majority which will merely strengthen the Communist grip."[42] The British told Mihai that they "did not wish to give any advice or encouragement . . . since they would be unable to protect the king and opposition leaders from the consequences."[43] The United States too recommended moderation, a spirit of collaboration, and trust in the Groza government. Mihai gave in, the two ministers without portfolio and also without power took their places in the cabinet, and the Allies, satisfied that they had resolved the crisis, recognized the Groza government (4 February 1946).

Now that it was officially recognized, the regime at once took steps to remove all opposition to a Communist Romania. These included the trial (May 1946) and execution (June) of Marshal Ion Antonescu, the passage of a new electoral law, the reduction of the parliament to a unicameral body (July), and the trial of fifty-six so-called war criminals (November), including General Alexandru Aldea, one of the organizers of the August 1944 coup against Antonescu.

Meanwhile preparations were made for parliamentary elections in an atmosphere of fear and coercion. They were held on 19 November 1946, and the National Democratic Front won with 80 percent of the vote, although all the Western observers recorded that at least three-quarters of the votes were cast for the opposition parties. Both the United States Department of State and the British Foreign Office issued protests declaring that the elections had been falsified and that the results did not represent the true wishes of the Romanians. But both countries went ahead and signed the Treaty of Paris, renewing the previous year's endorsement of the Romanian administration and of the parliament that they themselves had declared unrepresentative. With the treaty concluded, the Allied Control Commission, one of the last obstacles in the Communists' path to power, was removed. In July the leaders of the National Peasant Party were arrested and the party dissolved, and the National Liberal Party, whose youth organization had actively helped to organize the massive anti-Communist demonstration of 8 November 1945, prudently suspended operations. That did not, however, prevent their members' being arrested as well and spending many years in prison. As for the social democrats, they had already been neutralized by the split of March 1946, and were heading for "union" with the Communist Party, which took place in February 1948. At the end of October 1947 Gheorghe Tătărăscu and his faction of the Liberal Party were dropped from the government, and a few days later Iuliu Maniu, then seventy-five, was condemned to life imprisonment, as was his vice president, Ion Mihalache. The People's Democracy of Romania was established just one month later.

The People's Democracy. With its great social inequities, Romania provided fertile ground for a radical ideology that promised an end to class differences and the coming of a golden age. At a national conference in October 1945 the Communist Party adopted an ambitious modernization program, including accelerated development of heavy industry, nationwide electrification, and extensive agrarian reform, including encouragement for the formation of agricultural cooperatives. Gheorghiu-Dej, now first secretary, prudently did not mention collectivization in his report. Instead he spoke of bolstering private enterprise in all domains and permitting foreign investment in industry. It is not surprising that the program attracted general interest, for it promised everything, without revealing that most of the gains of the early reforms—appropriation of land in particular—would be taken away by later measures.

Agrarian reform came about in response to pressure from the peasants, whose hunger for land was sharpened by Communist calls for the immediate breakup of the remaining large estates. Before the agrarian reform was adopted in 1946, 19 percent of farmland was in parcels of over 50 hectares, 21 percent in 10–50 hectare plots, 24 percent in 5–10 hectare plots, and 36 percent in plots smaller than five hectares. The new law, under which 1,468,000 hectares were expropriated, limited ownership of rural property to fifty hectares and thus affected less than a fifth of the farmland, much less than the 1921 reform. The immediate result was that no great properties remained: now 76 percent of the farmland was in plots smaller than five hectares. Those who benefited from this reform became supporters of the Groza regime, little knowing that in only a few years the party would begin the drive for collectivization.

Having "won" the November 1946 elections, the Communist Party went on to adopt measures that would limit the economic power of the middle class. The National Bank was nationalized, monetary reform was initiated by the Soviet economist Evgenii V. Varga, and industrial commissions were created to set production plans and prices and to allocate raw materials. In November 1947 Gheorghiu-Dej replaced Petre Bejan, a Liberal Party collaborator, as minister of the national economy. With that, almost all the party's objectives had been reached. The one thing standing in the way of the People's Democracy was the monarchy.

On 12 November, a day after Maniu was sentenced, Mihai left for London to attend the wedding of Princess Elizabeth. No doubt he hoped for some good advice there, too. The government approved his trip in the belief that he might not return. That was indeed what most American and British politicians advised Mihai in London; only Churchill urged him to go where duty called, whatever the risks. Mihai had always considered the constitutional monarchy to be his duty, and now he returned to it, to find that the takeover had progressed considerably. Ana Pauker was now foreign minister, Emil Bodnăraş had been appointed minister of defense, and Tito had visited Bucharest. Even so, when Groza and Gheorghiu-Dej requested an audience on the morning of 30 December, Mihai did not guess that they would ask him to abdicate. They were very polite, but they had troops surrounding the palace. Isolated, with only a small loyal group to advise him, Mihai thought for a few hours and then signed the abdication statement that had been presented to him. Romania was declared a People's Democracy the same day. On 3 January 1948 the former king, aged twenty-six, left Peleş Palace in Sinaia for Switzerland.

CHAPTER SIX

Communism in Romania
(1948–83)

From Stalinism to Détente at Home and Abroad

The Stalinist Model: Economy, Politics, Culture. The Communist Party embraced the principles of Stalinist economics as early as October 1945, at the National Conference of the Romanian Communist Party (RCP), but they could not be applied until the monarchy had fallen and the party was in power. Once this had happened Stalinist principles were quickly put into practice: 1,060 companies were nationalized in June 1948. These represented 90 percent of national production and included mining and industry as well as banks and insurance companies. In November health institutions, film companies, and movie theaters were nationalized; in April 1949 pharmacies, laboratories, and chemical companies followed; and in April 1950 some housing was also affected. By the end of the fifties doctors' offices, restaurants, taxis, and small shops were state owned. The first one-year plan came out in 1948 and the second in 1950, after which came the first five-year plan (1951–55).

Vlad Georgescu was unable to revise and update this chapter for the English translation. The present version is based on the text of the Romanian edition of his *Istoria românilor de la origini pînă în zilele noastre* (Los Angeles, 1984), without the benefit of the author's subsequent improvements and without the endnotes that he added to the other chapters. For the interested reader, the lack of notes to this chapter is made up for, at least in part, by the section "Communism in Romania" in the bibliographical essay at the end of the volume, which was revised and updated by Georgescu in 1988. As explained in the preface, Georgescu intended to write a new chapter about Romania in the 1980s, which was to be based on his essay (published here as chapter 7) "Romania in the Mid-1980s." This chapter, together with the "Epilogue: The 1989 Revolution and the Collapse of Communism in Romania," written by Matei Calinescu and Vladimir Tismăneanu especially for this volume, will, we hope, answer questions about contemporary Romania—including bibliographical ones—left unanswered by "Communism in Romania (1948–83)."—ED.

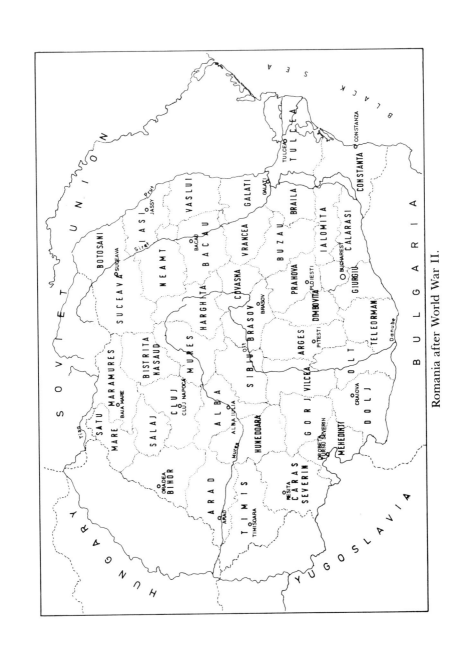

Romania after World War II.

In 1949 agricultural collectivization was begun, a measure that took thirteen years to complete. The first four years were particularly hard on the peasants. According to figures later released by the party, 80,000 peasants were arrested for resisting collectivization. The actual numbers were doubtless much higher. In addition to this direct repression, the regime employed indirect means to induce the villagers to form farming associations, where privately owned land was worked cooperatively, or collective farms. For example, in 1951 the government set quotas of goods that peasants were constrained to sell to the state at very low prices. These amounted to between 20 and 60 percent of peasant production—less for the poorer peasants and more for the middle-level peasants and the wealthy peasants, or kulaks.

In spite of constant pressure, agricultural collectivization proceeded slowly. When the plenary session of March 1949 resolved to accelerate it, there were only 55 collective farms in the whole country. The number grew to 1,070 in 1951 and to 1,980 by 1953, but in that year 92 percent of all peasant farms were still privately owned. In 1953 agricultural production finally reached its 1938 level, after which it fluctuated (1953, 101% of 1938 production; 1954, 98%; 1955, 119%; 1956, 89%). The government had expected to receive great profits from agriculture without investing much in modernizing it, and the figures reflect the problems of such an approach. Agriculture was allocated only 9 percent of all investment in 1949, 7 percent in 1950, and 7.5 percent in 1953. In 1956, fearing an uprising like those in Poland and Hungary, the government lowered its economic ambitions, reduced the planned rate of industrial growth from 10–12 percent in 1956 to 4 percent in 1957, and did away with the obligatory quotas on wheat, potatoes, sunflower seed, and milk.

The new approach brought stability and consolidation to the Communist Party, but it lasted only until 1958, when the Stalinist economic model was applied even more rigorously than before in both agriculture and industry. At the plenary session of November 1958 the Central Committee pronounced the country ready for a general effort at socialist modernization, with primary emphasis on developing the machine-tool and steel industries. The six-year plan of 1960–65 provided for 78 percent of all investment to go into heavy industry and energy.

The change of direction mandated by the plenary session of November 1958 ended the peasants' breathing spell. In 1958 collective farms accounted for less than 18 percent of land under cultivation, but only four years later, in 1962, the figure had soared to 96 percent, and collectivization was nearly complete. Both total production and pro-

duction per hectare were disappointing, however. Net agricultural production was only 110 percent of 1938 production in 1962 and 123
percent in 1965.

There was, however, clear economic progress. The percentage of
Romania's population living in the cities rose from 23 percent in 1948
to 39 percent in 1966, while the rural population fell from 77 percent
of the total to 61 percent during the same period. At the same time the
percentage of the gross value of output provided by industry rose from
39 percent in 1938 to 47 percent in 1950 and 57 percent in 1965. Per
capita income also rose, from $180 in 1950 to $653 in 1965.

Political Stalinism, the dictatorship of the proletariat, the monopoly
of power by a single party, the restriction of civil rights, the continual
"intensification" of the class struggle, the liquidation by terrorist means
of the old political and cultural elites and of all other opposition, all in
the name of building a new society and a new man, had already begun
before 1948 when the leaders of the Antonescu regime were arrested,
and the most important executed, followed by the leaders of the National Peasant Party, most of whom were arrested in 1947. A few attempts at military resistance occurred during this period. They were
organized by former or even active groups or officers—such as the
Transylvanian peasant organization Sumanele Negre (black coats) or
the National Resistance Movement led by General Aldea. These were
soon crushed. In 1948 the liberal leaders were arrested along with those
social democratic leaders who still refused to join with the Communists.
The dignitaries of old Romania, several thousand in number, were assembled in a prison camp in the town of Sighet. Most of them died
there and were buried in the prison's common grave, victims of age
and a regime bent on their extermination.

The repression of churches was carried out with particular virulence.
The Orthodox church was completely subordinated to the state through
the appointment of a patriarch sympathetic to the Communists. Church
property was nationalized, and all undesirable members of the clergy
were purged. Orthodox priests became one of the largest groups of
political prisoners. Other faiths met a similar fate, some an even more
tragic one. The Uniate church, for instance, was forced to unite with
Orthodoxy, and all five Uniate bishops were arrested (four would die
in prison), together with some six hundred Uniate clergy. A 1927 con-
cordat with the Vatican was annulled in July 1948 to permit the government to reduce the number of Catholic bishops to two, and then
those last two bishops were arrested. The spiritual leaders of the Jewish

community were imprisoned or forced into exile. A similar fate befell the leaders of the various Protestant churches.

In 1948 the security police was formed, and immediately its ranks swelled with Soviet agents who had become Romanian generals. Repression grew still harsher as those in power struck out indiscriminately—in keeping with the Stalinist principle of intensification of the class struggle. The peasants in particular paid dearly for their resistance to collectivization, and even some members of the Communist Party were destroyed by their own revolution. Between 1949 and 1953 many tens of thousands of political prisoners—exact figures cannot be established—died while forced to work on the Danube–Black Sea canal.

Repression in Romania may have been harsher than in any other Soviet satellite country in Europe. It eased slightly after the death of Stalin, but sprang up again, aimed especially at intellectuals and students, from 1956 through 1959 in reaction to the uprisings in Poland and Hungary. It is impossible even to estimate the number of people arrested from 1944 to 1964 (when the political prisons were closed), but it must have been at least several hundred thousand, to which must be added other victims of repression like the Swabians, who were deported to the Bărăgan steppe. The sustained terror explains in large part why no active resistance could be organized, although there were isolated groups of partisans in the mountains until 1956.

The Stalinist regime headed by Gheorghe Gheorghiu-Dej quickly went beyond the elimination of the monarchy, and as it worked to destroy the old ruling class and all opposition from any class, it worked too to build the new structures of the "people's democracy." In 1948 the first Communist constitution was adopted. In 1952 Gheorghiu-Dej issued a second after receiving, he claimed, 8,000 proposals from the workers. Both documents were modeled on Stalin's 1936 constitution. Elections were held, and the Communist Party candidates predictably won them all. The first, in 1948, they won with "only" 92 percent of the votes. Succeeding victories came ever nearer to perfection, 99.15% (1957), 99.78% (1961), 99.96% (1965), 99.97% (1969), 99.96% (1975), and 99.99% (1980). The party kept all power in its own hands because, as the Soviet deputy foreign minister Andrei Y. Vyshinsky said in 1948, Communism "rejects the bourgeois principle of the separation of powers." Domestic politics enjoyed relative stability. It was dominated by a totalitarian party whose ranks grew, once it had absorbed the social democrats (February 1948) and changed its name to the Romanian Workers' Party, from 720,000 in 1950 to 834,000 in 1960 and 1,450,000

in 1965. Within the ruling elite, however, among the few dozen apparatchiks who retained all power, there were ceaseless power struggles
from 1948 until 1957. Only in 1957 did Gheorghiu-Dej, surrounded
by a group of new "barons" and out of all danger from his rivals and
from Nikita Khrushchev's de-Stalinization program, see his authority
consolidated.

The first phase of the power struggle lasted from 1948 until 1952.
No new members were admitted to the party, and 192,000 people were
dropped from its ranks. In February 1948 even Lucreţiu Pătrăşcanu,
the representative of national Communism, was expelled from the
party and arrested on a charge of "national chauvinism." The national
Communists loyal to Gheorghiu-Dej united with Ana Pauker's Moscow
group against Pătrăşcanu. Gheorghiu-Dej's group regarded him as a
dangerous rival, Pauker's as an uncontrollable nationalist. But the fall
of Pătrăşcanu did not resolve the situation. Instead, the conflict between
Gheorghiu-Dej and the Moscow faction came to the fore. This power
struggle was affected by frequent changes in external circumstances,
especially in the Kremlin. Stalin's illness, his anti-Semitic outbursts, and
the Korean War all contributed greatly to the declining influence of
Pauker's faction and to the final victory of the home-grown Stalinists
over those trained in Moscow.

So it was that Gheorghiu-Dej undertook the Romanianization of the
party in 1950, and in 1952 Ana Pauker, Teohari Georgescu, and Vasile
Luca were accused of right-wing deviation and expelled. Luca was condemned to death, although the sentence was not carried out. It is an
indication of his complete victory that in June 1952 Gheorghiu-Dej
became prime minister in addition to his original position as first secretary of the party. The new secretariat, which now for the first time
included Nicolae Ceauşescu, had a clear majority of national Communists, to whom the Bessarabian group (Petre Borilă, Leonte Răutu, and
Iosif Chişinevski) rallied in spite of their traditional ties to the Moscow
faction.

After 1953 the principal threat to Gheorghiu-Dej's authority came
not from his party but from Moscow, reflecting the struggle taking place
in the Kremlin. Khrushchev would have liked to replace the Romanian
dictator as part of his process of de-Stalinization. Gheorghiu-Dej viewed
Khrushchev's de-Stalinization with evident concern. He took early defensive action in 1954 by obtaining the conviction and execution of
Pătrăşcanu, whom the Soviets could possibly have chosen to head a de-
Stalinized Communist Party.

The Twentieth Congress of the Soviet Communist Party, the congress of de-Stalinization and of Khrushchev's "secret speech," appears to have taken Gheorghiu-Dej by surprise. Until then he had resisted the new course on the grounds that de-Stalinization had already taken place in Romania in 1952. A divided Romanian delegation returned to Bucharest. Gheorghiu-Dej was determined to oppose liberalization, but the chief of planning, Miron Constantinescu, insisted at the plenary session of 23–25 March 1956 on the need for real reforms and for democratizing party and society. The uprisings in Hungary and Poland in October and November 1956 postponed any resolution of the new division. Students in Bucharest, Cluj, Timişoara, and the Autonomous Hungarian Region demonstrated in solidarity with the Hungarian uprising, demanding among other things an end to the Russian-language requirement at the universities. Over a thousand intellectuals and students were arrested after November 1956, underscoring the renewed breach between Gheorghiu-Dej and Constantinescu, who was now minister of education. At the party's plenary sessions of June and July 1957, under circumstances that are still unclear but probably were connected with the fall of Georgi Malenkov in the Soviet Union, Gheorghiu-Dej managed to eliminate all Khrushchevites from the party leadership. The fall of Constantinescu, among others, coincided with a new wave of terror directed largely against intellectuals and bringing increased dogmatism to cultural life.

As soon as the "people's democracy" was established, the third element of Stalinism, the cultural, inspired a radical restructuring of the value system and of the cultural institutions that reflect it. Like all eastern European Communist parties, the Romanian party had the ambition of creating a "new man." Since "the light comes from the east" (Mihail Sadoveanu, 1944), the only possible model was of course the Soviet one. "The shining beacon that must guide our scientists is the country with the most advanced culture, the Soviet Union," declared Gheorghiu-Dej in 1951, an axiom that no one would dare to question for more than a decade.

But the Romanian *homo sovieticus* could not be created until traditional national values had been destroyed and rewritten. A massive infusion of Marxist-Leninist values and a campaign of active Russification were necessary. The first manifestations of these were Mihai Roller's *History of Romania* (*Istoria României* [1947]), a complete revision of the country's past and its concepts of nationalism and patriotism; and a programmatic study by Leonte Răutu entitled *Against Cosmopolitanism and Objectivism in the Social Sciences* (*Împotiva cosmopolitanismului şi obiectivismului în ştiinţele sociale* [1949]), a Romanian application of the arguments of Andrei A. Zhdanov and a vehement attack on those who "hide the rot of cosmopolitanism inside a shell of verbiage about the national character."

Like its political and economic aspects, cultural Stalinism had to be imposed by force. The ties that bound the intelligentsia to the West were severed. The Romanian Academy was dissolved in June 1948 and replaced with a new one, a majority of whose members were docile party appointees, many with doubtful scientific qualifications. A new Education Law enacted in August 1948 eliminated uncooperative faculty members and reorganized both secondary and higher education on the Soviet model. The old research institutes were broken up in the summer of 1948, and replaced with new ones under the revamped Academy.

Purging of intellectuals was not restricted to the administrative level. A great many scientists, artists, and others involved in cultural activities went to prison. Some died there (Gheorghe Brătianu, Ioan Lupaş, Anton Golopenţia, and M. Vulcănescu). Others were released after many years' imprisonment (Ion Petrovici, Constantin C. Giurescu, and Nichifor Crainic). Some venerable figures of Romanian scholarly and intellectual life were marginalized and ended their days in isolation and poverty (Constantin Rădulescu-Motru, Simion Mehedinţi, Dimitrie Gusti, and Lucian Blaga, among others).

The number of censored authors and titles grew steadily as well. In July 1946 some 2,000 books and journals were banned, to which 8,000 more were added in the spring of 1948. The list of banned publications (publicaţiile interzise) filled a volume of 522 pages. For more than a decade the works of such great historians as Nicolae Iorga and Vasile Pârvan were forbidden reading. Of Mihai Eminescu's oeuvre just a few social poems were allowed in print, and Titu Maiorescu, one of the founders of modern Romanian culture, was declared a "rootless cosmopolitan" and a "court lackey" whose only goal was to ensure that "liberty and light not reach the masses." Other writers and scientists of the past fully or partially censored were Vasile Alecsandri, Grigore Alexandrescu, Costache Negruzzi, Petre Ispirescu, Panait Istrati, Liviu Rebreanu, Gheorghe Coşbuc, Virgil Madgearu, Victor Slăvescu, Constantin Rădulescu-Motru, Henri H. Stahl, Gheorghe Ionescu-Siseşti, and V. Vâlcovici. The blacklist of 1948 included many heroes of 1848, Mihai Kogălniceanu among them, and even Dimitrie Cantemir's *Chronicle of the Antiquity of the Roman-Moldavian-Wallachians* (*Hronicul vechimii romano-moldo-vlahilor* [1723]), which was probably too pro-Roman for the new pro-Slavic approach, was banned.

As traditional national values were obscured, the party made efforts to inject society with a new kind of socialist and internationalist patriotism, in which love of country and of tradition was replaced with love of Marxism and of the Soviet Union, the country of "victorious socialism." As a 1957 party pamphlet said, the Soviet Union "has won the right to teach others the characteristics of the new man." To develop these characteristics the party early set in motion its intensive campaign of Russification, setting up in rapid succession the Cartea Rusă (Russian Book) publishing house and bookstore (1946), the Institute of Romanian-Soviet Studies (1947), the Romanian-Russian Museum (1948), and the Maxim Gorky Russian Language Institute (1948). The aim of the publishing house, bookstore, and study institute was to popularize in Romania the achievements of Soviet science and culture, "the foremost in the world." The museum was intended to show that Romanian-Russian relations were long-standing and friendly. The language institute was set up to prepare the thousands of teachers who would be needed to teach Russian in the universities and schools, where it became a requirement in 1948.

The entire history of Romania was rewritten to play up the role of the Slavs, to diminish that of the Romans and the Latin elements, and to stress the support the Romanians had received through the ages from their eastern brother and liberator. A high point of Russification was the introduction of a new Slavicized orthography (1953), which replaced some of the language's Latin elements and even went so far as to change the spelling of the country's name from România to Romînia (both are pronounced the same in Romanian, but the second obscures the etymology). As the journal *Limba romînă* (Romanian language) wrote a year later, linguistic reform was necessary. The old spelling had become "intolerable," "a matter of concern to the working class," and "a national problem." Socialist patriotism even affected the national anthem, which now proclaimed, "Our people will always be the brothers of our liberators, the Soviet people; Leninism is our beacon and strength and inspiration."

From 1956 to 1959 cultural dogmatism increased, and the ideological campaign intensified. Probably this was a reaction to both the power struggles going on within the Communist Party and the need to give Khrushchev further evidence of the Gheorghiu-Dej group's loyalty. First came a wave of arrests of such noncomforming intellectuals as the philosopher Constantin Noica and his circle, as well as public exposure of cases of "cosmopolitanism" and "antiparty sentiment," like that of the composer Mihail Andricu (1959). In 1958 noisy public meetings were held in the universities, at which distinguished professors were "unmasked" and accused of failure to eliminate bourgeois influences. Many students were thrown out of school on the basis of their files. The fifties ended on the same note on which they had begun: pure Marxist orthodoxy. No one could have foreseen a political upset or imagined that in just a few years the "liberators" would be dropped from the national anthem, the Russian language from the schools, and the Soviet presence from Romanian cultural life.

Foreign Policy and the Beginnings of Liberalization. The first years of the "people's democracy," which coincided with Stalin's last years (1948– 53), were marked by absolute docility in Romanian foreign policy. Like its fraternal Communist countries Romania was diplomatically an absolute Soviet satellite. In February 1948 the government signed a treaty of friendship, collaboration, and mutual assistance with the Soviets that was binding for twenty years, and reached similar agreements with Bulgaria, Czechoslovakia, Poland, and Hungary. Romania's 1947 treaty with Yugoslavia was of course abrogated when that country was expelled from the Cominform—which had its headquarters in Bucharest—and Gheorghiu-Dej immediately embarked on a heated campaign to unmask "the traitor" Tito. From an economic point of view, the country had already been brought into the Soviet sphere of influence by an economic collaboration treaty and trade agreement signed in May 1945, and then by its membership in the Council for Mutual Economic Assistance (Comecon), established in 1949. Soviet military domination was also absolute. Direct military occupation of the country lasted until 1958. Romania signed the Warsaw Pact in 1955.

Stalin's death in March 1953 threw all eastern Europe into a period of uncertainty, which for Romania included the beginnings of discord with the Soviets. Although events, attitudes, and political initiatives remain unclear or contradictory, it seems certain that from the very beginning Gheorghiu-Dej and his new master in the Kremlin regarded each other suspiciously and without sympathy. Khrushchev consistently tried to replace eastern European Stalinists with his own people, supporters of détente and peaceful coexistence. This was easy in Poland and Czechoslovakia, though more difficult in Bulgaria. In Hungary the old leaders were finally purged in 1956 at Moscow's request. But it did not work at all in Romania, where the Stalinist leader had succeeded in neutralizing all possible adversaries at home while displaying absolute loyalty to the Kremlin. At the same time Gheorghiu-Dej declared emphatically that de-Stalinization had already taken place in Romania in 1952, when the Pauker faction was removed.

Gheorghiu-Dej's relations with Khrushchev seems to have become still more strained in 1955 as certain differences of opinion came to light while the Soviet leader was visiting Bucharest. For instance, the Soviets favored separating the positions of party first secretary and prime minister. Gheorghiu-Dej was only prime minister at the time of the visit, but in October of that year he assumed the function of party leader as well—over Soviet objections. At the Second Congress of the Romanian Workers' Party (Seventh Congress of the Romanian Communist Party) in 1955, there was talk for the first time of a Romanian road to socialism and of adapting Marxism to local needs. The congress affirmed that the principles of sovereignty, equality, and noninterference in the internal affairs of other countries must be respected. That same year Miron Constantinescu, probably Khrushchev's favorite, was removed from his important position as Romania's chief of planning.

These differences temporarily gave place to the uprisings in Poland and Hungary (October–November 1956), although those events posed no threat either to socialism in Romania or to Soviet interests in the area, while offering Gheorghiu-Dej a new pretext for opposing de-Stalinization. Romanian Communists had been hostile to Hungarian premier Imre Nagy from the first, and they heartily supported the Soviet repression of the revolt. But in December 1956 they were again talking of a Romanian road to socialism—while requesting increased economic assistance from Moscow. In 1956 the last combined Soviet-Romanian company, Sovromcuarțul, reverted to Romanian ownership. One form at least of direct economic exploitation by the Soviet Union had come to an end.

The Romanian road to socialism differed significantly from Khrushchev's plans for eastern Europe. Comecon had been dormant from 1949 to 1955, but now the Soviet leader reactivated it to create a division of labor and economic specialization among the socialist countries. The north became responsible for industrial production and the south for raw materials and agricultural production. This created conflict between north and south, between the developed socialist countries, Czechoslovakia in particular, and the developing socialist countries. Bulgaria quickly accepted Moscow's view, but the Khrushchev plan came up against Romanian decisions on national independence approved by the Second Congress. Prague had revealed its opposition to Romania's accelerated industrialization as early as 1956, when it opposed technological aid to that country. In 1957–58 Czechoslovakia openly criticized what it called Romania's "autarkical" and protectionist tendencies.

In spite of the friction between the two leaders, Khrushchev in 1958 granted Gheorghiu-Dej's long-standing request to withdraw Soviet troops from Romania. It is still not clear where this move originated, but it seems to have been made at the request of the Romanian Communist Party, which had been recommending the withdrawal of troops since 1953. Bucharest's principal negotiator was Emil Bodnăraş, a former Soviet agent who had parachuted into Romania in 1944 but who subsequently became a consistent supporter of Gheorghiu-Dej's foreign policy. The Soviet withdrawal must be understood in its international context as well. Romania's strategic value dropped significantly after the Soviet Union signed a peace treaty with Austria and withdrew its troops from that country. Khrushchev was also campaigning for favorable Western public opinion, and he probably considered it safe to end the direct occupation of a country that was anyhow surrounded by satellites and within easy striking distance of Soviet troops stationed in Bessarabia. The Soviets seem to have viewed the whole problem of keeping troops in Romania as a purely military and diplomatic issue. Apparently they did not realize that in withdrawing their troops they were losing a way to pressure Gheorghiu-Dej and his government. When the troops pulled out (July 1958), Gheorghiu-Dej gave one of his most fawning and servile speeches ever, perhaps to convince the Kremlin of his loyalty. But it is most likely that beneath the servility he was already planning the spectacular reorientation of domestic and foreign policy that occurred after 1960.

In 1958 the old seeds of strife between Bucharest and Moscow ripened into political action. This was made possible by the formation of a new ruling elite in Romania, dominated by Ion Gheorghe Maurer, chief of state from 1958 until 1961 and then prime minister. With the concurrence of Gheorghiu-Dej, the new team moved quickly toward a relatively liberal economic policy that would have been inconceivable a few years earlier. Foreign trade was gradually reoriented toward the West, and some Western firms pronounced themselves willing to grant Romania credit. An important economic delegation headed by Alexandru Bârlădeanu visited various Western capitals in 1958, to be followed by the prime minister himself the next year. In 1960 Romania concluded agreements with the principal Western governments on compensation for property nationalized in 1948. Once this obstacle to normal economic relations had been removed, imports from capitalist countries grew. The total value of imports from the West rose from

21.5 percent in 1958 to 40 percent in 1965. Exports went from 24 percent to 33 percent. During the same period imports from the Soviet Union fell from 53 percent to 38 percent, while exports declined from 50 percent to 40 percent.

The principles of national Communism were clearly formulated at the Third Congress of the Romanian Workers' Party (1960) with another statement of the country's right to industrialize rapidly, and the construction of the Iron and Steel Aggregate Works at Galaţi was made a test case in Romania's relationship with Comecon. Just after his return from the Twenty-Second Congress of the Soviet Communist Party in Moscow (October 1961), Gheorghiu-Dej launched an impassioned attack against the Moscow factions that had been purged in 1952 and 1957, reaffirming his position that political de-Stalinization had already been accomplished in Romania. From then until his death in March 1965, relations between Gheorghiu-Dej and the Kremlin steadily worsened, aggravated by Soviet rigidity in formulating Comecon's role.

At Khrushchev's insistence, Comecon adopted the Soviet plan as "Principles for the International Division of Labor" in June 1962. The Soviet leader reiterated his position in an article published in the journal *Kommunist* in August of the same year. These statements did not accord with Bucharest's idea of socialist economic collaboration, since they called for a division between the industrialized north and the agrarian south and for a supranational Comecon with broad powers to coordinate national economic policies. During 1962–63 a great deal of pressure was put on the Romanians, whether directly by Khrushchev and by Walter Ulbricht, party chief in the German Democratic Republic, or by means of individual economists and publications in economics. All strove to demonstrate the advantages of economic integration. The campaign came to a head in April 1964, when E. B. Valev published an article proposing an "interstate economic complex" in the lower Danube region. The land for the complex would be taken from the southern Soviet Union (12,000 square km), southeast Romania (100,000 square km), and northern Bulgaria (38,000 square km). Romania responded furiously, considering with good reason that the plan was an attempt "to dismember national economies and national territory."

The Valev plan and its rejection in the name of Romania's national interest were just the latest manifestation of a discord that had gone beyond the economic sphere and entered the political. The split between the Soviet Union and China had introduced a new element into

Romanian-Soviet relations and permitted Bucharest to distance itself from Moscow with little fear of retaliation. The Chinese Communist leadership had chosen the Romanian capital as the setting for a strong verbal attack on the Soviet Union (1960). In 1962 and 1963 they also sent a number of economic and political delegations there. We cannot know whether Gheorghiu-Dej or Mao was behind this. But in 1963 the Romanian leader moved toward rapprochement with other countries. He visited Yugoslavia and concluded an agreement to construct a hydroelectric plant at the Iron Gates on the Danube. The Romanian ambassador to Albania, withdrawn in May 1961, was reinstated. The British and French legations in Bucharest were upgraded to embassies. And this was the year when Romania first voted differently from the Soviet Union and its allies at the United Nations.

At the beginning of 1964 Gheorghiu-Dej offered to mediate in the Sino-Soviet conflict and sent Maurer to Beijing for that purpose, but if Khrushchev's memoirs are to be believed, Maurer's mission there and his subsequent meeting with Khrushchev at Pitsunda only increased the suspicions of all parties. The so-called memoirs are extremely hard on Maurer, accusing him of anti-Sovietism and bourgeois nationalism, and of irredentism with regard to Bessarabia. At Pitsunda Soviets and Romanians could not even agree to keep their disagreements secret. The next month the Valev plan came out, and the April statement of the Romanian position on the Sino-Soviet conflict was published in Bucharest. This document reiterated the need for independence and mutual noninterference among the socialist nations in such strong terms that it was virtually a proclamation of Romania's autonomy. Romanian foreign policy became ever more daring and separate from that of the eastern European satellite countries: there were economic delegations to Washington; Maurer visited Paris; independent voting at the United Nations increased. The Gheorghiu-Dej regime had achieved international respectability with surprising speed and had no intention of relinquishing it.

With the new orientation of foreign policy after 1960 came significant changes in domestic policy, starting with the relaxation of police rule. The authorities began to open the political prisons in 1962, when 1,304 prisoners were released (according to official records). In 1963 an additional 2,892 were freed, and in the first four months of 1964, the final 464 prisoners came out. The figures are of course too low to be credible.

An essential element in Gheorghiu-Dej's new course, intended primarily to win public approval, was de-Russification, which was completed in 1963 with the closing of all the institutions that had been created between 1946 and 1948 in order to further Russification: the Maxim Gorky Russian Language Institute, the Romanian-Russian Museum, the Institute of Romanian-Soviet Studies, the *Romanian-Soviet Annals* and the journal *New Times* (Timpuri noi). Russian names of streets, institutions, and movie theaters changed overnight. Gheorghiu-Dej organized public meetings in all workplaces at which high-level party apparatchiks hurled outrageous accusations at Moscow, blaming it for all the wrongs and ills of the preceding two decades: Stalinism, economic exploitation, perversion of national values, the country's isolation from the rest of the world, Slavicization of a Latin culture, and more. As the Russified institutions were dismantled, some of the older cultural institutions that had been dissolved in 1948 were again set up. Now that faculty members' files were less important, it became possible to draw on a large pool of technocrats who had been pushed to the edges of society for reasons of social origin, bourgeois political activities, or ideological sins. All these changes, in remarkable contrast to the situation in the fifties, gave rise to an apparent climate of harmony and national consensus, especially since all hopes of liberation from Communism seemed to have been postponed indefinitely.

By 1965 Gheorghiu-Dej's foreign and domestic policies were heading in a new direction—toward autonomy—a very different path from the one the other countries of eastern Europe were following. Economically, Romania opposed the integration and specialization called for by Comecon, obstinately driving for rapid industrialization and Western aid. Domestically there was a degree of liberalization. In foreign policy the party refused to support Moscow's wish for hegemony over the international Communist movement, instead drawing closer to China and to the industrialized nations. Finally, the Russian influence on culture disappeared almost entirely as the party prudently permitted the gradual recovery, rehabilitation, and dissemination of such traditional values as posed no direct threat to its authority.

Gheorghiu-Dej died suddenly in March 1965 with his new course barely begun, leaving to historians the task of explaining a contradictory personality and a policy whose source and motivations must remain for the present in the domain of speculation and hypothesis. His policies had evolved through many stages. Until the Communist takeover he had worked underground, representing the nationalist faction of the Communist movement. He had no contact with the Moscow faction and was free of Kremlin influence. After the takeover he wavered briefly between the nationalist line and that of the Moscow faction, but soon opted for Moscow, probably out of political realism. From 1948 to 1958 he was identified entirely with the Stalinist model and interests, including mass murder—we might mention that Yugoslavia's Tito and Hungary's János Kádár too engaged in bloodshed at certain periods of their regimes. After 1958, Gheorghiu-Dej gradually moved away from the Soviets, achieving the relative autonomy described above.

The position Gheorghiu-Dej reached by this circuitous route can be explained in various ways. It may have been the result of a clash with Khrushchev against Gheorghiu-Dej's wish. The Romanian leader was driven toward autonomy to keep the throne from which Khrushchev was trying to remove him. On the other hand, considering the earlier stages of his development, one could hypothesize that Gheorghiu-Dej had always been striving for the autonomy that he achieved in 1964, but could not succeed until the international situation was favorable. Both theories probably contain some truth, and they complement each other. The new core of leaders that formed the party after 1958, technocrats centered around Maurer, was also of great importance in establishing the new course. Gheorghiu-Dej was a simple, uneducated man, but one with excellent political instincts. He knew enough to follow the advice of the Maurer group and to combine autonomy in foreign affairs with a domestic ideological thaw and liberalization that would give autonomy abroad meaning to the people.

But Gheorghiu-Dej's reforms were extremely limited. His quarrel with Khrushchev arose not because the Romanians wanted to adopt a different model for development, but because the Soviets wanted to prevent them from holding fast to the classic Marxist/Stalinist model of industrialization in their country. The Romanian Communists had no thought of attempting any real reform of the Stalinist economic model. Their only wish was to apply it fully. Although by 1965 Gheorghiu-Dej and his circle were in disagreement with Moscow over national independence, the domestic structures they controlled did not differ from the Soviet ones in any essential way.

There is no knowing which way domestic policy might have gone but for the unexpected death of the first secretary in March 1965, with his new course just begun. In Hungary it took more than ten years for Kádár's policies to be fully established, time that Gheorghiu-Dej did not have. The most attractive hypothesis, in view of the influence the Maurer group had over him, is that once Romania's autonomy had been consolidated, Gheorghiu-Dej might have encouraged some real domestic reform as well.

The Rise of Neo-Stalinism

Détente. Gheorghiu-Dej himself had settled the matter of succession in the late fifties when he designated the young Nicolae Ceauşescu as the next leader of the Communist Party. Born in 1918 into a family of poor Wallachian peasants, Ceauşescu had risen through the party hierarchy under the protection of Gheorghiu-Dej, whom he had met in prison. He had been secretary-general of the Union of Communist Youth immediately after the war, deputy minister of the armed forces and chief of the army's political section (1950), secretary of the Central Committee (1952), and a member of the party's political bureau (1955) in charge of cadre personnel. When he became first secretary of the party at age forty-seven, however, he was just one member of the collective leadership that still included Ion Gheorghe Maurer as head of government and Chivu Stoica as president of the State Council. In 1965 Ceauşescu was only first among equals. The leading figure in the troika was without question the prime minister. Furthermore, the Ninth Congress of the Romanian Communist Party (1965) had tried to prevent concentration of power in one person by passing a statute prohibiting the top party official from holding government offices as well.

Gheorghiu-Dej's "barons," Maurer, Emil Bodnăraş, Chivu Stoica, and Gheorghe Apostol, thinking no doubt that they could control the young Ceauşescu, formed an alliance with him to eliminate the last Stalinists, starting with Alexandru Drăghici, minister for internal affairs since 1952. Drăghici lost his position immediately after the death of Gheorghiu-Dej and was expelled from the secretariat of the Central Committee as well in 1968. A large number of other apparatchiks from the old Stalinist days were dropped from both government and party at the Ninth Party Congress. A new generation of apparatchiks like Gaston Marin, Alexandru Bârlădeanu, Paul Niculescu-Mizil, Ilie Verdeţ, Corneliu Mănescu, Mihail Florescu, Virgil Trofin, and Maxim Bergheanu replaced them. All of these had been active in the party during the latter part of the Gheorghiu-Dej regime and were known to favor a degree of reform and technocracy.

Maurer and the other "barons" seem not to have considered Ceauşescu's accession to power as a threat to their vision of gradually diminished repression at home and disengagement from the Soviet Union, and so, hard though it is to explain, they encouraged a violation of the new restrictions against holding more than one top office and permitted the secretary-general of the Romanian Communist Party to become president of the State Council as well (1967). Ceauşescu skill-

Nicolae Ceauşescu, president of Romania
(1974–89).

fully used this office to broaden the State Council's sphere until he controlled the Economic Council (created in 1967) and the Defense Council (created in 1968). The State Council was transformed imperceptibly from a figurehead into an effective governing body, duplicating or taking over Maurer's government functions. When we further consider that two-thirds of the members of the Permanent Presidium at the Tenth Party Congress (1969) had been promoted after the preceding congress (1965) under Ceauşescu's guidance, it becomes clear that his circle was now fully in charge.

The domestic policy of the Maurer-Ceauşescu team tended to encourage the moderate optimism that had spread across the country under Gheorghiu-Dej. The new regime began with a number of symbolic but popular measures. The country's name was re-Latinized (to

România instead of Romînia), a new constitution was adopted (1965) that gave less weight to the "brother liberator," and the national Communist Lucreţiu Pătrăşcanu was rehabilitated along with many other political prisoners arrested between 1951 and 1958, whether Communist, non-Communist, monarchist, military, or other.

The next step in liberalization was a series of measures encouraging small-scale private enterprise and modifying the rigidly Stalinist relationship between state and individual. For instance, in July 1967 the party authorized private shops, restaurants, and boardinghouses, and within six months 183 private restaurants had opened. The construction of privately owned houses was legalized in 1967. In the universities the role of the dreaded personnel office was reduced, personal files were no longer kept, and the main criteria for hiring were no longer the biography and social origin of the candidates, but their merits and professional abilities. Finally, new passport regulations were adopted between 1968 and 1970, making it easier for Romanians to travel abroad, and police surveillance decreased significantly.

But perhaps the new orientation was most noticeable in the cultural domain. In the hands of several fairly enlightened ministers of education (1969–1972), there was progress, modernization, and some openness in education, with less weight given to Marxism and more to the hard sciences and technological fields. Russian disappeared almost entirely from schools and universities, to be replaced by English, French, and German, which had been little taught until then. Several high schools opened in which one of these was the language of instruction for all subjects. Equally innovative changes were permitted in the social sciences. Sociology, which had been scorned, appeared once again in research programs and on university course lists, and a research center and a journal of sociology were even established. History too enjoyed an unexpected renaissance, which was the more promising since the party and its secretary-general had for some years displayed a total lack of interest in the country's past. Unhindered by official attention, historiography flourished. The Stalinist concept of the "historical front" (as a locus of class struggle) was abandoned. Historians formed collectives and chose subjects for research according to their own inclinations and initiative, not the interests and directives of the party. Several histories of the country appeared during this period, as well as many studies in which recently taboo subjects were discussed and debated fairly freely, without either the Marxist dogmatism of the preceding era or quotations from the work of the party's head.

There were similar developments in letters, the arts, and music. The removal of the Stalinist poet Mihail Beniuc as head of the Writers' Union put an end for a while to socialist realism in literature and opened the door to a number of talented young writers. The novel, poetry, and criticism all entered a period of real originality.

The party shrewdly represented itself as eager to liberalize its own political organization, to eliminate dogmatism, and to achieve national consensus. In 1965 it opened its doors, shortening the probation period and seeking to attract people from the sciences and cultural areas as well as intellectuals in technology. This open-door policy took party membership over the two million mark for the first time, to 2,089,085 in 1970, or about 10 percent of the population.

These steps toward a real easing of repression were accompanied by some economic progress, which made them yet more promising. Industrialization was carried out in two separate phases, divided by the year 1970. The 1966–70 five-year plan provided for the rapid development, especially of heavy industry. The Galați steel plant (which went into partial production in 1968) became a symbol of that focus. At the time 28 percent of the national income (net material product excluding services) was reinvested in industry annually, and the growth rate was about 12 percent. Industry accounted for 49 percent of the national income in 1965 and 60 percent in 1970. Allocation of funds for it was increased to 49 percent of all investment in 1965 and 47.5 percent in 1970, while agriculture received only 16 percent. Nonetheless the agricultural yield was generally good, with a record grain harvest of sixteen million metric tons in 1972. Exports of food products were still low in 1970–71 (about 4 percent of the total value of exports in 1970, slightly less in 1971), which probably explains the relative abundance of food in Romania during the seventies—even of meat and meat products.

The sixties were a time of experiment and reform throughout eastern Europe, especially in the economy. In 1967 the Romanian Communist Party adopted what they considered to be a new system of economic planning and leadership. It was generally more conservative than those formulated by the other socialist countries. In theory, more decisions were permitted at the local level, and the number of central planning directives was reduced, but in fact strict centralization was still the rule, with detailed planning by the party. The ruling elite clearly believed, as Ceaușescu often said, that the economic system could be modernized more quickly with central bureaucratic control than under decentralization.

The government acted on this view in 1970, at Ceaușescu's urging and over Maurer's objections, by revising the 1971–75 five-year plan adopted just the year before. The proportion of the national income to be reinvested was raised to 34 percent, and industry's budget allotment went up to 49 percent. Agriculture's fell to 13 percent, although exports of meat and grain products were supposed to double between 1970 and 1974. The party set ambitious goals for industry, some of dubious economic value. Two such projects were the Danube–Black Sea Canal and the accelerated development of the steel and petrochemical industries, particularly oil refining. Steel and petrochemical expansion was undertaken despite the lack of domestic iron ore and the fact that Romanian oil production was falling and the price of imports rising. Without much reference to domestic conditions and resources or to economic laws, the party unhesitatingly committed the country to constructing nuclear power plants and new steel plants, and to producing, among other things, technologically obsolete or poor quality computers, helicopters, airplanes, automobiles, and ships of up to 100,000 metric tons, including oil tankers.

The unfortunate results of this economic overreach did not become apparent for several years. For the moment rapid industrialization created outlets for the work force that was leaving the villages en masse. It helped urbanize the towns and brought seeming prosperity. Along with reduced ideological and police surveillance, the economic development that followed 1965 was undoubtedly a factor in the atmosphere of internal stability, helping the public to accept the Ceauşescu regime resignedly.

Another factor contributing to public complaisance was the emphasis on autonomy in foreign policy. Romania undertook some spectacular diplomatic initiatives between 1965 and 1974, giving Bucharest greater standing in the eyes of the international community. Prestigious visitors to the Romanian capital—French president Charles de Gaulle in 1968, United States president Richard Nixon in 1969—brought goodwill and Western economic aid. The limits of Soviet tolerance were frequently tested as Romania remained neutral in the Sino-Soviet conflict, formed closer ties with Yugoslavia, and, without attempting to imitate it, defended the Prague Spring to the end. Romania was the only member of the Warsaw Pact not to participate in the invasion of Czechoslovakia in August 1968. Romania established diplomatic relations with the Federal Republic of Germany at a time (1967) when no other Warsaw Pact country had yet done so, and maintained diplomatic relations with Israel after the Six-Day War (1967). All these actions were certain to annoy the Kremlin. Romania also consistently refused to participate in military maneuvers with the Warsaw Pact or to permit maneuvers on Romanian territory, and it favored the simultaneous dissolving of the Warsaw Pact and NATO.

As it redirected its diplomatic efforts toward the West, Romania began to restructure its commercial ties. The first economic accords with the Federal Republic of Germany were signed in 1966, followed by others with the principal developed capitalist countries. Romania negotiated from 1968 to 1971 to become a party of the General Agreement on Tariffs and Trade (GATT). Discussions with the International Monetary Fund and the World Bank began in Washington that same year, and Romania joined both in 1972. Romanian delegations applied to the Common Market for preferential treatment in trade, which was granted in 1973. In 1971 the government passed legislation permitting joint ventures in order to attract capital and technology and to secure a market for Romanian products outside Comecon. These companies would be 51 percent Romanian-owned, the Western partner providing 49 percent of the capital and receiving a proportionate share of the profits. Twenty such companies had been formed by 1973. The foreign trade figures clearly show the changing orientation. In 1965 trade with Comecon accounted for 60 percent of the value of all Romania's foreign commerce—39 percent of it was with the Soviet Union—and trade with developed capitalist countries accounted for 29 percent. In 1974 these figures were 34 percent, 16 percent, and 45 percent, respectively.

Why did the Soviets tolerate this foreign policy? Why did they not restrain Romania as they had Hungary and Poland? The reason is largely that, appearances to the contrary, Romania's actions, though annoying, did not pose any real threat to Moscow's interests, or not enough to justify direct intervention. The lack of significant domestic reform relieved the Soviets. The changes within Poland and Czechoslovakia had caused them much more concern than did the rebelliousness of the little brother who might occasionally go against Soviet interests but who never acted against the interests of world Communism. Another hypothesis that should not be rejected out of hand is that Moscow sometimes used Bucharest to establish contacts and take action that it could not have undertaken on its own account. Several cases of Romanian espionage in the West have been revealed since 1969, and these were too far-reaching to have been for Bucharest's use alone. In spite of their differences the Romanians and the Soviets had some areas where their interests converged.

Romania's foreign policy from 1965 through 1974 raises a good many questions. There is no doubt that it wanted to escape Soviet protection, but only politically, for Romania had no desire to depart from the Soviet model. This was not entirely clear at the time, however, and many Romanians hoped that the gradual withdrawal from the Russian embrace would lead to basic changes in domestic policy. They were dazzled by the new leadership's nationalism and did not notice the ever more frequent signs that eased repression was coming to an end and that orthodox neo-Stalinism was about to come into its own again as it did after 1974.

The return to neo-Stalinism and the sudden increase of repression were probably connected with a disagreement between Ceauşescu and Maurer over the route Romania should follow in developing. Little is known about this quarrel, but Maurer unfortunately lost in the end. Central to the dispute was the pace of industrialization. The secretary-general wanted it increased, with even greater emphasis on heavy industry; the prime minister favored a more moderate pace and wanted some attention given to consumer industry. One generation after another, he felt, should not be sacrificed to a rigidly utopian plan without reference to the country's technological, natural, and human resources.

Ceauşescu's economic policy could not be reconciled with Gheorghiu-Dej's incipient liberal approach. Stalinist economics required absolute centralization, with all resources and energies concentrated in a single direction and all initiative placed in the hands of the small group that considered it held the key to the future. Stalinist economics made neo-Stalinist politics inevitable and brought the party apparatchiks to the fore again, displacing the technocrats. The new political course was first revealed in the July 1971 "theses" that Ceauşescu promulgated after his trip to China, a kind of mini–cultural revolution through which he struck at Maurer's group to hasten his fall. Like documents of the fifties, the theses assailed "cosmopolitanism," exalted ideological purity, and encouraged the deprofessionalizing of government positions. They marked the beginning of the pseudonationalism and jingoism that were to dominate Romanian cultural institutions and the mentality of the ruling elite.

The July theses were enthusiastically adopted at the party's plenary session of November 1971, and just a few months later Maurer and his economic approach were indirectly but publicly criticized when the secretary-general accused him of lack of faith in party policy and of economic defeatism. At about the same time (April 1972), Ceauşescu announced that as a basic principle of party policy official posts would now rotate. Government office-holders and apparatchiks at all levels were changed around periodically—increasingly at the whim of the secretary-general—and so were prevented from forming a power base. In June 1973 Elena Ceauşescu, wife of the secretary-general, was given a place on the Executive Committee and embarked on a career that in just a few years made her the second most powerful person in the party and in the government.

The careful investigator will find between the theses of July 1971 and the Eleventh Party Congress in November 1974 a growing number of signs that both a cult of personality and a new phenomenon, the presidential regime, were at hand. The secretary-general was no longer placed in the ranks of the "heroes of the working class," but began to appear at the end of a long line of princes, kings, and voivodes, claiming a different kind of legitimacy. Cultural apparatchiks went so far as to discover the remains of the first European man near Scorniceşti, Oltenia, the secretary-general's home town, and to give it the pretentious name of *Australanthropos olteniensis*. This, the numerous volumes of homage, and the adulation from the party, writers, poets, painters, and the press, show a consistent effort to construct the figure of a legendary leader with almost superhuman qualities, capable of finding the answers not only to the nation's questions but to those of all humanity.

For the cult really to blossom, it was necessary that Maurer's influence cease. He was replaced as prime minister by Manea Mănescu in March 1974, and at the Eleventh Party Congress (November 1974) he lost his place on the Central Committee as well. This ouster, and the March 1974 election of Nicolae Ceauşescu as president of Romania, seem the natural end to the power struggle begun in July 1971. The last of Gheorghiu-Dej's "barons" had fallen and the regime of the *conducător*, or leader, emerged victorious. Only foreign policy continued in the same direction, with a few changes. Otherwise, the Eleventh Congress marked the end of post-1960 enlightened despotism and a return to the methods, goals, and value systems of the fifties.

The Cult of Personality and Dynastic Socialism. Romanian neo-Stalinism of the seventies differed in several ways from the original model. First, it was less brutal, with generalized terror replaced by selective repression and often, as in other Communist countries, by the deportation of recalcitrant citizens. Another difference was the cult of personality, taken to the extreme of a family dynasty. These features were not present under Gheorghiu-Dej. They were then and are today absent from most Communist countries, especially those dependent on Moscow, although the cult of personality has prospered better in autonomous or independent socialist countries like Albania, North Korea, or Mao's

China. In Romania it appeared rather unexpectedly, for there was no such tradition among the old political elites or in Romanian socialism. On the contrary, for centuries the social elites had prevailed over the executive. There had been no cult of personality under the voivodes, the princes, or the statesmen of greater Romania. The only analogy in the country's history was the pre–World War II legionary movement's cult of its leader.

Beyond its picturesque aspects, the cult of personality was a political regime with specific characteristics. A small elite controlled first the party and later the whole country. The rise of the new political elite was probably one of the most interesting phenomena of the seventies in Romania. As we have seen, the top positions changed hands in 1974, when Ceauşescu became president and Maurer was removed from government leadership. At the same time many of Ceauşescu's original group were dropped. These included Virgil Trofin, Paul Niculescu-Mizil, Gheorghe Rădulescu, Ion Iliescu, and others he had helped at the time of his power struggle with Gheorghiu-Dej's "barons" after 1965, but who now posed a threat to the new "guiding light." All were relatively able administrators who had dared to question Ceauşescu's economic policy or suggest modifications to it. Within a few years they had lost their influential positions and were completely marginalized, their places filled by pliant apparatchiks whose only concern was to translate the *conducător*'s "precious directions" into reality. In order to keep these under control, the president stretched the rotation method to its limit. He made such frequent and disruptive changes in party and government officials that their roles became confused and the government could hardly function.

The only members of the political elite who were not constantly purged or rotated but steadily gained new posts and responsibilities were Ceauşescu's family members. The chief of state increasingly seemed to trust only his close relatives. The president's wife, brothers, children, and in-laws were placed in key positions controlling the party, the ministries of internal affairs, defense, and agriculture, the Planning Committee, the National Council on Science and Technology, and the Union of Communist Youth.

This dynastic socialism, without a precedent in the history of Romanian politics, was strengthened by a curious obsession with cultural prestige. The ruling family was now considered a repository not only of political wisdom but also of the highest scientific and cultural values. Dictators are usually satisfied to hold the reins of power without aspiring to intellectual repute, but Romania provided the exception to this rule. Nicolae Ceauşescu was listed as the author of books on philosophy, political economy, and history, and was proclaimed one of the greatest thinkers of the age. His wife, Elena, was made a member of the Romanian Academy and was given a doctorate in chemistry. She was the author of books published in many languages and was pronounced a "world-famous scholar." Two of the president's brothers and two of his children likewise boasted numerous titles and extensive bibliographies. All Romania's political leaders now joined in this culture obsession. When the Academy of Political and Social Sciences was founded in 1970, its charter members included the president, a vice prime minister, the foreign minister and his deputy, the minister of chemical industries, the governor of the National Bank, the minister of finance, many party secretaries at the regional level, and some of Ceauşescu's chief advisors. Professional scholars took back seats.

As in the cases of Josef Stalin, Kim Il Sung of North Korea, or Enver Hoxha of Albania, the president's personality went beyond the bounds of reality and took on mythic proportions. People made pilgrimages to his obscure home town and wove legends about it. The title *conducător* was always accompanied by extravagant adjectives. Ceauşescu's biography was constantly rewritten to improve the hagiography. Every 26 January the whole country celebrated the birthday of its "most beloved son" with delirious joy, pride, and recognition approaching deification. "He is ageless," "he is Romania, we are his children," wrote the newspaper *Scînteia* on his birthday in 1983.

Under such an extreme personalization of power the worst sufferer was probably the economy. The dispute between Ceauşescu and Maurer had concentrated on two problems: the degree of centralization in decision-making and the pace and extent of modernization. The triumph of the cult of personality and the transformation of the leader into a kind of omniscient oracle who also headed all committees and councils put an end to the timid decentralization initiated by the former prime minister. After 1974 the "precious directions" handed down on all subjects from agriculture and industry to science and the arts became the main factors influencing decisions. This made it difficult to reach any decision at all and destroyed initiative and willingness to take responsibility at every level. And considering the quality of this rule from the top, it was scarcely surprising that arbitrary or downright bad economic policies were adopted.

The fall of Maurer closed discussion, for the moment, on the issue of capital formation versus current consumption. In 1974 Ceauşescu instituted a policy of even faster and more diversified industrialization.

As early as July 1975 he revised the 1976–80 five-year plan, increasing the development budget from 30–32 percent of the national income, as provided by the Ninth Congress (1974), to 33.5 percent. In July 1976 the allocation rose to 34 percent, while the budgets for many other branches of industry, including the chemical industry, machine tools, and grain production, were also increased. The plan was revised again in February, October, and December 1977, with ever more ambitious goals. The next five-year plan (1981–85), adopted in 1979, was revised upward equally unrealistically, despite the already clear signs of an economic crisis.

This numbers game suggests complete chaos in planning, the more since behind it lay no attempt whatsoever at real economic reform. Romania's economy was without doubt the most strictly centralized and rigidly planned in the entire socialist camp. This led to inefficiency and inflexibility and discouraged initiative. The excessive emphasis on heavy industry created an economic imbalance. Although the country looked rich on paper, its inhabitants were extremely poor. Ironically, the factories of socialist industrialization had produced poverty instead of wealth. Even industrial development seemed to have come to a standstill when its sources—a work force transferred from agriculture on Western credit, and forced investment at the expense of consumption—gradually dried up.

After 1974 economic problems were aggravated by the government's inability to solve agricultural problems, and Romania gradually became a country with chronic food shortages. It had always been party policy to treat agriculture and the peasants with indifference and lack of understanding. No free enterprise had been permitted at the local level, nor had central control of the collective farms been relinquished. In spring 1983 the party leadership issued no fewer than five decrees on agriculture, all of them seeking to deal with the crisis, and all once again finding the "solution" only in still greater central control. The degree to which the natural order was being perverted can be seen in the preamble to one of these decrees, which states that the peasants should regard the care of cattle as an honor and a duty. Once again what ought to be a function of the market was made a moral and political issue. Under that same decree peasants were required to contract only with the state for the purchase and sale of animals, at prices fixed by the state. Another decree set harsh penalties—fines and imprisonment—for slaughtering animals privately, and required each peasant household to register all domestic animals at the town hall. Still another decree strictly regulated the prices peasants might ask for any of their products, with a very low price ceiling. In December 1982 Ceauşescu said in a speech that the peasants should be allowed to get rich if they could do so by their labor. But it is hardly likely that the regulations that he imposed on the villages in a manner reminiscent of the Phanariot period could have stimulated the peasants to work more and harder.

The troubled economy had an immediate effect on the standard of living, making the citizens of socialist Romania worse off in the eighties than they were in the sixties—and with far less hope that the situation would be remedied. Beginning in 1978, prices that until then had been stable were raised steadily. First food, services, public transportation, clothing, wood and wood products, including paper, went up. Then in 1979 gasoline, natural gas, fuel oil, and electricity rose. According to figures from the International Monetary Fund the standard of living fell in 1983 by 19–40 percent. But higher prices did not solve the problem of the food supply. Shortages of all kinds, most notably food, became chronic, and the party was forced to reintroduce the rationing it had discontinued in 1954, beginning, in fall 1981, with bread, milk, cooking oil, sugar, and meat. At the same time, on Ceauşescu's initiative, a "Rational Eating Program" was promulgated. It claimed that Romanians were eating too much, consuming too many calories, and set limits on per capita consumption for the period 1982–85. The program reduced calorie intake limits by 9–15 percent, to 2,800–3,000 calories per day. Following these guidelines, the dietary program for 1984, published in December 1983, set allowances even lower than the original "scientific plan." Soap and detergent allowances, however, were raised. The party almost doubled the allowable soap consumption between 1980 and 1983. But the standard of living had dropped significantly.

One of the ruling passions of Romanian neo-Stalinism was detailed planning and centralization of every aspect of existence. History offers few other examples of political leaders stating in an official document how many kilograms of vegetables a citizen had the right to, or how much soap would meet the hygiene needs of 365 days, as Romania did. Accepting this kind of "leadership," the party under Ceauşescu gave no sign that they realized the gravity of the situation to which they had brought the country or that they were concerned about ending the crisis.

On the contrary, instead of reforms they turned to new restrictive measures better suited to slavery than to "multilaterally developed" socialism, such as binding the worker to the workplace and making it more difficult for people to move from the country to the city. In 1976 fourteen towns were declared "large cities," with a special committee to regulate who might live in them. Two years later moving to a town, no matter how small, was made harder still. Another law made it almost impossible to change jobs. The problem of providing enough agricultural labor was resolved from year to year by taking millions of school children and university students out of class (2.5 million in 1981, 2 million in 1982) to work in the fields when needed, along with government workers and soldiers. This was done in spite of the fact that, theoretically, about 30 percent of the population was already working in agriculture. From 1981 on the army had more and more duties in the economic sector, and many economic departments and projects were wholly under the purview of the military (the Transfăgărașan highway, the Danube–Black Sea Canal, the Bucharest subway, and the national airline, Tarom).

The cult of personality had an unfortunate effect on cultural development as well. From the early sixties until the fall of Maurer's technocrats, many improvements had been made over the fifties. Greater openness toward the West, a diminished role for Marxist ideology, cultivation of national values, reduced censorship, modernization of education and research, and increased freedom for creativity in literature and the arts had all come into being. Dynastic Stalinism, however, closed the windows on the West, left education and research in disarray, and brought literature and science back under strict party control. All these measures made the years after 1974 more like the full Stalinism of the fifties than like the short, more liberal period. The state put less and less money into cultural activities. The allotment in the 1984 budget was 40 percent less than for 1983 and two million lei less than for 1965.

The most striking cultural change was probably the unqualified return to ideology as the primary instrument of social development. This gave rise to a new type of intellectual: the party apparatchik with degrees, titles, and pretensions, who treated culture as a kind of administrative domain to be planned, coordinated, and directed according to the demands of the ruling elite. In 1976, for instance, Ceaușescu declared, probably in order to stimulate scientists, "I am ready at any time to award the title of Hero of Socialist Labor for a discovery of genius." In 1981 a four-year plan for the "development of literature" was adopted.

The preferred field of these new intellectuals seemed to be history. Beginning with the party program of 1974, which had an eighteen-page historical-patriotic-nationalistic introduction, all programmatic texts dated their claims from the Dacians or the Thracians, for whom the party now felt it spoke directly. The first room of the Communist Party Museum of History was devoted to the Dacians and dominated by imposing busts of Decebalus and Trajan. Ceauşescu himself wrote about the past repeatedly, even publishing a volume called *Pages from the History of the Romanian People* (*Pagini din istoria poporului român* [1983]). A number of cultural apparatchiks, including a brother of the president, became official historians overnight, specializing in equal measure in contemporary, medieval, and ancient history. By using history the regime intended to demonstrate its legitimacy while at the same time diverting the public's nationalism to party use. But its crudeness (in creating, for example, commemorative holidays, jingoism, and false euphoria) tended to bring about the opposite effect.

Special attention was given to education, which was reorganized to the point of disorder, until almost all the progress made in the preceding period had been undone. The Education Law of 1978 introduced a principle dear to the president's heart, the integration of education with production. The theoretical fields, the social sciences, and the humanities were dropped almost entirely from school curricula, and each high school and university department was put under the guardianship of a factory and given a production plan. The institution of education survived from day to day, subject to the needs of the moment, and the quality of intellectual preparation in high school and university graduates declined. University enrollment fell steadily, and social background again became a factor in admission standards. A recommendation from the Union of Communist Youth was required for entrance into social science departments. The university faculty was purged beginning in 1974, when Ceauşescu declared, "No one may work in higher education who shirks the task of educating the younger generation in the spirit of Marxism-Leninism, of our Party's program." This policy was extended to all levels of education. Starting in 1975, admission for doctoral studies was possible only with the approval of the local party committee. Later a special commission of the Central Committee was given this authority. The ruling elite seems to have decided to grant access to higher education only to those who seemed loyal and whom they could hope to control. This kind of "cadre policy," rewarding political allegiance over merit, tended increasingly to provincialize Romania's intellectual life.

One of the few domains that the cultural apparatchiks could not entirely control, and which therefore still showed surprising vitality, was literature. Writers, although many were careful to conform, remained the principal force of intellectual opposition and the only relatively autonomous group in Romania. The very fact that they were so difficult to influence explained the calls for an end to the Writer's Union, as well as to the other unions in the creative fields. None of the writers who took orders from the ruling elite ever managed to attain the leadership of this union, which so often showed its independence. The so-called working meetings between writers and the secretary-general more than once included courageous discussions of official cultural policy.

The increasingly critical economic and cultural situation brought dissidence to Romania, but not until long after it had come to Poland, Hungary, and Czechoslovakia. Tactics and objectives had changed since the resistance and opposition of the forties and fifties. Then the resistance movement had hoped to overthrow Communism, in the conviction that the West would certainly intervene and that the regime set up by Moscow would be brought down by external forces. But these hopes faded away as détente and the Helsinki Accords (1975) gave the Communist governments some respectability. New efforts at change concentrated on reforming existing structures. Reform can lead to upheaval, as happened when the group formed around dissident writer Paul Goma called for free elections, or when free labor unions were proposed (several times, beginning in 1977). Such radical demands might have brought about changes in the system—and so were incompatible with the socialist regime. The brutality with which incipient dissident movements were put down showed that the party was well aware of the threat posed by legal tactics.

Dissidence did not appear in Romania until after 1975 for many reasons. The spirit of nationalism in Gheorghiu-Dej's regime after 1960, and under Ceauşescu, too, undoubtedly delayed its appearance. The absence of any real de-Stalinization was probably another reason. In the Soviet Union, Poland, Hungary, and Czechoslovakia, dissidence appeared only after repression was reduced, and in Romania any such diminution was superficial even in the 1960s. There were no left-wing Marxist dissidents within the party like those who had been so influential in Poland and Czechoslovakia, so there was no one to present alternatives. The Romanian dissident movement might never have seen the light of day if it had not been for détente and the Helsinki Accords. On the one hand these permitted the West to intervene in defense of human rights, while on the other they moderated the reactions of a president anxious to retain his place in the world as a reformer and enlightened spirit.

Where theory is concerned, the Romanian dissident movement produced some noteworthy documents. Open letters from Paul Goma and his followers (January–March 1977) and several studies of Romanian Communism, together with dozens of open letters and other writings by religious dissidents, are among them. All were extremely critical of the cult of personality and of dynastic socialism, and all recommended structural reforms that no Communist regime would agree to: freedom of thought and of the press, free elections, political pluralism, and democratic civil rights. It is doubtful whether at the time the intellectuals who put these demands on paper had any hope that they would be accepted. The numbers of such dissidents were small, which made it easier to neutralize them.

The threat from worker unrest was probably greater. The formation of the Free Union of the Working People of Romania (S.L.O.M.R.) in March 1979, with locals in Wallachia, the Banat, and Transylvania totaling over 2,000 members, was particularly remarkable. The union had an interesting program that called first for freedom of assembly and then for all kinds of rights denied to workers in Communist countries. But it lasted no more than two weeks before its leaders and many members vanished behind prison doors. The creation of this free trade union came just two years after the strike of 35,000 miners in the Jiu valley (August 1977), and the party leadership hastened to crush the movement before it could spread. After that isolated groups occasionally formed free unions, but until 1989 apparently none survived more than a few days after becoming public.

The religious dissident movement was very active between 1975 and 1983. Most notable in the Orthodox Church were the sermons given by Father Gheorghe Calciu Dumitreasa at Radu Vodă Church in Bucharest in 1979. Addressed especially to young people, these prudently avoided political questions to concentrate on the relationship of atheism, faith, and Marxism, but the government still considered them dangerous enough to condemn Father Calciu—who had already spent sixteen years in prison (1948–64)—to ten more. A number of Protestant groups, too, persistently demanded their rights, including the right to emigrate. That a religious renaissance was taking place in Romania was plain to any observer, and was no doubt the cause of the active, though probably ineffective, campaign for atheism in the official propaganda of the 1970s and 1980s.

Beyond the few organized dissident activities, individual dissatisfaction grew greatly. In the 1979 United Nations yearbook Romania led the world in suicides, with 66.5 per 100,000 inhabitants, ahead of Hungary (43.1), the German Democratic Republic (30.5), Finland (25.1), and Austria (24.8). Emigration reached massive proportions. Some

170,000 Romanian citizens left the country between 1975 and 1986. The Jewish community had fallen to about 30,000 in 1983, from about 400,000 in 1945. The Armenian and Greek populations were completely gone. Forsaking one's own country, that act of desperation, was a widespread phenomenon touching all ages and professions, and a novelty in the history of a country that had so long been attractive to immigrants and had not had much emigration.

The party's response to all this dissatisfaction was a series of administrative measures. For example, a new law (March 1981) assigned harsher penalties for attempted border crossing. In an effort to cut down on the number of applications for emigration, the State Council instituted (November 1982) an education fee to be paid—in hard currency—by anyone wanting to leave the country permanently. In response to pressure from Western governments this charge was suspended in June 1983. In exchange the Federal Republic of Germany agreed to increase economic aid, largely in the form of credit, and to pay seven or eight thousand marks per emigrant (twice the amount agreed on by Ceauşescu and Helmut Schmidt in 1978). Under the new agreement some 12,000 ethnic Germans were permitted to leave Romania annually.

Increased repression, together with the continuing economic crisis, overshadowed the autonomous foreign policy initiated under Gheorghiu-Dej and courageously expanded in the years of détente and internal liberalization. Although relations between Romania and the Soviet Union remained unchanged, those between Ceauşescu and Leonid Brezhnev improved somewhat after 1974. They reached a high point in 1976, when Ceauşescu visited Soviet Bessarabia and the Crimea and Brezhnev visited Bucharest. Apparently the reduced friction with Moscow set the tone for a new Romanian approach. Polemicizing about the Bessarabian problem, for example, stopped. In order to please Moscow, Bucharest may also have transmitted information to the Soviets on the activities of some Bessarabian nationalists who had approached Ceauşescu for support. As a result, these people spent many years in Siberian prison camps before some were permitted to emigrate to Romania.

The Romanian-Soviet rapprochement in foreign policy was short-lived, however, for the two Communist parties found themselves in conflict over such important questions as military integration under the Warsaw Pact and economic collaboration and integration under Comecon. Differences also arose over Afghanistan, Kampuchea, and the Middle East, although during the early eighties Bucharest began to draw closer to Moscow's position on these matters. Differences over international affairs became more a matter of rhetoric than of substance.

But disagreements about bilateral relations were more serious. The lack of concurrence about the Warsaw Pact went beyond the old issue of military maneuvers on Romanian territory. In November 1978, for example, the other pact members joined in condemning the peace negotiations between Israel and Egypt, but Romania refused to sign the declaration. Romania also refused to agree to increased military spending, a stance Bucharest maintained in spite of repeated Soviet calls for larger military budgets. Differences on economic questions were probably even greater. Comecon and Romania seemed to have returned to their 1962–64 positions, as Comecon once again called for economic specialization and integration among member nations and Romania rejected all such demands, insisting that economic relations be based on equality and mutual advantage.

The change in leadership in the Kremlin after Brezhnev's death did not improve the relationship between the two countries and their parties. On the contrary, Ceauşescu seemed to have hoped that Konstantin Chernenko, not Yuri Andropov, would replace Brezhnev, and he openly expressed his preference in a conversation with former United States President Richard Nixon. Bucharest viewed Andropov with uneasiness, since he was thought to sympathize with Hungary. As soon as Andropov was in place, the cultural presses of Romania and the Soviet Union engaged in a prolonged ideological dispute over problems of "building socialism," the relationship between nationalism and internationalism, and the right of each country to follow its own model of development. But for the Romanian people this dispute was of limited interest—the Soviet and the Romanian models were already like two peas in a pod.

CHAPTER SEVEN

Romania in the Mid-1980s

In 1984, in a speech delivered after a trip to eastern Europe, the then vice president George Bush was still praising Ceauşescu as one of eastern Europe's "good Communists." That speech was a belated echo of what had been the Western attitude toward Romania since the mid-1960s: a firm belief in and support for its foreign policy, perceived as autonomous; willingness to help economic modernization through credit and technology; and the hope that an independent and national-minded leadership would also favor a more liberal domestic model. The expectations, however, were not borne out. Domestically, the autonomous Romanian Communists continued to rely on the same old models, mismanaging the economy and impoverishing one of the potentially richest east European countries. This in turn gradually eroded the country's international standing and narrowed the margin of maneuver it had enjoyed vis-à-vis the Soviets.

The reports coming out of Romania in the mid-1980s seemed to be from another world: official proposals to move old people out of the cities, families living for weeks in unheated apartments, ration cards for bread, a law forcing the registration of typewriters with the police, Bibles turned into toilet paper, sixteenth-century churches and nineteenth-century synagogues demolished to make room for the "Victory of Socialism Boulevard," and so on. It was a very long way from the heyday of détente, when Ceauşescu was received at Buckingham Palace and at the White House and was treated as a courageous and innovative

Since Vlad Georgescu was unable to rewrite and update for the English translation the chapter on contemporary Romania of his *The Romanians: A History,* I have decided to include this essay, written independently during the last year of his life (1987–88). As I pointed out in the preface, he told me that he intended to use this essay as a basis for the last section of the chapter "Communism in Romania." To account for the 1989 December revolution in Romania—an epochal event no one could have predicted even a few months before—I have added an epilogue to the book, written by Vladimir Tismăneanu and myself.—ED.

leader. The image had changed. The Western press now called him a "tyrant" (*The Wall Street Journal, The Times* [London]), or "the sick man of communism" (*The Economist*); his rule was defined as a "lugubre fin de règne" (*L'Express*) or "le temps du délire" (*Le Figaro*), which had turned Romania into "das Aethiopien Europas" (*Frankfurter Allgemeine Zeitung*). And the same Romanian foreign-policy makers who only ten years before were considered sophisticated international mediators were now labeled "the yokels of Eastern Europe" (*PlanEcon Report* [June 1986]).

In such a short time span, the country had run the gamut from being received with open arms to denunciation, from the promise of accelerated modernization to the reintroduction of bread rationing. This was certainly an unusual case of political decay. How did it all come about?

Economic Performance. As the party so often liked to proclaim, "we have everything we need to overcome obstacles and continue our advance toward . . . prosperity and happiness." The goals were supposed to be clear enough. By 1990 Romania was supposed to become what the party leadership called a "medium-developed country," and by 2000 it was to prosper as a "multilaterally developed socialist country."

In order to reach these goals, the Romanian Communist Party (RCP) had since the 1970s been imposing record high investment rates, concentrating on heavy industry, as the Stalinist model prescribed. Romania strove to become one of the world's leading producers of steel, machinery, and chemicals. The needs of these industries greatly outstripped the domestic resources of energy and raw materials. Moreover, without securing a domestic or international market for its output, Romania began producing high-cost but low-quality goods that proved with few exceptions to be uncompetitive and could be exported to the world market only at a loss, if at all.

According to official statistics, about one-third of the national income, or the net material product (NMP) had been reinvested between 1970 and 1984. More than half the investments had been allotted to industry, with agriculture getting only a small fraction of the total.[1] Most of the overambitious plan objectives were never fulfilled, with both NMP and the gross industrial product (GIP) falling repeatedly behind projected levels. Nevertheless, the targets for the five-year plan ending in 1990 aimed as before, at extremely high annual growth rates for both the NMP (9.9% to 10.6%) and the GIP (13.3% to 14.2%). Fragmentary data released by the Romanian authorities, as well as their constant calls for "undeviating" pursuit of the plan targets, indicated year by year that the plan was not being fulfilled. The party, however, made no serious attempt to get at the causes of this situation, other than euphemistically admitting at regular intervals to unspecified "serious shortcomings" in the implementation of its infallible policies. Agriculture also failed constantly to meet its plan targets, although the official statistics kept reporting record outputs. Specialists concluded that real outputs had through the years been significantly lower than the figures reported.

When admitting to "shortcomings," the government preferred to blame them mainly on the "world economic crisis," on the alleged greed of Western creditors, and even on purported natural calamities. However, even though the world recession had been over for a long time, Romania's debt burden in the mid-1980s was comparatively low by eastern European standards, and the winters had been unusually clement for several years in a row. Romania's economic situation, though, went from bad to worse. Clearly, the main reasons for the malaise were internal rather than external. The Romanian Communists' approach to modernization belonged to the classical Stalinist pattern. The row with the Soviets over the strategy of economic development occurred not because of the RCP's wish to be more pragmatic or innovative, but because the Romanian leadership insisted on its unalloyed right to adhere strictly to that Stalinist model. The division of labor envisaged by Moscow under Khrushchev had actually been a diluted version of socialist development, centered not upon heavy industry with the machine-building industry as its pivot, but upon agriculture and the light and consumer industries.

Three sectors in particular reflected the unwise priorities chosen in the 1960s and pursued through the 1970s and the 1980s: these were the steel, petrochemical, and machine-building industries. Given the lack of a domestic resource base commensurate to the grand scale on which these sectors were developed, Romania had to rely on expensive imports, often from distant sources. The shrinking international demand for steel, machinery, and petrochemicals in the 1980s and the inability to compete of most Romanian products exposed the basic flaws in the leadership's development strategy. Poor quality and low technology forced Romania to sell its industrial products at prices well below production costs, largely on Third World markets, and often in barter deals and on credit. These three sectors also proved to be the cause of Romania's energy deficit, which assumed dramatic proportions during the 1980s.

Compounding the waste of resources on inefficient industries that were massive money losers, huge additional sums were poured into such noneconomic, prestige projects as grandiose canals and the politically inspired reconstruction of Bucharest.

The regime's policies and methods were inherently inimical to real modernization. Romania's economy had become the most rigid command economy in the Soviet bloc. The half-hearted attempts at relaxing the centralized planning and management and allowing at least some degree of enterprise autonomy initiated during the late 1960s under Prime Minister Ion Gheorghe Maurer were short-lived. Steps to create incentives for private-plot and noncollectivized peasant producers were also abandoned by the early 1970s. Strict centralization was the defining trait of Romania's mechanism. All decisions, even minor ones, were typically being referred to the highest levels. In agriculture, compulsory deliveries of produce to the state, abolished in 1956, were reimposed on the collective farms and the peasants in 1983. Cooperative farms became directly subordinated to the state sector. The size of the private peasant plot was reduced by decree, and the state imposed—and enforced with unprecedented strictness—price ceilings that removed all incentive to bring privately grown produce to the market. This coercive approach was no doubt an important cause of low agricultural productivity and of the food shortages plaguing the country.

The mismanagement of the economy inevitably led to a reorientation of Romania's trade with the Soviet Union and away from the West, reversing the trend of the 1960s and 1970s. At that time, trade with the developed market economies grew rapidly, at the expense of the Soviet Union and other Comecon states. Modernization and trade with the West, however, relied in large part on borrowed funds and technology transfers, without any reform of Romania's old economic mechanism. Western credit became readily available, especially after Romania was admitted into GATT (1971), joined the International Monetary Fund, and was granted most-favored-nation status by the United States (1975). Romania's Western indebtedness rose from 1.2 billion dollars in 1971 to a record of about 13 billion in 1982, but no economic improvements ensued from these borrowings. Neither did Romania manage to provide an attractive environment for joint ventures with Western firms, so that both the hoped-for transfers of capital and technology and expansion into Western and Third World markets failed to materialize.

All of this led Romania to return to barter trade on the less competitive socialist market. Its share in Romania's foreign trade grew from 33.8 percent in 1980 to 57 percent in 1985, while the share of the developed countries stagnated at an annual average of 27 percent from 1981 to 1985.[2] Romania's trade with the Soviets rose spectacularly from 17 percent in 1982 to 34 percent in 1986. Romanian exports to the

Soviet Union consisted mainly of steel and industrial machinery, weapons produced under Soviet license, rolling stock, oil equipment, consumer goods, and food. The Soviets in turn substantially increased deliveries to Romania of electricity, natural gas, oil, and other raw materials.[3] Under the "long-term program for the development of Romanian-Soviet economic, technological and scientific cooperation" signed by Ceauşescu and Soviet leader Mikhail Gorbachev in May 1986, the two sides were to set up a multitude of sectoral programs of bilateral cooperation in industry—joint resource development projects, scientific and technological research, industrial standardization, coordination of planning, and so forth. After some bargaining and delays, Bucharest also agreed in principle to develop "direct links between enterprises."

Such a course would have been unthinkable during the 1960s and the early 1970s. It was made possible by colossal mismanagement of the economy and by the incapacity of the ruling class to respond to the need for reforms.

The Standard of Living. The cost of supporting massive heavy industries working at a loss pauperized Romania's population. Romanians in the mid-1980s lived in a society which was clearly worse off economically than anything they had experienced since the Second World War. To deflect popular pressures for reform, the regime paid abundant lip service to progress, democracy, and modernization, using a strategy of political mobilization that Michael Shafir has aptly named one of "simulated change" in his book *Romania: Politics, Economics and Society* (1985).

In many respects, the state seemed to have given up its social functions. According to Comecon statistics, social spending in Romania declined steadily after 1980. For example, annual state expenditures on housing decreased by 37 percent, health care by 17 percent, and education, culture, and science by 53 percent from 1980 to 1985.[4] The authorities stopped providing these data after 1985.

But the state seemed intent on squeezing every ounce from its population, notwithstanding that this population had become eastern Europe's most impoverished. The Romanians were underfed, having to make do on meager food rations. Although they were overworked, their real incomes continued to shrink owing to both inflation and severe shortages of goods and services. This led to a prosperous black market, which priced out most ordinary consumers. Despite optimistic party announcements that the problem of housing had been solved, the law continued to allot only twelve square meters of living space per person.

In addition to these hardships, constantly recurring cuts in the permitted household consumption of electricity and heating made for unbearable winters, as people were forced to live and work in freezing temperatures and near darkness. Bans on private driving were regularly imposed, ostensibly to save fuel—which was severely rationed and often almost unobtainable even when driving was not legally banned.

Under the guise of austerity, the regime imposed on the country an almost bizarre process of demodernization. The media constantly appealed to the peasants to replace mechanical with manual work, and to use carts and horses instead of trucks and tractors. Commercial firms were advised to transport merchandise on tricycles. The use of refrigerators and washing machines was officially discouraged and restricted, and coal irons and oil lamps were recommended as energy savers, in preference to electrical appliances. In a state that produced cars but banned driving, built housing developments but withheld heat and running water, announced that it had harvested the biggest grain crop in history but put its people on meager bread rations, this paradoxical turning back of the clock belied the outward forms of modernization and exposed their lack of content.

The Role of the Ruling Class. The composition, outlook, and policy options of the Romanian ruling class underwent a marked change after the 1960s. As a self-appointed agent of change, empowered with an authority no Romanian elite had ever had before, the Communist ruling class had the means to impose almost unchallenged its political philosophy and strategy of development. Contrary to the Soviet approach, which still considered the party in Bolshevik terms as a vanguard of the working class, the Romanian leaders made it into a mass party. Membership swelled from less than a thousand in 1944, to a million and a half in 1965 (when Ceauşescu came to power), to over 3.6 million by 1987. Most undoubtedly joined for opportunistic reasons and largely in name only, gaining little real privilege or power from their party affiliation. The real holders of power and privilege, the "central nomenklatura," accounted for about 10,000, according to official figures. Inclusion of the "local nomenklatura" brought the figure to slightly under 200,000, according to the same official data. The political class was probably one of the smallest in Romanian history.[5] It was also one of the most provincial and least educated: 80 percent of the party members and 78.5 percent of what the plenum of March 1987 called the "party apparat" had a peasant or working-class background. The education of the elite was mostly ensured by the party academy, and recruiting policies clearly favored the apparatchiks over the technocrats.[6]

Under such circumstances, it should come as no surprise that the elite was antiintellectual, xenophobic, isolationist, antitechnocratic, and hostile to change. The nationally insulated ruling class of the 1980s stood in striking contrast to the Romanian elites of the nineteenth and early twentieth centuries, who were formed for the most part of highly educated, cosmopolitan, and active agents of change along the lines of the western European model. Nor did the political class resemble the earlier Communist elite, which had engineered the new course of the 1960s. In general, those individuals had been educated before the war. Many of them had a bourgeois background, and some belonged to ethnic minorities. Their domestic and foreign policy successes of the 1960s could also be explained by the ability with which they had been able to coopt a large number of technocrats and intellectuals belonging to the old educated classes.

Another peculiar trait of the new elite was its obsession with history. It fostered a neonationalism strongly reminiscent in some respects of the one practiced by the Romanian right in the 1930s: emphasis on Dacian, as opposed to Roman, ethnic roots; constant appeals to historical symbols and myths and affective identification with figures from the national past as devices to legitimate present policies; hyperbolic claims regarding Romanian historical and cultural achievements, promoting an inflated national ego; and indirect encouragement of xenophobic, pseudopatriotic attitudes, including anti-Semitic, anti-Russian, and anti-Hungarian ones. The regime's resort to these appeals was on the one hand manipulative, seeking to earn a semblance of national legitimacy. But on the other hand it reflected the personality of Ceauşescu, who would rather have been perceived as a traditional Romanian leader than as a successor of the first Romanian Communists. Ceauşescu discoursed at great length on Romanian history, beginning with the Dacians, on whom he was fond of quoting Herodotus. The party museum displayed the story of the Dacian kingdom in its first rooms.

No other European Communist leadership liked to display so openly a "touch of royalty."[7] As Mihai Botez, one of the most articulate Romanian dissidents, argued, such a regime all but precludes successful modernization. It lacks the ability to identify real needs and rational goals, perpetuating instead a fantasy world, and is therefore subject to a higher probability of error than other Communist regimes.[8] The country was being run on the basis of "cherished instructions" from Ceauşescu, who, on whirlwind inspection tours, dictated to farmers when and how to plow or harvest, to engineers how to build a nuclear power plant, and to historians what to write about the Middle Ages. While effective as an instrument for the exercise of Ceauşescu's personal power, his cult tended to generate even more centralism, favoring apparatchiks over technocrats and ideological mobilization over cost-benefit analysis in the formulation and implementation of policies.

Inevitably, as in Albania, North Korea, or Stalin's U.S.S.R., the cult helped to produce a closed society, repression, international isolation, and cultural decline. In Ceauşescu's Romania, failure to report a conversation with a foreigner was a criminal offense (decree no. 408 [1985]), possession of typewriters was subject to authorization by the police (decree no. 98 [1983]), and information policy was so restrictive that it limited television programming to two hours per weekday.

The structural changes within the ruling class also impaired its ability to carry on the highly successful foreign policy of the 1960s and the early 1970s. By skillfully resisting Soviet military and political pressure, as well as Comecon integration, the ruling elite had secured a certain degree of autonomy for the country that made the elite relatively popular both at home and in the West. But neither Romanian nor Western analysts seemed to notice the growing indications from the mid-1970s on that the same policies that had led to conflict with the Soviets in the 1960s were preparing the ground for a return to the fold in the 1980s. The main disagreement with Moscow had been over the strategy of modernization, but modernization could only have succeeded if it had been based on domestic reforms. It was not, because the Romanian Communists remained wedded to the classical Soviet economic and political model. As the personality cult grew in intensity, and economic failure grew more evident, it became clear that the prodigal son had no choice but to turn to the economic and political patron he had left twenty years earlier.

The Romanian-Soviet rapprochement in foreign policy seemed to be the dominant trend of the 1980s just as rapprochement with the West had been in the 1960s. The economy also gradually pulled back into reliance on the Soviet Union. This was not without certain advantages, since only the less demanding Soviet market could absorb the surplus production of Romania's mammoth heavy industries. Nor could these survive without the raw materials and energy supplied by the U.S.S.R. The rapprochement, however, was not only economic but also political.

Despite Ceauşescu's continued quest for recognition as a world statesman in his own right, his foreign policy aligned itself with Soviet positions on most topical international issues. If Ceauşescu's offices as an international intermediary had few takers and returned only modest political dividends even in the halcyon days of his diplomacy, his open embrace of the Soviet agenda on a variety of international issues did nothing but diminish his credibility. The main cause of the loss of international credibility and respect, however, was the West's gradual realization of the reactionary and repressive nature of the regime's domestic policies. The high expectations raised between 1964 and 1968 were not borne out, and the enormous amount of goodwill and political capital that still existed in the West through the 1970s was squandered. The same leadership that had once been praised for its presumed sophistication and innovative spirit managed to maneuver itself into a position of isolation from almost all its former friends and supporters.

With Deng's China, relations were correct but perfunctory. Yugoslavia expressed unusually open criticism on the full range of bilateral issues as well as on the Romanian regime's ideological dogmatism. West Germany tried hard to save what could be saved of their Romanian Ostpolitik, which reduced itself to buying the freedom of as many ethnic Germans as possible, as quickly as possible. Relations with France became downright cold, and French governmental as well as media criticism of the regime's policies was acerbic. In Washington, the policy of differentiation came to be invoked against Romania rather than in her favor, as the regime was no longer deemed worthy of rewards. Congress voted, and the executive branch concurred, to suspend Romania's most-favored-nation status, which was lost in 1988. Even the Communist parties in western Europe came to find the Ceauşescu regime an embarrassment to socialism and publicly criticized its dogmatism and unresponsiveness to workers' needs.

The reformist course launched by Mikhail Gorbachev in the U.S.S.R. after 1985 indirectly helped to highlight the Ceauşescu regime's resistance to innovation even more, and increased the regime's isolation. Ceauşescu and the leadership group around him emerged as the most vocal opponents of reform in the Soviet bloc. The Romanian media maintained complete silence about Soviet (as well as Hungarian or Chinese) political and economic reforms. In speech after speech, Ceauşescu denounced any reforms aimed at allowing greater scope for decentralization of planning and management, market mechanisms, and small private ownership. These, he claimed, were incompatible with socialism. He equally vociferously rejected any idea of scaling down the direct control of the Communist Party over society and any relaxation in the combat against religion and for the shaping of "new socialist man." Deploring the fact that these and similar ideas were current in "certain countries," Ceauşescu anathematized them as "rightist deviations" and "liquidationism" that "dismantle the foundations of socialism."

Bucharest adopted the position that the new Soviet course was not at all new for Romania, where democratization, self-management, and the break with "conservatism" and "obsolete models" were allegedly implemented long ago. But Ceauşescu's idea of in-system innovation clearly differed from everybody else's: his consisted, as he summed it up, of "expanding the leading role of the party in all areas of activity," greater centralization of economic planning and management, "strengthening and expanding socialist property," and stepped-up ideological mobilization.

Ceauşescu vowed in ringing tones to keep reformist heresies out of Romania, and his lieutenants in the party leadership faithfully echoed those vows. The Romanian media spewed out a constant flow of polemics against Soviet and eastern European reformism, without, however, naming the parties and countries being targeted.

The Soviet foreign minister, Eduard Shevardnadze, was quoted in the Western press as having said that "no one would believe . . . that there are no problems between Romania and the Soviet Union." Although Soviet leaders carefully avoided open criticism, the tenor of some Radio Moscow programs in Romanian, as well as Gorbachev's and then head of state Andrei Gromyko's public comments on their visits to Romania in 1987 and 1988, implied that sooner or later the Soviets expected their allies to follow the new Soviet line.

Societal Responses. As in most eastern European countries, Romanian dissent was encouraged by the relatively more tolerant atmosphere generated by the Helsinki Accords. Individual protesters and intellectual critics of the regime, who had previously been isolated from one another—writer Dumitru Tepeneag in the early 1970s was a case in point—now coalesced in the short-lived human rights movement spearheaded by novelist Paul Goma in 1977. That same year, some 35,000 miners went on strike in the Jiu Valley. In 1979 about two thousand blue- and white-collar workers from Bucharest and several provincial cities managed to join a fledgling free trade union before the police cracked down. The years 1978–79 witnessed a flurry of dissident religious activities by the Orthodox, the Baptists, and other evangelical Christians. Among them was the eloquent Orthodox priest Gheorghe Calciu, who became the standard-bearer in the struggle for religious rights before being sent back to the jails in which he had already spent so many years. Criticism of Ceauşescu's style of rule was even voiced within the highest-level party bodies by several members of the ruling elite. In addition, several ethnic Hungarian party officials criticized the regime's nationality policies. The situation offered a unique chance for creating a country-wide, institutionalized human rights movement. But the various individuals or groups—workers, intellectuals, religious activists, and Magyars—acted independently, with no attempt to create a united front. The security police, using both diplomacy and brutality, had little difficulty in repressing one by one these isolated attempts to challenge the established order. Some of the workers' leaders simply "disappeared," and have remained unaccounted for ever since. Religious dissidents were sentenced to prison. Some oppositionists were put into psychiatric hospitals, and many nonconformist intellectuals were allowed or pressured to emigrate. By 1980, what could have become a lively and interesting dissident movement seemed to have come to a complete halt.

Individual dissenters continued nevertheless to emerge all the time from amid an atomized populace, and they sought to express their views publicly despite the extremely repressive atmosphere of the 1980s. Mihai Botez, a professor of mathematics, formulated a solid, technocratically oriented critique of the party's economic strategies, emphasizing their unrealistic nature, lack of professionalism, and divorce from the country's needs. The poet Dorin Tudoran focused on the social position of the intelligentsia and its political passivity.

One noteworthy feature of the opposition movement of the 1980s was the reappearance of activists of the old political parties that had been banned in 1947. The liberals made themselves heard through the open letters of Ion I. C. Bratianu (who died in 1987) and through the programmatic documents of the group Romanian Democratic Action. Former leaders of the National Peasant Party managed to recruit some young people, including workers, and to establish a human rights association with mostly young members in Bucharest and in Transylvania. The political approach of these groups was strictly legalistic, demanding respect for the constitution and economic and political reforms leading toward a pluralistic order.

Religious dissent lost its political overtones around 1984–85 and centered mainly on fundamentalist communities with their preachers, networks of Bible smugglers, inspirational prayer meetings, and religion courses for the laity and for children. Fundamentalist Christian movements posed a challenge to the official ideology by their very existence, and especially by their growth. They had nearly half a million members in Romania, more than in all other eastern European countries combined. In addition, the banned Eastern Rite Catholic (Uniate) church retained an underground structure complete with bishops and priests. One Uniate believer, Doina Cornea, also became the best-known intellectual critic of the regime and a figure of great moral authority within the decimated community of political dissidents. But the Uniate church's organizational strength and political effectiveness declined markedly as a result of police repression and forced emigration.

Members of the Hungarian minority, under the growing pressure of the regime's policy of ethnic "homogenization,"[9] protested the violation of nationality and cultural rights. Some of them were sentenced to prison, while others died under suspicious circumstances. Members of the Hungarian minority succeeded in producing Romania's only samizdat periodicals. At the same time, the first-ever samizdat periodical in the Romanian language appeared and thrived in Budapest as the organ of Free Romania, an opposition group of ethnic Romanians from Romania who had found a haven in Hungary and linked up with the Hungarian democratic opposition.

Social unrest broke out in several parts of the country in 1987. In Braşov, Romania's second largest industrial center, thousands of workers staged a hunger march reminiscent of the industrial strikes of the nineteenth century and went on to devastate the party and administrative headquarters. The riot was put down by the military with armored vehicles and dogs; severe judicial reprisals followed. Strikes and other forms of protests, some involving violence, took place in Iaşi, Timişoara, Cluj, and Bucharest. For the first time since 1956, students joined in the protests in Iaşi and Timişoara. Yet the protests were uncoordinated and lacked any follow-up action, and the protesting groups failed to make connections with the intellectual dissidents or the political opposition. The disturbances turned out to be of an episodic nature and made no discernible impact on the leadership's policies or its hold over the party.

As the Ceauşescu regime approached its twenty-fifth jubilee, its rule appeared stable, and the leadership displayed greater determination than ever to perpetuate its policies and enforce its ideological values in defiance of the reformist trends at work in other countries in the Soviet sphere. Faced with the complete blockage of political change in their country, many Romanians pinned their hopes on the progress of reforms in the socialist world, which, they expected, would ultimately sweep up Romanian Stalinism in their course. But most Romanian as well as foreign observers also believed that after nearly twenty-five years under Ceauşescu, the damage to the social and even biological fabric of the Romanian people would take several generations to repair.

The 1989 Revolution and the Collapse of Communism in Romania

Matei Calinescu and Vladimir Tismăneanu

Over four decades of harsh Communist rule in Romania came to an abrupt end on 22 December 1989. The fall of Ceauşescu and the disintegration of the Romanian Communist Party as a formal organization were the result of an irresistible popular uprising that would have been unthinkable a few months or even a few weeks before. Indeed, many Romanians regard that day as a miracle, "the miracle of December." On that day the wave of popular anger that had started in mid-December in Timişoara reached its climax in Bucharest and swept away the Ceauşescu regime in a matter of hours. Significantly, the poet and former dissident Mircea Dinescu, who was the first to speak on liberated Romanian television on 22 December, began his statement with the words: "God has turned his face toward Romania again."[1] It is remarkable that normally skeptical, freethinking Romanian intellectuals should resort to such theological language. The sincere, intelligent need for religious terms and metaphors (a need not diminished by the awareness that they are often exploited for political purposes)[2] measures how deeply traumatic the character of Communism in Romania was, particularly in its last, grotesque, terrifying, and indeed demonic years, during which Ceauşescu ran the country as a virtual concentration camp. Other metaphors—psychological metaphors of madness, for instance—have also been used and misused in trying to explain what will, in the life of individual Romanians as well as of the nation as a whole, remain ultimately unexplainable.

But (before we ascend to the metaphysical level where all things that matter become mysterious) it is our intellectual duty to understand the

understandable and to explain the explainable. Seen in a broader international context, the events of December 1989 in Romania become
less miraculous and more comprehensible—yet lose nothing of their
drama and originality. After the so-called velvet revolution in Czechoslovakia, and after the October–November events in East Germany, including the spectacular collapse of the Berlin Wall on 9 November
1989, it became clear that Gorbachev's Soviet Union had renounced
the Brezhnev Doctrine both in word and in deed, and that it would not
intervene in Warsaw Pact countries to prop up crumbling Communist
regimes. Given the new situation, Ceauşescu's days in Romania were
numbered. Of course, he could have lasted a while longer, and the
specifics of his removal from power could have been different. But the
time had come for this primitive Stalinist to go. After all, the situation
in Romania was explosive, the population desperate, the economy in a
shambles, and the dictatorial-personalistic regime of Nicolae and Elena
Ceauşescu, based primarily on repression, was structurally fragile. A
spark was enough to ignite the whole edifice.[3]

The Romanian revolution began in Timişoara, and what sparked it was
the courage of one man, the Reverend László Tőkés, a minister of the
Reformed (Calvinist) church and a member of the Hungarian ethnic
minority. Tőkés, the spiritual leader of a small congregation, had been
repeatedly harassed by the Romanian secret police, or Securitate, for
his unyielding stance on human and religious rights. Still unintimidated
after numerous threatening telephone calls and after being beaten up
by Securitate thugs in November 1989, he decided to disobey an evic-
tion order. He had been transferred by his bishop to another parish in
a smaller town as a result of official manipulations and pressure. On
the day the order was to be carried out, 15 December, people from
Tőkés' congregation, spontaneously joined by Romanians, Serbs, and
other ethnic groups, formed a swelling crowd around his church. The
crowd kept growing, and the next day the Communist mayor of Timişoara, summoned by nervous Securitate officials, failed to persuade
them to disperse. The mood of the crowd was increasingly defiant, but
it was not before Tőkés himself (obviously under duress) told his supporters to go home that the first cries of "Down with Ceauşescu!" were
heard. During the night of 16–17 December, the city was virtually taken
over by anti-Ceauşescu and anti-Communist demonstrators, including
students of the Timişoara University and Polytechnic and massive
groups of workers.[4] A religiously inspired act of civil disobedience had

thus triggered a full-blown political rebellion against one of the most tightly controlled totalitarian societies in the world.

But on Ceauşescu's orders, a massacre took place.[5] On the same day, 17 December, the news of the Timişoara uprising and its bloody repression reached Budapest, Belgrade, and the Western capitals. Immediately it started to be beamed back toward Romania by Radio Free Europe, the BBC, Deutsche Welle, and others. From this moment the fate of the Ceauşescu regime was sealed. The dictator himself, in the middle of a political and social crisis whose significance apparently escaped him, decided to act as if nothing had happened: he went as scheduled on his official visit to Tehran, leaving on 18 December and returning on 20 December.

Back in Bucharest, Ceauşescu made what many Romanians regard as his first big mistake (although by that time anything he did would have been a mistake). On 20 December he addressed the nation on radio and television, blaming the events in Timişoara on "hooligans" and "fascists" instigated from abroad. He praised the army and the Securitate for their "utmost forbearance" before taking action and thus took personal responsibility, since he was supreme commander of the Romanian armed forces, for what (as by now everybody knew) had been a savage massacre of untold proportions.[6] His stern warning that demonstrators in other places would be fired on was seen as both a confirmation of the horrifying news about the Timişoara bloodbath and a humiliating challenge to a restless, edgy, deeply frustrated population. This was perhaps the magic moment when, in the consciousness of many Romanians, the threshold of fear was crossed. Revulsion, moral indignation, outrage, and contempt suddenly overcame fear.

Ceauşescu's second, and even more astonishing, mistake was his idea of organizing, that is, stage managing, a huge demonstration of popular support for his rule, as he had done only a month before after the eerie nonevent of the Fourteenth Party Congress. But this time, the tens of thousands of people who were herded into the palace square on the morning of 21 December under the tight supervision of Securitate and assorted party bosses were there to acclaim the man who only a day before had taken responsibility for the savage Timişoara repression. These people formed a highly volatile crowd, one on the brink of rebellion. When Ceauşescu started his live television address from the balcony of the Central Committee building, he obviously did not expect what he should have been prepared to expect. The television images, which were soon broadcast all over the world, captured the unique moments of the tyrant's utter surprise. With a mixture of incredulity and anger on his face and a bewildered waving of his arms, he heard the cheering multitude suddenly booing him, and the ritual chants of "Ceauşescu şi poporul" (Ceauşescu and the people) changed to "Ceau-şescu dictatorul" (Ceauşescu the dictator). Millions of people saw and heard this on television. The image was extinguished—though Mrs. Ceauşescu's voice could still be heard for a few seconds saying "Be calm! Be calm!"—and the broadcast was interrupted for three long minutes. When live transmission resumed, Ceauşescu was making lame prom-ises, for example, a raise in the minimum wage, to calm the angry crowd. But power had already slipped, invisibly, irreversibly, from the Central Committee building to the street.

There followed a sequence of revolutionary events: a string of stu-dent demonstrations in University Square, which went on through 22 December in spite of bloody repression; spontaneous anti-Ceauşescu marches through the streets of Bucharest, in which hundreds of thou-sands participated; the seizure of the television station with the help of army units that switched sides and supported the popular uprising. Virtually all the participants experienced feelings of extraordinary ela-tion and even ecstasy, which were described in an avalanche of inter-views, declarations, and statements published by the suddenly liberated media.[7] The resistance put up by isolated units of the secret police between 22 December and Christmas Day, when Ceauşescu and his wife were executed, provided a dramatic background to the popular eu-phoria but could not essentially affect the nearly universal sense of relief, enthusiasm, and hope sweeping the country. Despite the violence, less widespread than was at first thought, the revolutionary feast lasted well into the first days of January 1990, when disappointment and mis-trust in the new government, the self-appointed National Salvation Front (NSF), started to set in. The pace of disenchantment with the NSF increased in January and February, when its ruling council (in which former Communist officials held the key positions) was responsible for a series of blunders, broken promises, recantations, and contradictory actions, suggesting—beyond ideological disarray and vicious infight-ing—the decision of the old party apparatus to stay in power no matter what.

A more dispassionate observer might have figured out the NSF's in-tentions as early as the trial and execution of Nicolae and Elena Ceau-şescu on Christmas Day 1989. A public trial had been promised by an NSF spokesman when the Ceauşescus were captured soon after their flight by helicopter from the roof of the Central Committee building on the morning of 22 December. But on 25 December it was announced that a secret military tribunal had sentenced the two Ceauşescus to death and that they had been executed immediately. To justify the procedure the NSF invoked the resistance put up by Ceauşescu loyalists in the Securitate. In hindsight, however, one can see that this resistance was more sporadic and less intense than some spectacular television footage, which concentrated on the burning of the central university library in Bucharest and the extensive damage to the art museum located on the second floor of the old Royal Palace, suggested.[8] The execution of the Ceauşescus, the NSF argument went, saved many lives by making the Securitate "terrorists" stop fighting for a lost cause and surrender. Subsequently, though, since no such "terrorists" were brought to justice or otherwise heard about, some people started having doubts about their existence.

At any rate, the death of the tyrant was good news for the Romanians, and the fact that it coincided with Christmas added an intriguing symbolic dimension (people interviewed on television spoke of the "death of the Antichrist"). Unfortunately, instead of a clear-cut case of revolutionary tyrannicide, the people of Romania were faced with one of judicial murder. Disturbing details emerged after the execution which suggested that the death sentence had been imposed by key NSF leaders on 24 December—the day before the trial started.[9] The way the heavily and secretly edited videotape from the trial was released fragmentarily and with huge unexplained gaps (from a trial that lasted approximately nine hours only a total of fifty-odd minutes was shown for nearly four months), raised serious suspicions about the candor of the Front.

These were aggravated on 22 April 1990, when the government released a videotape with a more detailed but still secretly edited version of the trial (it lasted ninety minutes and was shown almost simultaneously on Romanian and French television).[10] Unlike the older version, the new tape showed the faces of the members of the military tribunal which sentenced the Ceauşescus to death. In addition to the judges and the lawyers, one could recognize General Victor Atanasie Stănculescu, a first deputy minister of defense at the time of the trial and the liaison between the army and the Securitate; one could also recognize Gelu Voican-Voiculescu, an enigmatic geologist who was supposed to have participated in the storming of the Central Committee building on 22 December, and Virgil Măgureanu, a professor of Marxism at the former Party Academy Stefan Gheorghiu and the man who had read the first official NSF proclamation on Romanian television after Ceauşescu's flight from Bucharest. Ceauşescu must have been familiar with

at least one face—that of General Stănculescu, whom he had known
for years as a docile subordinate—among those who decided his fate.
Stănculescu was one of the very last persons to have talked to Ceauşescu
on the morning of 22 December, when the dictator tried to escape by
helicopter from the besieged Central Committee building. In fact, Stănculescu had arranged the (false) escape and the delivery of the couple
to the military tribunal.[11] Under the circumstances, Ceauşescu may well
have seen his trial as a form of vengeance perpetrated by a treasonous
praetorian guard rather than an expression of revolutionary justice,
and his fury against the "putschists" was less absurd than it initially
sounded.

The newer videotape confirms the hypothesis that the revolutionary
upheaval was immediately followed by an anti-Ceauşescu coup organized by disenchanted members of the party, army, and Securitate bu-
reaucracies. After serving for a brief time after the revolution as
minister of economy, General Stănculescu replaced General Nicolae
Militaru as minister of defense (to whose department the Securitate was
now subordinate) in February 1990. Gelu Voican-Voiculescu emerged
as the number two man in Prime Minister Petre Roman's government.
In April 1990, Virgil Măgureanu was appointed director of the newly
created Romanian Intelligence Office. Direct involvement in the trial
seemed to have enhanced at least some political careers.

A mystery as profound as the one that surrounds the Ceauşescu trial
surrounds the origins of the NSF. Who appointed Ion Iliescu president
of the Front? How was he selected? Who decided, and how, to appoint
the original members of the Front? What were the criteria? How was
the prime minister, Petre Roman, selected? Such questions remained
without a credible official answer. The notion that these people had
been swept into power by a spontaneous revolutionary wave—as they
claimed—was less than convincing. Had there been a conspiracy? Did
Moscow play any role in it?[12] Had a genuine popular revolution been
the object of an attempted—and at least temporarily successful—ab-
duction by the old party apparatus, relying now on elements that had
protested the Ceauşescu regime or that had been in disfavor with it?
These are questions that only future historians will have the chance to
answer more fully.

The original NSF council included a number of genuine non-
Communist dissidents ready to endorse its initial platform promising
free elections, the establishment of a democratic system, and, more
broadly, the development of a civil society in Romania. As the chasm
between the Front's rhetoric and its Leninist practice became evident,

celebrated dissidents like Doina Cornea and Ana Blandiana resigned. Romanians began to realize that the new structure of power was in many ways a continuation of the old one. The Front's systematic ambiguities were criticized by outspoken journalists like Octavian Paler who took issue with the NSF ideologue Silviu Brucan on the question of democracy. While Brucan argued that Romania's transition to democracy would take at least two decades—an interval during which a paternalistic regime was necessary to keep the nation together—Paler emphasized the relevance of the country's democratic traditions and referred to the 1923 constitution as the best guide for a speedy return to the rule of law.

As was obvious from the early moments of the revolution, Communism as a system of government was dead in Romania. But the party nomenklatura—with the two outstanding exceptions of the Ceauşescus, to whom we might add the immediate members of their clan and their closest collaborators—were still around and held positions of power which they were not ready to abandon. When the Front leadership proclaimed its policy of abolishing one-party rule and allowing multiparty democracy, it offered the entire old party apparatus a model of instant conversion from Marxism-Leninism to "democracy," the "market," and, if necessary, even "Christianity" (see note 2). At the same time, and as alarmingly, the NSF was setting itself long-term goals exceeding by far the capacity of a provisional administration. It looked like the NSF was prepared to keep power for a long time. That it did not have a mandate or any legitimacy did not seem to matter.[13]

Unlike the other eastern European revolutions, the Romanian one was violent—shockingly so, even if the number of people who died in it was smaller than initially claimed. Romania was different from its neighbors in eastern Europe because it had never undergone real de-Stalinization. It had never passed through the process of moving from the absolute rule of one man to the slightly less absolute rule of a Communist politburo. To Westerners the distinction between these two forms of oppression may seem irrelevant, but it is very great to people who live under them. A single absolute ruler in the mold of Stalin, Mao, Kim Il Sung, Castro, or Ceauşescu means a rule unchecked and unmoderated in its arbitrariness, ignorance, and cruelty. The autocrat enters with impunity into the most erratic actions. A politburo, even one made up of cruel individuals, provides a moderating check against the worst depravities of any one member. Compare, for example, Stalin's rule to that of Khrushchev. The former terrorized not only the whole of society but also his closest collaborators. The latter returned to the alleged "Leninist norms of party life" precisely because the party bureaucracy could no longer tolerate Stalinist methods of intimidation and persecution. In the same vein, with all his sins, Erich Honecker was only the primus inter pares within a Mafia-like politburo in East Germany. Ceauşescu, however, not only monopolized power; he also dynasticized the Romanian party by appointing members of his clan to top party and government positions.[14] The degree of hatred oppressed people feel toward their masters is bound to be quite different in the two cases.

Some historical background may be useful here. Nicolae Ceauşescu did not emerge out of the blue. He was the product of Romanian Communist political culture,[15] and his extravaganzas did nothing but carry to an extreme its never-abandoned Stalinist features. He climbed the career ladder within the RCP under the protection of Gheorghe Gheorghiu-Dej, the party's general secretary between 1944 and 1965, and Gheorghiu-Dej, his mentor, was the one who avoided the de-Stalinization process initiated by Khrushchev in 1956. Ceauşescu, who became a politburo member in 1954, helped Gheorghiu-Dej to collectivize agriculture forcibly and organize repeated antiintellectual witch hunts.

Most of the original Romanian Communists, who before the arrival of the Soviet troops in August 1944 numbered no more than a thousand, preserved an uncompromising commitment to hard-line Stalinism. Under both Gheorghiu-Dej and Ceauşescu, the party suffered from a painful inferiority complex. Its leaders were perfectly aware that their coming to power was the result of Soviet diktat and that they lacked any genuine popularity and legitimacy. For a long time, this was their Achilles' heel: a total alienation from the Romanian nation. Scared by Khrushchev's anti-Stalin campaign, Gheorghiu-Dej simulated Romanian patriotism and defied Moscow's plans for economic integration within the Comecon. Instead of de-Stalinizing Romania, he de-Sovietized her. But by the end of his life, the country had the potential to become a second Yugoslavia. A good rate of economic growth and encouraging links with the West could have been used for a gradual dissolution of Stalinism. In 1964 Gheorghiu-Dej decided to release all the political prisoners and to start a cautious process of liberalization.[16] Even the national intelligentsia, viscerally anti-Communist, was ready to credit the party leadership for the break with Moscow.

Ironically, when Nicolae Ceauşescu took power in March 1965, it appeared that he would de-Stalinize the party. He condemned the holding of political prisoners, deplored the abuses of the past, and instructed the Securitate to abide by the law. In April 1968 he rehabilitated Lucrețiu Pătrășcanu, a former politburo member and Marxist thinker executed in 1954 under trumped-up charges of espionage. He also reinstated in the party many victims of Gheorghiu-Dej's terror and proclaimed—hypocritically, as would soon become clear—the need to write a true history of both the party and the country. It looked like an incipient glasnost, with Ceaușescu championing a self-styled version of reform Communism. But it was really hardly more than a ploy to consolidate his power. At the same time, Ceaușescu continued to de-Sovietize through his independent line in foreign policy. For example, he distanced his country from the Soviet Union by maintaining diplomatic relations with Israel after 1967 and by vehemently condemning the Soviet invasion of Czechoslovakia in 1968.

His stance won Ceaușescu early plaudits and even aid from Western governments. In April 1968 Charles de Gaulle visited Romania and congratulated Ceaușescu on his alleged independence. In August 1969, Richard Nixon went to Bucharest, where he was triumphantly received by an increasingly self-enamored Ceaușescu. The myth of the maverick diplomat, the supernegotiator and only trustworthy Communist leader, was naively believed by many Western analysts, who glossed over Ceaușescu's growing dictatorial propensities. This image also strengthened him by allowing him to portray dissidents as traitors.

Ceaușescu's Stalinist inclinations were catalyzed by a trip he made in May 1971 to China and North Korea. He appears then to have considered the possibility of importing into Romania the methods of indoctrination used during Mao's Cultural Revolution. This was as much a matter of personal preference as of long-term ideological considerations. Ceaușescu was trying to contain the liberalization movement in Romania, curb growing intellectual independence, and deter students from emulating their rebellious peers in other Communist states. He was also trying to consolidate his personal power and get rid of those in the apparatus who might have nourished dreams of "socialism with a human face." In July 1971, he published his infamous "theses" for "the improvement of ideological activity," a monument of Zhdanovist obscurantism. What followed was a radical re-Stalinization and the emergence of an unprecedented cult of personality surrounding first himself and then, after 1974, his equally autocratic wife, Elena.

Several thousand people in Romania—the hard core of his followers—came to believe the myth that Ceaușescu was the demiurge of national dignity and sovereignty. Above all, the myth was believed by his wife, who after 1979 became his second-in-command. Her influence catalyzed his Hitlerian personality, expunging the impulses that had

prompted his regime's early promises of liberalization. Many of Ceauşescu's initial supporters, party apparatchiks like Virgil Trofin, Ion Iliescu, and János Fazekas, the prime minister Ion Gheorghe Maurer, and
the defense minister-general Ion Ioniţă, were marginalized or fired.

The only criterion for political success in Ceauşescu's Romania became unconditional loyalty to the president. A permanent encomiastic
deluge was engineered by agitprop hacks: making Ceauşescu's name
synonymous with Communism, the sycophants heaped hagiographic
epithets on him. A victim of the mechanism he had created, Ceauşescu
himself came to believe in his providential role as "the savior of the
nation," "the hero of peace," "the genius of the Carpathians," "the Danube of thought," and "the most brilliant revolutionary thinker of all
times," to quote some of his supporters. In an attempt to ensure his
political immortality, he promoted his youngest son, Nicu, to high party
positions. The dictator dreamed of leaving his imprint on the Romanian
soul. He submitted Romanians to incredible humiliations by forcing
them to simulate joy in times of utter poverty and despondency. He
presided over the bulldozing of old Bucharest[17] and imposed the building of a giant palace, the apogee of monumental fascist/Stalinist kitsch.
Possessed by an overweening hubris, hypnotized by a self-image mag-
nified to grotesque proportions by the corrupt scribes of the presidential court, Ceauşescu completely lost touch with reality.

Ceauşescu was secretly obsessed with the ultranationalistic Iron
Guard and its leader, Corneliu Zelea Codreanu, while believing passionately in orthodox Stalinism. He merged these two horrifying lega-
cies into a personalized tyranny that ranked with any of this century.
Its basis, and the sole explanation for its longevity, was the feared,
omnipresent Securitate. As for the Communist Party, Ceauşescu managed to annihilate it by converting it into a passive body of almost four
million members whose sole duty was to worship him—or at least to
pretend to do so. Not only the party, but all sources of independent
social life were suppressed. In 1977, when coal miners in the Jiu Valley
organized a massive strike, their leaders were captured by the Securitate
and made to disappear permanently. Ten years later, in November
1987, when street demonstrations took place in Braşov, the Securitate
intervened, order was restored, and the organizers vanished. Prominent
intellectual dissidents were forced into either external or internal exile.
There was no possibility of engaging in anything similar to Czechoslovakia's Charter 77 or Poland's Committee for Workers' Defense. An
all-pervasive police terror thwarted any consistent, organized attempt
to launch democratic initiatives from below. After the quashing of the

embryonic Goma movement and of the parallel effort to start a free trade union in 1977, dissent was largely limited to courageous acts of individual defiance of the regime. Romania's civil society was almost completely paralyzed.

With Ceauşescu dead and most of his main acolytes in jail (the first trials of his henchmen were disturbingly reminiscent of Stalinist frame-ups rather than of the Nuremberg trials they were supposed to be modeled after), the question was how deeply the process of uprooting his regime would reach and how soon. Because the Romanian revolution had been a violent one, it was likely to be thoroughgoing. Its martyrs gave it a strong momentum. The first signals coming from post-Communist Bucharest, however, were mixed.

The council of the NSF was initially led by a group made up of old Communists, including army and Securitate generals who had been instrumental in the anti-Ceauşescu coup. Its chairman, Ion Iliescu, had studied in Moscow in the early 1950s and was Ceauşescu's protégé until 1971, when he fell into disgrace for "intellectualism." Although presumably anti-Stalinist, he was far from being anti-Communist. His model seemed to be Gorbachev, and his ideal a reformed version of the one-party system. After his coming to power, Iliescu did not hide these convictions, although he spoke of them rarely and without elaborating. In a conversation with student leaders on 21 January 1990, he described political pluralism as "an obsolete ideology of the nineteenth century." In this he was echoing not so much Gorbachev as the confused, contradictory political philosophy of the NSF's early ideologue, Communist veteran, and former Stalinist, Silviu Brucan.[18]

Brucan expressed his deep contempt for Western-style democracy. He was the author of the concept that the recent Romanian revolution was so original that its aftermath must essentially be different from those of other eastern European countries. Interestingly, for Brucan, as for Iliescu, terms like socialism, Communism, Marxism, Leninism, capitalism, and fascism appeared to have suddenly lost any sense. Both argued that the NSF was a supra-ideological body, a sort of mass party movement, a corporation of diverging but not necessarily incompatible interests. In light of this outlook, there was no real need for other parties to exist and compete for power with the "truly national exponent," that is, the NSF.

In the meantime, however, due to the strong momentum created by the revolution and the new laws on associations that the Front was compelled to pass, political parties started to form. Among them one could identify such historical parties linked to Romania's fragile inter-

war democracy as the National Peasant Party and the National Liberal
Party. The National Peasant Party was led by Corneliu Coposu, an old
activist who had spent nearly two decades as a political prisoner after
his party was outlawed by the Communists in 1947. The reborn National Peasant Party allied itself to a Christian group and immediately
affiliated itself with the Brussels International of European Christian
Democratic parties, to avoid the extreme right-wing connotations of the
term "Christian" in the Romanian political context (reminiscent of the
interwar anti-Semitic League for National Christian Defense led by
A. C. Cuza). The Liberal Party, initially weaker in terms of membership
and organizational structure, was led by perhaps the most articulate
and popular early opponent of the NSF, Radu Câmpeanu, a former
political prisoner and then an expatriate who returned from Paris in
the first days of the revolution. The third historical party, the Social
Democratic Party led by Sergiu Cunescu, was also revived, but it suffered from the handicap of being perceived as a party of the left in a
country where Marxism was synonymous with disaster.

By mid-April, more than sixty other political parties were registered.
Most were bound to disappear soon; others had better chances of sur-
vival (among these were two ecological groups). An intellectually and
politically interesting organization which saw itself as a sort of impartial
arbiter of political life in the fledgling Romanian democracy was the
Group for Social Dialogue. It expressed its views in the incisive weekly
22 (named for the date of the triumph of the revolution, 22 December).
For instance, *22* offered perhaps the most cogent critique of the position adopted by the NSF when, in January 1990, it declared its intention
of running its own candidates in the upcoming elections. What was
supposed to be a caretaker administration, it said, had all of a sudden
become a political party which masqueraded as a nonpolitical mass
movement in the making. In fact it was, in spite of vocal protestations
to the contrary, a reincarnation of the old RCP.

The Communists themselves refrained from trying to reestablish
their party, but it was likely that some of their activists would eventually
try to emulate the Hungarian, East German, or Polish strategy and
propose the formation of a "Socialist Party." Their handicap, however,
would be nearly insurmountable. The general mood among Romanians
was definitely anti-Communist. To dispel suspicions about their hidden
agenda, Front leaders went out of their way to emphasize their anti-
Communism. In January 1990 they even outlawed Communism, but
rescinded the decree a day later. Still the NSF looked increasingly like
the Romanian counterpart to attempts in other Eastern bloc countries

to create a socialism with a human face. In its official platform, the NSF pledged to have broken with the totalitarian system of the previous decades and with "the ideology characteristic of that system" (the term *Marxism-Leninism,* by now totally compromised, was not mentioned).

On 11 March 1990 a mass gathering took place in Timişoara, the cradle of the Romanian revolution. On that occasion representatives of a variety of workers' and students' associations adopted the "Proclamation of Timişoara," a thirteen-point political platform destined to become a watershed in Romania's struggle for democracy. The proclamation represented the most mature and comprehensive formulation of the true objectives of the Romanian revolution. Moreover, it was the most convincing refutation of the NSF's claim to legitimacy. According to the proclamation, which was soon adopted as a programmatic document by hundreds of independent groups and associations throughout the country, the December revolution did not aim merely to replace one clique of Communists with another: "Timişoara initiated a revolution against the entire Communist regime and its entire nomenklatura, and by no means in order to give an opportunity to a group of anti-Ceauşescu dissidents within the Romanian Communist Party to gain power" (art. 7).[19] The potentially devastating blow to the beleaguered bureaucracy came with article 8, which demanded the elimination of former RCP activists and Securitate officers from Romania's political life by banning them for three consecutive legislatures from every electoral list. And as if that had not made things clear enough, the proclamation went on to demand that the new electoral law ban former Communist activists—as opposed to simple party members— from running for the presidential office. This was an unmistakable denial of interim president Ion Iliescu's right to present himself as the heir of the Romanian revolution and the guarantor of social peace and political stability. By the end of April, the NSF had started to show more and more signs of nervousness. The headquarters of opposition parties were repeatedly ransacked, National Peasant and National Liberal activists in the provinces beaten up, and simple supporters harassed and threatened. The climate in Romania grew increasingly tense. In the meantime, millions of Romanians (almost four million by mid-May) registered their support for the Timişoara Proclamation.

The economic legacy of Ceauşescu and of the entire Communist period was disastrous—one might say worse than disastrous. After clear-cut calamities like wars, floods, or earthquakes, the survivors start over again from scratch with renewed energies and hopes. Economically, periods of reconstruction (such as the reconstruction of the western European economies after the devastation of World War II) offer chances of radical modernization. But what were the chances of real modernization in a country like Romania, which had to deal with a burdensome, almost paralyzing legacy? The Stalinist model forced on her after World War II and dogmatically reinforced over the last twenty years (while other Warsaw Pact countries—Hungary, Poland, and, since 1985, even the Soviet Union—were trying to find paths away from it) left the country with an economically unjustifiable and obsolete heavy industry employing hundreds of thousands of workers and with a totally collectivized, only marginally productive agriculture.

Immediately after the fall of Ceauşescu, the Front took some popular remedial measures. The supply of electricity and gas for private and public consumption was increased; the export of badly needed food-stuffs, such as meat, was temporarily halted; food supplies stashed away for party use were distributed to the people. But the leaders of the NSF seemed to assume that by relying on such measures and on direct or indirect handouts from the West, they could postpone indefinitely nec-essary economic reforms. Such an illusion could not last. The problems of what to do about the economy's centralized management, pricing, productivity, exports, imports, and other essential matters were grow-ing by the day, while the economy continued to operate by inertia along the lines established by the old regime.

Virtually all the new parties called for a speedy return to a market economy, but without having any clear idea what this meant. Under the best of circumstances, the process could only be exasperatingly slow, fraught with difficulties, and socially extremely painful. The hardest to face up to would certainly be the social question. In one of the most impoverished countries of Europe, the passage from a centrally planned economy to one oriented, even in part, toward the market would involve massive unemployment of industrial workers, since most of the Stalinist-conceived industries (the giant steelworks at Galaţi was typical) were plainly unviable. The very idea of the market is tied to the related notions of economic expectations (in a general atmosphere of mutual trust) and risk taking. The primitive, barbaric type of so-cialism introduced in Romania by Gheorghiu-Dej and pushed to gro-tesque extremes by Ceauşescu continuously lowered the economic ex-pectations of both the population and the leaders (who could not take seriously the extravagant statistics they cooked up) in an atmosphere of uni-versal distrust. At the same time it discouraged the taking of any econom-ically meaningful risks in a system in which every worker was guaranteed a job at subsistence wages. Over four decades of Stalinist industrialization had created a work force that lacked in many cases the training, discipline, and motivation to be competitive in a market environment.

Nor was the decollectivization of agriculture so simple as some of the new parties, including the National Peasant Party, seemed to have anticipated. Many former peasants, now agricultural workers on state or collective farms, had lost the desire to hold land and work it individually. They did not trust the political future, and their own experience of persecution as small landowners in the 1950s and early 1960s had been a nightmare. Again, one of the main obstacles was the lack of personal motivation, a state of general demoralization induced by the ruthless antipeasant policy of more than forty years.

But in a traditionally agricultural country like Romania, the post-Communist prospects for agriculture were on the whole better than those for industry. With adequate help from a reformed industrial sector and from newly created financial institutions, agricultural productivity could be raised, waste be reduced, and, after a bumpy period of a few years, an incipient real market for agricultural products, directed in part toward export, be created. This could become the starting point for a process of raising the low standard of living of the Romanian people (bringing it closer to that of, say, Greece; statistics show that pre-Communist Romania was, in the 1930s, considerably richer and more developed than Greece). It could also lead to the formation of a broader market of consumer goods and supporting industries, as the heavy industry bequeathed by Stalinism would shrink. Other necessary economic changes (the realization of a stable, convertible currency, the creation of a healthy banking system, and so on) would depend on how the most important natural resource of the country, its potentially rich land, would be managed and how the consumer industries directly linked to it (food processing, lumber, tanneries and leather products, certain mineral resources) would develop.

Uncertainties about the economy could explain, at least partially, some of the most characteristic social and political conflicts of post-revolutionary Romania. The NSF had the support of those—and their number was far from insignificant—who stood to lose from a transition to a competitive market economy. Primarily these were industrial workers in the giant factories that had been favored by Ceaușescu, miners (particularly of low-grade coal), and workers in other unprofitable, wasteful, unviable industries. In addition, the Front could count on the support of the former party bureaucracy, of a large part of the state bureaucracy, and of virtually the entire repressive apparatus of the old regime, which needed—beyond economic protection—some kind of guarantee that it would not be prosecuted for its crimes against the population.

Opposed to the Front were, in the first place, the young, and most visibly the students who had so valiantly fought for the triumph of the revolution. They were joined in their profound anti-Front feelings by most of the professionals (doctors, engineers, technical personnel, and many skilled workers whose services were likely to be in demand in a new market situation). For different reasons—reasons having to do with intellectual freedom—a part of the intelligentsia also turned against the Front, but only a part. The other part, even if not actively pro-Front, was reluctant to renounce certain advantages that the Front could continue to extend (through the so-called creation unions: the Writers' Union, the Artists' Union, the Journalists' Union, the Composers' Union, and others), all the more so as the Front seemed ready to grant such advantages without requiring anything specific in return. But even without this segment of the intelligentsia, opposition to the NSF was widespread and highly articulate. The young, the professionals, and many intellectuals of all generations were ready to demonstrate in the streets for full democracy and against what they called the "neo-Bolshevik" or the "crypto-Communist" tendencies of the Front. Their banners read: "The revolution has been confiscated," 'Beware of the chameleons," or even "Iliescu / Is a second Ceauşescu." To intimidate such vocal but peaceful opponents the Front organized (in a manner often reminiscent of both the Ceauşescu days and interwar governmental electoral tactics) large counterdemonstrations, busing in miners from the Jiu Valley or workers from around the country, and assisted by goons who were responsible for occasional outbreaks of violence.

In April 1990, after having initially approved a private visit of the former king Michael of Hohenzollern (in exile in Switzerland), the Romanian government withdrew his visa at the very last moment under the pretext that he intended to engage in political activities. This highlighted a major problem for Romania's difficult exit from totalitarianism. After the glowing mood of the first postrevolutionary weeks, internecine conflicts started to plague the country's budding democracy. There were rumors of a military takeover if the clashes between vying parties and groups continued to gather momentum. At the same time the absence of a figure of commanding moral-political prestige, comparable to that of Václav Havel in Czechoslovakia, became more and more conspicuous. Under such circumstances, the king represented a

symbol of continuity with Romania's democratic legacy, brutally interrupted by the Communists when they forced him to abdicate on
30 December 1947. The issue was not the monarchic institution as such,
but the person of King Michael as a dignified statesman, who had to
his credit such achievements as taking Romania out of the alliance with
Nazi Germany, engineering the coup against Marshal Antonescu's dictatorship, and ensuring the establishment of a democratic regime on
23 August 1944. By treating the king as an enemy of public order the
NSF achieved little more than making many Romanians think whether
the restoration of constitutional monarchy might not be the best solution for their country's predicament. Was not the king more likely to
bring about the necessary process of national reconciliation than any
of the groups, parties, and individual politicians active during the first
months of 1990?

During the last week of April another confrontation between the NSF
and the people took place. After a number of students organized a vigil
in University Square in Bucharest to protest the overwhelming presence
of former Ceauşescu cronies in the provisional government and to voice
support for the "Timişoara Proclamation," Ion Iliescu stigmatized the
demonstrators as "hoodlums." This was already too much for those who
had not forgotten Ceauşescu's televised speech of 20 December 1989,
when the dictator had called the protesters in Timişoara "hooligans."
From one day to the next, University Square became the center of a
new revolutionary wave. First students, then intellectuals and workers,
gathered there and called for Iliescu to resign. Initially reserved, the
opposition parties called for a dialogue between the NSF leadership and
the exponents of the public opinion. The prolonged occupation of University Square by the demonstrators was a healthy popular response to
the Front's political lie. The students and the intellectuals who joined
the occupation, including some of the country's most prominent cultural and scientific personalities, were asking for a recognition by the
government of the real nature of the revolution as a spontaneous, anti-
Communist uprising and not as a reformist movement within the same
execrated system. Iliescu's verbal and even practical toughness (the police tried to disperse the demonstrators by using truncheons and police
dogs) backfired: by lambasting his young critics as "tramps," he further
polarized the country and contributed to the degradation of the Front's
domestic and international image.[20] But the Front was not without its
strength. Its main source of support came from that new human type
created by Communism, whom the Russian dissident writer Alexander
Zinoviev called *homo sovieticus*: a man who automatically chooses security

(even at the price of enslavement to the state) over freedom with its risks.

Learning the democratic process could not but be difficult in a country whose fragile democratic traditions went back only to the last decades of the nineteenth century and had been brutally interrupted by a series of right-wing dictatorships (1938–44) and then by Communism. Deep-seated ethnic conflicts (particularly between the Romanian majority and the two-million-member strong Hungarian ethnic minority in Transylvania), which had been kept in check by the Ceauşescus' repressive regime and then temporarily overcome by the anti-Ceauşescu revolutionary fervor, reasserted themselves violently in Tîrgu Mureş (March 1990). A new kind of anti-Semitism seemed also to be on the rise, an anti-Semitism that gave a new twist to the old stereotype of Jews as Communists. The Jews, the argument of the new anti-Semites went, brought Communism to Romania from the Soviet Union, installed a system that gave absolute power to an illiterate utopian like Ceauşescu, and, seeing the mess they had created, emigrated to Israel or the West. Even though Romania had only a tiny Jewish community (less than 25,000 by 1990), the new type of anti-Semitism could have unfortunate consequences. It could not only poison cultural life but also become a catalyst for other kinds of bigotry and xenophobia. It came as no surprise that the former Communists saw a welcome opportunity in the rising xenophobic sentiments of a part of the population. By exploiting such sentiments and by playing the nationalist card they seemed to think that they might eventually regain full control of the country. Xenophobia of another type—hatred toward Romanians who had emigrated and had thus become "foreigners"—also received quasi-official encouragement. Irresponsibly, media dominated by the Front (including the daily *Adevărul*) tried to stir up resentment against Romanian emigrés who were returning, mostly for visits, during the first weeks of the revolution. These emigrés, it was suggested, had lived the good life in the West while their fellow Romanians had suffered heroically at the hands of a monstrous dictatorship. Of course, no serious attempt at a democratic reconstruction of the Romanian economy could afford to ignore this important asset, a large emigré community consisting mainly of professionals (the exodus during the Ceauşescu years had reached tens of thousands). These people should have been wooed, not driven away.

But encouraging signals were not absent. The students, who had spearheaded the overthrow of the dictatorship, created a Student League, which could well become a rallying point for Romania's democratic youth. Even though the intelligentsia was divided on the question of the Front, critical intellectuals of various persuasions could bring themselves to organize the Group for Social Dialogue, whose tasks were to reflect on the country's problems, monitor the government's observance of democratic procedures, and, most important, help the development of a civil society in Romania. Other groups patterned after it became active in the first months after the revolution and started publishing some thoughtful magazines. A vigorous free press, if not yet a truly free television, could help the process of democratization. Most encouraging of all, the "Timişoara Proclamation" explicitly condemned any kind of chauvinism (no interethnic conflicts were registered in the multiethnic city of Timişoara or in the Banat region), and the fact that it was endorsed by millions of Romanians of various ethnic backgrounds and religious persuasions showed that both politically and culturally there existed a real popular basis for democracy in Romania.

In a broader perspective, the events of December 1989 created a completely new and irreversible political situation in Romania. The fact that the transition to the post-Communist era was rockier than in other eastern European countries did not mean that a return to the forms and institutions of Communism as they had existed between 1947 and 1989 was possible. But the NSF, an improvised organization of former Communists left without an ideology, had positioned itself to become a kind of mass movement and was bent on trying to slow down the country's drive toward democracy and a market economy. This meant that dangerous and potentially explosive developments could not be ignored. With a divided society and with much of the old party apparatus still controlling the key positions in the state bureaucracy and in the army, neither the possibility of a military coup nor even that of a civil war could be ruled out. It was more likely, however, that the democratic forms and institutions adopted in the postrevolutionary rush to change would eventually help the people themselves to create the democratic content that at the beginning these forms lacked. The initial obstacles on Romania's road to democracy were enormous but not insurmountable.

NOTES

Chapter 1: Early Times

1. A detailed description of the Paleolithic, Neolithic, and Bronze ages appears in V. Dumitrescu, A. Bolomey, and F. Mogosanu, eds., "The Prehistory of Romania," in *The Cambridge Ancient History,* 2d ed. (London: Cambridge University Press, 1982), 3/1:1–74.

2. All the Greek and Latin references to the Getae and the Dacians have been recently republished in *Fontes Historiae Daco-Romanae* (Bucharest: Ed. Academiei, 1964–70), vols. 1 and 2 (henceforth *Fontes*). For references to the Getae and the Dacians in Herodotus, see *Fontes,* 1:47–51. For an English translation, see *Herodotus,* trans. A. D. Godley (New York: G. P. Putnam's Sons; London: W. Heinemann, 1921–24), 3:292–99. In his *Geography,* Strabo (63 B.C.–A.D. 19) explains the origin of the two names: "Some of the people are called Dacians, whereas others are called Getae. The Getae are located around the Pontus and in the East. The Dacians live in the opposite direction, toward Germany and the sources of the Ister" (*Fontes,* 1:237–38). An English version is found in *The Geography of Strabo,* trans. H. L. Jones (New York: W. Heinemann; London: G. P. Putnam's Sons, 1923), 3:213.

3. According to V. Pârvan, Dacia Felix had a surface of approximately 100,000 sq. km and a probable population density of ten inhabitants per sq. km. The number of Dacians living in Moldavia and the Danube plain (that is, outside Roman Dacia) cannot be estimated. V. Pârvan, *Începuturile vieţii române la gurile Dunării* (Bucharest: Cultura Naţională, 1923), 8.

4. *Istoria româniei* (Bucharest: Ed. Academiei, 1960), 1:385.

5. Eutropius wrote his *Breviarum ab urbe condita* in A.D. 368. Here is the passage on the disappearance of the Dacians: "Trajan, after having overpowered Dacia, transplanted thither a great number of men from the whole Roman world [*ex toto orbe romano*] to populate the country and cities since the land had been exhausted [*exhausta*] of inhabitants in the long war waged against Decebalus." *Fontes,* 2:37; English translation in John Selby Watson, trans., *Justin, Cornelius Nepos and Eutropius* (London: G. Bell and Sons, 1876), 510. An inventory of the Dacian and Daco-Roman archaeological findings such as cemetery inventories, coins, pottery, paleochristian objects appears in D. Protase, *Problema continuităţii în Dacia în lumina arheologiei şi numismaticii* (Bucharest: Ed. Academiei, 1966), 103–96. For an analysis of the literary sources dealing with these problems, see V. Iliescu, "Die Räumung Dakiens und die Anwesenheit

der romanischen Bevölkerung Nördlich der Donau im Lichte der Schriftquellen," *Dacoromania* 1 (1973): 5–28.

6. For the Bratei excavations see L. Bârzu, *Continuitatea populației autohtone în Transilvania în secolele IV–V: Cimitirul dela Bratei* (Bucharest: Ed. Academiei, 1973), 79–97.

7. The theory of Aurelian's total evacuation of the Roman and Romanized population from Dacia was also based on Eutropius: "The province of Dacia, which Trajan had formed beyond the Danube, he gave up, despairing, after all Illyricum and Moesia had been depopulated, of being able to retain it. The Roman citizens, removed from the town and lands of Dacia, he settled in the interior of Moesia, calling that Dacia which now divides the two Moesiae, and which is on the right hand of the Danube as it runs to the sea, whereas Dacia was previously on the left." *Fontes*, 2:39; Watson, *Justin, Cornelius Nepos and Eutropius*, 521. The Roman origin of the Romanians, as well as their continuity on the territory of the former Dacia, was not questioned by Byzantine, Italian, German, Transylvanian Saxon, Polish, and Hungarian historians who wrote about the Romanians until the end of the sixteenth century. The first historian to question the continuity theory seems to have been the Transylvanian Hungarian István Szamosközy (1565–1612). His *De Originibus Hungarorum,* written around 1600, was first published in 1667. See A. Armbruster, *La romanité des Roumains: Histoire d'une idée* (Bucharest: Ed. Academiei, 1977), 140–41. Most Hungarian historians continued to accept the continuity theory until the second half of the eighteenth century. All contemporary Hungarian historians claim that the Dacians were completely exterminated by the Romans and that the entire Roman population was transferred to Moesia in A.D. 271–75, leaving Dacia a *terra deserta*. See especially L. Makkai, *Histoire de la Transylvanie* (Paris: Presses Universitaires de France, 1945), 24–29, 67–72; I. Fodor, *In Search of a New Homeland: The Prehistory of the Hungarian People* (Budapest: Corvina, 1982), 278–85; and B. Köpeczi, ed., *Erdély története* (Budapest: Akadémia, 1986), 1:71–106.

8. P. Roussev, "La civilisation bulgare et les peuples balkaniques aux IXème–XIIème siècles," *Etudes Balkaniques* 5/1 (1969); J. Dujcev, ed., *Histoire de la Bulgarie* (Roanne: Horvath, 1977), 49, 170; V. Velkov, ed., *Istoriia na Bulgariia* (Sofia: Izdatelstvo na Bulgarskata Akademiia na Naukite, 1979), 1:298–99. For the Soviet position see especially L. V. Cherepnin, ed., *Istoriia Moldavskoi S.S.R.* (Kishinev: Kartea Moldoveneasca, 1965), 1:57–86; and V. J. Tzaranov, ed., *Istoriia Moldavskoi S.S.R.* (Kishinev: Shtiintza, 1982), 32–46.

9. I. Nestor, "Les données archéologiques et le problème de la formation du peuple roumain," *Revue roumaine d'histoire* 3/3 (1964): 387–417; E. Zaharia, *Săpăturile de la Dridu* (Bucharest: Ed. Academiei, 1967), 151–65; E. Zaharia, *Populația românească din Transilvania în secolele VI–VIII: Cimitirul no. 2 dela Bratei* (Bucharest: Ed. Academiei, 1967), 100–5. For the paleochristian churches discovered in the Banat, southern Transylvania, Wallachia, and the Dobrudja (third–seventh centuries), see D. Păcurariu, *Istoria bisericii ortodoxe române* (Bucharest: Ed. Institutului Biblic, 1980), 1:91, 165–67; and I. Barnea and C. Popa, *Arta creștină în România* (Bucharest: Ed. Institutului Biblic, 1979), 1:21–29, 31–36.

10. The words are quoted in Theophylaktus Simocatta's *Historiae* (A.D. 610–41): "A great confusion occurred among the soldiers, and there was a huge noise; everybody was shouting to turn back and they were encouraging each other, in their native language, to do so, screaming passionately 'torna, torna' [turn back, turn back]." Theophanes, who wrote his chronicles between 810 and 814, quotes a slightly different expression, "torna, torna frater," *Fontes*, 2:539, 604. For the Dacian-Thracian elements in Romanian see I. I. Russu, *Die Sprache der Thrako-Daker* (Bucharest: Ed. Ştiinţifică, 1969), 233–348; idem, *Etnogeneza românilor* (Bucharest: Ed. Ştiinţifică, 1981), 108–10. See also A. Graur, *The Romance Character of Romanian* (Bucharest: Ed. Academiei, 1967), 7–8; and A. Rosetti, *Istoria limbii române* (Bucharest: Ed. Ştiinţifică şi Enciclopedică, 1986), 200–1, 321–25.

11. For the references to the Romanians found in the Byzantine chronicles see *Fontes*, 2:663, and vol. 3 (Bucharest: Ed. Academiei, 1975): 41, 145, 239. A fourth volume of *Fontes* (1982) gives additional Byzantine sources (fourth to fifteenth centuries).

12. I. Szentpétery, *Scriptores rerum hungaricum* (Budapest: Academia Litter. Hungarica atque Societate Histor. Hungarica, 1938), 2:45; and G. Popa-Lisseanu, *Isvoarele istoriei românilor* (Bucharest: Ed. Bucovina, 1934), 1:32.

13. Nestor, "Povest vremenykh let," in *Polnoe sobranie russkikh letopisei*, 3d ed. (St. Petersburg, 1879), 1:9; and K. Lachman, ed., *Der Nibelungen Noth und Klage*, 4th ed. (Berlin, 1878), 173–74, 240, 310.

14. A story of the conquest written by Anonymus appears in Szentpétery, *Scriptores*, 2:33–117, and in Popa-Lisseanu, *Isvoarele*, 1:24–65. The Roman origin of the Romanians was also accepted by Simon of Kéza, the other important medieval Hungarian chronicler, who wrote his *Gesta Hunnorum et Hungarorum* around the end of the thirteenth century. Simon mentions the "Blackis" from Pannonia and Transylvania and, like Anonymus, considers them "pastores et coloni" of the Romans (Szentpétery, *Scriptores*, 2:156–57, 163; and Popa-Lisseanu, *Isvoarele*, 4:32, 37). These two early chroniclers' ideas on the Romanians are repeated in many Hungarian texts of the fourteenth and fifteenth centuries. For the modern Hungarian rejection of the Anonymus story, see Gy. Györffy, "Formations d'état au IXème siècle suivant les *Gesta Hungarorum du notaire Anonyme*," *Nouvelles études historiques* 1 (1965): 27–53.

15. I. Donat, "Aşezările din Ţara Românească în secolele XIV–XVI," *Studii* 11/6 (1956): 75–93; S. Olteanu, "State Formations on the Territory of Romania," in M. Constantinescu, S. Pascu, and P. Diaconu, eds., *Relations between the Autochthonous Populations and the Migratory Populations on the Territory of Romania* (Bucharest: Ed. Academiei, 1975), 35–53. For the still open discussion on the ethnic character of the Barladniks, Brodniks, and Bolokhovenians, of whom only the last were probably Romanians, see V. Spinei, *Moldavia in the XIth–XIVth Centuries* (Bucharest: Ed. Academiei, 1986), 57–58, 104–8, 130; V. Spinei, *Realităţi etnice şi politice în Moldova meridională în secolele X–XIII* (Iaşi: Junimea, 1985), 87–89.

16. *Istoria româniei* (1962) 2: 170.

Chapter 2: The Middle Ages

1. For an analysis of the issue by nineteenth- and twentieth-century Romanian historians, see F. Constantiniu, "Iobăgia în istoriografia română," *Studii și materiale de istorie medie* 10 (1983): 57–114. The classic Marxist interpretation is found in *Istoria României* (Bucharest: Ed. Academiei, 1962), 2:37–39. The counterpoint to this interpretation in found in C. C. Giurescu, *Probleme controversate în istoriografia românească* (Bucharest: Ed. Albatros, 1977), 13–18; and H. H. Stahl, *Controverse de istorie socială românească* (Bucharest: Ed. Științifică, 1969), 62–123.

2. S. Pascu, "Demografie istorică," in S. Pascu, ed., *Populație și societate: Studii de demografie istorică* (Cluj: Dacia, 1972), 1:39–70; S. Ștefănescu, "Conjuncturi socio-economice și situația demografică în țările române în secolele XIV–XVII," in the same volume, 78–88; I. Donat, "Așezările omenești din Țara Românească în secolele XIV–XVI," *Studii* 10/6 (1956): 77–81; C. C. Giurescu, *Țara Românească în secolele XIV–XV* (Bucharest: Ed. Științifică, 1973), 26.

3. I. Donat, "The Romanians South of the Carpathians and the Migratory People," in Constantinescu, Pascu, and Diaconu, *Autochthonous Populations*, 277, 297–98.

4. *Documenta Romaniae Historica: D. Relațiile între țările române* (Bucharest: Ed. Academiei, 1977), 20–21; M. Vlad, "Mișcări demografice în cadrul colonizării rurale din Țara Românească și Moldova," *Studii și materiale de istorie* 14 (1969).

5. V. Costăchel, P. P. Panaitescu, and A. Cazacu, *Viața feudală în Țara Românească și Moldova* (Bucharest: Ed. Științifică, 1957), 28–39; N. Edroiu and P. Gyulai, "Evoluția plugului în țările române," *Acta Musei Napocensis* 2 (1965): 307–43; V. Neamțu, *La technique de la production céréalière en Valachie et en Moldavie jusqu'au XVIIIème siècle* (Bucharest: Ed. Academiei, 1975), 118–38, 235–43.

6. Costăchel, Panaitescu, and Cazacu, *Viața feudală*, 16–23; L. Roman, "Les transylvanians en Valachie," *Revue roumaine d'histoire* 11/5 (1972): 774–82; C. Constantinescu-Mircești, *Păstoritul transhumant și implicațiile lui în Transilvania și Țara Românească* (Bucharest: Ed. Academiei, 1976), 12, 17–29, 66–68.

7. N. Iorga, *Istoria industriilor la români* (Bucharest: Datina Românească, 1927), 163–65; S. Pascu, *Meșteșugurile din Transilvania pînă în secolul al XVI-lea* (Bucharest: Ed. Academiei, 1954), 163–92, 224–30, 236–37; S. Olteanu and C. Șerban, *Meșteșugurile din Țara Românească și Moldova în evul mediu* (Bucharest: Ed. Academiei, 1969), 123–25, 223–29; S. Goldberg, "Comerțul, producția și consumul de postavuri de lînă în țările române, secolul XIV–jumătatea secolului XVIII," *Studii* 24/5 (1971): 886–94.

8. P. P. Panaitescu, "La route commerciale de Pologne à la Mer Noire au Moyen Âge," *Revista istorică romînă* 3/2–3 (1933): 172–93; S. Papacostea, "Începuturile politicii comerciale a Țării Românești și Moldovei (secolele XIV–XVI): Drum și stat," *Studii și materiale de istorie medie* 10 (1983): 9–10.

9. G. Brătianu, *Recherches sur le commerce gênois dans la Mer Noire au XIIIème siècle* (Paris: Geuthner, 1929), 197–208, 219–25; idem, *La Mer Noire: Des origines*

à *la conquête ottomane* (Munich: Societas Academica Dacoromana, 1969), 219–24, 274–76, 325–27; R. Lopez, "L'importance de la Mer Noire dans l'histoire de gênes," in S. Pascu, ed., *Genovesi nel Mar Nero* (Bucharest: Ed. Academiei, 1977), 13–31.

10. F. C. Nano, *Condica tratatelor și a altor legăminte ale României (1354–1937)* (Bucharest: Imprimeria Naţionala, 1938), 1:1, 5, 7–24; I. Ionaşcu, P. Bărbulescu, and G. Gheorghe, *Tratatele internaţionale ale României* (Bucharest: Ed. Politica, 1971), 81–83, 94–99, 105–9, 120–23.

11. For a general discussion on the character of Romanian-Ottoman relations see C. C. Giurescu, "Despre caracterul relaţiilor dintre români şi turci," in Giurescu, *Probleme,* 87–122.

12. R. Rosetti, *Despre originea şi transformările clasei stăpînitoare din Moldova* (Bucharest: C. Goebl, 1906), 1–38; C. Giurchescu, *Studii de istorie socială* (Bucharest: Universul, 1943), 227–31, 237–56, 348–49; I. C. Filitti, *Proprietatea solului în Principatele Române* (Fundaţia Regele Ferdinand I, 1935), 64–109; P. P. Panaitescu, *Interpretări românești: Studii de istorie economică şi socială* (Bucharest: Ed. Universul, 1947), 33–80; D. C. Giurescu, *Ţara Românească în secolele XIV–XV,* 213–45; M. Neagoe, *Problema centralizării statelor feudale româneşti* (Craiova: Scrisul Românesc, 1977), 133–50. For an excellent survey of the discussions regarding the origins of the Romanian aristocracy see N. Djuvara, "Les grands boyars ont-ils constitué dans les principautés roumaines une véritable oligarchie institutionelle et héréditaire?" in *Südost-Forschung* 46 (1987): 1–56. On the important family ties of the Romanian boyars with the Byzantine aristocracy see M. D. Sturdza, "Grandes familles de Grèce, d'Albanie et de Constantinople," *Dictionnaire historique et généalogique* (Paris: Imprimerie Alençonnaise, 1983), 127–58.

13. D. Prodan, *Iobăgia în Transilvania în secolul al XVI-lea* (Bucharest: Ed. Ştiinţifică, 1967), 1:166.

14. M. N. Tikhomirov, "Spisok russkikh gorodov dalnikh i blizhnikh," *Istoricheskie zapiski* 40 (1952): 223; reprinted in C. C. Giurescu, *Tîrguri sau oraşe şi cetăţi moldovene* (Bucharest: Ed. Academiei, 1967), 70; M. Costin, "Khronika ziem moldavskikh i multanskikh, 1677," in Miron Costin, ed. P. P. Panaitescu, *Opere* (Bucharest: ESPLA, 1958), 217; and Oţetea, *Istoria României,* 2:289–94, and 3:67–70.

15. *Documenta Romaniae Historica: B. Ţara Românească* (Bucharest: Ed. Academiei, 1966), 1:3–7.

16. S. Papacostea, "La fondation de la Valachie et de la Moldavie et les roumains de Transylvanie," *Revue roumaine d'histoire* 18/3 (1978): 390–401; N. Stoicescu, *Continuitea românilor* (Bucharest: Ed. Ştiinţifică şi Enciclopedică, 1980), 62. For the rise and fall of the Romanian nobility in southern Transylvania and Maramureş see R. Popa, "Structures socio-politiques roumaines au sud de la Transylvanie au commencement du Moyen-Âge," *Revue roumaine d'histoire* 14/2 (1975): 293–314; R. Popa, *Ţara Maramureşului în secolul al XIV-lea* (Bucharest: Ed. Academiei, 1970), 50–53, 192, 232–33.

17. Despot's letter to the boyars (1561) in *Documente privitoare la istoria românilor* in *Colecţia E. de Hurmuzaki* (Bucharest: 1887–1942; henceforth *Hur-*

muzaki) 2/1:415–16; Michael the Brave's treaty with Sigismund Báthory at Alba Iulia (1595) is given in ibid., 3/1:209–13.

18. Aron's treaty with Casimir IV of Poland (1456) appears in M. Costăchescu, *Documente moldoveneşti înainte de Ştefan cel Mare* (Bucharest: Viaţa Românească, 1932), 2:779–88. The Despot letter and the treaty of Alba Iulia have already been quoted. For Costin see *Opere*, 214–15. For Prince Cantemir's treaty with Peter the Great signed at Lutsk (1711), see *Polnoe sobranie zakonov rossiskoi imperii* (St. Petersburg, 1830), 4:659–62; M. Mitilineu, *Collecţiune de tratatele şi convenţiunile României cu puterile străine* (Bucharest: Nova Typographie, 1874), 76–77; and E. Lozovan, "Le traité russo-moldave de 1711," *Revue des études roumaines* 16 (1981): 64.

19. Letter to Ivan III of Russia, in I. Grosul and A. Oţetea, eds., *Istoricheskie svyazi narodov SSSR i Rumynii v XV–nachalo XVIII v.: Dokumenty i materialy* (Moscow: Nauka; Bucharest: Ed. Academiei, 1965–70; henceforth *Istoricheskie svyazi*), 1:61–63.

20. The Moldavian acceptance of Ottoman suzerainty (1456) can be read in *Documenta Romaniae Historica: A. Moldova*, 2 (1976):85–88; Prince Stefăniţă's letter to the Polish king in N. Iorga, *Scrisori de Boieri. Scrisori de Domni*, 2d ed. (Vălenii de Munte, 1925), 186–89; Prince Neagoe's opinions on the Ottomans in *Teachings to His Son Teodosie (1512–1521)*, in P. P. Panaitescu, *Cronicile slavo-române din secolele XV–XVI publicate de I. Bogdan* (Bucharest: Ed. Academiei, 1959), 239.

21. See especially Stephen the Great's letter to the Hungarian king and other European princes (1475), in M. Costăchescu, *Documente moldoveneşti dela Ştefan cel Mare* (Bucharest: Viaţa Românească, 1933), 2:321.

22. See especially Prince Brâncoveanu's letters to Peter the Great of 31 December 1688, 16 September 1697, and 10 September 1698; also *Istoricheskie svyazi*, 3:105, 118–21, 127–30.

23. I. Matei, "Quelques considérations concernant le régime de la domination ottomane dans les pays roumains," *Revue des études sud-est européennes* 10/1 (1972): 68–73 (part 1); and 11/1 (1973): 82–86 (part 2); S. Gorovei, "Moldova în casa păcii," *Anuarul Institutului de Istorie şi Arheologie "A. D. Xenopol"* 17 (1980): 639–43, 664.

24. M. Berza, "Haraciul Moldovei şi Ţării Româneşti în secolele XV–XIX," *Studii şi materiale de istorie medie* 2 (1957): 7–45; idem, "Variaţiile exploatării Ţării Româneşti de către Poarta otomană în secolele XVI–XVII," *Studii* 11/2 (1958): 59–70. Berza's studies, the only ones to cover the whole period of Ottoman suzerainty, are based mostly on Western sources, especially on Venetian ones. For recent attempts at analyzing economic relations between the Romanians and the Ottomans, using Turkish sources, see M. Guboglu, "Le tribut payé par les principautés roumaines à la Porte jusqu'au début du XVIème siècle," *Revue des études islamiques* 37 (1969): 49–80; M. Maxim, "Regimul economic al dominaţiei otomane în Moldova şi Ţara Românească în secolul al XVI-lea," *Revista de istorie* 32/9 (1979): 1731–65; T. Gemil, "Date noi privind haraciul Ţărilor române în secolul al XVII-lea," *Revista de istorie* 30/8 (1977): 1433–46; M. Berindei and G. Veinstein, *L'empire ottoman et les pays rou-*

mains, 1544–45: Etudes et documents (Paris: Editions de l'Ecole des Hautes Etudes en Sciences Sociales, 1987).

25. *Hurmuzaki*, 12:290–91; M. Berza, ed., *România în sud-estul Europei* (Bucharest: Ed. Politică, 1979), 16; A. Pippidi, *Tradiţia politică bizantină în ţările române în secolele XVI–XVIII* (Bucharest: Ed. Academiei, 1983), 184–89.

26. P. P. Panaitescu, *D. Cantemir: Viaţa şi opera* (Bucharest: Ed. Academiei, 1958), 102–17.

27. N. Iorga, *Byzance après Byzance* (Bucharest: Association Internationale d'Etudes du Sud-Est Européen, 1971).

28. Prince Movilă's letter to the Polish envoy I. Herbult (August 1598) is reprinted in P. P. Panaitescu, *Documente privitoare la Mihai Viteazul* (Bucharest: Fundaţia Regală Carol I, 1936), 52–56.

29. A. Camariano-Cioran, *Les académies princières de Bucharest et de Iassy* (Thessaloniki: Institute for Balkan Studies, 1974), 356–62.

30. Preface to the Gospels (1512); see I. Bianu, N. Hodos, and D. Simonescu, *Bibliografia românească veche* (henceforth *BRV*) (Bucharest: Socec, 1903–44), 1:17.

31. Introductions to the prayer book (1635) and Psalms (1637), *BRV*, 1:105, 139; and *Carte de învăţătură* (1643), 4:184.

32. B. Theodorescu, "Cartea românească veche," *Mitropolia Olteniei* 9–12 (1959): 590 ff; idem, "Repertoriul cărţii vechi româneşti," *Biserica ortodoxă română* 3–4 (1960): 340 ff; C. Tomescu, *Istoria cărţii româneşti de la începuturi pînă la 1918* (Bucharest: Ed. Ştiinţifică, 1968), 21.

33. Coresi, *Tîlcul evangheliilor* (Commentary on the Gospels [1564]), *BRV*, 1:516–17; idem, *Molitvenic* (Prayer book [1564]); see M. Gaster, *Chrestomaţie română: Texte tipărite şi manuscrise, secolele XVI–XIX* (Bucharest: Socec, 1891), 1:24.

34. Udrişte Năsturel, "Preface to the Slavic edition of Thomas à Kempis's *Imitatio Christi* (1647)," *BRV*, 4:197–98.

35. D. Cantemir, *Descriptio Moldaviae* (1716), ed. G. Guţu (Bucharest: Ed. Academiei, 1973), 371–73.

36. Stephen the Great, "Letter to the doge of Venice (1478)," *Hurmuzaki*, 8:23–25; Despot, letter to the boyars (1561), in ibid., 2/1:415–16; Coresi, *Introduction to the Apostles* (1563), *Tîlcul evangheliilor* (1564), and *Psaltirea slavo-română* (1577), all in *BRV*, 1:51, 64, 516–17; the letter of the Wallachian boyars (1599) is in *Hurmuzaki*, supp. 2, vol. 1:488.

37. See Varlaam, *Carte de învăţătură* (Book of instructions [1643]); Dosoftei, *Liturghier* (Missal [1679]); and Simion Ştefan's edition of the New Testament (1648), all in *BRV*, 1:139–40, 170, 224.

38. Grigore Ureche, *Letopiseţul ţării Moldovei*, 2d ed., ed. P. P. Panaitescu (Bucharest: ESPLA, 1958), 67, 134.

39. The great Moldavian boyar expressed his views on Romanian history especially in "De neamul moldovenilor" (1675), "Cronica ţărilor Moldovei şi Munteniei" (1677), and "Istorie în versuri polone despre Moldova şi Ţara Românească" (1684), the last two written in Polish. All have been edited by P. P. Panaitescu and appear in Costin, *Opere*.

40. Cantemir wrote two lengthy studies dealing especially with these questions: *Historia Moldo-Vlahica* (1717), and *Hronicul vechimii a romano-moldo-vlahilor* (1717–1723). In D. Cantemir, *Opere complete* (Bucharest: Ed. Academiei, 1983), 9/1–2.

41. Vasile Lupu, letter to the sultan (1642), in N. Iorga, *Documente românești din arhivele Bistriței* (Bucharest: Socec, 1899), 1:144.

42. Constantin Brâncoveanu and Constantin Cantacuzino, letter to Peter the Great (1702), in *Istoricheskie svyazi*, 3:184–90.

43. Ureche, *Letopisețul*, 68.

44. Miron Costin, "Letopisețul țării Moldovei" (1675), in Costin, *Opere*, 158.

Chapter 3: Despotism and Enlightenment

1. I. Neculce, *Letopisețul țării Moldovei* (1745), ed. I. Iordan (Bucharest: ESPLA, 1959), 148, 196–97, 323–24; C. Daponte, "Catalogul istoric al oamenilor însemnați din veacul al XVIII-lea (1784), in C. Erbiceanu, ed., *Cronicarii greci care au scris despre români în epoca fanariotă* (Bucharest, 1888), 172–73; V. Georgescu, *Political Ideas and the Enlightenment in the Romanian Principalities, 1750–1831* (Boulder, Colo.: East-European Monographs, 1971), 90–91.

2. S. Vianu, "Din acțiunea diplomatică a Țării Românești în Rusia în anii 1736–1739," *Romanoslavica* 8 (1963): 40–43.

3. D. Eclesiarhul, *Cronograful Țării Românești*, ed. C. S. Nicolaescu-Plopșor (Râmicul-Vîlcea, 1934).

4. E. Vîrtosu, "Napoleon Bonaparte și dorințele moldovenilor la 1807," *Studii* 18/2 (1965): 416–18.

5. M. Berza, *Haraciul Moldovei și Țării Românești în secolele XV–XIX*, 43–45; M. Alexandrescu-Dersca-Bulgaru, "Rolul hatiserifelor de privilegii în limitarea obligațiilor către Poartă," *Studii* 11/6 (1958): 105–11; G. Zane, *Un veac de luptă pentru cucerirea pieții românești* (Iași, 1926), and Oțetea, *Istoria României*, 3:858.

6. A. Oțetea, "Un cartel fanariot," *Studii* 12/3 (1959): 111–18; idem, *Tudor Vladimirescu și revoluția dela 1821* (Bucharest: Ed. Științifică, 1971), 39–40. For a detailed contemporary description of Moldavia's financial losses during the last years of Phanariot rule see I. Rosetti-Rosnovanu, "Exposé des tributs de toute nature et des pertes supportées par la Moldavie depuis 1812," in V. Georgescu, *Mémoires et projets de réforme dans les principautés roumaines, 1769–1830* (Bucharest: Association Internationale d'Etudes Sud-Est Européennes, 1970), 1:47–69.

7. T. Holban, *Documente românești în arhivele franceze* (Bucharest, 1939), 39; G. Ungureanu, "Catagrafia locuitorilor Moldovei din 1825," *Revista de statistică* 17/10 (1969): 70.

8. G. Platon, "Cu privire la desvoltarea pieții interne a Moldovei," *Analele științifice ale universității "Al. I. Cuza"* 5 (1959): 27; V. A. Urechia, *Istoria românilor* (Bucharest: C. Goebl, 1891–1902), 8:303.

9. W. Wilkinson, *An Account of the Principalities of Wallachia and Moldavia* (London, 1820), 75.

10. Charter for the founding of the Ciorogârla paper factory, January 1796, in Urechia, *Istoria românilor,* 6:688–89.

11. Urechia, *Istoria românilor,* 9:591; 12:409–13; and A. Oţetea, ed., *Istoria românilor,* 3:648–49.

12. C. Şerban, "Înterprinderea manufacturieră de postav dela Pociovalişte," *Studii* 5/3 (1952): 89–90.

13. G. Zane, *Un veac de luptă,* 21–24; P. Cernovodeanu, "Les échanges économiques entre les pays roumains et l'occident, 1650–1829," in *Contributions roumaines au VIème Congrès International d'Histoire Economique, Leningrad, août 1970* (Bucharest: Ed. Academiei, 1971), 65–66.

14. C. Şerban, "Le rôle économique des villes roumaines au XVII–XVIIIème siècles," *Studia Balcanica* 3 (1970): 141; F. Georgescu, D. Berindei, and A. Cebuc, eds., *Istoria Bucureştilor* (Bucharest: Muzeul de Istorie al Oraşului Bucureşti, 1966), 1:150; N. Bogdan, *Oraşul Iaşi,* 2d ed. (Iaşi: Tipografia Naţională, 1915), 74; V. Mateescu, "Populaţia oraşului Bucureşti în secolele XIX–XX," *Revista de statistică* 12/9 (1959): 57–61; G. Platon, "Populaţia oraşului Iaşi," in S. Pascu, ed., *Populaţie şi societate: Studii de demografie istorică,* 1:281–82; G. Retegan, "Evoluţia populaţiei urbane," *Revista de statistică* 18/7 (1965): 57–62.

15. I. C. Filitti, *Catagrafia oficială de toţi boierii Ţării Româneşti la 1829* (Bucharest, 1929), 70; G. Ungureanu, *Catagrafia locuitorilor Moldovei,* 69–70.

16. S. Diamandi, "O gospodărie moşierească din Moldova din prima jumătate a secolului al XIX-lea," *Studii* 9/2–3 (1956): 79.

17. A. Oţetea, "Consideraţii asupra trecerii dela feudalism la capitalism," *Studii şi materiale de istorie medie* 4 (1960): 331; H. H. Stahl, *Contribuţii la studiul satelor devălmaşe româneşti* (Bucharest: Ed. Academiei, 1958), 1:34; V. Mihordea, *Maîtres du sol et paysans dans les principautés roumaines au XVIIIème siècle* (Bucharest: Ed. Academiei, 1971), 129–44; F. Constantiniu, *Relaţiile agrare din Ţara Românească în secolul al XVIII-lea* (Bucharest: Ed. Academiei, 1972), 121–28. The charters abolishing serfdom are found in V. Mihordea, ed., *Documente privind relaţiile agrare în veacul al XVIII-lea* (Bucharest: Ed. Academiei, 1961–66), 1:287–89.

18. *Regulamentele Organice ale Valahiei şi Moldovei* (Bucharest, 1944), 1:15 ff.; N. Bălcescu, *Question économique des principautés danubiennes* (Paris, 1850), 33; M. Emerit, *Les paysans roumains depuis le traité d'Adrianople jusqu'à la libération des terres, 1829–1864* (Paris: Librairie du Recueil Sirey, 1937), 251–58; I. Corfus, *L'agriculture en Valachie durant la première moitié du XIXème siècle* (Bucharest: Ed. Academiei, 1969), 16–37.

19. Cantemir, *Descriptio Moldaviae,* 297.

20. V. Mihordea, "Date cu privire la începuturile industriei din oraşul Bucureşti," *Revista de statistică* 8/9 (1959): 50–51; S. Columbeanu, "O statistică negustorească şi fiscală dela 1824 in Ţara Românească," *Studii* 13/4 (1960): 195.

21. D. Prodan, *Les migrations des roumains au-delà des Carpathes* (Sibiu: Centrul de Studii privitoare la Transilvania, 1945); D. Giurgiu, "Populaţia Transilvaniei la sfîrşitul secolului al XVIII-lea şi începutul secolului XIX," in S. Pascu, *Populaţie şi societate,* 1:101–14; C. Daicoviciu and S. Pascu, eds., *Din istoria Transilvaniei* (Bucharest: Ed. Academiei, 1960), 1:193.

22. L. Roman, "Aşezarea statornică a românilor transilvănei în Ţara Ro-

mânească, 1738–1831," *Studii* 15/5 (1971): 902–15; idem, "Les transylvains en Valachie," *Revue roumaine d'histoire* 12/5 (1972).

23. For a definitive history of the 1784 uprising see D. Prodan, *Răscoala lui Horia*, 2d ed. (Bucharest: Ed. Științifică, 1984), vols. 1 and 2.

24. The *Supplex* has been published several times since the Eder edition of 1791. The Latin text was recently republished by D. Prodan, ed., *Supplex Libellus Valachorum* (Bucharest: Ed. Științifică, 1984), 455–67. For an English translation see D. Prodan, Supplex Libellus Valachorum *and the Political Struggle of the Romanians of Transylvania during the 18th Century* (Bucharest: Ed. Academiei, 1971), 455–66.

25. Urechia, *Istoria românilor*, 1:101–3.

26. A catalogue of the programs of reform written between 1769 and 1830 is in Georgescu, *Mémoires et projets*, 1:3–34.

27. N. Iorga, "Francmasoni și conspiratori în Moldova în secolul al XVIII-lea," *Analele Academiei Române, memoriile secțiunii istorice*, 3d ser. (1928), 8:301–4; P. P. Panaitescu, "Medaliile francmasonilor din Moldova în secolul al XVIII-lea," *Revista istorică* 14/10–12 (1928): 354–55; A. Camariano-Cioran, *Spiritul filozofic și revoluționar francez combătut de patriarhia ecumenică și Sublima Poartă* (Bucharest: Imprimeria Națională, 1941); G. Serbanesco, *Histoire de la Franc-Maçonnerie* (Paris: Editions Intercontinentales, 1966), 3:317.

28. A. Duțu, "L'image de la France dans les principautés roumaines pendant les campagnes napoléoniennes," *Nouvelles études d'histoire* 3 (1965): 224–33.

29. *Hurmuzaki*, n.s. 1:767–68; T. Codrescu, *Uricariul* (Iași, 1852–95), 3:61–68; A. Oțetea, ed., *Documente privind istoria României: Răscoala din 1821* (Bucharest: Ed. Academiei, 1959–62), 1:187.

30. Oțetea, *Răscoala din 1821*, 1:196–97.

31. N. Stetcu and I. Vătămanu, "Un manuscris necunoscut al ponturilor lui T. Vladimirescu," *Revista arhivelor* 47/2 (1970): 601–04. For a contemporary German translation of the "Demands," see Oțetea, *Răscoala din 1821*, 1:274–78; the proclamation to the pandours appears in C. D. Aricescu, *Acte justificative privind istoria revoluției române dela 1821* (Craiova, 1874), 91.

32. E. Vîrtosu, *Din scrierile inedite ale lui I. Tăutu* (Bucharest, 1939), 6–11.

33. B. P. Mumuleanu, *Rost de poezii* (Bucharest, 1820), 1.

34. Prince Ghica's letter to the Austrian diplomat F. von Gentz, February 1824, is reprinted in V. Georgescu, *Din corespondența diplomatică a Țării Româ-nești, 1823–1878* (Bucharest: Muzeul Româno-Rus, 1962), 121. Tăutu's "Constitution" appears in A. D. Xenopol, "Primul proiect de constituție al Moldovei," *Analele Academiei Române, memoriile secției istorice* (1898) 20:4–23.

35. Cantemir, *Descriptio Moldaviae*, 135.

36. *BRV*, 2:406.

37. Letter of the Wallachian boyars of 1 June 1821, Oțetea, *Răscoala din 1821*, 2:191–92; D. Golescu, *Însemnare a călătoriei mele, 1826* (Bucharest: Minerva, 1915), 65; E. Poteca, speech delivered 20 July 1827, in G. D. Teodorescu, *Viața și operele lui E. Poteca* (Bucharest, 1883), 57.

38. A. Alexianu, *Mode și vestminte din trecut* (Bucharest: Meridiane, 1971), 2:90.

39. G. Ungureanu, "Veniturile şi cheltuielile unei mari case boiereşti din Iaşi în anul 1816. Casa Rosetti-Rosnovanu," *Studii şi articole de istorie* 1 (1956).

40. *Catalogue of the Rosetti-Rosnovanu Library, 1827* (Bucharest: State Archives), A.N. 260/16; P. Poenaru, *Catalog de cărţile ce s-au găsit în biblioteca Sfîntei Mitropolii, 1836* (Bucharest: Library of the Academy), MSS. Rom. no. 2683.

41. Urechia, *Istoria românilor,* 1:83–84; Tomescu, *Istoria cărţii româneşti,* 87; Camariano-Cioran, *Les académies princières,* 279–80.

42. N. Soutzo, "Notions statistiques sur la Moldavie (Iassy, 1849)," *Hurmuzaki,* 18:464.

43. N. Albu, *Istoria învăţămîntului românesc în Transilvania* (Blaj, 1944), 148.

44. Theodorescu, *Repertoriul cărţii vechi româneşti,* 341–42; Tomescu, *Istoria cărţii româneşti,* 110.

45. D. Fotino, *Istoria vechii Dachii, 1818,* ed. G. Sion (Bucharest: Imprimeria Naţională, 1859), 1:45; N. Râmniceanu, "Despre origina românilor, 1820," in Erbiceanu, *Cronicarii,* 245–46; N. Râmniceanu, *Cronică inedită, 1802,* ed. S. Bezdechi (Cluj, 1944), 84, 87–88, 92.

46. Transylvanian Saxon historians, beginning with G. Reichersdorffer, questioned the unadulterated breeding of the Romanians.

47. Georgescu, *Mémoires et projets,* 1:38.

48. Vîrtosu, "Napoleon Bonaparte," 415–16.

49. N. Râmniceanu, "Cronica Ţării Româneşti, 1802," in Erbiceanu, *Cronicarii,* 90; for I. Budai-Deleanu's plans see D. Prodan, *Înca un Supplex Libellus Valachorum, 1804* (Cluj: Dacia, 1970), 42, 81; M. Nicoară's letter in C. Bodea, *Moise Nicoară* (Arad, 1943), 166–67.

50. In a letter written in October 1838, A. G. Golescu calls Bucharest "la capitale future de la Grande Dacie." In C. Bodea, *Lupta românilor pentru unitate naţională, 1834–1849* (Bucharest: Ed. Academiei, 1967), 209.

51. "The origin, the same religion, the customs and the same language of the inhabitants of these two principalities, as well as their common needs, are sufficient elements to justify their closer union." *Regulamentele Organice,* 1:130; 2:341.

52. BRV, 2:44.

53. Ibid., 321; A. Donici, *Manualul de legi, 1814* (Bucharest: Ed. Academiei, 1959), 21.

54. BRV, 3:631–32.

55. Oţetea, *Răscoala din 1821,* 1:211–12, 228–30, 258–59; I. Tăutu, *Scrieri social-politice,* ed. E. Vîrtosu (Bucharest: Ed. Ştiinţifică, 1974), 279.

56. Urechia, *Istoria românilor,* 1:83–84; 2:154–55.

57. T. Thorton, *Starea de acum a principatelor Valahiei şi Moldovei,* trans. D. Golescu (Buda, 1826). Cf. *BRV,* 3:522; Ursu, *O disertaţie,* 163–70.

58. G. Şincai, "Hronica românilor, 1808–1809," in G. Şincai, *Opere,* ed. F. Fugariu and M. Neagoe (Bucharest: Minerva, 1967–73), 2:337–38; N. Râmniceanu, "Tratat important, 1822," in *Biserica ortodoxă română,* 27 (1903): 26; C. Erbiceanu, *Viaţa şi activitatea literară a lui N. Râmniceanu* (Bucharest, 1900), 22.

59. G. Pleşoianu, "Preface to Marmontel," *Aneta şi Luben* (Bucharest, 1829). Cf. *BRV,* 3:658.

Chapter 4: The Age of National Revival

1. L. Colescu, *Recensămîntul general al populaţiei României din 1899* (Bucharest: Inst. de Arte Grafice M. Eminescu, 1905), xviii; idem, *La population de la Roumanie* (Bucharest: Institut Central de Statistique, 1903), 16–19; I. Scărlătescu, *Statistica demografică a României: Populaţia regatului român după recensamîntul făcut la 19 decembrie 1912* (Bucharest, 1921), 5–52; I. Adam, "La structure de la population de Transylvanie du point de vue des recensements hongrois de 1900 et 1910," in Pascu, *Populaţie şi societate*, 3:99–103; B. Köpeczi, ed., *Erdély története*, 3:1742. The 1910 Hungarian census did not register the 195,000 Jews (4.2%) of the Transylvanian population as a separate ethnic group, but as Hungarians. See J. Ancel, "The Jewish Presence in Transylvania According to the 1910 Hungarian Ethnic Census of the Region," *Romanian Jewish Studies* 1/2 (1987): 107–8.

2. E. Illyés, *National Minorities in Romania* (Boulder, Colo.: East-European Reports, 1982), 22; S. Columbeanu, "Economia domeniului feudal," *Studii* 18/2 (1965): 349; D. Gusti and N. Cornăţeanu, *La vie rurale en Roumanie* (Bucharest: Imprimeriile Naţionale, 1940), 63; *Statistica agricolă a României pe anii 1911–1915* (Bucharest, 1918), 3:24.

3. *Anuarul statistic al României, 1915–1916* (Bucharest, 1916), 38.

4. *Lucrări statistice făcute în anii 1859–1860*, 323; *Desvoltarea economică a Moldovei între anii 1848 şi 1864* (Bucharest: Ed. Academiei, 1963), 71–72; C. D. Creangă, *Proprietatea rurală în România* (Bucharest: C. Goebl, 1907), 17; *La Roumanie économique* (Bucharest: Ministerul Industriei, 1921), 13–14; G. D. Cioriceanu, *La Roumanie économique et ses rapports avec l'étranger de 1860 à 1915* (Paris: Giard, 1928), 331–32.

5. *La Roumanie: Guide économique* (Bucharest: Union des Chambres Agricoles, 1936); C. Boncu, *Contribuţii la istoria petrolului românesc* (Bucharest: Ed. Academiei, 1971), 90, 183–89; G. Ravas, *Din istoria petrolului românesc*, 2d ed. (Bucharest: Ed. de Stat pentru Literatură Politică, 1957), 53–56; C. C. Kiriţescu, *Sistemul bănesc al leului* (Bucharest: Ed. Academiei, 1967), 2:64.

6. C. Băicoianu, *Istoria politicii noastre vamale şi comerciale* (Bucharest, 1904), 1/1.

7. *Desvoltarea economică*, 352–57; S. Columbeanu, *Economia domeniului feudal*, 350; *Comerţul exterior al României* (Bucharest: Banca Naţională, 1939), 1/1:48; V. Jinga, *Principii şi orientări ale comerţului exterior al României* (Cluj: Dacia, 1975), 55; M. Popa-Veres, *Situaţia producţiei şi exportului de cereale* (Bucharest: Independenţa Economică, 1939), 3–53.

8. Băicoianu, *Istoria politicii*, 1/1:397 ff.

9. N. Şuţu, "Despre utilitatea unei căi ferate, 1854," in N. Şuţu, *Opere economice* (Bucharest: Ed. Ştiinţifică, 1957), 334. According to J. Hagemeister, the cost of transporting 1000 oca from Cerneţi in western Wallachia to Brăila was between 33 and 36 rubles in 1834; from Ismail to Sulina it was only two rubles. J. Hagemeister, *Report on the Commerce of the Ports of New Russia, Moldavia and Wallachia* (London, 1836), 83–84.

10. G. D. Cioriceanu, *La Roumanie économique*, 124–27, 256; B. Tincu, "Contribuții la istoria căilor ferate în România," *Studii* 24/5 (1971): 951–62.

11. G. Vulturescu, *Despre societățile de credit funciar și institutirea lor în România* (Bucharest, 1889); N. Petra, *Băncile românești din Ardeal și Banat* (Sibiu: Cartea Românească, 1936), 31, 99; Kirițescu, *Sistemul bănesc*, 2:67–68. I. Totu, ed., *Progresul economic în România* (Bucharest: Ed. Politică, 1977), 148–50.

12. D. Pop-Marțian, "Recesiunea din 1860," *Analele statistice* 1/2 (1860): 109; *Lucrări statistice făcute în anii 1859–1860*, 124, 188; *Anuarul statistic al României, 1904* (Bucharest, 1905), 137; Colescu, *La population de la Roumanie,* 30; L. Colescu, *Statistica profesiunilor din România* (Bucharest, 1913), iv ff.; O. Constantinescu and N. N. Constantinescu, *Cu privire la problema revoluției industriale în România* (Bucharest: Ed. Științifică, 1957), 175; C. Daicoviciu and M. Constantinescu, eds., *La désagrégation de la monarchie austro-hongroise, 1900–1918* (Bucharest: Ed. Academiei, 1965), 258–59.

13. For what was probably the most eloquent presentation of this position see B. Catargiu, *L'état social des principautés danubiennes* (Brussels, 1857).

14. L. Colescu, *La loi rurale de 1864* (Bucharest, 1900), v; N. Adăniloaie, *La réforme agraire de 1864* (Bucharest: Ed. Academiei, 1966).

15. Creangă, *Proprietatea rurală în România*, 43; *Relațiile agrare și mișcări țărănești în România, 1908–1921* (Bucharest: Ed. Politică, 1968), 49.

16. R. Rosetti, *Pentru ce s-au răsculat țăranii* (Bucharest: Socec, 1907), 507–9.

17. Daicoviciu and Constantinescu, *Désagrégation*, 19–37; I. Kovacs, *Desființarea relațiilor feudale în Transilvania* (Cluj: Dacia, 1973), 161–68; *Relațiile agrare și mișcări țărănești*, 93; I. Popescu-Puțuri and A. Deac, *Unirea Transilvaniei cu România*, 3d ed. (Bucharest: Ed. Politică, 1978), 258–59.

18. G. Brătianu, *Sfatul domnesc și adunarea stărilor în Principatele Române* (Evry: Academia Română, 1977), 414.

19. L. Colescu, *Statistica electorală* (Bucharest: A. Baer, 1913), 8–9, 126–27.

20. Câmpineanu's programs are given in French and Romanian in Bodea, *Lupta românilor*, 216–23.

21. Filipescu's "Profession de foi" appears in E. Vîrtosu, "Réformes sociales et économiques proposées par M. Filipescu en 1841," *Revue des études sud-est européennes* 8/1 (1970): 116–20.

22. *Anul 1848 în Principatele Române: Acte și documente*, 1 (Bucharest: C. Goebl, 1902–10). For a contemporary French translation see Georgescu, *Mémoires et projets*, 2:144–54.

23. Georgescu, *Mémoires et projets*, 1:490–501.

24. See especially D. Bolintineanu, *Les principautés roumaines* (Paris, 1854); C. Filipescu, *Mémoire sur les conditions d'existence des principautés danubiennes* (Paris, 1854); G. Gănescu, *La Valachie depuis 1830 à nos jours* (Brussels, 1855); V. Boerescu, *La Roumanie d'après le Traité de Paris* (Paris, 1856).

25. A. Papiu-Ilarian, *Istoria românilor din Dacia Traiană*, 2d ed. (Vienna, 1852), 1:243–46.

26. Bărnuțiu's speech as well as the sixteen demands have been recently republished in C. Bodea, *1848 la Români* (Bucharest: Ed. Științifică și Enciclopedică, 1982), 1:446–86.

27. K. Hitchins, "The Rumanians of Transylvania and the Constitutional Experiment in the Habsburg Monarchy, 1860–1865," *Balkan Studies* 1 (1964): 95–107.

28. V. Netea, *Istoria memorandului românilor din Transilvania și Banat* (Bucharest, 1947).

29. See, for example, I. Ghica, *Poids de la Moldovalachie dans la question d'orient* (Paris, 1838), and A. G. Golescu, "Historique du protectorat russe dans les principautés roumaines," in *Anul 1848 in Principatele Române,* 4:35–47.

30. See Georgescu, *Mémoires et projets,* 2:139–42.

31. L. Kossuth, *Souvenirs* (Paris, 1880), 236 ff; V. A. Urechia, *L'alliance des roumains et des hongrois en 1859* (Bucharest, 1894); A. Marcu, *Conspiratori și conspirații în epoca renasterii României, 1848–1877* (Bucharest: Cartea Româneascâ, 1930), 324–27; I. Lupaș, *Problema transilvană în timpul lui Cuza și Carol I* (Bucharest, 1946).

32. A. G. Golescu's letter appears in *Anul 1848 în Principatele Române,* 2:732–33; the Bălcescu plans in N. Bălcescu, *Opere,* ed. G. Zane (Bucharest: Ed. Academiei, 1964), 276–84, 291–94, 310–17, 344–45; I. Ghica's letter of 4 January 1850, to Bălcescu in I. Ghica, *Scrisori câtre N. Bălcescu* (Bucharest, 1943), 37–41; the letter to General Wissoski, 1 February 1850, in *Documente și manuscrise literare* 2 (Bucharest: Ed. Academiei, 1969), 2:91–98. For Maniu's Latin Federation, see his *La mission de l'occident latin dans l'orient de l'Europe* (Paris, 1859).

33. Carol I, *Cuvîntări și scrisori* (Bucharest, 1909), 1:8–9, 465–67.

34. D. Brătianu, "Notice à l'appui de la demande de neutralité adressée par la Roumanie à la Conférence Européenne réunie à Constantinople," in R. Rosetti, *Documente privitoare la misiunea lui D. Brătianu la Constantinopol* (Bucharest: Academia Română, 1943), 17–20.

35. The Romanian-Russian convention is reprinted in *Documente privind istoria României. Războiul pentru independență* (Bucharest: Ed. Academiei, 1952), 2:112.

36. *Monitorul Oficial,* no. 118 (8 June 1877), 3451–53.

37. S. Rădulescu-Zoner, *Rumänien und der Dreibund, 1878–1914* (Bucharest: Ed. Academiei, 1983), 202, 260.

38. Râmniceanu, *Cronica inedită,* 90; Prodan, *Înca un* Supplex Libellus Românesc, *1804,* 79–81.

39. C. Bodea, "Lupta pentru unitatea națională a românilor," *Anuarul Institutului de Istorie Națională* 13 (1946): 89–90.

40. The phrase was first reported by N. Bălcescu in his "Mișcarea românilor din Ardeal la 1848" written in 1851. In Bălcescu, *Opere,* ed. G. Zane (Bucharest: Fundațiile Regale, 1940), 1/2:216.

41. "Manifesto of the Romanian Revolutionary Committee, London, September 10, 1852" in A. Cretzianu, *Din arhiva lui D. Brătianu* (Bucharest: Imprimeriile Naționale, 1933), 1:289–301.

42. B. P. Hașdeu, "Răsboiul franco-german și o eventuală împărțire a Austriei," in *Columna lui Traian,* 29 July 1870.

43. A. D. Xenopol, *Scrieri sociale și filozofice,* ed. N. Gogoneață and Z. Ornea (Bucharest: Ed. Științifică, 1967), 204–16.

44. In Alexandre Boldur, *La Bessarabie et les relations russo-roumaines* (Paris: J. Gamber, 1927), 136.

45. "Haracterul epohi noastre," in *Curierul românesc* 2 (1830): 399–400.

46. D. Buga, "Populaţia Olteniei în secolele XIX şi XX," *Revista de statistică* 17/6 (1968): 62–63.

47. L. Colescu, *Statistica clădirilor şi locuintelor din România* (Bucharest: Cartea Românească, 1920), 12–51; G. Banu, *Sănătatea poporului român* (Bucharest: Fundaţia pentru Literatură şi Artă "Regele Carol II," 1935), 121–22; Gusti and Cornăţeanu, *La vie rurale en Roumanie*, 151–52.

48. For everyday life in the Old Kingdom around the turn of the century see Ion Bulei, *Lumea românească la 1900* (Bucharest: Ed. Eminescu, 1984).

49. *Regulamentele Organice,* 1:18; 2:190; *Buletinul Oficial al Ţării Româneşti,* no. 45 (September 1833): 244; Banu, *Sănătatea,* 47–57; M. Iosa and T. Lungu, *Viaţa politică în România, 1899–1910* (Bucharest: Ed. Politică, 1977), 146.

50. The total student population in 1900–01 was 440,431. *Hurmuzaki,* 18:383; *Anuarul statistic al României, 1904,* 79, 92; *Contribuţii la istoria desvoltării universităţii din Iaşi* (1960), 1:182–83, 215; Tomescu, *Istoria cărţii româneşti,* 129.

51. I. Slavici, *Die Rumänen in Ungarn* (Vienna: K. Prohaska, 1881), 234–36; S. Polverejan, "Contribuţii statistice privind şcolile româneşti din Transilvania în a doua jumătate a secolului al XIX-lea," *Cumidava* 2 (1968): 161.

52. Colescu, *Statistica ştiutorilor de carte,* ix; C. Angelescu, *Activitatea Ministerului Instrucţiunii* (Bucharest, 1926), 4; S. Manuilă and M. Georgescu, "Populaţia României," in *Enciclopedia României* (Bucharest: Imprimeriile Naţionale, 1938–43), 1:142.

53. D. Grăsoiu, "O cercetare sociologică asupra stratificării publicului românesc în prima jumătate a secolului al XIX-lea," *Revista de istorie şi teorie literară* 23/2 (1974): 229–37.

54. (Prince) Grigore V Ghica, "Aperçu sur les principales réformes à introduire en Moldavie, 1854," in D. A. Sturdza, ed., *Acte şi documente relative la istoria renaşcerei României* (Bucharest, 1889–1909), 9:578–86. For the anti-church policy advocated by the 1857 Moldavian ad hoc assembly, see Sturdza, *Acte şi documente,* 6/1:160, 169; and M. Kogălniceanu, *Discursuri parlamentare din epoca unirii* (Bucharest: Ed. Ştiinţifică, 1959), 66–78. The political and economic rights of the church were defended mainly by the archimandrites N. Scriban and Melchisedec, as is pointed out in Sturdza, *Acte şi documente,* 6/1:102–7, 435–42. For Prince Cuza's church laws see C. C. Giurescu, *Viaţa şi opera lui Cuza-Vodă,* 2d ed. (Bucharest: Ed. Ştiinţifică, 1970), 149–64, 199–210, 338–39, and Păcuraru, *Istoria bisericii ortodoxe române,* 3:113–27.

55. Sturdza, *Acte şi documente,* 11/1.

56. M. Kogălniceanu, "Cuvînt pentru deschiderea cursului de istorie naţională," in idem, *Opere,* ed. A. Oţetea (Bucharest: Imprimeria Naţională, 1946), 1:634–35; T. Maiorescu, "Observări polemice," in his *Critice* (Bucharest: Minerva, 1908), 1:117–42; G. Panu, "Studii asupra atîrnării sau neatîrnării politice a românilor," *Convorbiri literare* (1872), nos. 4–7.

57. T. Maiorescu, "În contra direcţiei de astăzi în cultura română," in idem, *Critice,* 1:152–64.

58. Xenopol, *Scrieri sociale şi filozofice*, 146–55. Xenopol later developed these ideas on social development in *La théorie de l'histoire* (Paris: Leroux, 1908).

59. I. Ghica, *Scrieri economice* (Bucharest, 1879), 82–83, 242.

60. For the Romanian avant-garde movement, see Ion Pop, *Avangardismul poetic românesc* (Bucharest: Ed. pentru Literatură, 1969).

61. Colescu, *Recensămîntul general*, xliv; Scărlătescu, *Statistica demografică*, 52. For the history of Romanian nineteenth-century anti-Semitism, especially the opposition to full naturalization for Jews, see C. Iancu, *Les juifs en Roumanie, 1866–1919: De l'exclusion à l'émancipation* (Aix-en-Provence: Editions de l'Université de Provence, 1978), 175–80, 186–205.

Chapter 5: From Greater Romania to Popular Democracy

1. *Recensămîntul general al populaţiei României din 29 decembrie 1930* (Bucharest: Institutul Central de Statistică, 1938–41), 1:xxiv; S. Manuilă, *Ethnographical Survey of the Population of Romania* (Bucharest: Imprimeria Naţională, 1938), xxiii–xxxvii. After the loss of Bessarabia, northern Transylvania, and southern Dobrudja in 1940, the population fell to 13,535,757, of which 87 percent were Romanians, 4 percent Germans, 3 percent Hungarians, 2 percent Jews, and 3 percent other. *Die Bevölkerungszählung in Rumänien, 1941* (Vienna: Staatsdruckerei Wien, 1943), 22; Daicoviciu and Pascu, *Din istoria Transilvaniei*, 1:12.

2. *Anuarul statistic al României, 1937 şi 1938*, 130–31; ibid., 1939–40, 192.

3. *Recensămîntul din 29 decembrie 1930*, 5:xiv; S. Manuilă and D. C. Georgescu, *Populaţia României* (Bucharest: Imprimeria Naţională, 1937), 17–20.

4. *Anuarul statistic al României, 1937 şi 1938*, 34–35.

5. *Documente din istoria Partidului Comunist din România* (Bucharest: Ed. P.M.R., 1951), 37–38, 49–51, 70–76, 112–33, 266–68; *Congresul al V-lea al P.C.R.* (Bucharest: Ed. P.C.R., 1932), 35–47; M. Muşat and I. Ardeleanu, *România după marea unire* (Bucharest: Ed. Ştiinţifică, 1986), 195–96, 607–8; R. King, *History of the Romanian Communist Party* (Stanford, Calif.: Hoover Institution Press, 1980), 31–36.

6. King, *Romanian Communist Party*, 22. At the fifth Party Congress in Kharkov in 1931, A. Danieliuc-Stefanski (Gorn) admitted that "our party in Romania is less than numerous, and what is even more important is that its proletarian core among the Romanian workers from large industries is very weak." Muşat and Ardeleanu, *România după marea unire*, 634.

7. Percentages have been rounded to the nearest whole number. N. Petraşcu, *Evoluţia politică a României în ultimii 20 de ani, 1918–1938* (Bucharest: Ed. Bucovina, 1939), 139–40.

8. C. Z. Codreanu, *Eiserne Garde* (Berlin: Brunnen, 1939), 440–41; I. Scurtu, "Acţiuni de opoziţie ale unor partide şi grupări politice burgheze faţă de tendinţele dictatoriale ale regelui Carol al II-lea," *Revista de istorie* 27/3 (1978): 412.

9. O. Parpală, *Aspecte din agricultura României, 1920–1940* (Bucharest: Ed. Academiei, 1966), 69; I. C. Vasiliu, "Structura economică a agriculturii româneşti," in *Enciclopedia României*, 3:303.

10. D. Şandru, *Reforma agrară din 1921* (Bucharest: Ed. Academiei, 1975), 19–20, 98–130, 146–67; G. Ionescu-Siseşti and N. Cornăţeanu, *La réforme agraire en Roumanie* (Bucharest: Académie Roumaine, 1938), 17–38.

11. *La Roumanie agricole* (Bucharest, 1929), 427; "L'agriculture en Roumanie," in H. Lupan, *La production agricole en Roumanie* (Bucharest: Bureau of Statistics(?), 193?), 28–30, 82; M. Popa-Veres, *Situaţia producţiêi şi exportului de cereale* (Bucharest, 1939), 9; I. Vasiliu, *Rentabilitatea agriculturii României* (Bucharest, 1942), 4–6; Parpală, *Aspecte*, 47.

12. "Tabele statistice generale," in *Enciclopedia României*, 3:1067; Gusti and Cornăţeanu, *La vie rurale en Roumanie*, 23; I. Vasiliu, *Politica de valorificare a grîului* (Bucharest, 1940), 5–13, 28; I. Vasiliu, *Problema inventarului agricol în România* (Bucharest, 1941), 7; Parpală, *Aspecte*, 107–8; N. N. Constantinescu, *Capitalul monopolist în România* (Bucharest: Ed. Politică, 1962), 89.

13. Totu, *Progresul economic*, 307.

14. *Transilvania, Banatul, Crişana, Maramureşul* (Bucharest: Cultura Naţională, 1929), 1:490–91; N. P. Arkadian, *Industrializarea României* (Bucharest: Imprimeria Naţională, 1936), 219; V. Madgearu, *Evoluţia economiei româneşti după primul răsboi mondial* (Bucharest: Independenţa Economică, 1940), 137, 146; I. Puiu, "Le développement de l'industrie roumaine dans les années qui ont précédé la Seconde Guerre Mondiale," *Revue roumaine d'histoire* 10/3 (1971): 493.

15. *Anuarul statistic al României, 1937–1938*, 452; Madgearu, *Evoluţia economiei*, 102.

16. *Anuarul statistic al României, 1937–1938*, 570–91; ibid., 1939–40, 596–600; Madgearu, *Evoluţia economiei*, 276; Puiu, "Développement," 496–97.

17. M. Manoilescu, *Rostul şi destinul burgheziei româneşti* (Bucharest: Cugetarea, 1942), 151–54.

18. S. Manuilă, *Statistica preţurilor de detaliu în 1940* (Bucharest: Institutul de Statistică, 1942), 2–5; *L'agriculture en Roumanie* (Bucharest: Album Statistique, 1927), 38; I. Claudian, *Alimentaţia poporului roman* (Bucharest: Fundaţia Regele Carol II, 1939), 11–127, 135–43; D. C. Georgescu, *L'alimentation de la population rurale en Roumanie* (Bucharest, 1940); R. Moldavan, "Bunurile de consum," in *Enciclopedia României*, 4:920–23.

19. *Recensămîntul din 29 decembrie 1930*, 3:xxxvi; 5:lxxxv; S. Manuilă, *Stiinţa de carte a populaţiei României* (Bucharest: Institutul Social Român, 1932), 4–32.

20. I. I. C. Brătianu, *Activitatea corpurilor legiuitoare şi a guvernului, 1922–1926* (Bucharest, 1926), 97; Angelescu, *Activitatea Ministerului Instrucţiunii*, 3–8; *Statistica învătămîntului în România pe anii 1921–1922, 1928–1929* (Bucharest, 1931), 488–89, 744–50.

21. "Noua constituţie promulgată la 27 februarie 1938," in Petraşcu, *Evoluţia politică*, supp. 4:142; *Codul Calimah* (Bucharest: Ed. Academiei, 1958), art. 41–42, p. 81.

22. V. Moisiuc, *Diplomaţia României şi problema apărării suveranirăţii şi independenţei naţionale în perioada martie–mai 1940* (Bucharest: Ed. Academiei, 1971), 177.

23. *Documente din istoria Partidului Comunist*, 308, 309–11.

316   NOTES TO PAGES 210—21

24. C. Hamangiu, *Codul general al României* (Bucharest: Alcalay), 18/2:1272–89, 1428–31, 1764–65; B. Vago, *The Shadow of the Swastika: The Rise of Fascism and Anti-Semitism in the Danube Basin, 1936–1939* (Farnborough, England: Saxon House, published for the Institute of Jewish Affairs, 1975), 71.

25. G. Barbul, *Mémorial Antonescu, le troisième homme de l'Axe* (Paris: Editions de la Couronne, 1950), 82.

26. The letters exchanged by Antonescu and Sima were published, after the crushing of the Guardist rebellion, in *Pe marginea prăpastiei* (Bucharest: Ed. Ministerul de Propagandă Naţională, 1942), 1:144–61; see also E. Weber, "Romania," in E. Weber and H. Rogger, *The European Right* (Berkeley: University of California Press, 1965), 560–61.

27. M. Carp, *Cartea neagră: Fapte şi documente. Suferinţele evreilor din România, 1940–1944* (Bucharest: Socec, 1946–48), 1:68; *23 August 1944: Documente* (Bucharest: Ed. Ştiinţifică, 1984), 1:157–60.

28. *Pe marginea prăpastiei,* 2:44–45.

29. Barbul, *Mémorial Antonescu,* 104–5; M. Sturdza, *The Suicide of Europe: Memoirs* (Boston: Western Blands, 1968), 217; A. Hillgruber, *Hitler, König Carol und Marschall Antonescu: Die deutsch-rumänischen Beziehungen, 1938–1944* (Wiesbaden: F. Steiner, 1954), 118–21; N. Nagy-Talavera, *The Green Shirts and Others: A History of Fascism in Hungary and Romania* (Stanford, Calif.: Hoover Institute Press, 1970), 324–28.

30. *23 August 1944. Documente,* 1:342–45; A. Cretzianu, *The Lost Opportunity* (London: J. Cape, 1957), 83; N. Penescu, *La Roumanie de la démocratie au totalitarisme* (Paris: Contrepoint, 1981), 24–25.

31. Barbul, *Mémorial Antonescu,* 140–41. *Policies towards Romania, 1938–1947* (Los Angeles: Romanian-American Academy, 1977), 83–85; Penescu, *De la démocratie au totalitarisme,* 38 ff.

32. Barbul, *Mémorial Antonescu,* 163.

33. A. Karetki and M. Covaci, *Zile însîngerate la Iaşi, 28–30 iunie 1941* (Bucharest: Ed. Politică, 1978), 105. The official Romanian historians have given figures varying from 3,233 to "over 8,000." G. Zaharia, "Quelques données concernant la terreur fasciste en Roumanie, 1940–1944," in I. Popescu-Puţuri, ed., *La Roumanie pendant la Deuxième Guerre Mondiale* (Bucharest, 1969), 37 ff.

34. According to a May 1943 official report from the ministry of the interior, 110,033 Jews from Bessarabia, Bucovina, Dorohoi, and Hertza had been "evacuated" to Transnistria since 1941; 50,741 were still there on September 1, 1943. Carp, *Cartea neagră,* 3:447–50, 457. W. Filderman, the president of the Federation of the Jewish Communities, put the figures of the deported at 136,000 and of the dead at 60,000. M. Gilbert, *Auschwitz and the Allies* (New York: Holt, Rinehart and Winston, 1981), 114.

35. J. Ancel, "Plans for deportation of Romanian Jews, July–October 1942," *Yad Vashem Studies* 16 (1984): 381–90; R. Hilberg, *The Destruction of the European Jews,* 3 vols. (New York: Holmes and Meier, 1985), 3:782–87.

36. Establishing the exact number of victims is a difficult task. Figures vary from author to author. W. Filderman considered 209,214 Jews unaccounted for

by the end of the war: 15,000 in the Old Kingdom and southern Transylvania, 103,919 in Bessarabia, northern Bucovina, and the Hertza region, and 90,295 in Hungarian-occupied northern Transylvania. Cf. S. Manuilă and W. Filderman, *Regional Development of the Jewish Population in Romania* (Rome: F. Failli, 1957), 4–12.

M. Carp, another wartime leader of the Romanian Jewish community, gives higher figures: 385,170 dead, of whom 263,900 were from Romania and 121,270 from northern Transylvania. Carp believes that 592,418 Jews were living in Romania and northern Transylvania in 1941, a figure well above the official Romanian and Hungarian censuses. The number of survivors would thus be only 207,248 (Carp, *Cartea neagră*, 1:18–20). This figure is contradicted by Safran, chief rabbi of Romania from 1940 to 1947, who puts the number of survivors at 370,000. See A. Safran, *Resisting the Storm: Romania, 1940–1947 (Memoirs)* (Jerusalem: Yad Vashem, 1987), 177. Vago gives a figure of up to 126,125 killed in northern Transylvania, out of the 151,125 registered in 1941. Cf. B. Vago, "The Distribution of the Jews of Transylvania," in R. L. Braham, ed., *Hungarian-Jewish Studies* (New York: World Federation of Hungarian Jews, 1966), 1:181, 211. Braham thinks the Hungarians deported 164,052 Jews, most of them to Auschwitz, where the great majority were killed. See R. L. Braham, *Genocide and Retribution: The Holocaust in Hungarian Ruled Northern Transylvania* (Boston: Kluwer-Nijhoff, 1983), 10, 223. According to Filderman and to the former Cluj (Kolozsvár) chief rabbi, the number of survivors may have been greater. Filderman mentions the existence in the Soviet Union in 1947 of about 100,000 Romanian Jews, most of them Bessarabians who had apparently fled before the advancing German and Romanian armies in 1941. M. Carmilly-Weinberger mentions that up to 80,000 northern Transylvanian and Central European Jews escaped into Romania between 1941 and 1944 on their way to Palestine. Cf. M. Carmilly-Weinberger, *Memorial Volume for the Jews of Cluj/Kolozsvár* (New York, 1970), 293. For the number of Jews in Romania in April 1941, see *Bevölkerungszählung in Rumänien, 1941*, 22. For the number of Jews in 1945, see Manuilă and Filderman, *Jewish Population*, 4.

37. *Foreign Relations of the United States* (Washington, D.C.: U.S. Department of State, 1944), 4:236–37.

38. W. Churchill, *The Second World War: Triumph and Tragedy* (Boston: Houghton Mifflin, 1953), 227.

39. M. Djilas, *Conversations with Stalin* (New York: Harcourt, Brace and World, 1962), 114.

40. *Foreign Relations of the United States*, 5:566; L. Holborn, *War and Peace Aims of the United Nations, 1943–1945* (Boston: World Peace Foundation, 1948), 2:353–54.

41. *Foreign Relations of the United States*, 5:550.

42. A. S. Gould Lee, *Crown against Sickle: The Story of King Michael of Romania* (London: Hutchinson, 1950), 135.

43. Ibid., 134; P. Quinlan, *Clash over Romania: British and American Policies towards Romania, 1938–1947* (Oakland, Calif.: American Academy of Arts and Sciences, 1977), 143.

Chapter 7: Romania in the Mid-1980s

1. According to Romanian official sources, the structure of investments for four of the years in the last completed quinquennial plan was as follows:

	1981	1982	1983	1984 (planned)
Industry	50.7%	46.9%	48%	51.7%
Agriculture	15.8%	15.6%	17.2%	14.9%

In 1985, 48.3% of total investments were allocated to industry and 17.7% to agriculture (*Anuarul statistic, 1986,* 222–23). See also S. Orescu, "Multilaterally Developed Romania: An Overview," in Vlad Georgescu, ed., *Romania: 40 Years, 1944–1984* (New York: Praeger, 1985), 13.

2. Comecon Secretariat, *Statisticheskii ezhegodnik stran chlen soveta ekonomicheskogo vzaimopomoshchi, 1986* (Moscow, 1986); see also Wharton Economic Forecasting Associates, "Romanian Foreign Trade Performance," *Centrally Planned Economies Current Analysis* 40 (7 June 1984): 1–7, and "Romanian Foreign Trade Performance," *PlanEcon Report* 23 (6 June 1986): 1–8.

3. In both 1987 and 1988, various Soviet sources consistently reported the U.S.S.R.'s share in Romania's foreign trade as "about one-third," or roughly five billion rubles. However, Romanian-Soviet trade grew in volume far more than the figures would indicate, since the ruble-denominated prices of some of the main categories of mutually traded commodities and goods fell during this period. In order to disguise the dramatic increase in its economic reliance on the U.S.S.R., Romania ceased publishing the relevant data after 1984.

4. Comecon Secretariat, *Statisticheskii ezhegodnik, 1986,* 51–53, 143–56, 289–91; cited by Vladimir Socor, "Social Hardships Reflected in Comecon Statistics," *RFE Research, Romania SR/1* (6 February 1987), 11–13.

5. Figures made public following the Romanian Communist Party's Central Committee Plenum of 24–25 March 1987. The ruling class numbered 204,535 individuals, or 5.6% of party members and 0.9% of the total population.

6. From 1950 to 1985, the percentage of "intellectuals and administrative personnel" fell from 24% to less than 21%. See *Munca de Partid,* no. 8 (1986): 89; *Scînteia,* 26 March 1987, p. 3, and 29 March 1987, p. 2. The very phrasing of the entry gave away the party's view of the proper function of the intelligentsia. The data failed to provide a numerical breakdown between the two categories or even to define them.

7. Dan Ionescu, "A Touch of Royalty," *RFE Research, Romania SR/2* (22 February 1985), 13–19.

8. Mihai Botez, "Lumea a doua: Introducere în comunismologie structurala" (manuscript, 1980), 26. These trends set in as part of the Ceaușescu regime's own "cultural revolution" launched in 1971. Ceaușescu defined the ideal apparatchik as "a party and state activist possessing the kind of knowledge that enables him to perform satisfactorily any kind of activity" (*Scînteia,* 26 March 1981, pp. 1–3). Romania's "cultural revolution" called for a society in which "political criteria, not professional ones, must be decisive" (*Scînteia,*

5 November 1971, p. 5). See also Mihai Sturdza, "Reds Squeeze Out the Experts," *RFE Research, Romania SR/11* (2 October 1986), 37–39.

9. At the Romanian Communist Party National Conference of 1972, Ceauşescu declared that "although the rights of the [ethnic] minorities should be protected . . . we should always keep in mind . . . the necessity . . . to reach a more homogeneous society, both socially and nationally." *Conferinţa naţională a PCR* (Bucharest: Ed. Politică, 1972), 79; see also Anneli-Ute Gabanyi and Dan Ionescu, "Minorities Issues," *RFE Research, Romania SR/3* (22 April 1987), 3–22. For a roundup of religious dissident activities in the 1980s, see Vladimir Socor, "Mounting Religious Repression in Romania," *RFE Research Background Report* (30 August 1985), 1–16; and idem, "Romania," *RFE Research Background Report (Eastern Europe)* (1 October 1986), 49–53.

Epilogue: The 1989 Revolution and the Collapse of Communism in Romania

1. See Robert Cullen, "Report from Romania," *The New Yorker,* 2 April 1990, p. 104.

2. Interestingly, the first to exploit religious metaphors after 22 December were the former Communists, who became good Christians literally overnight. This metamorphosis was graphically illustrated by the former party newspaper *Scînteia* (The spark), reborn after the December revolution as *Adevărul* (The truth), and now calling itself "an independent daily." *Adevărul* replaced the old atheistic propaganda with an unctuous lowbrow display of religiosity. Every day it featured, in large type and in an obvious place to the right of the logo, a quotation from the Bible. It saluted the removal of the huge statue of Lenin from the former Scînteia Square, renamed "Square of the Free Press" (March 1990) and, for its Easter 1990 issue (15 April), had "Christ is risen" superimposed across the first page in huge pink letters. Former Communists like Ion Iliescu, who served both as president of the "mini-parliament" (the Provisional Council of National Unity) and as chairman of the National Salvation Front (NSF), and Prime Minister Petre Roman participated conspicuously in religious services. During the electoral campaign in May 1990, Iliescu attended religious services in most of the cities where he participated in electoral meetings. It seemed that the National Salvation Front was trying to appropriate the symbols of Romanian Orthodox Christianity to persuade the population of its leaders' radical break with their Communist past.

3. For an analysis of the revolutionary situation in Romania on the eve of the December uprising, see Vladimir Tismăneanu, "Personal Power and Political Crisis in Romania," *Government and Opposition* 24/2 (Spring 1989): 177–98. For different but converging interpretations of the political and moral decay of the Romanian leadership during Ceauşescu's last years in power, including the nauseating pageants of the cult of personality and the unprecedented concentration of power in the hands of the Ceauşescu clan, see J. F. Brown, *Eastern Europe and Communist Rule* (Durham: Duke University Press, 1988), 274–82; Mark Almond, *Decline without Fall: Romania under Ceauşescu* (London: Institute

for European Defence and Strategic Studies, 1988); Vladimir Tismăneanu, "Byzantine Rites, Stalinist Follies: The Twilight of Dynastic Socialism in Romania," ORBIS 30/1 (Spring 1986): 65–90; Mary Ellen Fischer, *Nicolae Ceauşescu: A Study in Political Leadership* (Boulder, Colo.: Lynne Rienner, 1989), 224–70.

4. For a detailed account of the revolution in Timişoara in English, see Vladimir Socor, "Pastor Toekes and the Outbreak of the Revolution in Timişoara," *Report on Eastern Europe* 1/5 (2 February 1990).

5. A transcript of the 17 December emergency meeting of the Political Executive Committee of the RCP, published after the revolution, shows that Ceauşescu himself ordered the massacre. What he had in mind was clearly the model of the Tiananmen Square massacre ordered by the Chinese leaders in June 1989, an action he had publicly praised.

6. The initial rumors of thousands of dead in Timişoara turned out to be exaggerated, but the conditions for such gruesome exaggeration were part and parcel of the regime's systematic policy of misinformation and the spreading of suspicion through terror and of terror through suspicion. At his secret and selectively videotaped trial, Ceauşescu was accused of genocide, more specifically of the death of over 60,000 people, but weeks later, at the trial of four of his closest advisers, the official figure of the dead was revised downward to fewer than seven hundred. Massacres of innocent civilian demonstrators, however, took place in Timişoara and, a few days later, in several other cities, including Bucharest, Cluj, and Braşov. Any serious efforts to establish the real number of victims and the identities of those responsible for the killings were sabotaged by the National Salvation Front in its attempt to whitewash the crimes of the Securitate and promote a broader policy of amnesia.

7. Freedom of the press became a real possibility as of 22 December, but what this meant must be carefully qualified. "Free Romanian Television," as Romanian television was renamed on 22 December, was largely free and credible in its reporting of the revolution, whose actions it actually helped coordinate. But high-level censorship and control of information continued to exist (for instance, in the case of the Ceauşescu trial and execution and in regard to high-ranking members of the National Salvation Front and key decisions made by its executive council). In less than a month after the revolution, attempts by the Front to manipulate television news programs became more evident, and popular distrust increased. (See Crisula Stefanescu, "'Free Romanian Television' Losing Its Credibility," *Report on Eastern Europe* 1/12 [23 March 1990]).

As for the print media, they became highly diversified. Some newspapers were clearly controlled by the Front (for example, *Scînteia*, reborn as *Adevărul*), but there were genuinely independent ones (such as *România liberă* [Free Romania]). By mid-April, as reported in the *New York Times* (21 April 1990), more than nine hundred newspapers and journals were being published in Bucharest alone. Most of these were genuinely independent, but they had very small circulations (print runs and distribution continued to be controlled by the government), and their precarious existence did "not stop many [Romanians] from complaining loudly about the lack of freedom of the press." An indirect de facto censorship continued to regulate a theoretically (and on occasion practically) free press by denying it an adequate supply of paper to satisfy demand and by limiting its distribution. This censorship was less indirect in regard to media with large circulation or widespread public access—television first of all.

8. As the respected journalist Octavian Paler noted in an interview with the French newspaper *Le Monde* (1 April 1990, pp. 1–3), the harm done by the so-called Securitate terrorists (or Ceauşescu loyalists) may have been deliberately exaggerated: "There were certainly some fanatics. But the myth has been exaggerated, if not fabricated. . . . The myth of the 'terrorists' had two consequences: on the one hand, the revolution was masked, interrupted, as many people stayed at home; on the other hand, the authors of this masking got out of it the moral capital of having resisted the terrorists." Another hypothesis was that the army, which was defending the revolution, overreacted to fire from a few isolated snipers, destroying whole buildings in the process. But then, as Paler pointedly asks: How does one explain the extensive damage to houses in the area where the television building is located and the lack of any damage— even the slightest bullet traces—on the television building itself?

9. See Michael Shafir, "The Revolution: An Initial Assessment," *Report on Eastern Europe* 1/4 (26 January 1990); and Dan Ionescu, "Old Practices Persist in Romanian Justice," *Report on Eastern Europe* 1/10 (9 March 1990). For an early discussion of the Ceauşescu trial and execution—seen essentially as a "party execution" in an attempt by the party apparatus to cut its losses and preserve its hold on power in its new disguise as the National Salvation Front— see Matei Calinescu and Nicolas Spulber, "In Rumania, an Old Stalinist Charade?" *New York Times*, 30 December 1989, op-ed page. Later on, when the NSF announced its decision to run candidates for the 20 May 1990 elections, many Romanians rallied and went into the streets demonstrating against it under such banners as "The revolution has been confiscated" and "The only solution / Another revolution." For a discussion of NSF politics once it had become clear that the organization was a reincarnation of the old party nomenklatura, see M. Calinescu and N. Spulber, "Romanians Don't Want Warmed-Over Communism," *Philadelphia Inquirer*, 31 January 1990, editorial page; and Vladimir Tismăneanu, "New Masks, Old Faces" and "Between Revolutions," *New Republic*, 5 February and 23 April 1990, respectively.

10. For an examination of Ceauşescu's trial and of the handling of the videotape of the trial as a mockery of justice, see Michel Tatu, "La seconde mort de Ceauşescu," *Le Monde*, 24 April 1990; and the article "Nausée," signed with the initials T. D., *Le Figaro*, 23 April 1990. After the film's appearance on French television, forensic experts claimed that certain key sections were faked. According to these experts, the Ceauşescu couple may not have died by firing squad but their deaths may have resulted from other causes. Their corpses would have been later propped up for a staged execution by firing squad, videotaped some four hours after the actual deaths occurred. Subsequently it was rumored that Ceauşescu died from a heart attack during the trial or during a separate interrogation, possibly under torture. This rumor was judged newsworthy enough to be picked up by some French newspapers and the National Public Radio (NPR) in the United States (13 May 1990). If this were true, it

would go a long way toward explaining some gaps in the theory of the French forensic specialists. For one thing, it would explain the need to stage the execution by firing squad. This might have been done to create an impression of legality (although legality was absent from the very beginning). The trial was supposed to have come to a conclusion, the defendant found guilty, and the death sentence imposed and carried out. If the dictator died indeed of a heart attack, Elena Ceauşescu, in a state of hysterical anger understandable under the circumstances, might have been killed on the spot, gangland style. The chief judge of the trial would have had to sentence two corpses to death! For a judge such an act would be tantamount to professional suicide. The actual suicide on 1 March 1990 of the judge presiding at the Ceauşescu trial was explained by the pro-Front newspaper *Adevărul* as due to a state of mental imbalance. If the hypothesis suggested above is correct, the judge's suicide would be the act of desperation of an essentially honest man who had been forced to go through a criminal charade.

11. For the role General Stănculescu may have played in the palace revolution that followed the popular revolution, see *Le Monde*, 26 April 1990, p. 5.

12. See Michael Shafir, "Ceauşescu's Overthrow: Popular Uprising or Moscow-Guided Conspiracy?" *Report on Eastern Europe* 1/3 (19 January 1990).

13. See Dan Ionescu, "The National Salvation Front Starts to Implement Its Program," *Report on Eastern Europe* 1/5 (2 February 1990).

14. For a discussion of the political situation of Romania just a year or so before the revolution, see *Romania: A Case of "Dynastic" Communism* (New York: Freedom House, 1989).

15. For a more detailed view of Romanian Communist political culture, see Vladimir Tismăneanu, "The Tragicomedy of Romanian Communism," *East European Politics and Societies* 3/2 (Spring 1989): 329–76.

16. In the early days of the revolution, some former Communists thought that it would be possible to go back to the mid-sixties—the years of quasi-liberalization started by Gheorghiu-Dej in 1964 and continued by Ceauşescu during the period of his consolidation of power—and go on from there. From this point of view, the revolution had called into question only the last twenty-odd years of the Ceauşescu dictatorship, not the entire four decades of Communism. Ceauşescu himself was the focus of evil, not the system. An interpretation of the revolution consistent with this point of view was proposed in English by Pavel Campeanu in "The Revolt of the Romanians" (*New York Review of Books*, 1 February 1990). For a critique of such an approach, see the letter of M. Calinescu et al. to the editor of the *New York Review of Books*, 12 April 1990.

17. A careful documentation of the destruction of historical monuments by Ceauşescu, with abundant iconographic material, appears in Dinu C. Giurescu, *The Razing of Romania's Past* (Washington: U.S. Committee, International Committee on Monuments and Sites, 1989).

18. Silviu Brucan articulated his views on intrasystemic reforms in Soviet-style societies and the role of the party intelligentsia in these changes in his book *World Socialism at the Crossroads: An Insider's View* (New York: Praeger,

1987). According to him, pluralism in post-Stalinist societies did not mean the building of a multiparty system but merely the development of democratic mechanisms within the Communist Party, which would play the role of a "collective intellectual." The book reflected Brucan's fascination with the strategy of reforms from above and his deep distrust of independent social movements and reforms from below. As the chief NSF ideologue, Brucan corrected the most controversial points of his neo-Bolshevik doctrine by accepting the rationale for a multiparty democracy in Romania. He never renounced, however, the belief that an enlightened avant-garde could and should play the role of national pedagogue. Whether this avant-garde was called the Romanian Communist Party or the National Salvation Front was, for Brucan, irrelevant.

19. The complete text of the proclamation was translated into English and published in *Report on Eastern Europe* 1/14 (6 April 1990): 41–45. For the passage quoted, see p. 43.

20. See Marc Semo, "La commune de la Place de l'Université," *Libération*, 30 April 1990.

BIBLIOGRAPHICAL ESSAY

General Works

Although outdated in terms of information, pre–World War II general studies still provide fascinating reading. See especially A. D. Xenopol, *Istoria românilor,* 12 vols. (1925–30); N. Iorga, *Histoire des roumains,* 10 vols. (1937–44); C. C. Giurescu, *Istoria românilor,* 3 vols. (1938–46); and R. Seton-Watson, *A History of the Roumanians* (1934; reprinted 1963). M. Roller's *Istoria României* (1947) is the first Marxist attempt at interpreting the country's history, but is of interest only as a piece of historiography. C. Daicoviciu and A. Oţetea, eds., *Istoria României,* 4 vols. (1960–64), is probably the most interesting product of Marxist Romanian historiography. Of the studies published during the liberalization of the late sixties and early seventies, M. Constantinescu, C. Daicoviciu, and S. Pascu, eds., *Histoire de la Roumanie* (1970); C. C. Giurescu and D. C. Giurescu, *Istoria românilor* (1971); and A. Oţetea, ed., *The History of the Romanian People* (1975), are probably the most interesting. See also D. C. Giurescu, *Illustrated History of the Romanian People* (1981).

Bibliographies
Very useful: *Bibliografia istorică a României,* 6 vols. (1970–85); S. Stefănescu, ed., *Enciclopedia istoriografiei româneşti* (1978); A. Deletant and D. Deletant, *Romania* (1985). See also S. Fischer-Galaţi, *Romania, a Bibliographic Guide* (1968); P. Horecky, *South-Eastern Europe: A Guide to Basic Publications* (1969); E. Keefe, *Area Handbook for Romania* (1972); and K. D. Grothusen, "Rumänien," in *Südosteuropa Handbuch,* 2 (1977).

Regional Studies. Transylvania: C. Daicoviciu and S. Pascu, eds., *Din Istoria Transilvaniei,* 2 vols. (1960–61); C. Daicoviciu and M. Constantinescu, *Brève histoire de la Transylvanie* (1965); and S. Pascu, *A History of Transylvania* (1982), all reflect the Romanian position on the history of this much-disputed province. For the Hungarian point of view see especially L. Makkai, *Histoire de la Transylvanie* (1946); and B. Köpeczi, ed., *Erdély Története,* 3 vols. (1986).

Bessarabia: Z. Arbore, *Bessarabia and Bukowina: The Soviet-Romanian Territorial Dispute* (1982); M. Manoliu-Manea, ed., *The Tragic Plight of a Border Area: Bessarabia and Bukovina* (1983); G. Ciorănescu, *Bessarabia: Disputed Land between East and West* (1984). For the Soviet position on the "disputed land," see L. V. Cherepnin, ed., *Istorija Moldavskoi S.S.R.,* 2 vols. (1965); A. M. Lazarev, *Moldavskaya sovetskaya gosudarstvenost i bessarabskij vopros* (1974); and V. I. Tsaranov, ed., *Istorija Moldavskoi S.S.R.* (1982).

Dobrudja: A. Rădulescu and I. Bitoleanu, *A Concise History of Dobruja* (1984).

The Macedo-Romanians: T. Capidan's books, especially *Origina macedo-românilor* (1939) and *Macedo-românii: etnografie, istorie, limbă* (1942), are still fundamental. See also M. D. Peyfuss, *Die aromunische Frage* (1974), and G. Murnu, *Studii istorice privitoare la trecutul românilor de peste Dunăre* (1984). An excellent Macedo-Romanian bibliography was published in 1984 by the Rumänischer Forschungsinstitut, Freiburg.

Social and Economic History: Institutions. The chapters dealing with Romania in J. Lampe and M. Jackson, *Balkan Economic History, 1550–1850* (1982), are probably the best general survey of Romanian economic history. For the history of specific branches, see *Istoricul dezvoltării tehnice în România*, 2 vols. (1931); *Contribuții la istoricul industriei miniere în România* (1971); M. Pearton, *Oil and the Romanian State* (1971); C. Boncu, *Contribuții la istoria petrolului românesc* (1971); O. Iliescu, *Moneta în România* (1971); N. Iorga, *Opere economice* (1982).

General studies of social history are not so numerous as the subject deserves. For the peasantry, see the still useful studies of R. Rosetti, *Pămîntul, sătenii și stăpânii în Moldova* (1907), and idem, *Pentru ce s-au răsculat țăranii* (1908; reprinted 1987); and C. D. Creangă, *Propietatea rurală în România* (1907). For a more modern sociological interpretation see H. H. Stahl, *Traditional Romanian Village Communities* (1980). S. Zeletin, *Burghezia românească: Originea și rolul ei istoric* (1925); M. Manoilescu, *Rostul și destinul burgheziei românești* (1942), are probably the two best studies on the origins and role of the middle class in Romanian history. Useful data can also be found in C. C. Giurescu, *Contribuții la studiul originilor și dezvoltării burgheziei românești* (1973); I. Peretz, *Curs de istoria dreptului român*, 3 vols. (1926–31); D. Ionescu, G. Tutui, and G. Matei, *Dezvoltarea constituțională a poporului roman* (1957); and I. Ceterchi, ed., *Istoria dreptului românesc*, 2 vols. (1980–87), are solid studies of constitutional history. For the church, see N. Iorga, *Istoria bisericii române și a vieții religioase a românilor*, 2 vols. (1908–09); and M. Păcurariu, *Istoria bisericii române*, 3 vols. (1980). For military history, see N. Iorga, *Istoria armatei românești*, 2 vols. (1929–30); and R. Rosetti, *Essai sur l'art militaire des roumains* (1935). The recent flurry of books published by the Bucharest-based Center of Studies and Research for Military History contain interesting documentary material, but their excessive nationalism makes them difficult to use.

Culture and Civilization. The Romanian mentality and psychology have been studied by several distinguished sociologists and philosophers. See D. Drăghicescu, *Din psihologia poporului roman* (1907); G. Rădulescu-Motru, *Psihologia ciocoismului: Psihologia industriașului* (1911); and idem, *Etnicul românesc* (1942). For a provocative approach to the subject, see G. Ibrăileanu, *Spiritul critic în cultura românească* (1909; reprinted 1922). Less useful are the recent studies of the history of Romanian philosophy, such as *Istoria gîndirii sociale și filozofice din România* (1965) or *Istoria filozofiei românești*, 2 vols. (1972–80). Although less rigidly Marxist than similar studies published in the 1950s, they are still rather dogmatic. For the history of literature see N. Iorga, *Istoria literaturii românești*, 2 vols. (1925–26); and especially G. Călinescu, *Istoria literaturii române* (1941;

reprinted 1982). For other cultural developments see G. Ionescu, *Histoire de l'architecture en Roumanie* (1970); M. Tomescu, *Istoria cărții românești* (1968), *Istoria artelor plastice în România,* 2 vols. (1968–70), and *Pictura românească* (1976); V. Drăguț, *L'art roumain: Préhistoire. Antiquité. Moyen-Âge. Renaissance. Baroque* (1984). A. Rosetti has published several editions of his *Istoria limbii române* over the last fifty years; the 1968 edition seems to be the most useful. The first volume of a new edition, called "definitive," was published in 1986.

Sources. Impressive multivolume collections of documents have been published since the middle of the nineteenth century: T. Codrescu, *Uricariul,* 24 vols. (1852–95); *Documente privitoare la istoria românilor: Colecția E. de Hurmuzaki,* 45 vols. published between 1876 and 1942, with a new series from 1962; D. A. Sturdza, D. Sturdza-Scheianu, and G. Petrescu, *Acte și documente relative la istoria renascerii României,* 10 vols. (1888–1909); N. Iorga, *Acte și fragmente,* 3 vols. (1895–97); and N. Iorga, *Studii și documente,* 29 vols. (1901–16); D. Sturdza-Scheianu, *Acte și legiuiri privitoare la chestia țărănească,* 4 vols. (1907–10); G. Ghibănescu, *Surete și izvoade,* 25 vols. (1906–33); and idem, *Ispisoace și zapise,* 6 vols. (1906–26). The international treaties and conventions signed by the Romanians have been published in several collections. See especially M. Mitilineu, *Tratatele și convențiile României de la 1368 pîna în zilele noastre* (1874); F. C. Nano, *Condica tratatelor și a altor legături ale României (1354–1937),* 3 vols. (1937–42); I. Ionescu, ed., *Tratatele internaționale ale României, 1354–1920* (1971). For constitutional developments and the history of institutions, see C. Hamangiu, ed., *Codul general al României, 1393–1942,* 38 volumes published between 1899 and 1944, and still invaluable. No valid study of cultural history could be undertaken without consulting I. Bianu, N. Hodoș, and D. Simionescu, *Bibliografia românească veche, 1508–1830,* 4 vols. (1903–44). N. Hodoș and S. A. Ionescu published a still useful inventory of the Romanian press under the title *Publicațiile periodice românești* (1913), an endeavor supplemented recently by the *Bibliografia analitică a periodicelor românești, 1790–1858,* 4 vols. (1966–72). Travelers' accounts of the principalities have been published by N. Iorga, *Istoria românilor prin călători,* 4 vols. (1928–29); and by M. Holban, ed., *Călători străini despre țările române,* 8 vols. (1968–83).

Early Times

V. Pârvan's pioneering studies on pre-Roman Dacia, although outdated especially in terms of archaeological data, still provide interesting reading. See in particular *Începuturile vieții romane la gurile Dunării* (1923), *Getica* (1926), and *Dacia: Civilizațiile străvechi din regiunile carpato-danubiene* (1937). R. Vulpe, *Histoire ancienne de la Dobroudja* (1938), and C. Daicoviciu, *La Transylvanie dans l'antiquité* (1945), are fundamental for the study of the two provinces. V. Dumitrescu, ed., "The prehistory of Romania, from earliest times to 1000 B.C." in *The Cambridge Ancient History. The Prehistory of the Balkans* (1982), is probably the best introduction to Romanian prehistory. Also useful is M. Petrescu-Dâmbovița's *Scurtă istoriea a Daciei preromane* (1978).

For the Dacians, before and after the Roman conquest, see I. H. Crişan, *Burebista and His Time* (1978); H. Daicoviciu, *Dacii* (1972); R. Vulpe and I. Barnea, *Românii la Dunarea de jos* (1968); and M. Macrea, *Viaţa în Dacia romană* (1968).

The continuity theory and the history of the rise of the Romanian people have been in the midst of heated arguments ever since R. Rössler published his *Rumänische Studien* (1871) and A. D. Xenopol his rebuttal, *Une énigme historique: Les roumains au Moyen-Âge* (1885). G. Brătianu, *Une énigme et un miracle historique: Le peuple roumain* (1937) and N. Stoicescu, *The Continuity of the Romanian People* (1983) are excellent presentations of the historiography of the problem. Because the written evidence has not changed much since the Rössler-Xenopol dispute, the most interesting new contributions have come from the archaeologists: I. Nestor, "Les données archéologiques et le problème de la formation du peuple roumain," *Revue roumaine d'histoire* 3/3 (1964); E. Zaharia, *Săpăturile de la Dridu* (1967), and *Populaţia românească din Transilvania în secolele VI–VIII: Cimitirul nr. 23 de la Bratei* (1977); D. Protase, *Problema continuităţii în Dacia în lumina arheologiei şi numismaticii* (1966), and *Autohtonii în Dacia* (1980), vol. 1; L. Bârzu, *Continuitatea populaţiei autohtone în Transilvania în secolele IV–V* (1973). Also useful are S. Pascu and P. Diaconu, eds., *Relations between the Autochthonous Populations and the Migratory Populations on the Territory of Romania* (1975); V. Spinei, *Moldavia in the XIth–XIVth Centuries* (1986); V. Spinei, *Relaţii etnice şi politice în Moldova meridională in secolele X–XIII: Românii şi turanicii* (1985); and P. Diaconu, *Les Petchenegues au Bas-Danube* (1970), and *Les Coumans au Bas-Danube* (1978).

The Roman, Greek, and Byzantine references to the Dacians and early Romanians have recently been republished in *Fontes Historiae Daco-Romaniae* (1964–83), vols. 1–4; still useful is G. Popa-Lisseanu, *Izvoarele istoriei românilor*, 14 vols. (1934–39). For English translations of the important references from Herodotus and Strabo, see *Herodotus*, trans. A. D. Godley (1966) and *The Geography of Strabo*, trans. J. L. Jones (1960); for other significant literary sources see E. Szentpetery, *Scriptores Rerum Hungaricum* (1937), *Polnoe sobranie russkich letopisei* (1879), vol. 1; and K. Lachman, *Der Nibelungen Noth und Klage* (1878).

For the linguistic developments of the period see I. I. Rusu, *Die Sprache der Thrako-Daker* (1969), and *Etnogeneza românilor* (1981), as well as A. Graur, *The Romance Character of Romanian* (1967), and A. Rosetti, *Les origines de la langue roumaine* (1974).

The continuity theory has been a bone of contention for many historians of eastern Europe. Some of the Russian and Hungarian positions were mentioned along with the bibliography on Transylvania and Bessarabia. For more detailed Hungarian arguments see G. Gyorffy, "Formations d'états au XIème siècle suivant les *Gesta Hungarorum* du notaire Anonyme," *Nouvelles études historiques* 1 (1965); and I. Fodor, *In Search of a New Homeland: The Prehistory of the Hungarian People and the Conquest* (1982). For the Bulgarian point of view, which accepts the continuity theory, see P. Rousse, "La civilisation bulgare et les peuples balkaniques aux IXème–XIIème siècles," *Études balkaniques* 5/1 (1969); I. Dujcev, ed., *Histoire de la Bulgarie* (1977); and V. Velkov, ed., *Istoriia na Bulgariia*, 2 vols. (1979–81).

The Middle Ages

For excellent overviews of an old and controversial topic, Romanian feudalism, see F. Constantiniu's "Geneza feudalismului românesc: Incadrare tipologică," *Revista de istorie* 31/7 (1978), and his "Iobăgia în istoriografia română," *Studii şi materiale de istorie medie* 10 (1983). Opposed to the very concept of Romanian feudalism are H. H. Stahl, *Controverse de istorie socială românească* (1969), and C. C. Giurescu, *Probleme controversate în istoriografia românească* (1977).

Sources. All the known documents from Romania have been catalogued and published. I. R. Mircea, *Catalogul documentelor Ţării Româneşti, 1369–1600* (1947), and *Catalogul documentelor moldoveneşti,* 5 vols. (1957–75), are probably the most complete such catalogues. Between 1951 and 1960 the Romanian Academy published 32 volumes under the title *Documente privind istoria României* and covering the period 1251–1625. A new collection is in the process of being published now under the general title *Documenta Romaniae Historica*; 28 volumes were published between 1966 and 1988. The aim is to republish all internal documents to the end of the seventeenth century. Until this ambitious plan is completed, the older collections of documents cannot be overlooked. See for example I. Bogdan, *Documentele lui Ştefan cel Mare,* 2 vols. (1931–32); and C. Costăchescu, *Documente moldoveneşti înainte Ştefan cel Mare,* 2 vols. (1931–33); C. Costăchescu, *Documente moldoveneşti de la Ştefan cel Mare* (1933). For Transylvania see A. Veress, *Bibliografia româno-ungară,* 3 vols. (1931–35); and *Documente privitoare la istoria Ardealului, Moldovei şi Ţării Româneşti,* 9 vols. (1929–39).

For the minorities—Saxons, Hungarians, and Jews—see the collections more or less completed: F. Zimmermann and G. Gündisch, eds., *Urkundenbuch zur Geschichte der Deutschen in Siebenbürgen,* 7 vols. (1892–1981); L. Demény and J. Pataki, eds., *Székely oklevéltár* (1983), vol. 1; V. Eskenazy and M. Spielmann, eds., *Izvoare şi mărturii referitoare la evreii din România,* 2 vols. (1986–88). For Transylvania, see A. Veress, *Bibliografia româno-ungară* and *Documente privitoare la istoria Ardealului, Moldovei şi Ţării Româneşti;* and V. Eskenazy and M. Spielmann, eds., *Izvoare şi mărturii referitoare la evreii din România* (1986), vol. 1.

The Economy. I. Donat, "Aşerzările omeneşti din Ţara Românească in secolele XIV–XVII," *Studii* 10/6 (1956), and idem, "The Romanians South of the Carpathians and the Migratory People," in M. Constantinescu, S. Pascu, and P. Diaconu, *Relations between the Autochthonous Populations and the Migratory Populations on the Territory of Romania* (1975); S. Pascu, ed., *Populaţie şi societate* (1972), vol. 1; S. Stefănescu, "Conjuncturi socio-economice şi situaţia demografică în ţările române în secolele XIV–XVII" in Pascu, *Populaţie şi societate;* S. Stefănescu, *Demografia, dimensiune a istoriei* (1974); S. Meteş, *Emigrări româneşti în Transilvania în secolele XIV–XX* (1977), are all sound introductions to the demographic trends of the period. For a general survey of economic development, see N. Iorga, *Istoria industriilor la români* (1927). M. Popescu, *Fabrici româneşti de hîrtie* (1941); S. Pascu, *Meşteşugurile din Transilvania pînă în secolul al XVI-lea* (1954); S. Olteanu and C. Şerban, *Meşteşugurile din Ţara Românească şi Moldova în evul mediu* (1969); and S. Goldenberg, "Comerţul, producţia şi consumul de postavuri de lînă în ţările române, secolul al XIV-lea-jumătatea secolului al

XVIII-lea," *Studii* 24/5 (1971), provide useful information on the history of medieval crafts and manufacturing industries. For agriculture, see especially N. Edroiu and P. Gyulai, "Evoluţia plugului în ţările române," *Acta Musei Napocensis* 2 (1965); V. Neamţu, *La technique de la production céréalière en Valachie et en Moldavie jusqu'au XVIIIème siècle* (1975); and C. Constantinescu-Mirceşti, *Păstoritul transhumant şi implicaţiile lui în Transilvania şi Ţara Românească* (1976). On trade, see G. Brătianu, *Recherches sur le commerce gênois dans la Mer Noire* (1929), and idem, *La Mer Noire: Des origines à la conquête ottomane* (1969); P. P. Panaitescu, "La route commerciale de Pologne à la Mer Noire au Moyen-Âge," *Revista istorică română* 3/2–3 (1933); S. Meteş, *Relaţiile comerciale ale Ţării Româneşti cu Ardealul pînă în secolul al XVIII-lea* (1921); S. Papacostea, "Începuturile politicii comerciale a Ţării Româneşti şi Moldovei, secolele XIV–XVI: Drum şi stat," *Studii şi materiale de istorie medie* 10 (1983).

Social History. C. C. Giurescu, *Studii de istorie socială* (1943); P. P. Panaitescu, *Interpretări româneşti: Studii de istorie economică şi socială* (1947); idem, *Obştea ţărănească în Ţara Românească şi Moldova* (1964); R. Rosetti, *Despre originea şi transformările clasei stăpînitoare din Moldova* (1906); I. C. Filitti, *Proprietatea solului în Principatele Române* (1935); H. H. Stahl, *Contribuţii la istoria satelor devălmaşe româneşti*, vols. 1–2 (1958–59); and idem, *Traditional Romanian Village Communities* (1980), are probably the best studies of the social classes in the principalities. For Transylvania see the definitive works by D. Prodan, *Iobăgia în Transilvania în secolul al XVI-lea*, 2 vols. (1967–68); and idem, *Iobăgia în Transilvania în secolul al XVII-lea*, 2 vols. (1988).

For the history of the cities see especially C. C. Giurescu, *Tîrguri s-au oraşe şi cetăţi moldoveneşti din secolul al X-lea şi pînă la mijlocul secolului al XVI-lea* (1967); and M. Matei, *Studii de istorie orăşenească medievală: Moldova, secolele XIV–XVI* (1970).

Institutions. G. Brătianu, *Sfatul domnesc şi adunarea stărilor în Principatele Române* (1977), is probably the best single study of the central government's functioning. For other aspects of medieval institutional and constitutional history, see E. Vîrtosu, *Titulatura domnilor şi asocierea la domnie în Ţara Românească şi Moldova în secolele XIV–XVII* (1960); N. Stoicescu, *Sfatul domnesc şi marii dregători din Ţara Românesca şi Moldova în secolele XIV–XVII* (1968); idem, *Dicţionar al marilor dregători în Ţara Românească şi Moldova: Secolele XIV–XVII* (1971); N. Grigoraş, *Instituţii feudale din Moldova: Organizarea de stat pînă la mijlocul secolului al XVIII-lea* (1971); M. Neagoe, *Problema centralizării satelor feudale româneşti, Moldova şi Ţara Românească* (1976); V. A. Georgescu, *Bizanţul şi instituţiile româneşti* (1980); A. Pippidi, *Tradiţia politică bizantină în ţările române* (1983).

General studies of church history have already been mentioned. For relations with other Orthodox churches see A. I. Elian and I. Rămureanu, "Legăturile mitropoliei Ungrovlahiei cu patriarhia de la Constantinolpol şi celelalte biserici ortodoxe," *Biserica ortodoxă română*, nos. 7–10 (1959). For the two opposing interpretations of the union of the Transylvanian Orthodox Church with Rome, see S. Dragomir, *Românii din Transilvania şi unirea cu biserica Romei* (1963); O. Bârlea, "Die Union der Rumänen" in W. de Vries, ed., *Rom und die Patriarchate des Ostens*. Orbis Academicus 3/4 (1963); and P. S. Năsturel, *Le Mont Athos et les roumains* (1986).

Political History. For the founding of the principalities of Wallachia and Moldavia and their relations with the kingdom of Hungary during the fourteenth century, see S. Papacostea, "La formation de la Valachie et de la Moldavie et les roumains de Transilvanie," *Revue roumaine d'histoire* 18/3 (1970); N. Stoicescu, ed., *Constituirea statelor feudale românești* (1980); and M. Holban, *Din cronica relațiilor româno-ungare* (1981). Good general studies covering the fourteenth through sixteenth centuries have been written by S. Ștefănescu, *Țara Românească de la Basarab întemeitorul pînă la Mihai Viteazul* (1971); D. C. Giurescu, *Țara Românească în secolele XIV–XVI* (1973); and N. Grigoraș, *Țara Românească a Moldovei pînă la Ștefan cel Mare* (1978). Information about the most important reigns is found in P. P. Panaitescu, *Mircea cel Bătrîn* (1944); C. Mureșan, *Iancu de la Hunedoara și vremea sa* (1957, 1968); N. Stoicescu, *Vlad Țepeș* (1976); and idem, *Matei Basarab* (1988); I. Ursu, *Ștefan cel Mare* (1925); S. Papacostea, *Stephen the Great, Prince of Moldavia, 1457–1504* (1980); S. Gorovei, *Petru Rareș* (1982); M. Neagoe, *Neagoe Basarab* (1971); D. C. Giurescu, *Ioan Vodă cel Viteaz* (1966); N. Iorga, *Istoria lui Mihai Viteazul* (1936); N. Iorga, *Viața și domnia lui Constantin Dimitrie Cantemir* (1958).

Foreign Policy. Relations with the Ottoman Empire were obviously the dominant factor during the Middle Ages. C. Giurescu, *Capitulațiile Moldovei cu Poarta otomană* (1908), is still a basic introduction to the study of the political relationship between the two countries. See also I. Matei, "Quelques problèmes concernant le régime de la domination ottomane dans les pays roumains," *Revue des études sud-est européennes* 10 (1972); 11/1 (1973); S. Gorovei, "Moldova în casa păcii," *Anuarul Institutului de Istorie A. D. Xenopol* 18 (1980); S. Papacostea, "Tratatele Țării Românești și Moldovei cu Imperial Otoman în secolele XIV–XVI: Ficțiune politică și realitate istorică," in N. Edroiu et al., eds., *Stat, societate, națiune* (1982); and M. Berindei and G. Veinstein, *L'empire ottoman et les pays roumains, 1544–1545* (1987), a volume of documents with an excellent general introduction.

For the history of the economic relations between the empire and its vassal Romanian states, see M. Berza, "Haraciul Moldovei și Țării Românești în secolele XV–XIX," *Studii și materiale de istorie medie* 2 (1957); and idem, "Variațiile exploatării Țării Românești de către Poarta otomană in secolele XVI–XVIII," *Studii* 11/2 (1958); M. Maxim, "Regimul economic al dominației otomane în Moldova și Țara Românească în a doua jumătate a secolului al XVI-lea," *Revista de istorie* 32/9 (1979); T. Gemil, "Date noi privind haraciul țărilor române în secolul al XVII-lea," *Revista de istorie* 30/8 (1977). Very useful is M. Guboglu, "Le tribut payé par les principautés roumaines à la Porte jusqu'au début du XVIème siècle," *Revue des études islamiques* 37/1 (1969).

For relations with other neighboring powers, see S. Papacostea, "De la Calomeea la Codrul Cosminului: Poziția internațională a Moldovei la sfîrșitul secolului al XV-lea," *Romanoslavica* 17 (1970); V. Ciobanu, *Relațiile româno-polone între 1699 și 1848* (1980); L. E. Semeonova, *Russko-valashskije otnoshenija v kontse XVII–nachale XVIII v* (1969); G. Lebel, *La France et les principautés danubiennes du XVIème siècle à la chute de Napoléon Ier* (1955); and M. Berza, ed., *România în sud-estul Europei* (1979). Very useful is the work of the common Romanian-

Soviet undertaking published under the title *Relaţiile istorice dintre popoarele U.R.S.S. şi România*, 3 vols. (1965–70).

Medieval Culture. Fundamental studies are those of M. Berza, ed., *Cultura moldovenească în timpul lui Ştefan cel Mare* (1964); P. P. Panaitescu, *Einführung in die Geschichte der rumänischen Kultur* (1977); and R. Theodorescu, *Civilizaţia românilor între medieval şi modern*, 3 vols. (1987). See also P. P. Panaitescu, *Inceputurile sî biruinţa scrisului în limba română* (1969); I. Gheţie, *Originea scrisului în limba română* (1985); N. Cartojan, *Istoria literaturii române vechi*, 3 vols. (1940–45); E. Turdeanu, *Études de littérature roumaine* (1985). The medieval chronicles have been catalogued by I. Crăciun and A. Ilieş, *Repertoriul manuscriselor de cronici interne, secolele XV–XVIII* (1963); P. P. Panaitescu, *Cronici slavo-române din secolele XV–XVI* (1959); and M. Gregorian, *Cronicari munteni*, 2 vols. (1961). Gregorian's volumes have an excellent general introduction by E. Stănescu. There are several excellent editions of the important seventeenth- and early eighteenth-century historians.

History of Ideas. C. Tsourkas, *Les débuts de l'enseignement philosophique et de la libre pensée dans les Balkans* (1948); V. Cândea, "L'humanisme d'Udrişte Năsturel et l'agonie des lettres slavonnes en Valachie," *Revue des études sud-est européennes* 6/2 (1968); and "Les intellectuels d'Europe du sud-est au XVIIème siècle," *Revue des études sud-est européennes* 8/2 (1970). See also D. Zamfirescu, *Neagoe Basarab şi învăţăturile către fiul s-au Teodosie: Probleme controversate* (1973).

History of the Book. Interesting statistics are found in B. Theodorescu, "Cartea românească veche, 1508–1830," *Mitropolia Olteniei* nos. 9–12 (1959); and idem, "Repertoriul cărţii vechi româneşti," *Biserica ortodoxă română* nos. 3–4 (1960). Also useful are the two books published by C. Dima-Drăgan on seventeenth-century libraries, *Biblioteca unui umanist roman: C. Cantacuzino-Stolnicul* (1967) and *Biblioteci umaniste româneşti* (1974).

Art History, Civilization. V. Vătăşianu, *Istoria artei feudale româneşti* (1959), vol. 1, and the treatise published by the Romanian Academy, *Istoria artelor plastice in România*, 2 vols. (1968–70), are good general histories. Very useful is I. D. Ştefănescu, *Iconografia artei bizantine şi a picturii feudale româneşti* (1973). Provocative points of view are found in R. Theodorescu's two books, *Bizanţ, Balcani şi Occident la începuturile culturii medievale româneşti, secolele X–XIV* (1974) and *Un mileniu de artă la Dunărea de Jos, 400–1400* (1975), as well as in P. Chihaia's *Tradiţii răsăritene şi influenţe occidentale în Ţara Românească* (1983). For different aspects of everyday life in the medieval Romanian principalities, see especially C. Nicolescu, *Istoria costumului de curte în ţările române* (1971); and idem, *Case, conace şi palate vechi româneşti* (1979); A. Alexianu, *Mode şi vesminte din trecut*, 2 vols. (1971); P. Chihaia, *Din cetăţile de scaun ale Ţării Româneşti* (1974).

The medieval origins of modern national consciousness has been a favorite topic of Romanian historians. Probably the most interesting studies are those by E. Stănescu, "Premizele medievale ale conştiinţei naţionale româneşti," *Studii* 5 (1964), and "Roumanie. Histoire d'un mot. Développement de la conscience d'unité territoriale chez les roumains aux XVIIème–XIXème siècles," *Balkan Studies* 2 (1969); S. Papacostea, "Les roumains et la conscience nationale de leur romanité au Moyen-Âge," *Revue roumaine d'histoire* 1 (1965); A. Armbruster, *La romanité des roumains: Histoire d'une idée* (1977).

Despotism and Enlightenment

Few topics have been as passionately debated by historians as the role of the Phanariots in Balkan and Romanian history. Such traditional anti-Phanariot studies as M. Zallony, *Essai sur les phanariots* (1824), and A. D. Xenopol, *Epoca fanariotă, 1711–1821* (1892), have been challenged by N. Iorga, "Le despotisme éclairé dans les pays roumains au XVIIIème siècle," *Bulletin of the International Committee of Historical Sciences* 1 (1937), and more recently by F. Constantiniu and S. Papacostea, "Les réformes des premiers princes phanariotes en Moldavie et en Valachie: Essai d'interprétation," *Balkan Studies* 13 (1972), and S. Papacostea, *Oltenia sub stăpînirea austriacă* (1971). For a more critical point of view see V. Georgescu, *Political Ideas and the Enlightenment in the Romanian Principalities, 1750–1831* (1971).

For internal, especially constitutional, developments see V. A. Urechia, *Istoria românilor*, 13 vols. (1891–1901); D. V. Barnoski, *Originile democrației române: Cărvunarii și constituția Moldovei din 1822* (1922); E. Vîrtosu, "Napoléon Bonaparte și proiectul unei republici aristo-dimocraticești în Moldova la 1802," *Studii* 18/2 (1965); V. Georgescu, *Mémoires et projets de réforme dans les principautés roumaines*, vol. 1 (1769–1830) (1970); V. Șotropa, *Proiectele de constituție, programele de reforme și petițiile de drepturi din țările române în secolul al XVIII-lea și prima jumătate a secolului al XIX-lea* (1976). For the fascinating role played by the Freemasons during this period of national revival, see N. Iorga, *Francmasoni și conspiratori în Moldova în secolul al XVIII-lea* (1928); P. P. Panaitescu, "Medaliile francmasoniilor în Moldova în secolul al XVIII-lea," *Revista istorică* 14/10–12 (1928); and G. Șerbanesco, *Histoire de la franc-maçonnerie*, 3 vols. (1966).

The bibliography for the 1821 revolution is enormous. A. Oțetea, *Tudor Vladimirescu și mișcarea eteristă în țările române* (1945; reprinted 1971); and D. Berindei, *L'année révolutionnaire 1821 dans les pays roumains* (1973), are the best general studies. The most important sources concerning the uprising and its relation with the Greek revolution have been republished in *Documente privind istoria României: Răscoala de la 1821*, ed. A. Oțetea, 4 vols. (1959–68). For the postrevolutionary years see I. C. Filitti, *Frămîntările politice în Principatele Române de la 1821 la 1828* (1932); and I. C. Filitti, *Les principautés roumaines sous l'occupation russe, 1828–1834* (1904).

Social and Economic Developments. V. Mihordea, *Maîtres du sol et paysans dans les principautés roumaines au XVIIIème siècle* (1971); F. Constantiniu, *Relațiile agrare din Țara Românească în secolul al XVIII-lea* (1972); and S. Columbeanu, *Grandes exploitations domaniales en Valachie au XVIIIème siècle* (1974), are excellent not only for facilitating understanding of the relations between landlords and peasants, but also for the study of agriculture.

For industrial and commercial developments see E. Pavelescu, *Economia breslelor în Moldova* (1939); G. Penelea, *Les foires de Valachie pendant la période 1774–1848* (1973); A. Oțetea, "Considerații asupra trecerii de la feudalism la capitalism," *Studii și articole de istorie medievală* 4 (1960); A. Oțetea, *Pătrunderea comerțului românesc în circuitul internațional* (1977).

Foreign Policy. I. C. Filitti, *Rôle diplomatique des phanariotes de 1700 à 1821*

(1901); and A. Oţetea, "Influenţa Moldovei şi Ţării Româneşti asupra politicii Porţii," *Revista arhivelor* 1 (1960), are good general introductions. Relations with the Ottomans have been extensively covered by M. Alexandrescu-Dersca, "Rolul hatiserifelor de privilegii în limitarea obligaţiilor faţă de Poartă," *Studii* 11/6 (1958), and idem, "Sur le régime des ressortissants ottomans en Moldavie, 1711–1829," *Studia et acta orientalia* 5–6 (1967); T. Ionescu, "Hatiseriful din 1802," *Studii şi articole de istorie* 1 (1956); A. Vianu, "Aplicarea tratatului de la Kuciuk-Kainardji cu privire la Moldova şi Ţara Românească," *Studii* 13/5 (1960). For other aspects of the international position of the principalities, see A. Vianu, "Acţiuni diplomatice ale Ţării Româneşti în Rusia în anii 1736–39," *Romanoslavica* (1963); V. Georgescu, *Din corespondenţa diplomatică a Ţării Româneşti, 1823–1828* (1962); A. Duţu, "L'image de la France dans les pays roumains pendant les campagnes napoléoniennes et le Congrès de Vienne," *Nouvelles études d'histoire* 3 (1965).

The Enlightenment. N. Iorga, *Istoria literaturii române în veacul al XVIII-lea*, 2 vols. (1901); and D. Popovici, *La littérature roumaine à l'époque des lumières* (1945), are basic introductions to the study of the Romanian Enlightenment. Other important general contributions include A. Duţu, *Coordonate ale culturii româneşti în veacul al XVIII-lea* (1968); and A. Duţu, *Les livres de sagesse dans la culture roumaine* (1971); P. Teodor, ed., *Enlightenment and Romanian Society* (1980); R. Munteanu, *La culture roumaine, la littérature occidentale: Recontres* (1982); E. Turczynski, *Von Aufklärung zum Frühliberalismus* (1985). For specific issues, especially for the impact of Greek and French ideas on the Romanian intellectuals, see C. Erbiceanu, *Cronicarii greci care au scris despre români în epoca fanariotă* and *Bibliografia greacă sau cărţile greceşti imprimate în Principatele Române în epoca fanariotă* (1903); N. Camariano, "Influenţa franceză în Principatele Române prin filiera neogreacă," *Revista fundaţiilor regale* 9 (1942). A. Camariano-Cioran has written several studies which should be considered a model for the comparative understanding of the Balkan Enlightenment: *Spiritul filozofic şi revoluţionar francez combătut de patriarhia ecumenică şi Sublima Poartă* (1941), *Spiritul revoluţionar francez şi Voltaire în limbile greacă şi română* (1946), "L'oeuvre de Beccaria 'Dei delitti e delle penne' et ses traductions en langues grecque et roumaine," *Revue des études sud-est européennes* 5/1–2 (1967), and especially the fundamental *Les académies princières de Bucharest et de Jassy* (1974).

The Enlightenment had a direct influence on the rise of the national consciousness. N. Iorga, *Origine et développement de l'idée nationale surtout dans le monde oriental* (1934); idem, *Penseurs révolutionnaires roumains de 1804 à 1830* (1934); V. A. Georgescu, "La philosophie des lumières et la formation de la conscience nationale dans le sud-est de l'Europe," *Association Internationale d'Etudes Sud-Est Européennes* nos. 1–2 (1969); and S. Lemny, *Originea şi cristalizarea ideii de patrie în cultura română* (1986), are among the most interesting studies dealing with the subject.

Transylvania. D. Prodan, *Les migrations de roumains au-delà des Carpates au XVIIIème siècle: Critique d'une théorie* (1945), is an excellent study of demographic history. Still very useful are A. Treboniu-Laurian, *Die Rumänen der Österreichischen Monarchie*, 3 vols. (1849–52); and T. Păcăţian, *Cartea de Aur s-au luptele naţionale ale românilor de sub coroana maghiară*, 8 vols. (1904–15). Very good general surveys covering not only the eighteenth century but also the first half of the nineteenth have been published by K. Hitchins, *The Romanian National Movement in Transylvania, 1790–1848* (1969); and idem, *The Idea of Nation: The Romanians of Transylvania* (1985); and L. Gyemant, *Mişcarea naţională a românilor din Transilvania, 1790–1848* (1986). For religious and church-related developments, see S. Dragomir, *Istoria desrobirii religioase a românilor din Ardeal în secolul al XVIII-lea*, 2 vols. (1929–30); and K. Hitchins, "An East-European Elite in the 18th Century: The Romanian Uniate Hierarchy," in Frederic Cople Jaher, ed., *The Rich, the Well Born and the Powerful* (1973). The two main political events of the period, the Horia revolt of 1784 and the *Supplex* of 1791, are discussed by D. Prodan in Supplex Libellus Valachorum *and the Political Struggle of the Romanians during the XVIIIth Century* (1971) and in *Răscoala lui Horia*, 2 vols. (1984), which is the definitive analysis.

L. Blaga, *Gândirea românească din Transilvania în secolul al XVIII-lea* (1966), is a brilliant essay on Romanian-Transylvanian intellectual life. For the "Transylvanian School" see I. Lungu, *Scoala Ardeleană* (1978); and especially F. Fugariu, *Scoala Ardeleană*, 2 vols. (1983). N. Albu, *Istoria învăţămîntului românesc din Transylvania pînă la 1800* (1944), and L. Protopopescu, *Contribuţii la istoria învăţămîntului românesc din Transilvania, 1774–1805* (1966), are probably the most useful studies on the history of education. The rise of Romanian nationalism in Transylvania has been extensively covered by M. Bernath, *Habsburg und die Anfänge der rumänischen Nationsbildung* (1972), and E. Turczynski, *Konfession und Nation: Zur Frühgeschichte der serbischen und rumänischen Nationsbildung* (1976).

The Age of National Revival

For a collection of challenging articles about the process of modernization in Romania, see K. Jewitt, ed., *Social Change in Romania, 1860–1918* (1978). Valuable statistics were published by L. Colescu, *La population de la Roumanie* (1903); L. Colescu, *Recensămîntul general al României din 1899* (1905); and G. Retegan, "Evoluţia populaţiei urbane a României," *Revista de statistică* 14/7 (1965). N. Bălcescu, *Question économique des principautés danubiennes* (1850), and G. D. Cioriceanu, *La Roumanie économique et ses rapports avec l'étranger de 1860 à 1915* (1928), G. Zane, *Un veac de luptă pentru cucerirea pieţii româneşti* (1926), and G. Zane, *Economia de schimb în Principatele Române* (1930), are still fundamental for the understanding of nineteenth-century economic developments. For specific branches see C. Mănescu, *Istoricul căilor ferate în România*, 2 vols. (1906); G. Paşcanu, *Istoria uzinelor electrice din România* (1929); Ş. Imre, *Despre începuturile industriei capitaliste din Transilvania în prima jumătate a veacului al XIX-lea* (1955); A. Cebuc and C. Mocanu, *Din istoria transportului de călători în România* (1967); I. Corfus, *L'agriculture en Valachie durant la première moitié du XIXème siècle* (1969); G. Zane, *L'industrie roumaine au cours de la seconde moitié du XIXème siècle* (1973); V. Dinculescu, ed., *Relaţiile Ţării Româneşti cu peninsula balcanică, 1829–1858* (1970); V. Jinga, *Principii şi orientări ale comerţului exterior al României, 1859–1916* (1975).

For monetary and financial matters, see C. I. Băicoianu, *Istoria politicii noastre vamale şi comerciale de la Regulamentele Organice şi pînă în prezent*, 2 vols. (1904); C. I. Băicoianu, *Istoria politicii noastre monetare şi a Băncii Naţionale*, 4 vols. (1932); N. Petra, *Băncile româneşti din Ardeal şi Banat* (1936); C. C. Kiriţescu, *Sistemul bănesc al leului şi percursorii lui*, 3 vols. (1964–71); and M. Dreciu, *Banca Albina din Sibiu, 1871–1918* (1982).

Most of the studies dealing with social history have concentrated on the peasantry. M. Emerit, *Les paysans roumains depuis le traité d'Adrianople jusqu'à la libération des terres, 1829–1864* (1927), N. Adăniloaie and D. Berindei, *Reforma agrară din 1864* (1967), and P. Eidelberg, *The Great Romanian Peasant Revolt of 1907* (1974), are probably the most useful. For Transylvania, see especially I. Kovacs, *Desfinţarea relaţiilor feudale în Transilvania* (1973); A. Egyed, *Ţărănimea din Transilvania la sfîrşitul secolului al XIX-lea* (1975).

There are no general studies about the nineteenth-century boyars: I. C. Filitti's *Catagrafie de toţi boierii Ţării Româneşti la 1829* (1929), is an interesting statistical analysis of the size of the Romanian ruling class at the beginning of the century. Also useful is G. Bezviconi, *Boierimea Moldovei dintre Prut şi Nistru*, 2 vols. (1940–43). The lack of studies on the aristocracy is somewhat compensated for by several excellent works on the middle class. Ş. Zeletin, *Burghezia românească: Origina şi rolul ei istoric* (1925), and M. Manoilescu, *Rolul şi destinul burgheziei româneşti* (1942), are especially controversial. For a more strictly factual treatment, see G. Retegan, "Structura social-economică a burgheziei româneşti din Transilvania în anii regimului liberal," *Acta Musei Napocensis* 8 (1971); C. C. Giurescu, *Contribuţii la istoria, originiile şi dezvoltarea burgheziei româneşti pînă la 1848* (1973). The history of the working class was ignored almost completely by pre–World War II historians, while the Marxist ones tended to exaggerate its role. For a more balanced approach, see L. Fodor and L. Vaida, *Contribuţii la istoria mişcării sindicale din Transilvania, 1848–1917* (1957); N. N. Constantinescu, ed., *Din istoria formării şi dezvoltării clasei muncitoare din România* (1959); N. N. Constantinescu, *Mişcarea muncitorească şi legislaţia muncii în România, 1864–1944* (1972); and I. Cicală, *Mişcarea muncitorească şi socialistă din Transilvania, 1901–1921* (1976).

Political History. The bibliography of the political history of the period from the introduction of the Organic Statutes to the end of the First World War is very rich. For institutional changes see G. Nicolescu, *Parlamentul român, 1866–1901* (1903); L. Colescu, *Statistica electorală* (1913); A. Stan, V. Stan, and P. Câncea, eds., *Istoria parlamentului şi a vieţii parlamentare din România pînă la 1918* (1983); and I. Bulei, *Sistemul politic al României moderne: Partidul conservator* (1987). The pre-1848 period has been extensively covered by I. C. Filitti, *Domniile române sub Regulamentul Organic* (1915); P. P. Panaitescu, "Planurile lui I. Câmpineanu pentru unitatea naţională a românilor," *Anuarul Institutului de Istorie Naţională din Cluj* 3 (1924); G. Zane, *Le mouvement révolutionnaire de 1840* (1964); and C. Bodea, *The Romanians' Struggle for Unification, 1834–1848* (1970). The Romanian version of Bodea's book, *Lupta românilor pentru unitate naţională, 1834–1848* (1967), should nevertheless be consulted for the important documents it contains. The most important texts of the 1848 revolution are published in *Anul 1848 în Principatele Române: Acte și documente*, 6 vols. (1902–10). For Transylvania see S. Dragomir, *Studii și documente privitoare la revoluția românilor din Transilvania în 1848–1849*, 5 vols. (1946). C. Bodea, *1848 la români*, 2 vols. (1982), is also a useful collection of documents. For a general survey of the revolution, see V. Cherestesiu, *Adunarea națională dela Blaj* (1966); N. Adăniloaie and D. Berindei, eds., *Revoluția romănă de la 1848: Culegere de studii* (1974); and Ș. Pascu and V. Cherestesiu, *Revoluția de la 1848–1849 din Transilvania* (1977), vol. 1. I. Deak's *The Lawful Revolution: L. Kossuth and the Hungarians, 1848–1849* (1979) is a masterpiece of comparative history with interesting views on the sour Hungarian-Romanian relations during the revolution.

The Union of 1859. W. T. Riker, *The Making of Romania: A Study of an International Problem, 1856–1866* (1931), D. Berindei, *L'union de principautés roumaines* (1967), C. C. Giurescu, *Viața și opera lui Cuza-Vodă* (1970), and G. Bobango, *The Emergence of the Romanian National State* (1979), are all useful studies. P. Cancea, *Viața politică din România în primul deceniu al independenței de stat* (1974), T. Lungu, *Viața politică din România la sfîrșitul secolului al XIX, 1899–1910* (1977), and A. Iordache, *Viața politică a României, 1910–1914* (1972), cover the reign of Carol I in great detail. For the war of independence see A. Adăniloaie, *Independența națională a României* (1986). Older studies of diplomatic history, such as R. Bossy's *Agenția diplomatică a României la Paris și legăturile franco-române sub Cuza-Vodă* (1931) and his *L'Autriche et les Principautés Unies* (1938), should be supplemented with more recent studies such as L. Boicu's *Geneza chestiunii române ca problemă internațională* (1975) and S. Rădulescu-Zoner's *Rumänien und der Dreibund, 1878–1914* (1983). Very useful is B. Jelavich, *Russia and the Formation of the Romanian National State, 1821–1878* (1983).

For the history of Transylvania during the nineteenth century, see E. Brote, *Chestiunea romănă in Transilvania și Ungaria* (1895); V. Netea, *Lupta românilor din Transilvania pentru libertate națională, 1848–1881* (1974); and V. Netea, *Istoria Memorandumului românilor din Transilvania și Banat* (1947). Also very good are K. Hitchins, *Orthodoxy and Nationality: A. Șaguna and the Romanians of Transylvania, 1846–1873* (1977); and I. Popescu-Puțuri and A. Deac, eds., *Unirea Transilvaniei cu România*, 3d ed. (1978).

World War I and the Formation of Greater Romania. The military events have been described by C. Kirițescu, *La Roumanie dans la guerre mondiale, 1916–1919*, 3 vols. (1934). S. Spector, *Romania at the Paris Peace Conference* (1962), is an excellent study of diplomatic history. For the union of 1918, see M. Constantinescu, ed., *Unification of the Romanian National State: The Union of Transylvania with Old Romania* (1971); and S. Pascu, *Făurirea statului unitar romăn*, 2 vols. (1983).

Minorities. This is an issue that became important only after independence in 1878. On Romanian-Jewish relations, see I. Barasch, *L'émancipation israélite en Roumanie* (1861); I. B. Brociner, *Chestiunea israeliților romăni* (1910), vol. 1; E. Schwarzfeld, *Din istoria evreilor* (1914). C. Iancu's *Les juifs en Roumanie, 1866–1919: De l'exclusion à l'émancipation* (1978) and his *Bleichröder et Crémieux, le combat pour l'émancipation des juifs de Roumanie* (1987) are probably the best general works on the topic. Also interesting are V. Bănățeanu, *Armenii în istoria și viața românească* (1938); and G. Potra, *Contribuții la istoricul țiganilor din România* (1939).

Cultural Modernization. E. Lovinescu, *Istoria civilizației române moderne,* 3 vols. (1924–25), is undoubtedly the most provocative study written so far on the intellectual origins of modern Romanian society. Still useful are P. Eliade, *Histoire de l'esprit publique en Roumanie,* 2 vols. (1905–14); and V. Jinga, *Gîndirea economică românească în secolul al XIX-lea* (1938). V. Curticăpeanu, *Die rumänische Kulturbewegung in der österreichischen Monarchie* (1966), covers Romanian cultural activities within the Habsburg Empire. For the very rich literary culture of the period, see D. Păcurariu, *Clasicismul românesc* (1971); P. Cornea, *Originile romantismului românesc* (1972); C. Ciopraga, *Literatura română intre 1900 și 1918* (1970), vol. 1; and D. Micu, *Modernismul românesc* (1984), vol. 1. Z. Ornea has devoted much work and talent to some of the main nineteenth-century intellectual currents and personalities. See especially his *Curentul cultural de la contemporanul* (1977), *Semănătorismul* (1971), and *Titu Maiorescu,* 2 vols. (1986). The new generation of literary historians seems to prefer a more sociological approach, as exemplified by D. Grăsoiu, "O cercetare sociologică asupra stratificării publicului românesc în prima jumătate a secolului al XIX-lea," *Revista de teorie literară* 2 (1974); and E. Sipiur, "L'écrivain roumain au XIXème siècle: Typologie sociale et intellectuelle," *Cahiers roumains d'études littéraires* 2 (1980).

Education. V. A. Urechia, *Istoria școalelor* (1892–1901); S. Polverjan, "Contribuții statistice privind școlile românești din Transilvania în a doua jumătate a secolului al XIX-lea," *Cumidava* 2 (1968); S. Polverjan, *Contribuții la istoria universității din Iași,* 2 vols. (1960); G. Retegan, "Contribuții la istoria statisticii învățămîntului în România, 1830–1918," *Revista de statistică* 9 (1963); and V. Popeanga, *Școala românească din Transilvania în perioada 1867–1918* (1974), are all sound works on the history of education.

Lifestyles. See especially I. Felix, *Istoria igienei românești în secolul al XIX-lea și starea ei la începutul secolului al XX-lea,* 2 vols. (1901–03); E. Ghibu, *Sportul românesc de-a lungul anilor* (1971); I. Cantacuzino, ed., *Contribuții la istoria cinematografului în România, 1896–1948* (1971).

Greater Romania

Society. There is no book yet to match V. Madgearu's *Evoluția economiei românești după primul război mondial* (1940), or S. Manuilă's statistical analyses, such as *Populația României* (1937), *Etudes ethnographiques sur la population de la Roumanie* (1938), and *Structure et évolution de la population rurale* (1940). The multiauthor volumes *La Roumanie agricole* (1929), *Transilvania, Banatul, Crișana și Maramureșul, 1918–1928,* 3 vols. (1929), and *La Roumanie: Guide économique* (1936) contain valuable information about the economy. D. Turnock, *The Romanian Economy in the 20th Century* (1986), is one of the very few topical surveys. For particular industrial changes, see N. P. Arkadian, *Industrializarea României* (1936), M. F. Iovanelli, *Industria românească, 1934–1938*; I. Saizu, *Politica economică a României între 1922 și 1928* (1982); and M. Jackson, "National Product and Income in South-Eastern Europe before the Second World War," *A.C.E.S. Bulletin* 14/2 (1982). The agrarian reform of 1921 and the general performance of interwar agriculture are discussed in D. Mitrany, *The Land and the Peasant in Romania: The War and Agrarian Reform, 1917–1921* (1930); G. Ionescu-Sişeşti and N. D. Cornăţeanu, *La réforme rurale en Roumanie* (1940); D. Gusti and N. D. Cornăţeanu, eds., *La vie rurale en Roumanie* (1940); M. Popa-Vereş, *Producţia şi exportul de cereale în ultimii zece ani* (1939); O. Parpală, *Aspecte din agricultura României, 1920–1940* (1966); D. Şandru, *Reforma agrară din 1921* (1975); and M. Jackson, "Agricultural Output in South-Eastern Europe, 1910–1938," *A.C.E.S. Bulletin* 14/2 (1982). For trade and financial matters see G. Dobrovici, *Evoluţia economică şi financiară a României în perioada 1934–1938* (1943); and I. Puiu, *Relaţiile economice externe ale României în perioada interbelică* (1982).

Serious research was done between the wars on the living conditions of the population. G. Banu, *Sănătatea poporului român* (1935), and D. C. Georgescu, *L'alimentation de la population rurale en Roumanie* (1940), are among the most useful; see also *Statistica preţurilor* (1942).

Domestic Policies. H. L. Roberts, *Rumania: Political Problems of an Agrarian State* (1951), is an excellent survey also covering the first post–World War II years. Very good as well is P. Shapiro's "Romania's Past as a Challenge for the Future: A Developmental Approach to Interwar Politics," in D. Nelson, ed., *Romania in the 1980s* (1981). Studies by official Romanian historians, the only ones with access to the archives, are uneven and should be used with caution. See especially A. Savu, *Sistemul partidelor politice din România, 1919–1940* (1976); M. Muşat and I. Ardeleanu, *Political Life in Romania, 1918–1921* (1982); M. Muşat and I. Ardeleanu, *Romania după Marea Unire, 1918–1933* (1986); F. Nedelcu, *De la restauraţie la dictatura regală* (1981); F. Nedelcu, *Viaţa politică din România în preajma dictaturii regale* (1973); M. Rusenescu and I. Saizu, *Viaţa politică în România, 1922–1928* (1978); E. Sonea and G. Sonea, *Viaţa economică şi politică în România, 1933–1938* (1978); I. Scurtu, "Acţiuni de opoziţie ale unor partide şi grupări politice burgheze faţă de tendinţele dictatoriale ale regelui Carol al II-lea," *Revista de istorie* 31/3 (1978). If confused by the often biased interpretations of most of these authors, the reader should consult *Politics and Political Parties in Romania* (1936), an excellent documentary published in London about Romanian politics after Versailles.

Political Parties. Doctrinele partidelor politice (1924) is a collective effort offering an interesting description of the platforms of the major parties as given by their leaders. For the National Peasant Party, see P. Şeicaru, *Istoria partidelor naţional, ţărănist şi naţional-ţărănist,* 2 vols. (1963); I. Scurtu, *Din viaţa politică a României: Întemeierea şi activitatea partidului ţărănesc, 1918–1926* (1975); I. Scurtu, *Din viaţa politică a României, 1926–1947: Studiu critic privind istoria partidului naţional-ţărănesc* (1983); K. Beer, *Zur Entwicklung des Parteien- und Parlamentsystems in Rumänien, 1928–1933: Die Zeit der national-bäuerlichen Regierungen* (1986). There is no satisfactory history of the Iron Guard in Romanian. The Marxist approach is insulting instead of being analytical, and the Guardists themselves are self-serving. For two samples see A. Fătu and I. Spălăţelu, *Garda de Fier, organizaţie teroristă de tip fascist* (1971); and the writings of H. Sima, *Histoire du mouvement légionnaire* (1972), *Sfîrşitul unei domnii sîngeroase* (1977), and *Era libertăţii* (1982); C. Z. Codreanu, *Die Eiserne Garde* (1939) also provides instructive reading. For a scholarly approach to the history of the Romanian Fascist movement, see E. Weber, "Romania," in E. Weber and H. Rogger, *The European Right* (1966); N. Nagy-Talavera, *The Green Shirts and Others: A History of Fascism in Hungary and Romania* (1970); and A. Heinen, *Die Legion "Erzengel Michael" in Rumänien* (1986).

The official history of the Communist Party has been rewritten so many times that it would be useless to keep track of the ever-changing interpretations. Sound scholarly studies have been published only in the West. See especially T. Gilberg, "The Communist Party of Romania," in S. Fischer-Galati, ed., *The Communist Parties of Eastern Europe* (1979); R. King, *A History of the Romanian Communist Party* (1980); and V. Frunză, *Istoria P.C.R.,* 2 vols. (1980). The only work on the Socialist Party, *Socialismul în România,* was published in the 1930s by T. Petrescu.

Foreign Policy. E. Campus, *Mica înţelegere* (1968), *Înţelegerea balcanică* (1972), and *Din politica externă a României, 1913–1947* (1980), provide a complete picture of Romania's diplomatic history from Versailles to the treaty of Paris. Also useful are V. Moisiuc, *Diplomaţia României şi problema apărării suveranităţii şi independenţei naţionale în perioada martie–mai 1940* (1971); and D. Funderburk, *Politica Marii Britanii faţă de România, 1938–1940* (1983).

Literature, Culture, Arts, Ideas. E. Lovinescu, *Istoria literaturii române contemporane,* 4 vols. (1926–29); S. Cioculescu, V. Streinu, and T. Vianu, *Istoria literaturii române moderne* (1944); and O. S. Crohmălniceanu, *Literatura română între cele două războaie mondiale,* 3 vols. (1972–75), are interesting general studies on literary developments. For particular ideological trends, see D. Micu, *Gîndirea şi gîndirismul* (1975); and especially Z. Ornea, *Traditionalism şi modernitate în deceniul al treilea* (1980). M. Eliade's *Autobiography,* 2 vols. (1981–88), provides a vivid picture of the challenging intellectual atmosphere of the 1920s and 1930s.

The Authoritarian Regimes

P. Quinlan, *Clash over Romania: British and American Policies towards Romania, 1938–1947* (1977), and N. Penescu, *La Roumanie de la démocratie au totalitarisme, 1938–1948* (1981), are probably the best studies on the period from the fall of the parliamentarian system to the Communist takeover. For King Carol's dictatorship, see A. Savu, *Dictatura regală, 1938–1940* (1970); and A. Simion, *Dictatul de la Viena* (1972). Ion Antonescu's evaluation of the short-lived Iron Guardist regime appears in *Pe marginea prăpastiei,* 2 vols. (1942) (the Guardist view can be found in H. Sima's already cited memoirs). The official Marxist interpretation is reflected in A. Simion, *Regimul politic din România în perioada septembrie 1940–ianuarie 1941* (1976); and M. Fătu, *Contribuţii la studierea regimului politic din România (septembrie 1940–august 1944)* (1984).

World War II military history has been treated so far only by P. Chirnoagă, *Istoria politică şi militară a războiului României contra Rusiei Sovietice* (1965). For diplomatic aspects see G. Gafencu, *Préliminaires de la guerre à l'Est* (1944); G. Barbul, *Mémorial Antonescu: Le troisième homme de l'Axe* (1950); A. Cretzianu, "The Romanian Armistice Negotiations, Cairo, 1944," *Journal of Central European Affairs* 3 (1951); I. Gheorghe, *Rumäniens Weg zum Satelliten Staat* (1952); A. Cretzianu, *The Lost Opportunity* (1957); A. Hillgruber, *Hitler, König Carol und Marschall Antonescu: Die deutsch-rumänischen Beziehungen, 1938–1944* (1954; reprinted 1965); A. Resis, "The Stalin-Churchill Percentages Agreement on the Balkans, Moscow, October 1944," *American Historical Review* 83/2 (1978). Official Romanian historiography is rather unreliable for the 23 August 1944 coup. For partial exceptions, see A. Simion, *Preliminarii ale actului de la 23 August* (1979); and I. Ceauşescu, F. Constantiniu, and M. Ionescu, *A Turning Point in World War II: 23 August 1944 in Romania* (1985). Interesting documents have been published recently in *23 August 1944: Documente*, 4 vols. (1984); and in I. Drăgan, *Antonescu, Mareşalul României şi războaiele de reîntregire: Mărturii şi documente*, 2 vols. (1986–88). See also E. Bantea, ed., *La Roumanie dans la guerre anti-hitlérienne, août 1944–mai 1945* (1970); and V. Dobrinescu, "Der Waffenstillstand zwischen Rumänien und die Vereinten Nationen, Moskau, 12 September 1944," *Südostforschungen* (1986).

The Communist takeover is analyzed in almost all the books mentioned above. For a more detailed discussion of King Michael's last years in power, see A. S. Gould Lee, *Crown against Sickle: The Story of King Michael of Romania* (1950); and N. Frank, *La Roumanie dans l'engrenage, 1944–1947* (1977). Also useful are E. Ciurea, *Le traité de paix avec la Roumanie du 10 février 1947* (1954); and I. Alexandrescu, *Economia românească în primii ani postbelici, 1945–1947* (1986).

The Holocaust. The most significant documents were published by M. Carp, *Cartea neagră: Fapte şi documente. Suferinţele evreilor din România*, 3 vols. (1946–48); and J. Ancel, *Documents Concerning the Fate of Romanian Jewry during the Holocaust*, 12 vols. (1987). Precious information comes from the memoirs of the two wartime rabbis, A. Safran, *Resisting the Storm: Romania, 1940–1947. Memoirs* (1987); and M. Carmilly-Weinberger, *Memorial Volume for the Jews of Cluj/Kolozsvar* (1970). The bibliography on the subject is huge. Suggested readings: S. Manuilă and W. Filderman, *Regional Developments of the Jewish Population in Romania* (1957); G. Zaharia, "Quelques données concernant la terreur fasciste en Roumanie, 1940–1944," in I. Popescu-Puţuri, *La Roumanie pendant la deuxième guerre mondiale* (1964); J. Fischer, *Transnistria: The Forgotten Cemetery* (1969); B. Vago, "The Destruction of the Jews of Transylvania," in R. L. Braham, ed., *Hungarian Jewish Studies*, vol. 1 (1966); and B. Vago, *The Shadow of the Swastika: The Rise of Fascism and Anti-Semitism in the Danubian Basin, 1936–1939* (1975); A. Karetki and M. Covaci, *Zile însîngerate la Iaşi, 28–30 iunie 1941* (1978); R. L. Braham, *The Politics of Genocide: The Holocaust in Hungary*, 2 vols. (1981); R. L. Braham, *Genocide and Retribution: The Holocaust in Hungarian Ruled Northern Transylvania* (1983); M. Gilbert, *The Holocaust: The Jewish Tragedy* (1986); M. Gilbert, *Auschwitz and the Allies* (1984); E. Mendelsohn, *The Jews of East-Central Europe between the World Wars* (1983); J. Ancel, "Plans for Deportation of Romanian Jews, July–October, 1942," *Yad Vashem Studies* 16 (1984); J. Ancel, "The Roma-

342   BIBLIOGRAPHICAL ESSAY

nian Way of Solving the 'Jewish Problem' in Bessarabia and Bukovina, June–
July 1941," *Yad Vashem Studies* 19 (1988); R. Hilberg, *The Destruction of the European Jews*, 3 vols. (1985).

Communism in Romania

Dealing with the past in Marxist Romania is an adventurous undertaking. The
official view has changed quite often between 1947 and 1989, and the fabri-
cation of myths seems to have been an obsession with the ruling class. For an
analysis of this trend, which makes the past more unpredictable than the future,
see M. Rura, *Reinterpretation of History as a Method of Furthering Communism in
Romania* (1961); V. Georgescu, *Politică și istorie: Cazul comuniștilor români, 1948–
1977* (1981); and S. Fischer-Galati, "Myths in Romanian History," *East European
Quarterly* 15/3 (1981).

  General Works. A. Cretzianu: *Captive Romania* (1956); G. Ionescu, *Communism
in Romania, 1944–1962* (1964); S. Fischer-Galati, *The New Romania: From People's
Democracy to Socialist Republic* (1967); S. Fischer-Galati, *Twentieth Century Romania*
(1970); K. Jowitt, *Revolutionary Breakthrough and National Development: The Case
of Romania 1944–1965*(1971); V. Georgescu, ed., *Romania: 40 Years (1944–1984)*
(1985); D. Nelson, "Romania in the 1980s: The Legacy of Dynastic Socialism,"
East European Politics and Societies 2/1 (1988); and M. Shafir, *Romania: Politics,
Economics and Society* (1985), are all useful general introductions to the study of
Romanian Communism. For the economy, see J. Montias, *Economic Development
in Communist Romania* (1970); J. Spingler, *Economic Reform in Romanian Industry*
(1973); and T. Gilberg, *Modernization in Romania since World War II* (1975). All
deal with a period of relative economic growth and progress. For the changing
picture in the early 1980s see M. Jackson, "Romania's Economy at the End of
the 1970s: Turning the Corner on Intensive Development," in *East European
Assessment: A Compendium of the United States* (1981), as well as the papers published by V. Socor in Radio Free Europe's *Situation Reports* and *Background
Reports* series since 1983. The official Romanian position on economic development can be found in N. Giosan, ed., *Agricultura României, 1944–1964*
(1964); idem, *Dezvoltarea agriculturii României în cifre* (1965); V. Malinschi et al.,
eds., *Industria României, 1944–1964* (1964); V. Trebici, *Populația României și
creșterea economică* (1971); C. Moisiuc, *Coordonate principale ale dezvoltării economice, 1971–1990* (1972).

  Foreign Policy. This field has been monitored with interest and sympathy,
especially by Western scholars. F. David, *Russia's Dissident Ally* (1965); A. Braun,
Romanian Foreign Policy since 1965: The Political and Military Limits of Autonomy
(1978); A. Braun, *Small State Security in the Balkans* (1985); G. Linden, *Bear and
Foxes: The International Relations of the East-European Communist States* (1979); I.
Volgyes, *The Political Reliability of the Warsaw Pact Armies: The Southern Tier* (1982),
are all interesting, although outdated, in regard to developments in Romania
and the Communist world in the mid-eighties. For a provocative approach to
the general question of Romanian autonomy, see V. Socor, "Romania's Foreign

Policy Reconsidered," *Orbis* 3 (1983). G. Haupt has tried to explain the origins of the Romanian-Soviet conflict in "La genèse du conflict soviéto-roumain," *Revue française de sciences sociales* 18/4 (1968). No serious study on the relations between Bucharest and Moscow in the 1980s could be undertaken without consulting the articles published by V. Socor in Radio Free Europe's *Situation Reports* and *Background Reports* since 1983.

Dissidents. T. Gilberg, "Social Deviance in Romania," in I. Volgyes, ed., *Social Deviance in Eastern Europe* (1978); V. Georgescu, "Romanian Dissent: Its Ideas," in J. F. Curry, *Dissent in Eastern Europe* (1983); and M. Shafir, "Political Culture, Intellectual Dissent and Intellectual Consent: The Case of Romania," *Orbis* 3 (1983), are useful general surveys. Firsthand descriptions of the gulag of the 1950s are published in S. Crăciunaş, *The Lost Footsteps* (1961); and I. Cârjă, *Canalul morţii, 1949–1954* (1974). See also V. Ierunca, *Piteşti* (1981).

The texts of the Goma movement have been published in the journal *Limite* 24–25 (1977), and by V. Tănase, *Le dossier P. Goma.* See also P. Goma's own account in *Le tremblement des hommes* (1979). Other documents about the writings and activity of Romanian dissidents have appeared in *Limite* 26–27 (1978) and *L'alternative* (January 1983).

Cultural Trends. I. Negoiţescu, *Scriitori români* (1966); A. Piru, *Panorama deceniului literar românesc, 1940–1950* (1968); E. Simion, *Scriitori români de azi,* 3 vols. (1976–78); G. Grigurcu, *Poeţi români de azi* (1979); G. Grigurcu, *Critici români de azi* (1981); and N. Manolescu, *Arca lui Noe,* 3 vols. (1980–83), are valuable studies. See also A. U. Gabany, *Partei und Literatur in Rumänien seit 1945* (1975).

INDEX

Additional Article, 106, 160; appended by Russia to Organic Statutes, 141

Adevarul, NSF-backed newspaper, 296

Adrianople, Treaty of (1829), 21, 105, 122, 131, 160, 186; commerce under, 82, 85, 86, 127

Agrarian law, 133, 134, 150, 191; of 1921, 199

Agriculture: domestic investment in, 252, 253; early history of, 2, 15, 21, 23; and foreign trade, 83, 128, 132, 200; grain, 22, 83, 122, 125, 199; reforms in, 133–34, 198–200, 224; in Romanian economy, 81–82, 122–25, 198, 235–36, 259, 261, 268–69, 270, 292, 293

Alba Iulia: site of Transylvanian declaration of union, 172; treaty of (1595), 36

Alexander I (emperor of Russia, r. 1801–25): denies support for 1821 uprising, 102

Alexander II (emperor of Russia, r. 1855–81), 162; signs military convention with Romania, 163

Allied Control Commission, 223, 230–31

Allied powers: diplomatic relations with Romania, 219, 228; recognize Soviet-backed government in Romania, 230

Andropov, Yuri, 266

Anti-Semitism, 208, 210, 221, 238; promoted by Iron Guard, 194, 214, 215; resurgence of after 1989 revolution, 296

Antonescu, Ion, 209, 295; *conducător*, 211; and diplomatic relations, 213, 218; execution of, 230; government of, 210, 211–12, 219–21; military background of, 215–16

Apponyi Laws (1907), 158, 178

Archeology: evidence of Romanian culture, 3, 5, 7, 8–10, 11, 12–13, 15, 16, 27, 59

Architecture, 33, 34, 68, 108, 109, 172–74

Arts: innovations in, 185–86

Assemblies, Romanian national, 79, 135, 144; and convention of Balta Liman, 145

Association of Christian Students, 194

Association of Romanian Writers, 180

ASTRA (Transylvanian Association for Romanian Literature and the Culture of the Romanian People), 180; nationalist values of, 179

Atheneum, the, Bucharest, 174

Austria: cultural influences of, 107, 109, 111; diplomatic relations with Romania, 46, 49, 71, 77, 147, 148; and Romanian economy, 27, 80–81, 83, 85. *See also* Austria-Hungary, dual monarchy of; Habsburgs

Austria-Hungary, dual monarchy of, 157–58; diplomatic relations with Romania, 164, 165, 168; union of Transylvania and, 171–72. *See also* Austria; Habsburgs; Hungary

Averescu, Alexandru: leader of People's Party, 192; and peasant uprising, 139

Bălcescu, Nicolae, 141; organizer of Frăţia, 142

Balkan Entente, 197

Balkans, the, 17, 22, 25, 53, 88; diplomatic relations with, 47–48, 161, 164–65; instability in, 138, 165; religion in, 35, 41; revolutionary movement in, 100

Balş, Theodor: Moldavian regent under Treaty of Paris, 147

Balta Liman, convention of, 145

Banat, the, 167; and Bucharest convention, 168

Banffy Law (1896), 158

Banks and banking: and economic development, 129; nationalization of, 233

BIOGRAPHICAL NOTE

Vlad Georgescu was born on October 29, 1937, in Bucharest. He received his B.A. in history from the University of Bucharest in 1959 and his Ph.D. in history from the same institution in 1970. After having been a researcher at the Romanian-Russian Museum in Bucharest (1960–63) and then a senior researcher at the Institute of South-East European Studies in Bucharest (1963–79), Georgescu was forced into exile by the government of Nicolae Ceauşescu in 1979 on account of his dissident activities, for which he had already been arrested and briefly detained in 1977. Both before and after his exile he taught at several American universities as a visiting faculty member: at the University of California at Los Angeles (1967–68); at Columbia University (1973); and at the University of Maryland (1981–82). In 1979–80 he held a Woodrow Wilson Fellowship in Washington, D.C. During the last years of his life he was director of the Romanian Service of Radio Free Europe in Munich, West Germany. Taken suddenly ill in the summer of 1988, he died in Munich on 13 November 1988.

Vlad Georgescu had published extensively before his exile from Romania in Romanian, French, and English on such topics as the diplomatic correspondence of Wallachia (*Din corespondenţa diplomatică a Ţării Româneşti* [Bucharest, 1962]); projects of social reform in the Romanian principalities between 1769 and 1848 (*Mémoires et projets de réforme dans les principautés roumaines*, vol. 1, 1769–1830; and vol. 2, 1831–1848 [Bucharest, 1970, 1972]); and the political ideas of the Enlightenment in Romania (*Political Ideas and the Enlightenment in the Romanian Principalities, 1750–1831* [New York, 1971]).

His important dissident essay on Communist politics and history, *Politică şi istorie*, which dealt with successive distortions of the Romanian historical record to fit Marxist ideological schemes, could be published only after he arrived in the West (it ran through two editions [Munich, 1981, 1983]). It was also in the West that he was able to publish his massive study on the history of political ideas in Romania from 1369 to 1878 (*Istoria ideilor politice româneşti (1369–1878)* [Munich, 1987]), which he had virtually completed during his last years in Romania. The most significant work written by Vlad Georgescu in exile is certainly his *Romanians: A History*, first published in Romanian as *Istoria românilor de la origini pînă în zilele noastre* (Los Angeles, 1984) and now made available to the English-speaking reader. Other works completed during his last years of life include the volume *Romania: 40 Years (1944–1984)*, which he edited and introduced (New York, 1985).